Coaching
FOOTBALL
Technical and Tactical Skills

American Sport
Education Program
with Rob Ash

HUMAN KINETICS

Library of Congress Cataloging-in-Publication Data

Coaching football technical and tactical skills / American Sport Education
  Program.
    p. cm.
  Includes index.
  ISBN 0-7360-5184-8 (soft cover)
  1. Football--Coaching.   I. American Sport Education Program.
GV954.4.C63 2006
796.332'077--dc22

2005028758

ISBN-10: 0-7360-5184-8
ISBN-13: 978-0-7360-5184-2

Acquisitions Editor: Amy Tocco; **Project Writer:** Rob Ash; **Developmental Editor:** Laura Floch; **Assistant Editors:** Mandy Maiden and Scott Hawkins; **Copyeditor:** Bob Replinger; **Proofreader:** Anne Rogers; **Indexers:** Robert and Cynthia Swanson; **Permission Manager:** Carly Breeding; **Graphic Designers:** Bob Reuther and Nancy Rasmus; **Graphic Artist:** Sandra Meier; **Photo Manager:** Dan Wendt; **Cover Designer:** Keith Blomberg; **Photographer (cover):** Dan Wendt; **Photographer (interior):** Dan Wendt; **Art Manager:** Kareema McLendon-Foster; **Illustrator:** Argosy; **Printer:** Sheridan Books

We thank Valley High School in West Des Moines, Iowa, for assistance in providing the location for the photo shoot for this book.

Copies of this book are available at special discounts for bulk purchase for sales promotions, premiums, fundraising, or educational use. Special editions or book excerpts can also be created to specifications. For details, contact the Special Sales Manager at Human Kinetics.

Printed in the United States of America   10   9   8   7   6   5

The paper in this book is certified under a sustainable forestry program.

Human Kinetics
Web site: www.HumanKinetics.com

United States: Human Kinetics
P.O. Box 5076
Champaign, IL 61825-5076
800-747-4457
e-mail: humank@hkusa.com

Canada: Human Kinetics
475 Devonshire Road, Unit 100
Windsor, ON N8Y 2L5
800-465-7301 (in Canada only)
e-mail: info@hkcanada.com

Europe: Human Kinetics
107 Bradford Road
Stanningley
Leeds LS28 6AT, United Kingdom
+44 (0)113 255 5665
e-mail: hk@hkeurope.com

Australia: Human Kinetics
57A Price Avenue
Lower Mitcham, South Australia 5062
08 8372 0999
e-mail: info@hkaustralia.com

New Zealand: Human Kinetics
P.O. Box 80
Torrens Park, South Australia 5062
0800 222 062
e-mail: info@hknewzealand.com

contents

preface

If you are a seasoned football coach, surely you have experienced the frustration of watching your players perform well in practice, only to find them underperforming in games. In your playing days, you likely saw the same events unfold. Teammates, or perhaps even you, could find the open receiver and throw accurately to him nearly every time in seven-on-seven drills or shed blockers and make crunching tackles in scrimmages but could not transfer that kind of performance to games. Although this book will not provide you with a magical quick fix to your team's problems, it will help you prepare your players for game day. Whether you are a veteran coach or are new to coaching, *Coaching Football Technical and Tactical Skills* will help you take your game to the next level by providing you with the tools you need to teach your team the game of football.

Every football coach knows the importance of technical skills. The ability of a player to make an effective block, catch a pass off the turf, hurry the quarterback into making a poor pass or sprint downfield to cover a punt can significantly affect the outcome of a game. The book discusses the basic and intermediate technical skills necessary for your team's success, including offensive, defensive and special teams skills. You will learn how to detect and correct errors in your athletes' performance of those skills and then help them transfer the knowledge and ability that they gain in practice to execution in games.

Besides covering technical skills, the book focuses on tactical skills, including offensive skills like the option pitch read, crossing route adjustments and picking up the blitz; defensive skills such as defending the option, reads and reactions in zone pass coverage and defending the play-action pass; and special teams skills like the onside kick, sky punt and wall return. The book discusses the tactical triangle, an approach that teaches players to read a situation, acquire the knowledge that they need to make a tactical decision and apply decision-making skills to the problem. To advance this method, the book covers important cues that help athletes respond appropriately when they see a play developing, including important rules, game strategies and the strengths and weaknesses of opponents.

Although rigorous technical and tactical training prepares athletes for game situations, you can improve their game performance by incorporating gamelike situations into daily training. The book offers many traditional drills that can be effective but also shows you how to shape, focus and enhance scrimmages and minigames to help your players transfer their technical skills to tactical situations that occur during games. For example, you can change a tedious pass-timing drill into an exciting, competitive contest by keeping score of completions, pass break-ups and first downs.

The book also covers planning at several levels—the season plan, practice plans and game plans. A set of practice plans are offered based on the games approach which lay out a description of eight practice sessions, covering elements such as the length of the practice session, the objective of the practice, equipment needed, warm-up, practice of previously taught skills, teaching and practicing new skills, cool-down and evaluation.

Of course, playing the games is what your practices eventually lead to. The book shows you how to prepare long before the first game, including issues such as communicating with players, parents, officials and the media, scouting your opponent and motivating your players. You will learn how to control your team's performance on game day by establishing routines and how to manage such elements as the sideline area, coin toss, signaling, substitutions, halftime adjustments, time-outs and end-of-game decisions.

STAYING SAFE

Football is an exciting, thrilling, and physically challenging game. Yet, it can also be a dangerous game with a constant threat of injury. Safety precautions must be taken and proper technique for skills must be taught, emphasized, and re-emphasized in order to keep the players as safe as possible.

Even when safety procedures are carefully followed, participants in the sport of football must be aware that the game has inherent dangers. Although it rarely happens, the risk does exist that a player could suffer paralysis, brain injury, or even death while playing football. Players, parents, and coaches must discuss these risks, and the reduction of risk, prior to every season. Proper equipment, correct teaching and training methods, and common sense can minimize the risk. However, even with the best equipment and training, the chance of an accidental catastrophic injury still exists and must be clearly understood by everyone involved with the game.

Guidelines for coaches:

- Understand and explain the intent and correct application of safety rules in football. Specifically, remind all players prior to the season and frequently throughout the season that the helmet (including the facemask) should never be driven into an opponent as the initial point of contact. In particular, head-down contact (initiating contact with the top, or crown, of the helmet), also known as spearing, greatly increases the risk of catastrophic injury.

- Make graphically clear to players that paralysis, brain injury, or even death could result from violating the safety rules. Constantly reinforce that the use of proper techniques for contact greatly reduces the risk of catastrophic injury.

- Clearly explain that even with proper equipment, training, and technique, the risk of accidental catastrophic injury still exists and cannot be completely eliminated.

PART I

Teaching and Evaluating

Being a good coach takes more than knowing the sport of football. You have to go beyond that and find a way to teach your athletes how to be better players. To find effective ways to improve your players' performance, you must know how to teach and evaluate them.

In chapter 1 we go over the fundamentals of teaching sport skills. We first provide you with a general overview of your sport and talk with you about the importance of being an effective teacher. Next, we define some important skills, helping you gain a better understanding of technical and tactical skills, and the traditional and games approaches to coaching.

We build on the knowledge of how to teach sport skills with the evaluation of technical and tactical skills in chapter 2. We discuss the importance of evaluating athletes and review the core skills that you should assess and how you can best do so. This chapter stresses the importance of preseason, in-season and postseason evaluation and provides you with sample tools that you can use to evaluate your players.

By learning how to teach and evaluate your players, you will be better prepared to help them improve their performance.

chapter 1

Teaching Sport Skills

Football is an exceptionally complex and diverse sport. On any given play, 11 players on each team, with varying body shapes and sizes, use a wide range of skills to try to move a strange-shaped pigskin ball down the 100-yard field. Big linemen battle each other one-on-one in physical, hand-to-hand contests; smaller skill-position players, such as wide receivers, run a race down the sideline; a running back carries the ball and tries to outrun, fake out or run over defenders who are trying to take him to the ground; and another player, the quarterback, barks commands, directs traffic and often tries to throw the ball down the field to a teammate being guarded by an opponent. No other sport requires such diverse body types and skills; consequently, the game of football provides an opportunity for athletes of virtually every shape and size to compete.

The objective of the game is fairly simple: to move the ball down the field and score a touchdown by taking the ball across the goal line or by kicking a field goal. The game seems evenly matched, 11 against 11, but moving the ball down the field the required 10 yards in four downs can be challenging for the offense. The defense really outnumbers the offense because one of the offensive players has the ball and therefore the offense has only 10 players to block the 11 defenders. Even if every offensive player blocks his defender successfully, which is easier said than done, the player with the ball ultimately has to beat the unblocked defender to gain yards. Furthermore, if the quarterback just hands off the ball to a runner and does not carry out a fake or otherwise occupy a defender, the defense has two unblocked defenders and an even more significant advantage. The offense must be both creative and consistent in its blocking schemes, techniques and assignments to have a chance to move the ball consistently.

Clearly, then, football is complex and multifaceted. Despite all this variety, the game of football provides an opportunity for coaches and players to work together and mold the diverse members of the team into a unified, organized and efficient unit that performs with cohesion and symmetry. The beauty of the game is to see this unity develop from the varying elements that make up the separate parts of the whole. The symbolic snapshot of the sport of football is the huddle, where players of all types and sizes, all races and religions, all socioeconomic levels, hold hands and communicate their plan for success. In the huddle, no player is an individual, and no one is different from anyone else; each player is a member of the team, striving to do his job to the best of his ability.

Effective Teaching

Given the complexity and variety of football, the process of teaching this game to a group of young men might seem daunting. No matter what position you may have played or studied, you will eventually have to learn the intricacies of several other positions that are quite different from your area of expertise. The former wide receiver who was an expert at route running and pass catching may find the offensive line schemes and techniques or the linebackers' progression of pass and run keys to be nearly as unfamiliar as an entirely different sport. Furthermore, if you, like most coaches, are a former player, you must master the transition from playing the game to teaching the game, a more difficult step than most people realize. The athlete gradually gains a sense of how each skill feels—how he has to move and think—to perform successfully. As a teacher, you have to search for ways to help athletes gain that sense, that feeling, of how to perform skills, and you must understand that different athletes often perceive the same skill in different ways.

Additionally, you cannot be an effective teacher until you can accept responsibility for the performance of your athletes and team. If you hide behind the tired excuse that your athletes just can't play, you will never be motivated to find the teaching strategy that will produce improvement. But if you adopt the following credo—"The team will reflect everything the coach has taught the players, or everything the coach has allowed them to do"—you will understand that every player can improve. Even if the athlete's skill level is average, you can motivate him to hustle and give great effort, you can drill him until he carries out his assignments perfectly, and you can inspire him to help the whole be greater than the sum of the individual parts. And if you continually search for new ways to teach the same skill, you will eventually find a phrase, drill or concept that triggers the athlete's reactions in such a way that he finally starts showing improvement in areas where he previously struggled. You have the responsibility to find a way to teach, or motivate, the athlete to improve his skills. This concept alone—your acceptance of responsibility for the athlete's performance—will produce creative, exciting and extremely effective teaching, the kind of teaching that in turn results in improvement of skills and improved performance by both the individual and, ultimately, the team.

Technical and Tactical Skills

As a coach, you have the responsibility of patiently and systematically explaining and drilling the athletes on the basic skills, position by position, that make up the game. These skills, called technical skills, are the fundamentals that provide each player with the tools to execute the physical requirements of the game. Each day at practice, you also must create scenarios on the field in which players have to use their technical skills in a gamelike situation, forcing them to make decisions that simulate the choices that they will have to make in a game. These skills, called tactical skills, are the bridge between practice performance and game performance. Although the proper execution of technical skills is necessary for success, the tactical skills, the ability of the athletes to make the appropriate decisions, are the key to having everything come together when it counts—in the game.

Obviously, other types of skills, such as pure physical capacity, mental skills, communication ability and character traits, all contribute to athletic performance (Rainer Martens, *Successful Coaching, Third Edition*, Champaign, IL: Human Kinetics, 2004). Although all these skills are important, effective teaching of the technical and tactical skills of the game still provides the foundation for successful football coaching.

The number and variety of skills used by the different players in football is massive and impossible to chronicle in one text. Consequently, this book will focus on the essential basic to intermediate technical and tactical skills in football. These skills were compiled with the help of the American Football Coaches Association. The goal is to provide a resource that will help you improve your understanding and instructional methods as you strive to teach your players the great game of football.

Technical Skills

Technical skills are defined as "the specific procedures to move one's body to perform the task that needs to be accomplished" (Martens, *Successful Coaching*, p. 169). The proper execution of the technical skills of football is, obviously, crucial to successful performance. Most coaches, even those with little experience, know what the basic technical skills of football are: blocking, tackling and ball skills, such as throwing, catching, kicking and running with the football. But the ability to teach athletes how to perform those skills usually develops only over a long period, as a coach gains experience.

The goal of this book is to speed up the timetable of teaching skills, improving your ability to

- clearly communicate the basic elements of each skill to the athlete,
- construct drills and teaching scenarios to rehearse those skills,
- detect and correct errors in the athletes' performance of skills, and
- help athletes transfer knowledge and ability from practice into games.

Effective coaches have the capacity to transfer their knowledge and understanding of skills into improved performance of those skills by their athletes. This book will outline a plan that will help you do just that by teaching you how to become a master of the basic to intermediate technical skills of football and assisting you in providing your athletes with the resources necessary for success.

Tactical Skills

Mastery of the technical skills of football is important, but athletes must also learn the tactics of the game. Tactical skills are defined as "the decisions and actions of players in the contest to gain an advantage over the opposing team or players" (Martens, *Successful Coaching*, p. 170). Many football resources overlook the tactical aspects of the game. Coaches even omit tactical considerations from practice because they focus so intently on teaching technical skills. Another reason for this omission is that tactics are difficult to teach. One way that you can approach tactical skills is by focusing on the three critical aspects, the "tactical triangle":*

- Reading the play or situation
- Acquiring the knowledge needed to make an appropriate tactical decision
- Applying decision-making skills to the problem

This book as a whole provides you with the knowledge that you need to teach players how to use the tactical triangle. Part III covers important cues that help athletes respond appropriately when they see a play developing, including important rules, game strategies and opponents' strengths and weaknesses that affect game situations, as well as ways to teach athletes how to acquire and use this knowledge. Part III will also help you teach athletes how to make appropriate choices in a given situation and show you how to empower players to recognize emerging situations on their own and make sound judgments.

Perhaps the greatest frustration for a coach is to witness athletes making errors in games on skills that they have repeatedly drilled in practice. For example, the quarterback who has perfect footwork and accuracy in throwing the curl and flat patterns in practice either rushes his steps or throws indecisively to one of the two receivers on the curl–flat read in the game. This transfer of skills from practice to the game can be difficult, but you can reduce errors by placing the athletes in gamelike situations in practice to work on tactical skill decisions. Only after rehearsing the tactical decision repeatedly in practice will the athletes be prepared to execute those decisions (while maintaining their execution of the related technical skills) in the game.

Traditional Versus Games Approach to Coaching

As mentioned previously, transferring skills from practice to games can be difficult. A sound background of technical and tactical training prepares athletes for game situations. But you can surpass this level by incorporating gamelike situations into daily training, further enhancing the likelihood that players will transfer skills from practices to games. To understand how to accomplish this, you must be aware of two approaches to coaching—the traditional approach and the games approach.

Part IV of this book provides examples of both the traditional approach and the games approach to coaching. Although each style has its particular advantages, the concept favored in this book is the games approach. The games approach provides athletes with a competitive situation governed by clear objectives and focused on specific individuals and concepts. The games approach creates a productive and meaningful learning environment in which athletes are motivated by both the structure of the drills and the improvement that they make. Finally, the games

---

*Reprinted, by permission, from R. Martens, 2004, *Successful Coaching*, 3rd ed. (Champaign, IL: Human Kinetics), 215.

approach prepares athletes for competition because they have experienced settings that closely resemble the tactical situations that they will see in the game.

Traditional Approach

Although the games approach to coaching has much merit, the traditional approach to coaching also has value. The traditional approach often begins with a warm-up period, followed by individual drills, group drills and then a substantial team period, or scrimmage, at the end of the practice. The traditional approach can be helpful in teaching the technical skills of football. But unless you shape, focus and enhance the team period, the athletes may be unable to transfer the skills that they learn in the drills into the scrimmage situation in practice or, worse, into effective performance, especially of tactical skills, in games.

Games Approach

The games approach emphasizes the use of games and minigames to help coaches provide their athletes with situations that are as close to a real game as possible (Alan G. Launder, *Play Practice*. Champaign, IL: Human Kinetics, 2001). But this method requires more than just putting the players on the field, throwing out a ball and letting them play. You should use the following three components any time you use the games approach:

1. Shaping
2. Focusing
3. Enhancing

Shaping play allows you to modify the game in a way that is conducive to learning the skills for that particular concept. You can shape play by modifying the rules, the environment (playing area), the objectives of the game and the number of players (Launder, p. 56). In scrimmage situations the stronger players often dominate, and the weaker players merely get through the scrimmage without playing a strong, active role. If you shape play by reducing the playing area or number of players, every athlete will have the opportunity to learn and practice the skills for his position.

You also need to be sure to focus the athletes on the specific objectives of the game. Players are more apt to learn, or at least be open to learning, if they know why they are playing the game and how the tactics they are rehearsing fit into the bigger picture. Provide the athletes with clear objectives and a straightforward explanation of how those objectives will help them become better football players.

Finally, you must play an active role throughout the game, enhancing the play by stopping the game at the teachable moment and instructing the athletes about how they could improve their decision making, or technical skills.

An example of a games approach to teaching tactical skills is a game called the Curl Read Game. This game involves a quarterback, three offensive players (a tight end, a wide receiver and a running back) and three defensive players (an inside linebacker, an outside linebacker or strong safety, and a cornerback). The objective of the game is to refine the execution of the curl–flat pattern against a traditional zone defense. Using cones, mark off the drill area into a rectangle from just inside one hash mark to the sideline, so that the players are using one-third of the width of the field. The situation is third down and 7. The ball is placed

2 yards behind one line so that the players have a clearly defined first-down line. The offense runs the same play every time: The tight end runs an 8-yard hook over the middle, the wide receiver runs a 12-yard curl on the outside (with the option to go deep if the defensive back plays him too tightly) and the running back runs a flare (or flat) pattern outside the curl. The defense has an inside linebacker defending the hook, a strong safety who is the curl–flat defender and a cornerback who is responsible for any deep pattern but can help defend the curl as long as he doesn't get beat deep.

To make this drill a game, award points as follows: The offense scores 1 point for a completion and 1 extra point if the completion results in a first down; the defense scores 1 point for an incomplete pass or a pass that is short of the first down and 1 extra point for an interception. The game goes to 10 points, with all players on the losing side of the ball doing some quick but annoying form of penalty, such as 10 up-downs. (The penalty is not important; the competition is!)

So, you have shaped the play into a smaller field with a smaller number of players, with points to be scored and an objective—to get to 10 points first. The game is clearly focused on the critical third-down situation. And you have the opportunity to enhance the game by observing the players' decisions and skills as they compete and directing them in ways that they can improve their ability to execute or defend the play.

The game seems simple, but some fascinating scenarios invariably unfold, creating vivid opportunities for teaching. For example, after the offense gets an early first down for a 2-point lead in the game, the defense settles in, with the line-backer defending the tight end successfully and the curl–flat defender hanging in the curl, forcing the quarterback to make the throw to the flare back, short of the first down. But because the offense scores 1 point for every completion, the curl defender becomes impatient and ventures out of the curl area to stop the throw to the back. The quarterback then drills a completion to the wide receiver on the curl pattern to win the game. The defense has to learn to be patient and force the short throw every time! By the same token, the quarterback might become impatient in the game because he is forced to throw the short route every time. Realizing that he can't win the game unless he gets a first down, he forces a pass to the hook or the curl, and a defender intercepts it for a defensive victory. The quarterback must learn to take the completion that the defense gives him, patiently waiting for them to make a mistake and vacate an area.

This example of the Curl Read Game illustrates some intriguing dimensions of the games approach to coaching. Later sections of the text offer more examples of this approach for you to use in creating great learning experiences for your athletes.

Coaching football is a tough yet rewarding job. Football coaches are responsible not only for the development of good players but also for the development of young men who know right from wrong and know how to make good behavioral decisions. The emphasis of this book is on the concepts and strategies of teaching the essential basic to intermediate technical and tactical skills of football, using both the traditional and games approaches to that teaching. The foundation of effective teaching that this book provides will help you master the art of helping your athletes refine and improve the array of skills and techniques that make up the diverse, complex, fascinating and great game of football.

chapter 2

Evaluating Technical and Tactical Skills

Football is a team sport. In building your team, you should use specific evaluation tools to assess the development of the individual parts that make up the whole of the team. You must remember that basic physical skills contribute to the performance of the technical and tactical skills. In addition, a vast array of nonphysical skills, such as mental capacity, communication skills and character training, overlay athletic performance and affect its development (Rainer Martens, *Successful Coaching, Third Edition*). In this chapter we will examine evaluation guidelines, exploring the specific skills that should be evaluated and the tools to be used to accomplish that evaluation. Evaluations as described in this chapter will help you produce critiques of your players that are more objective, something that you should continually reach for.

Guidelines for Evaluation

Regardless of the skill that you are measuring and the evaluation tool that you are using, you should observe the basic guidelines that govern the testing and evaluation process. First, the athletes need to know and understand the purpose of the test and its relationship to the sport. If you are evaluating a technical skill, the correlation should be easy. But when you are evaluating physical skills, or mental, communication or character skills, you must explain the correlation between the skill and the aspect of the game that will benefit.

Second, you must motivate the athlete to improve. Understanding the correlation to his game will help, but sometimes the games seem a long ways away during practices and training. In the physical skills area, elevating the status of the testing process can help inspire the athletes. If you can create a game-day atmosphere with many players present and watching as you conduct the testing, the athletes will compete with more energy and enthusiasm than they would if you ran the tests in a more clinical fashion. Goal boards and record boards with all-time best performances can also motivate the athletes. The best of these boards have several categories (separating the linemen from the backs, for example, to give the backs a chance to compete in strength contests and the linemen a chance to compete in speed tests) and list several places, such as the Top Five or Top Ten performances, to give more athletes a reasonable chance to compete for a spot on the board.

The best motivation, though, is the concept of striving for a personal best effort in physical skills testing, or an improved score, compared to his own last evaluation, on measurement of technical, tactical, communication and mental skills. When the athlete compares himself today to himself yesterday, he can always succeed and make progress, regardless of the achievements of his teammates. And when he sees himself making progress, he will be motivated to continue to practice and train. This concept, while focusing on the individual, is not antithetical to the team concept. You simply need to remind the team that if every player gets better every day, the team must be getting better every day!

Third, all testing must be unbiased, formal and consistent. Athletes will easily recognize flaws in the testing process and subsequently lose confidence in the results. You must be systematic and accurate, treating every athlete the same way, for the test to have any integrity. No athlete can be credited with a test result on a physical skill if he does not execute the test regimen perfectly. You must mandate good form and attention to the details of the test. The same is true of evaluation tools that are not quantitatively measured. A position coach who wants to evaluate technical skills must use the same tool for all athletes at the position and score them fairly and consistently for them to trust the conclusions reached.

Fourth, you must convey the feedback to the athletes professionally and, if possible, personally. No athlete wants to fail, and all are self-conscious to a certain extent when they don't perform to their expectations or the expectations of their coach. At the same time, all athletes have areas that they need to improve, and you must communicate those needs to the athlete, especially if the athlete does not see or understand that he needs to make the improvement! Personal, private meetings with athletes are crucial to the exchange of this information. Factual results, comparative charts ranking the athlete, historical records of previous test results and even study of videotape of the athlete's performances can discreetly communicate both the positive areas of improvement and the areas where progress needs to be made. If you have a large number of athletes, you can accomplish these individual meetings in occasional and subtle ways—by asking the athlete to stay for a few minutes in the office after a position group meeting, by finding the athlete after practice or a workout in the locker room, by going out to practice early and creating an opportunity to talk to the player individually or by calling the player in to the office at random times just to talk. These in-person, one-on-one meetings are by far the best method to communicate to athletes the areas in which they need to improve.

Finally, you must apply the principles that you are asking of your players to the process of evaluating them. You must be an expert in your field in terms of your knowledge of the technical and tactical skills for your sport, and for your position group in particular, so that you can accurately and consistently evaluate the skill that you see your players perform. You must understand the value and importance of the physical skills (perhaps even in your personal lifestyle and health habits!) to convey the importance of these skills to the game. You must exhibit outstanding communication skills to be effective in your teaching, and you must exhibit those same skills in your dealings with other staff members, especially when you are visible to the players, so that you can establish credibility with the players regarding communication.

Evaluating Skills

Clearly, players must know the technical skills demanded by their sport, and they must know how to apply those skills in tactical situations when they compete. You must remember, however, that basic physical skills contribute to the performance of the technical and tactical skills, and must be consciously incorporated into the athlete's training plan. In addition, an array of nonphysical skills such as mental capacity, communication skills and character training also overlay athletic performance and affect its development.

As you evaluate your athletes, one concept is crucial: Each athlete should focus on trying to improve his own previous performance, as opposed to comparing his performance to those of his teammates. Certainly, comparative data helps an athlete see where he ranks on the team and perhaps among other players at his position, and this data may motivate him or help him set goals. But all rankings place some athletes on the team below others, and the danger of focusing on this type of system is that athletes can easily become discouraged if they consistently rank in the bottom part of the team or position group. Conversely, if the focus of the evaluation is for every player to improve, compared with himself at the last testing, then every player on the team can be successful every time tests are conducted. Whether you are looking at physical skills or nonphysical skills, encourage your athletes to achieve their own personal bests.

Evaluating Physical Skills

The essential physical skills for football are strength, speed, agility, power and flexibility. The training and evaluation of those five physical skills is especially important in the off-season and preseason periods, when athletes are concentrating on overall improvement. In-season evaluation, however, is also important, to ensure that any off-season gains, especially in strength, do not deteriorate because the players and coaches are devoting much of their time and attention to game-plan preparation and practice.

Testing should occur at least three times a year—once immediately before the football season begins to gauge the athlete's readiness for the season, once after the season to measure the retention of physical skills during competition and once in the spring to evaluate the athlete's progress and development in the off-season program. In addition, you will be constantly evaluating your athletes throughout the season to make slight adjustments, as you will learn more about in chapter 9.

Of course, training programs can positively affect several skills. For example, improvements in leg strength and flexibility will almost certainly improve speed. Furthermore, no specific workout program will ensure gains for every athlete in each of the five skill areas. Consequently, testing and measurement of gains in these areas is critical in showing you and the athlete where he is making gains and where to place the emphasis of subsequent training programs.

Strength

Strength testing can be done safely and efficiently using multiple-rep projections of the athlete's maximum performance. The risk of injury for the athlete is minimal because he is working with a weight that is less than his maximum load. After a proper warm-up, the athlete should select a weight that he believes he can rep at least three but no more than seven times. Using a chart of projected totals, the number of reps that he accomplishes will yield his max. This type of test is slightly less accurate than a one-rep max, in which the athlete continues to work with heavier weights until he finds the highest load that he can rep one time. But the one-rep test takes much longer to administer and is less safe because the athletes are working with peak loads. Furthermore, the accuracy of the test would be critical only if the athletes were competing with each other. Because the focus of the off-season training program is the development and improvement of each athlete, the multiple-rep projection is adequate for determining comparisons for each athlete with his own previous performances.

CORE STRENGTH

Like the proverbial chain that is only as strong as its weakest link, the core ultimately determines whether the athlete can put it all together and translate his strength, speed or agility into successful football performance. The core refers to the midsection of the body—the abdominal muscles, the lower-back muscles and the muscles of the hip girdle—that connect lower-body strength and functions with upper-body strength and functions. Core strength, then, is essential for football, but at the same time it is extremely difficult to isolate and test.

Football coaches repeatedly use the phrase "low pad wins" to emphasize the importance of keeping the legs bent and the center of gravity close to the ground for improved balance, leverage and transition from one direction to another. Without a strong core, the football athlete will experience great difficulty in keeping his pads low as he plays the game. The core also must be strong for the football athlete to be able to play with great explosiveness—combining strength, power and speed into decisive and effective blocks, tackles, runs and kicks. Every physical training program for football, therefore, must include exercises that strengthen and develop the core. This training program must go beyond sit-ups and crunches, which are important but not comprehensive enough to develop true core strength. Football athletes must incorporate active exercises such as lunges, step-ups and jump squats to focus on development of the core.

As mentioned before, isolating core strength is difficult because it is involved in the performance of every physical skill. But any exercise that recruits one or more large muscle areas and two or more primary joints (such as the bench press) can be used to test core strength (NSCA, *Essentials of Personal Training*). The ultimate evaluation of core strength, however, is the athlete's performance of football skills on the practice field and on game day in the stadium.

Speed

Speed testing for football has always focused on the 40-yard dash. Rarely does a football athlete have to run longer than 40 yards on a play, so longer distances are not indicative of the type of speed needed to play the game. But pass plays, kicking plays and runs from scrimmage that break into the open all require sprints that are in the 40-yard range, so the athlete's time over that distance is crucial. Still, the majority of runs that a football player makes in a game are short bursts, so a test of the player's initial 10-yard speed from a standing start also correlates well with the type of speed needed to play the game. The 10- and 40-yard tests can be administered simultaneously, with a coach or electronic timer stationed at each of those distances to record times for both yardages on the same trial. If the players are in the full-pad part of the season, test them in full pads. You want the test situation to resemble the game situation as closely as possible.

Agility

Football also requires the athlete to change direction quickly in short spaces and use quality footwork to get into proper position to make tackles, break tackles, block and shed blocks, cover receivers and get open on pass routes. So agility and footwork are physical skills that must be trained and measured. The most common agility test for football is the pro shuttle, a 20-yard lateral shuttle run. In this test, the athlete starts on a designated line, runs 5 yards to his left or right, returns through his starting point to a spot 5 yards on the other side of that starting point and then moves back to finish at the point where he started (yardage run is 5, 10 and 5). This test measures the athlete's ability to plant and change directions and requires him to keep the core low, in the athletic body position frequently mentioned throughout the skills in this book. The time on the pro shuttle should be about two-tenths of a second less than the athlete's 40-yard dash time. If the margin is greater, the athlete should emphasize speed development in his program; if the margin is less, the athlete should emphasize agility drills in his training program.

Power

Power is the fourth primary skill required for football. The emphasis here is on the lower-body explosiveness that helps the football athlete sustain blocks, finish tackles, break tackles, win on a pass rush, or jump to catch or intercept a pass. The two simplest and best tests for power are the standing long jump and the vertical jump. Administer both tests with the athlete in a stationary position so that the test measures pure explosiveness unassisted by a running start. Allow the athlete to take several trials at each event, using his best effort as his recorded score.

Flexibility

Flexibility is the most neglected physical skill but one of the most important. Increases in flexibility will help the athlete improve his performance in just about every other physical skill. Off-season programs should stress stretching, and you should encourage, or mandate, athletes to stretch for at least 15 minutes each day. In addition, the training program should include exercises that require the athlete to bend and move, such as lunges, step-ups, and so on, so that the athlete is stretching and training the hip girdle and lower-back area as he works on strength and power. Flexibility is difficult to measure, but the classic sit-and-reach test provides a reasonable indication of the athlete's range and gives him a standard to improve on.

Evaluating Nonphysical Skills

Athletic performance is not purely physical. A number of other factors influence it. You must recognize and emphasize mental skills, communication skills and character skills to enable your athletes to reach peak athletic performance.

Despite the importance of the physical, mental, communication and character skills, however, the emphasis in this book is on the coaching of essential technical and tactical skills. For an in-depth discussion of how to teach and develop both physical and nonphysical skills, refer to chapters 9 through 12 in Rainer Martens' *Successful Coaching, Third Edition*.

Mental Skills

Football is a complex game because of the large number of players on the field at one time; the vast number of possibilities for alignment, formations and plays; and the huge diversity of athletic types and abilities that make up a team. Consequently, football requires excellent mental skills, if for no other reason than for memorizing and remembering the plays and assignments!

More important, however, the successful football player has to have the mental ability to sort out and isolate the cues that allow him to execute those assignments. Linebackers have to see only one or two key blockers and ignore the rest, so that they can read what the play is and where it is going. Quarterbacks have to find only one or two key defenders and ignore the rest, so that they can determine where to throw the ball on a pass play. Defensive backs have to focus on only one or two receivers and resist the temptation to peek into the backfield after a pass play begins, so that they can cover their area or their man. And field goal kickers have to focus entirely on the ball and ignore the onrushing defenders, so that they can successfully execute their kick. The performance of these skills takes study, discipline, focus and belief that the system of cues will produce the desired results. The term mental toughness might be the best and simplest way to describe the concentration and determination required to perform these skills in the dangerous, high-risk intensity of football.

Communication Skills

Football also requires communication skills at several levels—among the players on the field and between the coaches and the players in classrooms, in practices and on the sidelines in games—to get the desired skills accomplished. Football teams use numerous and specific forms of communication to get all players on the same page on every play. Coaches send plays on to the field by messengers or by hand signals; both offense and defense have a huddle in which the play is conveyed to every teammate on the field; both sides of the ball use oral or signaled checks or audibles at the line of scrimmage to react to schemes that they see. You have to convey adjustments to the game plan and strategy in sideline meetings and halftime talks. All these communication skills are essential to football, and you must spend considerable time coordinating your system of communication.

Character Skills

Finally, character skills help shape the performance of the team. Although the game is tough, physical and hard hitting, officials regulate it so that it is fair and as safe as possible within the rules. Football athletes must play hard and aggressively, but they also must stop at the whistle and keep all contact in front of the player whom they hit. Failure to follow the rules results in major penalties or disqualification, and both outcomes clearly affect the team's performance. Football players also must avoid becoming distracted by any pushing, shoving or talking that might go on between plays. In all these cases, the team that has the most character among its players will have the best chance for success.

Evaluation Tools

Football coaches, perhaps more than coaches of any other sport, use recordings of practices and games to evaluate athletes' performance of basic technical and tactical skills. Recording is useful because so many players are participating at one time and it is difficult, if not impossible, to watch each of them on every play. The problem is compounded, especially on game days, because the players are a considerable distance away and you cannot see from the sideline precisely what is happening on the line of scrimmage and on the far side of the field. Recording allows you to review reps in practice or plays in a game repeatedly, enabling you to evaluate each player on each play. The recording also becomes an excellent teaching tool in individual, group or team meetings because the players can see themselves perform and listen to your comments evaluating that performance.

You can use many different systems to evaluate what you see on the recording. The most common system isn't really a system at all—it is the subjective impression that you get when you watch the recording, without taking notes or systematically evaluating every player on every play. Because of limitations of time and staff, many coaches use the recording in this manner, previewing the recording, gathering impressions and then sharing those impressions with the player or players as they watch the recording together later.

Other coaches systematically grade the recording, evaluating the athlete's performance on every play as to whether he executed the correct assignment, technique and tactical decision. The grading process can be simple; for example, you can simply give the athlete a plus or a minus on each play and score the total number of pluses versus the total number of minuses for the game. Alternatively, you can score the athlete on each aspect of the play, giving him a grade for his assignment, a grade for his technique and a grade for his tactical decision making. More elaborate grading systems keep track of position-specific hidden statistics such as knockdowns on blocks, plus yards for ball carriers after encountering the first tackler, pass breakups for defenders, hurries of the quarterback for defensive linemen, hustle plays in which an athlete gives extra effort, and bonus points for big plays such as touchdowns, interceptions or blocked kicks.

Regardless of the level of sophistication or detail of the grading instrument, most coaches use a grading system of some kind for evaluating game tape. Most grading systems are based on a play-by-play (or rep-by-rep in practices) analysis of performance, possibly coupled with an analysis of productivity totals such as the ones listed previously. Rarely does a coach systematically evaluate the technical and tactical skills required for football on a skill-by-skill basis.

Furthermore, when coaches evaluate a skill, they generally evaluate only the result (did the wide receiver catch the ball or not?), not the key elements that determine the player's ability to catch the ball (eye contact, hand position and so on).

Figure 2.1, *a* and *b*, are examples of an evaluation tool that allows you to isolate technical and tactical skills. By breaking down the whole skill into its component parts, this tool enables a more objective assessment of an athlete's performance in a skill than can be produced by statistics. By using these figures and the technical and tactical skills in parts II and III as a guide, you can create an evaluation tool for each of the technical and tactical skills that you want to evaluate during your season. In figure 2.1a, using the technical skill of drive blocking as an example, we have broken down the skill by pulling out each of the key points from the skills found in chapters 3 through 5 so that you can rate your players' execution of the skill in specific targeted areas.

As you may already know, evaluating tactical skills is more difficult because there are many outside influences that factor into how and when the skill comes into play. In figure 2.1*b*, rather than listing each of the various possibilities, we have targeted the general areas that need to be addressed when evaluating tactical skills. The breakdown of these general areas, as shown using the pass-run option as an example, is consistent with the format for how the tactical skills have been broken down in chapters 6 through 8. The hope, then, is that the more you work with chapters 6 through 8, the more automatic the information in those chapters will become, making figure 2.1*b* an effective guide for you as you evaluate your players' execution of tactical skills.

This evaluation tool, and the process of scoring that it advocates, may help you avoid the common pitfall of becoming preoccupied with the result of the skill and coaching and evaluating only the final outcome. This tool will help you pinpoint where errors are occurring and enable you to focus on correcting those errors with your athletes.

The tool is admittedly somewhat subjective because it asks the evaluator to rate on a scale of 1 to 5 how well the athlete executes the basic elements of each technical or tactical skill, and ratings would simply be an opinion based on observation. But you can add some statistical weight to the process by scoring the player on each play in which the skill came into use. For example, a linebacker involved in 40 plays during a game might have 10 opportunities to make a tackle. You could then score the linebacker on each of those 10 opportunities and calculate an average score. Most coaches would simply grade the linebacker on whether or not he made the tackle, but this tool allows you to organize your evaluation of the elements of tackling. You can pinpoint where the player is making mistakes by breaking down the skill and analyzing the component parts.

Likewise, if a wide receiver who plays 40 plays in a game has five opportunities to run crossing routes, you could use the evaluation tool to grade each of those five plays on the tactical skill of recognizing man or zone coverages and making the correct adjustment. This score would give both you and the receiver an excellent evaluation of his ability to perform this tactical skill, regardless of whether he caught the ball or even whether it was thrown to him.

You must go beyond the result and focus your teaching on the cues and knowledge needed to execute a specific skill, giving the athlete an evaluation that alerts him to the key elements of the skill that need improvement. An important corollary to this teaching and evaluation strategy, then, is that sometimes when the result is positive, the evaluation of the athlete's technique might be substantially critical.

For example, if the wide receiver is working in a practice session on catching the chest-high pass in the hands instead of on the pads, you need to reinforce the key point of using the hands, whether or not he catches the ball. If the receiver drops the ball but uses his hands, you must be positive about his effort to use that technique and avoid comments about his dropping the ball. Likewise, if the receiver catches the ball but uses his pads, you need to tell him that he is using an unacceptable technique. You cannot give the receiver mixed messages; you must focus on the process of catching the football, not the result, if you truly want the receiver to catch the ball in his hands.

This lesson was graphically illustrated to me, a career college football coach, at a Little League baseball game. I was coaching a team of 10-year-olds, including my son. After completing several practices, we were playing our first real game. I was excited about coaching this team of eager youngsters and confident about my ability to help them be successful. In the top of the first inning, our best pitcher was on the mound, and he, too, was excited and probably a bit nervous. His first four pitches were too high, so he walked the first batter. The next batter stepped

Figure 2.1a Drive Blocking Evaluation

| | SKILL RATING | | | | | |
| | Weak | | | | Strong | |
Drive blocking	**1**	**2**	**3**	**4**	**5**	**Notes**
Creates a base of power	1	2	3	4	5	
Uses proper footwork	1	2	3	4	5	
Contacts the defender at the landmark	1	2	3	4	5	
Follows through	1	2	3	4	5	

From *Coaching Football Technical and Tactical Skills* by ASEP, 2006, Champaign, IL: Human Kinetics.

Figure 2.1b Pass–Run Option Evaluation

| | SKILL RATING | | | | | |
| | Weak | | | | Strong | |
Pass–run option	**1**	**2**	**3**	**4**	**5**	**Notes**
Avoids distractions as discussed in "Watch Out!"	1	2	3	4	5	
Reads the situation	1	2	3	4	5	
Uses the appropriate knowledge about the team strategy and game plan	1	2	3	4	5	
Uses the appropriate knowledge about the rules	1	2	3	4	5	
Uses the appropriate knowledge about physical playing conditions	1	2	3	4	5	
Uses the appropriate knowledge about opponent's strengths and weaknesses	1	2	3	4	5	
Uses the appropriate knowledge about himself and his team	1	2	3	4	5	

From *Coaching Football Technical and Tactical Skills* by ASEP, 2006, Champaign, IL: Human Kinetics.

in, and the first two pitches were also high. By now, his teammates, the assistant coaches, and more than a few parents were shouting advice to the young pitcher: "Throw strikes!" or "Get the ball down!" Although I knew that he was nervous, another thought occurred to me—he's only 10 years old, but he knows that he needs to throw strikes, and he knows that he needs to get the ball down! The comments that he was hearing were not only unhelpful but also contributing to his anxiety. What he needed was some advice from his coach on how to get the ball down—some instruction on the key focal points of the technical skill of pitching a baseball. And that's when I realized that I didn't know enough about pitching a baseball to tell him what to do. I have never felt more powerless or ineffective in my entire life as a coach.

The sample evaluation tool shown in figure 2.1, *a* and *b*, constitutes a simple way to use the details of each technical and tactical skill, providing an outline for both the player and you to review and a mechanism for understanding the areas in which improvement is needed. The tool also can be used as a summary exercise. After a game, after a week of practice, or after a preseason or spring practice segment, the athlete can score himself on all his essential technical and tactical skills, including all the cues and focal points, and on as many of the corollary skills as desired. You can also score the athlete and then compare the two score sheets. The ensuing discussion will provide both the player and you with a direction for future practices and drills, and help you decide where the immediate focus of attention needs to be for the athlete to improve his performance. You can repeat this process later, so that the athlete can look for improvement in the areas where he has been concentrating his workouts. As the process unfolds, a better consensus between the athlete's score sheet and your score sheet should also occur.

You must display the identical mental skills you ask of your athletes—skills such as emotional control, self-confidence and motivation to achieve—because the players will mirror your mental outlook. Likewise, players will model your character, in terms of your trustworthiness, fairness and ability to earn respect. You are a role model, whether you want to be or not, and the athlete will develop the proper mental and character skills only if you display those skills.

You must evaluate athletes in many areas and in many ways. This process of teaching, evaluating and motivating the athlete to improve his performance defines the job of the coach: "taking the athlete somewhere he could not get to by himself." Without you, the athlete would not have a clear direction of the steps that he needs to take, or how he should proceed, to become a better player. You provide the expertise, guidance and incentive for the athlete to make progress.

One final rule, however, caps the discussion of evaluating athletes. Athletes in every sport want to know how much you care before they care how much you know. You need to keep in mind that at times you must suspend the process of teaching and evaluating to deal with the athlete as a person. You must spend time with your athletes discussing topics other than their sport and their performance. You must show each athlete that you have an interest and a concern for him as a person, that you are willing to listen to his issues and that you are willing to assist him if doing so is legal and he wants to be helped. Events in the athlete's personal life can overshadow his athletic quests, and you must be sensitive to that reality.

Another reality is that athletes will play their best and their hardest for the coach who cares. Their skills will improve, and their performance will improve, because they want to reward the coach's caring attitude for them with inspired performance. They will finish their athletic careers for that coach having learned a lifelong lesson that care and concern are as important as any skill in the game of football.

PART II

Teaching Technical Skills

Now that you know how to teach and evaluate sport skills, you are ready to dive into the specific skills necessary for success in football. This part focuses on the basic and intermediate skills necessary for your team's success, including offensive technical skills related to throwing, receiving and evading tacklers and defensive technical skills related to tackling, coverages and blitzing. This part also focuses on the essential special teams technical skills related to kicking, punting, and receiving kicks and punts.

Chapters 3, 4 and 5 present the material in a way that is clear and easy to understand. More important, you can immediately incorporate the information into your practices. Whether you are a seasoned veteran or a new coach, you will find the presentation of skills in this part helpful as you work with your athletes.

For each skill we first present what we call the "Key Points" for the particular skill. These points highlight the most important aspects of the skill, providing you and your players with a roadmap to proper execution of the skill. The remainder of the skill is a detailed explanation of these essential components, including instructional photos and diagrams to guide you along the way.

At the end of each skill we include a table to teach you to detect common errors and correct those errors in your athletes. To close each skill, we include a useful "At a Glance" section to guide you to other tools in the book that will help you teach your athletes this particular skill—whether it is another technical skill that they need to be able to perform to be successful, a tactical skill that uses this technical skill, or a practice plan or drill that helps you teach the skill.

chapter 3

Offensive Technical Skills

This chapter covers the offensive technical skills that you and your players must know to be successful. In this chapter, you will find the following skills:

Stance and Start for Offense

One of the greatest advantages that offensive players hold over defensive players in football is knowing the snap count and when the play will start. Regardless of whether the player is in a three-point, two-point or quarter-back stance, he must be able to explode out of his stance on any snap count in any direction to make the most of this advantage.

CHOOSING THE APPROPRIATE STANCE

The three-point stance (see figure 3.1) is used primarily by linemen, tight ends and fullbacks. This stance helps keep the player's pad level down and promotes a quick, explosive start, especially straight ahead. For run blocking, the three-point stance is ideal; its limitations are that from it, the lineman's pass set is more difficult and players cannot see the defensive alignments as well before the snap.

The two-point stance (see figure 3.2) is used primarily by wide receivers and tailbacks. This stance allows the player to have excellent vision of the defensive deployment, which is far more important for these positions than a low, explosive start.

Quarterbacks use a specific version of the two-point stance (see figure 3.3) with feet more parallel to the line of scrimmage and hands under the center. Again, being able to see the defense is far more important to the quarterback than the quickness of his start.

Figure 3.1   Three-point stance.   **Figure 3.2   Two-point stance.**

Figure 3.3 Two-point stance for quarterbacks.

ACHIEVING BALANCE

On the snap, balance is required for quick, sudden movement in any given direction. Players may feel more comfortable moving in one direction—for example, they may prefer moving to their left instead of to their right—but all players need to strive to be skilled at moving in both directions, as well as straight ahead, with equal quickness.

In the three-point stance, as shown previously in figure 3.1, linemen must keep enough weight on the down hand so that they have some forward lean, but not so much that they fall forward if someone knocks the hand out from under them. This balanced position allows the player to start to his left, right or straight ahead with a low pad level.

Players positioned in the two-point stance, as shown previously in figure 3.2, should keep some weight on each foot to stay balanced, with slightly more pressure on the foot that will stay on the ground when they take their first step. In a traditional two-point staggered stance, the player should move his back foot first, leaving the front foot on the ground. Therefore, before the snap the player should have slightly more weight on his front foot, but not so much that he risks losing his balance forward before the snap.

The quarterback's stance, as shown previously in figure 3.3, requires the quarterback to keep his weight evenly distributed between his feet, with slightly more weight and pressure on the foot that will stay on the ground when he takes his first step. If his first step is to his right, he should keep his left foot on the ground at the snap of the ball, pivoting slightly on that foot as he takes his first step with his right foot, opening up to the right.

The two-point stance used by a tailback, or halfback, involves all the same elements of balance and pressure as the two-point stance for wide receivers or quarterbacks.

(continued)

However, the tailback's feet should not be staggered in his alignment. Both feet should be parallel to the line of scrimmage and his hands can rest comfortably on his thigh pads as he bends slightly at the knees. At the snap, the tailback must push off the foot that is opposite his starting direction and take his first step with the foot closest to the direction he is going.

In all stances, players should remember to keep weight on the balls of their feet, even if that means taking a somewhat pigeon-toed stance, because doing so will eliminate false steps. In addition, to take advantage of knowing the snap count, the offensive team needs to start plays at different times within the cadence, hoping that someone on defense will jump offside and that all defensive players will become hesitant about their start because they won't know when the ball will be snapped. Of course, if offensive players commit a false start and incur illegal procedure penalties because of the changing snap count, the advantage swings the other way!

FEELING COMFORTABLE IN THE STANCE

Comfort in a stance is imperative. Offensive players must be able to remain poised and stable on a long snap count. They need to develop a poised, comfortable stance that is solid while at the same time being coiled—weight forward, hips low—for an explosive start. The knees must be bent slightly, weight evenly distributed, with just enough pressure on the plant foot to keep that foot on the ground at the snap. Regardless of whether the player is in a three-point, two-point or quarterback stance, feeling comfortable improves the chances for a positive start to the play.

At a Glance

The following parts of the text offer additional information on stances and starts for offense.

KEEPING THE HEAD AND EYES UP

Regardless of the stance that they are using, all offensive players must keep their head and eyes up so that they can see the alignment of the defenders and process as much information as possible about the defense's tactics before the snap. Offensive players should remember that they do *not* need to see the ball to know when the play is going to start (with the possible exception of wide receivers playing in stadiums with large, noisy crowds). The oral command of the quarterback will start the play. So, as the quarterback starts his cadence, the other 10 offensive players should be assessing the defense for clues about their intentions on the play. Remember, too, that without having a solid, comfortable stance, your players will probably be unable to use this crucial element of offensive strategy.

Common Errors

You may run into several common errors when teaching your athletes the proper stance and start for offense.

Error	Error correction
Player tips off his direction.	Emphasize using the same balanced stance on all plays. The player must not lean left or right if he is going to move laterally on the snap, he must not put too much weight on his down hand when he is going to move forward at the snap, and he must not take too much weight off his down hand when he is going to pass set because any of these errors might give away his intentions.
Defense surprises offense with a line game.	Emphasize keeping the head up in the stance and on the start, focusing on the defender, specifically the landmark for the block on the defender, so that if the landmark moves at the snap, the blocker can adjust.
Player jumps offside.	Emphasize not leaning too far forward in the initial stance because the player might lose his balance and fall forward if he is overeager to start at the snap. The offense should practice snapping the ball on different snap counts (some short, some long) every day so that the blockers get used to remaining poised in their stances for a different amount of time on each play and therefore will not jump offside on longer snap counts.
Player takes false steps.	Emphasize keeping weight on the balls of the feet so that the pushoff foot does not come off the ground on the first step. Practice going left more often (for right-handed players) to eliminate the tendency to take the first step with the right foot on every play, which is incorrect on plays going to the left.

The center–quarterback exchange starts every offensive play in football and is therefore the single most important offensive skill in the game. Nothing is more frustrating to players and coaches, or more detrimental to offensive performance, than a fumble or mishandle of the snap. At worst, the other team might take the ball away; at best, the play breaks down, wasting the efforts of the nine other offensive players. A seemingly simple skill, the center–quarterback exchange is deceptively technical and must be practiced daily to be perfected.

HAND POSITIONING

The quarterback must be sure to keep his hands far enough under the center, without any separation, so that a forceful snap will not push the quarterback's hands backward or cause him to lose the ball between his hands. The quarterback should be sure that his entire top hand, as far back as his wrist, is underneath the center (see figure 3.4). The center should position his dominant hand on the side of the football, with thumb up and fingers pointed down, and far enough forward that he can get a secure one-handed grip on the ball.

The quarterback must also ensure that the heels of his hands are always touching, so that the ball does not slip between his hands (see figure 3.5). He should press up with his bottom hand to prevent any separation, keeping the fingers of the bottom hand extended toward the ground so that ample room is available between his hands for the ball.

Additionally, the quarterback's passing hand should be on top when he receives the snap from the center. This hand position ensures that when the ball hits his hands with the laces up, on top of the ball, the laces will hit on the fingers of his passing hand. The center will naturally rotate the ball 90 degrees from a position perpendicular to the line of scrimmage when it is on the ground to a position parallel to the line of scrimmage when he completes the snap. With practice, the center can adjust the ball when

Figure 3.4   Quarterback's entire top hand positioned underneath the center when receiving the snap.

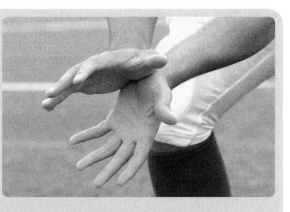

Figure 3.5   The heels of the quarterback's hands should touch when receiving the snap.

it is on the ground before the snap so that the laces will rotate perfectly to line up with the fingers of the quarterback's throwing hand. If the snap is properly executed, the quarterback will not have to rotate the ball around in his hands after the snap to get the laces in the proper alignment. Eliminating this extra ball movement helps ensure ball security because the quarterback can grip the ball tightly immediately after the snap.

LOWER-BODY POSITIONING

Quarterbacks and centers are not always evenly matched in height, so the quarterback must adjust the depth of his stance to the height of the center. He must bend his knees enough so that he is able to fit his hands properly under the center (see figure 3.6).

Figure 3.6 Proper quarterback lower-body positioning prior to the snap.

The quarterback should keep his feet close to parallel, keeping his weight on the balls of his feet so that he can push off properly in any direction. The quarterback can use a slightly staggered stance if he prefers, but he must use that same stance regardless of the play call so that he does not tip off the defense about which direction he is going.

RECEIVING THE SNAP

The center's stance should be a balanced, poised three-point stance (see "Stance and Start for Offense" on page 22). When the center snaps the ball, he must simultaneously take his first step toward his blocking assignment, which means that his hips will move forward slightly as he snaps. The quarterback must be sure to follow this movement by reaching his hands forward with the center, keeping his hands together and in the proper position.

After receiving the snap, the quarterback must immediately secure the ball by bringing it into his midsection with both hands (see figure 3.7). This action is called seating the ball, and

Figure 3.7 Quarterback bringing the ball into his midsection after receiving the snap.

(continued)

At a Glance

The following parts of the text offer additional information on the center–quarterback exchange.

the quarterback must do it every time he takes a snap. If the ball is properly seated, no passing lineman or back has a chance to knock the ball loose before the play can be properly executed.

Common Errors

You may run into several common errors when teaching your athletes how to execute the center–quarterback exchange.

Error	Error correction
Ball doesn't hit the quarterback's hands.	Emphasize the forcefulness of the snap. Make sure that the center thinks about snapping the ball all the way back to his own hips, not just to the quarterback's hands. Also, remind the quarterback that he must get his hands in the proper position under the center's hips.
Ball goes between the quarterback's hands.	Remind the quarterback that if he presses upward with his bottom hand, no separation will occur.
Ball hits the quarterback's fingertips.	If the quarterback occasionally gets his fingers smashed, he probably does not have his hands open far enough. Remind him to point the fingers of his bottom hand toward the ground.
Quarterback bobbles the ball.	Have the center practice rotating the laces so that the ball is in the proper position when the quarterback receives it.
The ball is knocked loose from the quarterback right after the snap.	The quarterback probably keeps the ball too far from his body after taking the snap. Have the quarterback practice seating the ball (bringing it into his belly with both hands) after taking practice snaps, so that this action becomes a habit in games and passing blockers or running backs do not knock the ball loose.

KEY POINTS

The most important components of ball security are

o forming a pocket on handoffs,

o securing the ball and

o catching the pitch.

Ball exchanges from the quarterback to the running backs, whether by handoffs or pitches, must be consistent, and the offense must consciously protect the ball at all times. Proper ball handling allows the offense to maintain control of the ball and have a chance to run successful plays.

After the running back receives the ball, his most important objective is keeping it secure; holding on to the ball is more important than gaining any amount of yards. Ball security keeps the offense on the field and prevents the defense from gaining valuable field position by recovering a fumble. The techniques of properly running with the football are all based on the principles of sound ball security.

FORMING A POCKET ON HANDOFFS

If the running back is going to receive a handoff from the quarterback, he uses the arm nearest the quarterback to form the upper part of the pocket for the handoff (see figure 3.8). The running back should raise the elbow of this upper arm to chest height, keeping his forearm parallel to the ground and his hand angled slightly toward the ground. He should place the other arm at about belt level, forming the bottom part of the pocket with the palm upward. The running back must concentrate on keeping this pocket open until he feels the ball against his belly, but he must keep his eyes looking at the blocking scheme in front of him so that he can see where to run the ball.

The quarterback should look at the pocket formed by the running back's arms and concentrate on placing the ball against the running back's belly without hitting his arms. The quarterback's arms should give as the ball hits the running back's belly, so that the ball does not bounce off or slow down the running back. The quarterback must not let go of the ball until it is in contact with the running back's belly.

Figure 3.8 Running back forming a pocket for the handoff.

SECURING THE BALL

When the running back feels the ball against his belly, he should fold his upper arm over the top of the ball and bring his lower arm up over the ball (see figure 3.9). The hands should grasp and cover the opposite points of the ball, and both elbows should press the ball against the belly. As the running back approaches the hole or opposing players, the arms and hands should continue to grasp the ball in this manner to prevent

(continued)

Figure 3.9 **Running back securing the ball after the handoff.**

Figure 3.10 **Running back carrying the ball in a one-arm grip.**

defenders from jarring it loose or taking it away.

When the running back is not in traffic (near other players, such as linemen, defenders or others), he can carry the ball with one arm. He should always carry the ball in the arm farther from the nearest defender who is a threat, with the hand covering the front point of the ball, the arm pressing the ball against the body and the elbow covering the back point of the ball, squeezing it against his side (see figure 3.10). The running back must maintain these three pressure points (front point of the ball, back point of the ball and the side of the ball) throughout the entire play. Although the one-arm grip is most acceptable when no defenders are nearby, the running back may use the free arm, if necessary, to ward off potential tacklers and further protect the ball.

Usually, when the ball carrier is carrying the ball in the arm farther from a defender, he should be carrying it in the arm closer to the sideline, or in what is referred to as the outside arm. If a tackler approaches from the side where the ball carrier is holding the ball, however, the ball carrier can switch the ball to the other hand by sliding the ball to the opposite side of his body. To make this shift, the ball carrier slides the ball to the center of the stomach, covers the ball with both arms and then removes the original carrying arm, leaving the ball in the opposite arm, as shown in figure 3.11 *a-c*. In making the shift, he should be sure to keep constant contact over the point of the ball. If the ball carrier finds himself in the open field, either before he reaches the line of scrimmage or after breaking through, he may shift the ball in this manner as well.

CATCHING THE PITCH

If the quarterback pitches the ball to him, the running back must keep his eyes on the ball instead of on the blocking scheme in front of him. The running back's hand position for the catch depends on the height of the pitch. If the pitch is below the jersey numbers, the little fingers are together (see figure 3.12*a*); if the pitch is above the jersey numbers, the thumbs are together (see figure 3.12*b*). Regardless of which hand position he is using, the running back must watch the ball all the way into his hands, secure the

Figure 3.11 *(a-c)* Ball carrier shifting the ball to the opposite side of the body.

Figure 3.12 Running back *(a)* catching a low pitch and *(b)* catching a high pitch.

(continued)

catch, slide the ball to one side of his body (probably the outside arm) and lock in the three pressure points.

When making a pitch, the quarterback must make the toss firm enough to get there quickly but soft enough that it's easy to catch. Ideally, the ball should be just above waist height so that the running back can catch it at the level where he will be carrying it, and where his arms do not have to overextend to make the catch.

Common Errors

You may run into several common errors when teaching your athletes proper ball exchange.

Error	Error correction
Running back reaches for the ball.	Remind the running back to keep his eyes on the blocks; he should not see the ball being handed to him. Remind the running back that he must allow the ball to hit his stomach, not his arms. The running back should never try to grab the ball.
Ball bounces off the running back's stomach.	Remind the quarterback to hand off the ball softly so that he doesn't knock the wind out of the running back when giving him the ball. The running back must also remember to fold his arms over the ball as soon as he feels it touch his midsection.
Ball hits the running back's arms.	The running back must be sure that his inside elbow is up. The quarterback must keep his eyes on the running back's belly, which is the pocket for the ball, as he hands off. This action is called looking the ball into the pocket.
Running back fumbles in traffic.	Remind the running back to return to two-handed ball security when surrounded by defenders.
Running back drops a pitch.	The running back probably took his eyes off the ball to look for defenders coming at him. Remind him that he will be in more trouble if the ball is on the ground!
Defender punches the ball out.	The running back must squeeze the elbow against the body to protect the ball from a punch. A simple demonstration will show the player this concept: Have the player hold the ball away from his body with the front tip properly covered but the back tip not pressed against the body. In this position, you can easily punch the ball out of his grasp. If he holds the ball with the back tip pressed against his body, you will be unable to punch the ball away.

Option Pitch Mechanics

On an option play, the final ball carrier is not determined in the huddle. Instead, the quarterback reads the defense and then decides either to keep the ball or to pitch it to a running back. The basic option play is the speed option, in which the quarterback attacks the defensive end or outside linebacker and decides what to do with the ball based on how the defender plays. "Option Pitch Read" on page 177 discusses the quarterback's decision-making process on this play. Here, we will cover the quarterback's mechanics for the play.

INITIAL HESITATION

After taking the snap from the center, the quarterback hesitates initially before attacking down the line of scrimmage toward the defender whom he is going to read. This initial hesitation allows the pitch back to get slightly ahead of the quarterback into proper position to receive the pitch, in what is commonly known as pitch relationship. The quarterback can accomplish the hesitation in several ways.

The two most common techniques are a reverse pivot, in which the quarterback pivots away from the center and spins around 270 degrees to attack down the line, or a technique that requires the quarterback to take two steps backward before starting down the line. The disadvantage of the reverse pivot is that the quarterback turns his back briefly on the defender whom he is going to attack, thus delaying his assessment of the defender's reaction. By using the backward steps technique the quarterback can more quickly pick up the defender whom is going to attack, but the steps take the quarterback away from the line of scrimmage instead of toward it.

ATTACKING THE END MAN

Before the quarterback can make his read and decide what to do with the ball, he must attack the unblocked defender on the end of the line (a common shorthand reference for this defender is EMOL, meaning "end man on the line"). As the quarterback attacks this defender, he must be running a downhill course, a lateral run that is slightly angled toward the line of scrimmage (see figure 3.13). If the quarterback runs parallel to or away from the line of scrimmage, he will be too deep to cut upfield inside the defender and successfully run the football.

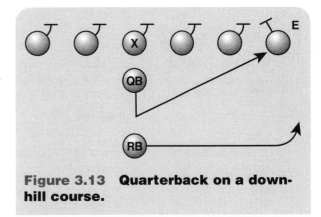

Figure 3.13 Quarterback on a downhill course.

Only by taking the downhill course can the quarterback threaten the inside shoulder of the defender. Because the quarterback's running lane, if he keeps the ball, will be inside the defender, the quarterback's course must appear to be going inside, or underneath, the defender. Attacking the inside shoulder should also cause the defender to turn toward the quarterback, which makes for an easy pitch read.

On the other hand, the quarterback must be prepared to pitch early in the play, as he takes his first steps away from the center, if the defender attacks him. If the

(continued)

At a Glance

The following parts of the text offer additional information on option pitch mechanics:

Feathering	p. 114
Option Pitch Read	p. 177
Reacting When Unblocked	p. 232
Defending the Option	p. 235

EMOL tries to feather, or stall, the option, the quarterback should attack him aggressively, close the gap and then, at a distance of 2 to 3 yards from the defender, turn slightly upfield inside him. The defender, who is probably assigned to the quarterback, will likely have to stop feathering the option and commit to the quarterback. As this happens, the quarterback should settle on his inside foot and prepare to make the pitch to the running back.

MAKING THE PITCH

The quarterback should carry the ball in both hands, at chest level, and be ready to deliver it quickly. Some defenders will attack the quarterback and try to cause an errant pitch, so the quarterback must be ready to pitch as soon as he turns to face the defender, realizing that the defender might be blitzing right at him.

The quarterback makes the pitch with the upfield or back hand (right hand going to the right; left hand going to the left). The quarterback should settle slightly, brake his run toward the defender and push off the foot opposite the pitching hand as he makes the pitch. The hand should pronate—in other words, the thumb should be down—on the pitch, giving the ball a gentle, end-over-end rotation.

Common Errors

You may run into several common errors when teaching your athletes option pitch mechanics.

Error	Error correction
Quarterback attacks parallel to the line or drifts away from the line.	Quarterbacks may tend to distance themselves from the line blocking that is going on right next to them and may not realize that they are taking an incorrect course. They must attack downhill at a slight angle toward the line of scrimmage as they move laterally toward the man whom they are going to attack. Observe the quarterback's course from the side of the play to be sure that his path is correct.
Quarterback fails to settle and step.	The quarterback should not keep running full speed when he pitches; he must settle and step. Quarterbacks can work in pairs and jog 5 yards apart, taking turns pitching to each other. On each pitch, they settle and step, which allows the partner to get ahead of the player who is pitching.
Quarterback fails to hesitate after the snap.	If the quarterback does not hesitate, the pitch back will not be able to get ahead of the quarterback. If the ball is pitched, the pitch back will not be able to outrun the EMOL defender toward the sideline. The quarterback must allow the pitch back to get ahead by hesitating. You must slow down the quarterback at the snap.

Quarterback Drops

KEY POINTS

The most important components of quarterback drops are

- number and length of strides,
- foot positioning,
- determining hit and throw versus hitch and throw and
- reacting to pressure.

The quarterback's drop is the number of steps that he takes away from the line of scrimmage before he sets up in the pocket on a drop-back pass. Each pass in the offense requires the quarterback to take a specific drop, or number of steps, for that particular play, based on the depth and location of his receivers' primary pass routes. A correct drop by the quarterback helps ensure proper timing between the quarterback and the receivers. To execute both short and long passes properly, the quarterback must match his drop with the routes called.

NUMBER AND LENGTH OF STRIDES

Short, quick passes use a three-step drop, whereas intermediate and deep passes require a five-step or even a seven-step drop. All drops use the same basic footwork. For a three-step drop, the quarterback takes one long step with the foot on the same side as his throwing hand (see figure 3.14a), followed by two quick steps—a crossover step with the opposite foot (see figure 3.14b) and a plant step with the initial foot (see figure 3.14c). These two quick steps stop the quarterback's drop and put him in position to step toward his target and throw the ball.

Figure 3.14 *(a-c)* **Quarterback three-step drop.**

(continued)

For a five-step drop, the quarterback simply takes three long steps backward, crossing over on the second step (see figure 3.15), before executing the same two quick final steps as he did in the three-step drop. For a seven-step drop, the quarterback takes five long steps backward, crossing over on the second and fourth steps, before stopping his drop with the same two quick steps that he used before.

FOOT POSITIONING

For the quarterback to throw the ball to the side of the field on his throwing-hand side, the final step of the last two quick steps should open up the foot somewhat in the direction of the throw, as shown in figure 3.16a, so that the front hip can start to rotate in the direction of the target before he takes his step to deliver the ball. When the throw starts, the back foot should be perpendicular to the line from the quarterback to the target.

To throw to the side of the field opposite the throwing hand, the final step of the last two quick steps should point the toes of the back foot toward the line of scrimmage, as shown in figure 3.16b, opening up the front hip in the direction of the target before the quarterback takes his step to deliver the ball. Again, when the throw starts, the back foot should be perpendicular to the line from the quarterback to the target.

a   b

Figure 3.15 **Crossover action on the second step of a five- or seven-step drop.**

Figure 3.16 **Quarterback throwing (a) to the same side of the field as his throwing hand and (b) to the side of the field opposite his throwing hand.**

Some plays may call for the quarterback to roll out or bootleg, running toward the sideline and looking for pass receivers while on the run. When throwing on the run, quarterbacks should still use proper footwork so that they can throw the ball on the correct step and deliver it on time. When preparing to throw on the run, the quarterback should keep both hands on the ball and keep the ball at chest height (see figure 3.17*a*). Just before the release, the quarterback should turn his hips and chest toward the target and then step directly toward the target with the foot opposite his passing hand (see figure 3.17*b*), following through with the opposite foot (see figure 3.17*c*).

a   b   c

Figure 3.17 *(a-c)* **Quarterback passing on the run.**

DETERMINING HIT AND THROW VERSUS HITCH AND THROW

To match the depth and location of each pass route, the quarterback must know whether to throw immediately on the conclusion of his drop using a maneuver called a hit and throw, or whether to take a hitch step before he throws, a maneuver called a hitch and throw. Quarterbacks should be able to execute both techniques and match them to the timing required for the pass route that they are trying to throw.

(continued)

The hit and throw technique should be used every time the quarterback employs a three-step drop, since these plays involve short, quick-hitting routes and release time is crucial. The hitch and throw technique should be used every time the quarterback employs a seven-step drop, because the quarterback gains too much backward momentum on a seven-step drop to be able to hit and throw. Both techniques, the hit and throw and the hitch and throw, are used in conjunction with five-step drops, depending on the depth of routes and the timing of play.

At the conclusion of any straight drop, the quarterback may have to throw the ball with no extra steps because the quickness of the pass route requires a quick delivery. This technique is called hit and throw because as soon as the last step in the drop hits the ground, the quarterback rolls forward on the back foot without resetting it (see figure 3.18*a*), pushes forward (see figure 3.18*b*) and steps in the direction of his target to throw the ball on time (see figure 3.18*c*).

a   b   c

Figure 3.18 *(a-c)* **Hit and throw.**

If the timing of the route is slightly slower, the quarterback may have time to hitch and throw. In this case, on the last step of his drop, he plants the back foot (see figure 3.19a), rolls his weight forward onto his front foot briefly to gain his balance (see figure 3.19b) and then skips forward with his back foot, making the hitch step (see figure 3.19c) before stepping in the direction of his target (see figure 3.19d).

REACTING TO PRESSURE

The timing for a pass can break down at any time because of good defensive coverage or a good defensive pass rush. The quarterback must be prepared for this occurrence. When a quarterback can't throw on time, he must feel the pressure around him without looking at the pass rushers, keeping his eyes downfield to see whether one of his receivers can find a way to get open. As the quarterback quickly scans the field, he must keep his feet alive by bouncing lightly on the balls of his feet. That way, if he does see an open receiver, he can immediately plant his back foot and step in the direction of his target for his throw.

Figure 3.19 *(a-d)* **Hitch and throw.**

(continued)

At a Glance

The following parts of the text offer additional information on quarterback drops.

If the quarterback cannot find a target or the pass rush closes in, he should tuck the ball away securely under his arm and escape the pocket. But he should never turn and run laterally or backward to escape because he will take a big loss if he is tackled. Instead, he should try to escape the pocket out the front door by finding an opening toward the line of scrimmage between his guard and tackle or between his guard and center. That way, he can still see potential receivers in front of him, and if he is tackled he will lose less yardage.

Common Errors

You may run into several common errors when teaching quarterback drops.

Error	Error correction
Quarterback fails to match drops with routes.	Timing is everything in the pass game, so you must insist on the proper drop for every pass route in the offense. Even on a completed pass, correct any error.
Quarterback makes all steps the same length.	The key to good pass drops is for the quarterback to gain depth on his long steps and gain balance on the final two quick steps. Insist on seeing a difference between the initial long step or steps and the finishing quick steps.
Quarterback confuses the hit and hitch steps.	The hitch step feels natural once learned, but initially it is awkward. Slow things down and have the quarterback perfect the footwork for the hitch step before he ever throws a ball in drills. The hit step is also awkward if the quarterback does not make his last two steps short so that he becomes balanced. Watch for extra steps and eliminate them if they occur.

Throwing

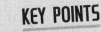

KEY POINTS

The most important components of throwing are

- o proper footwork,
- o hand positioning and arm action and
- o follow-through.

Only one player on the football field throws the football, the quarterback, and if he is ineffective, modern offensive football is rendered unproductive. Proper throwing mechanics are crucial to your quarterback's success in passing the football. These mechanics must be so ingrained that they become nothing less than natural and automatic. As you already know, the quarterback has many other things to think about when the game is under way.

PROPER FOOTWORK

Before concentrating on hand and arm mechanics, the quarterback must establish solid footwork. In proper throwing position, the feet are shoulder-width apart, and the line between the back and front shoulder, as well as the line between the back and front hip, should be pointing toward the target (see figure 3.20a). As the throw begins, the quarterback should push off the inside of his back foot, stepping directly toward his target with the front foot (see figure 3.20b). The back hip and back shoulder should start to move forward before the arm begins the throwing motion.

a   b

Figure 3.20 *(a-b)* **Proper footwork for quarterback when throwing.**

(continued)

HAND POSITIONING AND ARM ACTION

As the quarterback sets up to make the pass, he should hold the ball in both hands at chest height, with the fingers of the passing hand slightly on top of the ball and located on the laces (see figure 3.21*a*) When the throwing motion commences, the nonthrowing hand comes off the ball and the throwing hand takes the ball back with the elbow still bent and the ball remaining above the elbow (see figure 3.21*b*). The quarterback should rotate the ball slightly as he takes it back, so that the back point of the ball points toward his helmet. After taking the proper step and starting the hips forward, he brings the throwing arm forward with the ball remaining above the elbow (see figure 3.21*c*). The ball rotates so that the front nose of the ball is pointing to the target.

The football travels most quickly and accurately when it is thrown in a tight spiral. To achieve this effect, the quarterback must keep his fingers on top of the ball throughout the entire throwing motion. At the point of release, the throwing hand and arm should be fully extended toward the target. The little finger of the throwing hand begins the spiral rotation by pulling on the laces, and each finger of the throwing hand follows in succession, pulling down on the ball. The index finger is the last finger to leave the football, and it should briefly point to the target as it leaves the ball.

a   b   c

Figure 3.21 *(a-c)* **Quarterback hand and arm positioning when throwing.**

As a coach, watch for the ball being carried too low, at waist level instead of being carried chest high, as shown in figure 3.21a. Be sure that the ball does not drop to the waist at the "break" when the throwing hand comes off the ball. Also be sure that the back point of the football rotates; some younger quarterbacks take the ball straight back as if they are throwing a dart, and their delivery is severely compromised.

FOLLOW-THROUGH

Proper follow-through helps maintain velocity and accuracy while reducing strain on the throwing arm. After the quarterback releases the ball, the palm of the hand should continue to rotate to the outside with the thumb down in what is known as a pronated rotation (see figure 3.22). The back hip and leg should also rotate forward as the throw is completed.

The quarterback must be sure not to transfer his weight to his front foot too early; the throwing motion must commence while the back foot is still in contact with the ground, pushing forward to transfer the power of the lower body into the throw. After the ball leaves the quarterback's hand, the back foot may come up on the toes or it may come off the ground completely, depending on the force and trajection of the throw.

At a Glance

The following parts of the text offer additional information on throwing.

Center–Quarterback Exchange	p. 26
Quarterback Drops	p. 35
Running Shallow and Intermediate Routes	p. 51
Running Deep Routes	p. 55
Progression of Receivers	p. 174
Crossing Route Adjustments	p. 200
Curl Route Adjustments	p. 204

Figure 3.22 **Proper quarterback hand positioning on the follow-through.**

(continued)

Common Errors

You may run into several common errors when teaching your quarterbacks how to throw.

Error	Error correction
Quarterback drops the ball to his waist (called a windup) before releasing it.	Remind the quarterback that speed of release is crucial and that an elongated windup will significantly slow that release. Show players video of this release and drill short throws until the quarterback eliminates the windup.
Quarterback has dart-throwing habit.	Some quarterbacks fail to rotate the ball as they bring it back, meaning that the front point of the football always faces the target. This dart-throwing habit reduces velocity dramatically. Take the player through slow-motion drills with proper rotation and drill many short throws until the habit is gone.
Quarterback's elbow drops.	If the elbow drops as the throwing hand moves backward, the quarterback will pass with an inaccurate and slow sidearm motion. Drill the concept of keeping the elbow up using short passes and video.
Quarterback has a flat wrist.	At the release point, or top of the throwing motion, the wrist of the throwing hand should be vertical, not laid back at an angle. This flat-wrist problem places the hand under the ball instead of beside it and places the fingers on the side of the ball instead of on top of it. These problems make throwing a spiral difficult. Drill short passes with proper form to correct this habit.

Faking

Successful play-action passing depends on good faking by your players. The quarterback, the running back and the offensive blockers must all make the play look exactly like a run, so that the defense will react forward and in the direction of the movement that they believe is a run. Then, when the quarterback keeps the ball and either sets up to pass or rolls out to pass (see "Pass–Run Option" on page 180), the defense will be out of position to effectivly defend the pass. Without effective faking, however, the defense will tend not to believe that the play is a run, and they will slow their reactions to the run direction, putting them in better position to defend the pass.

INITIAL POSITIONING AND MOVEMENT

When preparing to execute a play-action pass fake, offensive linemen must keep their pads low as if they are executing a drive block. They must keep their pads low, commonly known as "low hat," for as long as possible so that the play looks like a run. If they pop up to pass protect, the defense will read this movement as a "high hat" or pass set and drop into pass coverage. The initial movement of the offensive line must "sound like a run," meaning that they must aggressively contact the defensive linemen across from them.

The most difficult aspect of the play-action fake for an offensive lineman is, by far, the fact that he is uncovered (no defensive lineman aligned over him). Without a defender to contact, the offensive lineman must convince himself to stay low and keep his pads down, while going nowhere and blocking no one! He must realize that one or more linebackers will be "reading" him for run or pass and he must stay low.

QUARTERBACK FAKING

Good faking by a quarterback on play-action passing is a beautiful part of offensive football. The quarterback must remember to take exactly the same steps and hold the ball in exactly the same manner as he would on a run until he passes the decoy ball carrier. Some coaches prefer an open-hand fake (see figure 3.23a), in which the quarterback hides the ball in his midsection with his off hand and extends the empty hand nearer the ball carrier toward him to make the fake. Although this is the safest way to fake a handoff, the defense will know that the play is a fake if they see the quarterback's empty hand. Other coaches prefer a true ball fake (see figure 3.23b) in which the quarterback extends the ball toward the running back, usually keeping both hands on the ball as the runner goes by to be sure that the ball is not knocked loose. This fake is more deceptive but somewhat more risky.

(continued)

Figure 3.23 Quarterback executing an *(a)* open-hand fake and a *(b)* ball fake.

Figure 3.24 Running back arm positioning to fake receiving a handoff.

RUNNING BACK FAKING

Faking by a running back is an important skill often overlooked by runners who would rather be carrying the ball than letting a teammate handle it. A good fake by a running back is one of the most effective tools that an offense can use to get the defensive players out of position. The running back should first make a pocket for the ball with both arms, exactly as he does when receiving a handoff, as shown in figure 3.8 on page 29. When the quarterback fakes the handoff, the running back should fold his arms over the imaginary ball in the same manner as he would if the ball were there (see figure 3.24). Keeping the arms folded over the midsection, the running back should maintain a low pad level and run hard to the line of scrimmage, as if he were carrying the ball and looking for a hole. A good fake by the running back can induce several defensiveplayers to attack the line of scrimmage to defend the running play that they think they see. A running back can probably block only one player at a time, but a good fake can occupy several defenders. The goal of the running back should be to get tackled by a defender.

WIDE RECEIVER FAKING

The wide receiver or receivers who will be the intended targets on play-action passing should simulate their stalk block, or slow block, before running a pass route. For the first few seconds, the backfield action and line blocking will look like a run, so the receiver should also simulate a running play. By coming off the line at three-quarter speed and breaking down while looking at the defender, the receiver sets up the play. When the defender stops backpedaling and begins to attack the line of scrimmage to defend the run, the receiver should burst by him, avoiding contact, and run to the designated area for the pass play.

At a Glance

The following parts of the text offer additional information on faking.

Center–Quarterback Exchange	p. 26
Ball Security	p. 29
Throwing	p. 41
Defending the Play-Action Pass	p. 254

Common Errors

You may run into several common errors when teaching your athletes how to fake.

Error	Error correction
Linemen stand up to pass protect.	When a play-action pass play is called, linemen must block using run-blocking techniques. Watch videotape of the play and study the linemen's pad level, or helmet level, to be sure that they are staying low.
Running back drops his arms.	After the quarterback passes by the running back without giving him the ball, many young running backs drop their arms because they do not have a ball to carry. This action immediately tells the defense that the play is a pass. Emphasize to the running back the importance of keeping his arms folded as if he had the ball.
Quarterback changes ball action.	Some quarterbacks handle the ball differently on play action than they do on a running play, either by failing to make a good fake or by not getting close enough to the running back to simulate a handoff. Tell the quarterback to do everything just as he would on a running play.

KEY POINTS

The most important components of catching are

○ hand positioning,

○ watching the ball and

○ securing the ball.

Catching the football is an offensive skill that also pertains to defensive players at times during a game. Many players on both sides of the ball use this skill, but wide receivers on offense must become specialists at it. Proper hand position and technique combined with focused concentration will provide the pass catcher with an excellent chance to be successful at this skill.

HAND POSITIONING

Pass catching requires various hand positions, depending on the location of the ball as it approaches the receiver. The two general types of hand positions are referred to as thumbs together and pinkies together.

Receivers should keep their thumbs together, as shown in figure 3.25, for passes as high as their jersey numbers or higher, if they are facing the quarterback. They should spread the fingers with hands open and thumbs touching. The hands should be relaxed and the wrists cocked back so that the fingers are pointing into the air, not toward the ball. The receiver should catch the front point, or stripe, of the ball in the noose formed by the thumbs and the index fingers. He should catch the ball away from his body, and the hands should give gently with the ball on the reception.

Coaches should talk to receivers about having "soft hands," meaning that the hands do not resist or fight the catch—they absorb the catch. Proper hand positioning on passes at the numbers or higher also helps prevent the dreaded "chest catch" or the catch "on the pads" that some receivers use for what they believe is a more secure catch than one in the hands. In truth, the catch on the pads is less consistent and secure because any contact by a defender tends to jostle the body and knock the ball loose. Plus, the ball is in the air slightly longer and gives the defender a split second more time to make a play on the ball. Receivers must learn to trade the short-term feeling of security that comes from catching the ball against the body for the long-term gain of making more and better catches in the hands.

Figure 3.25   Receiver hand positioning for high passes.

Receivers should keep their little fingers, or pinkies, together, for passes that are below the numbers (see figure 3.26a) or over the shoulder when the receiver's back is to the quarterback (see figure 3.26b). The receiver should also use this hand position when running laterally across the field. Again, the fingers of the hands should be spread out and relaxed, with the wrists cocked back to keep the fingers out of the way. The little fingers should be touching, and the receiver should catch the ball away from his body. On crossing routes, the placement of pinkies together prevents the receiver from bringing an arm across his body, which might briefly block his vision of the ball.

a   b

Figure 3.26 **Receiver hand positioning on *(a)* low and *(b)* over-the-shoulder passes.**

WATCHING THE BALL

The receiver must concentrate on the football as it approaches, focusing on the point of the football and literally watching the ball hit the hands. The receiver should reach out for the ball so that he can see his hands when the ball arrives. Of course, to adjust to its trajectory, the receiver must also be able to see the ball and concentrate on its path.

Additionally, if the receiver allows the ball to hit his body or his pads, his chances to finish the catch will diminish. He will have more difficulty seeing the ball when it is close to his body.

(continued)

SECURING THE BALL

As soon as he catches the ball, the receiver must transfer it to the ball-secure position with both points of the ball covered and the ball pressed against his body (as shown in figure 3.9 on page 30. At this point, the receiver becomes a running back and could benefit from referring to "Ball Security" on page 29.

Common Errors

You may run into several common errors when teaching your athletes how to catch a ball.

Error	Error correction
Receiver has his pinkies together for a ball at the numbers.	This common mistake will necessarily lead to an ill-advised catch against the body or on the pads. The receiver must discipline himself to put his hands in the proper noose position (thumbs together) so that he can see the ball and catch it in his hands.
Receiver takes his eyes off the ball.	Concern that an opposing player is closing in for a collision or simple lack of concentration can cause the receiver not to follow the flight of the ball all the way to his hands. Set up drills in which receivers can practice watching the ball all the way into their hands.
Receiver fails to secure the ball.	Some receivers tend to carry the ball away from the body after the catch even after they've been drilled to avoid making this mistake. Receivers should work with partners who try to strip the ball from them after a catch, so that they learn to tuck the ball away securely.
Receiver has his thumbs together for a ball thrown over his shoulder.	When a receiver tries to make the "over the shoulder" catch with his thumbs together, his inside arm invariably covers part of his face and often causes the receiver problems seeing the ball. Using a stationary demonstration, show the receiver this problem and have receivers run a "Pinky Drill," catching 2 to 3 balls over the shoulder at half speed every day, keeping the pinkies together.

The ability to run good shallow and intermediate pass routes elevates the best receivers above the average ones. To gain separation from a defender, regardless of whether he is playing man-to-man or zone defense, the route must attack the defender's coverage and force him away from the final destination. No route will be effective, however, unless the receiver runs it with the depth and speed that will time it up with the quarterback's drop and throw. An excellent curl route that is too shallow will leave the receiver waiting too long for the ball, whereas an excellent curl route that is too deep or is run at half speed will result in the arrival of the ball before the receiver is ready to make the catch. To achieve perfect coordination with the quarterback, receivers must discipline themselves to run every shallow and intermediate route at precisely the correct depth and at full speed. See examples of routes in Appendix A on page 355.

ROUTE STEM

As the receiver comes off the line, he must adjust the initial course of his route to play into the defender's alignment. If the defender is playing inside, the stem of his route should include an angling step or two that helps the receiver eliminate the defender's inside leverage. The same is true for an outside defender, with an outside angling step or two to attack the defender's outside leverage.

At the same time, the receiver must be mindful of his final destination and be sure to attack the shoulder of the defender that is on the side of the final break of the route. The final cut, of course, depends largely on the type of route being run and the defender's positioning, but, for example, on inside breaking routes like curls and digs, the receiver should attack the defender's inside shoulder. On outside breaking routes like comebacks and flags, the receiver should attack the defender's outside shoulder. This concept offers the receiver the best chance to get open because he does not have to break all the way across the defender's body after his final cut.

BREAKING DOWN

On intermediate routes in which the receiver comes back to the ball (for example, curls and comebacks), the receiver has to threaten the defender as if the route is going deep and then break down at the proper depth for the route and get open. At the break point, the receiver has to sink his hips (see figure 3.27) to lower his weight and change his steps from long strides to three short, choppy steps and a pressure step to get himself stopped. If his intended break

Figure 3.27 **Receiver sinking his hips as he begins to break down.**

(continued)

is to the left, the breakdown starts on the left foot. The first three steps would be left, right, left and the fourth step would be with the right foot at a 45-degree angle. The receiver uses this pressure step to gain separation from the defender back toward the line of scrimmage, the quarterback and the ball.

As the receiver is planting his foot on the pressure step, he must keep his weight balanced, chin over his knees (see figure 3.28a), and then snap his head, shoulders and hands around (see figure 3.28b). He must stay low with his knees bent and his weight on the balls of his feet so that he can accelerate back to the football.

a   b

Figure 3.28 *(a-b)* **Receiver making a pressure step.**

A variation of the breakdown is the speed cut, which relies on speed rather than a sharp-breaking cut to gain separation from the defender. The speed cut is used for quick or intermediate outs and crossing routes. On the speed cut, the defender does not use the three short, choppy steps to slow down. Instead, when he gets to the break point of the route (the depth for the route stem to end and the cut to begin) he starts right away with the pressure step (see figure 3.29a), using the foot away from the direction of his final break (right foot on a break to the left and vice versa). After this 45-degree angle pressure step, the receiver snaps his head back to the quarterback while taking his second step and placing it perpendicular to the sideline (see figure 3.29b). The third step is an acceleration step coming out of the cut directly toward the sideline (see figure 3.29c).

UNDERSTANDING MAN-TO-MAN AND ZONE DEFENSES

Shallow and intermediate routes differ somewhat depending on whether the coverage is man-to-man or zone. When facing man coverage, the receiver must know the importance of good head and shoulder fakes and changes of speed (called bursts) to

Figure 3.29 *(a-c)* **Receiver making a speed cut.**

gain separation from the man assigned to cover him. The receiver must also keep running hard throughout his route to avoid being caught from behind. When facing zone coverage, the receiver must first sprint toward the nearest deep defender, eliminating the defender's cushion so that he cannot break easily or comfortably to the ball. The receiver must then adjust his route to find the soft spot, or open area, in the coverage. In addition, when facing zone coverage when running a crossing route, the receiver must "sit down," or stop running, in an open area of the zone, so that he is not at risk of being hit unexpectedly by a defender from the opposite side of the field. See "Crossing Route Adjustments" on page 200 for more information.

(continued)

At a Glance

The following parts of the text offer additional information on running shallow and intermediate routes.

Quarterback Drops	p. 35
Crossing Route Adjustments	p. 200
Curl Route Adjustments	p. 204

If the defender is playing loosely in man-to-man coverage, the receiver should forget his fakes and simply attack the defender's leverage before making the appropriate break. If the defender is playing tight, the receiver must threaten him with speed and fakes to force him to turn his hips the wrong direction. For example, the receiver could threaten the defender as if the route is going deep and when the defender turns his hips to run upfield, the receiver can make his break to an intermediate cut. Or, the receiver could fake an inside break, forcing the defender to open his hips to the inside, and then break to the outside. The receiver must make sharp changes of direction with great quickness and speed to capitalize on the deception of the route.

In zone defenses, the key for the receiver is to run straight-line stems (directly toward a defender). The receiver should not use specific moves but should simply stretch the defender's area as much as possible, either horizontally or vertically, so that the defender has to cover more territory. At the proper depth for the route, the receiver should find the open area, or seam, and settle a bit while looking for the ball.

Common Errors

You may run into several common errors when teaching your athletes how to run shallow and intermediate routes.

Error	Error correction
Receiver rounds off breaks.	The receiver must slow down his practice routine and rehearse the three-step breakdown and pressure step repeatedly, on both sides, until the footwork is automatic. Then he can run the route at full speed and execute a sharp, decisive cut.
Receiver fails to break down a cushion.	The receiver should not make any fakes or moves if the defender is playing deep man coverage or zone coverage. Before making a move or break on his route, the receiver must attack upfield like a sprinter to eliminate the defender's cushion.
Ball arrives early.	Regardless of the route, if the ball arrives early the receiver either ran the route too deep or ran the proper depth but was slow getting there. The quarterback will deliver the ball "on time," so the receiver has to adjust to be in the proper position when the ball arrives.
Ball arrives late.	Regardless of the route, if the ball arrives late the receiver probably ran the route too shallow. To correct this common error, use cones to indicate the correct depth for the route on the practice field until the receiver memorizes proper depth.
Defender disrupts the route.	The receiver may have failed to attack the route-side shoulder of the defender, meaning that he had to work across the defender's body to get to his route. Teach receivers to make their breaks on the same side of the defender's body as the direction of the route (this is the route-side shoulder rule).

Deep pass routes require different skills for the receiver than shallow or intermediate routes do. On deep routes, the receiver does not make a plant and a cut move or break down to gain separation as he would on a shallow or intermediate route, as discussed in "Running Shallow and Intermediate Routes" beginning on page 51. Instead, the receiver uses slight changes in direction and subtle changes of speed to cause the defender either to hesitate or to open his hips in the wrong direction so that the receiver can accelerate past him for a long completion. The two most common deep routes are the post, in which the receiver bursts inside his defender, and the streak, in which the receiver bursts outside his defender. See examples of routes in Appendix A on page 355.

ROUTE STEM

As the receiver comes off the line, he must adjust the initial course of his route to play into the defender's alignment. If the defender is playing inside, the stem of the receiver's route should include an angling step or two that helps eliminate the defender's inside leverage. Against an outside defender, the receiver uses an outside angling step or two to attack the defender's outside leverage.

ERASING THE CUSHION

If the defender is playing man coverage in an off position (a normal alignment is 7 to 10 yards from the receiver) or zone coverage with a similar alignment, the receiver's first job is to attack the defender with as much speed as possible to erase his cushion. The receiver does not make any moves or fakes in the first few yards of his route, except to move slightly into the defender's leverage in the stem as described earlier. When the receiver closes the gap to within 3 or 4 yards of the defender, the defender is taught to open his hips, turn, and run with the receiver. The receiver must try to get the defender either to hesitate before making this turn or to turn the wrong way, before the receiver bursts past him for the long completion.

CREATING HESITATION

A receiver can attempt to gain an advantage over the defender on a deep route using changes in speed. The receiver's goal is to make the defender think that he will be defending an intermediate route. To do this, the receiver accelerates off the line of scrimmage, increasing his speed as he attacks the defender's cushion, to a depth of about 10 or 12 yards. At that point, the receiver slows down slightly to give the defender the idea that the receiver is about to break down and make a cut. The hope is that the defender will slow his backpedal or hesitate to turn and run because he senses that the receiver is going to run an intermediate route. Instead, after going slower for just a few steps, the receiver suddenly bursts back into full speed and accelerates past the defender on his deep route. The receiver must be sure to change speed on the correct side of the defender—outside for a streak and inside for a post.

(continued)

Figure 3.30 **Jab step to cause the defender to make a wrong turn.**

CREATING A WRONG TURN

The receiver can use two techniques to get the defender to turn his hips the wrong way. The most common is a jab step, in which the receiver gets close to the defender and then takes a hard step in the direction opposite the way that he really wants to go (see figure 3.30). The receiver makes this step at full speed without slowing down; the intention is simply to make the defender open his hips the wrong way. After the jab step, the receiver bursts by the defender in the other direction. So, on a post route, the receiver would jab outside before bursting by the defender on the inside; on a streak route, the receiver would jab inside before bursting by on the outside.

The receiver can also use a weave technique, in which just before he closes the gap on the defender, he attacks the defender's shoulder on the side where he intends to run his route (see figure 3.31*a*). After one or two steps, the receiver bursts back to the other shoulder of the defender (see figure 3.31*b*), hoping that the combination of these moves will convince the defender that the first move was a fake and that the second move is the final direction of the route. But the receiver only takes three or four steps in the second

a   b   c

Figure 3.31 *(a-c)* **Weave technique to cause the defender to make a wrong turn.**

direction before bursting back past the defender on the original side (see figure 3.31c). So, for example, on a post route the receiver would take one or two steps inside, three or four steps outside and then burst back past the defender on the inside. The receiver makes all steps at full speed and with full-length strides; he does not take the short, choppy steps that he would use on an intermediate route. Furthermore, the receiver does not travel very far left or right on these steps; he moves laterally just enough to make the defender think that he is going to try to run past him on that side.

HAND POSITIONING

After the receiver bursts past the defender, he accelerates to top speed and then takes a quick look back over his inside shoulder for the ball. As he looks, and even as he tracks the ball with his eyes as it approaches him, he must continue to move his hands forward and back in good running form and resist the temptation to raise his hands in preparation for the catch. Raising the hands too early slows him down and gives the defender time to catch up. The receiver should wait as long as he possibly can before he puts up his hands for the catch. Of course, he must get his hands in position in time to make the catch comfortably.

At a Glance

The following parts of the text offer additional information on running deep routes.

Running Shallow and Intermediate Routes	p. 51
Man Pass Coverage	p. 120
Speed Turn	p. 123
Finishing Plays in Man Pass Coverage	p. 244
Reads and Reactions in Zone Pass Coverage	p. 248

Common Errors

You may run into several common errors when teaching your athletes how to run deep routes.

Error	Error correction
Defender stays in a smooth backpedal with no hesitation.	The receiver failed to reduce the defender's cushion enough to get the defender to react to his change-of-speed maneuver. The receiver should not change speeds until he has approached within 3 or 4 yards of the defender.
Defender fails to open his hips in the wrong direction.	The receiver failed to reduce the defender's cushion enough to get the defender to react to his jab or weave maneuvers. The receiver should not jab or weave too early in the route; he must attack, erase the defender's cushion and get close enough to threaten to run past the defender on one side or the other.
Receiver collides with the defender.	The receiver may have waited too long to change speeds or try his jab or weave technique. The receiver should start these techniques before he completely erases the defender's cushion. Also, the receiver may have used too much lateral movement on his stem or weave, so that he has to come back across the defender's body too much as he tries to make his final burst into his deep route. The receiver must keep all moves subtle, working from one shoulder of the defender to the other, and not get farther than 1 or 2 feet outside or inside the defender at any time.

When a defender plays press, or bump and run, the receiver must escape, or release, from that defender at the line of scrimmage to run an effective pass route and get open to make a reception. The receiver's initial movements at the snap are crucial for the success of the release, and he must remember to play with quickness, strength and aggressiveness.

HAVING A PLAN

Before the snap, the receiver must know whether his route is an inside or outside route, because he must end up on that side of the defender after his release. He also must choose which type of release he intends to use and think through the motions for the release before the play begins.

The receiver has four basic choices for releases. First, he can use a direct release, in which he immediately attacks the defender to the side of his intended route. A direct outside release is called a fade release (see figure 3.32*a*), and a direct inside release is called a burst release (see figure 3.32*b*). This type of release is best when the defender's technique is opposite the side where the receiver needs to be (for example, the defender is playing inside and the receiver needs to be on his outside for the route).

Second, the receiver can step one way to hold the defender and then release past him to the opposite side (see figure 3.33). This step needs to be dramatic and forceful, giving the defender the impression that the receiver is doing a direct release to that side.

Third, the receiver can employ a double move, in which his first step is in the direction that he eventually wants to go, his second step is opposite that direction and his release is back in the original direction (see figure 3.34 *a* and *b*). This move should freeze the defender momentarily and allow the receiver a decent chance to escape.

Fourth, if the defender is aligned where the receiver needs to go (for example, the defender is aligned inside and the receiver has to run an inside route), the receiver can start upfield 3 or 4 yards as though he is going to run a fade release, enticing the defender to turn and run upfield with him (see figure 3.35). After the defender commits to running upfield, the receiver can plant the outside foot, drive the outside arm underneath the defender and drive underneath to the desired inside position.

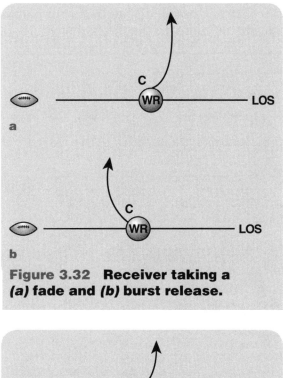

Figure 3.32 Receiver taking a
(a) fade and (b) burst release.

Figure 3.33 Receiver releasing past the defender.

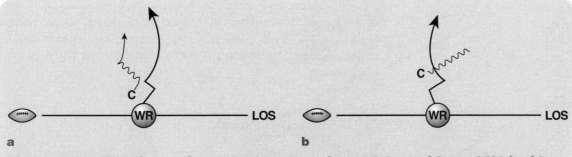

Figure 3.34 **Receiver using a double move for an (a) outside and (b) inside breaking route.**

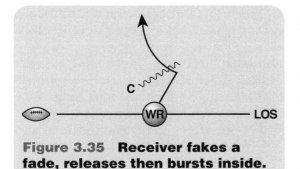

Figure 3.35 **Receiver fakes a fade, releases then bursts inside.**

AVOIDING THE DEFENDER'S HANDS

As the receiver moves past the defender, the most critical part of the release occurs. The receiver must not allow the defender's hands to contact him on the release and slow him down. If the defender's hands get past the receiver and contact him on the numbers on the front of his jersey, the defender can slow the receiver and destroy the timing of the route.

The receiver must use his own hands to knock down the defender's hands. The receiver can also use the rip technique, in which he hits the defender's hands with one hand and then rips his other hand underneath the defender's hands and past him, as shown in figure 3.36a. Or the receiver can try the swim technique, as shown in figure 3.36b, in which he hits the defender's hands with one hand and then punches his other hand over the defender's hands and past him.

Figure 3.36 **Receiver executing the (a) rip and (b) swim techniques.**

(continued)

At a Glance

The following parts of the text offer additional information on releases.

Running Shallow and Intermediate Routes	p. 51
Running Deep Routes	p. 55
Press Man Coverage	p. 125

In all cases, the receiver must dip the shoulder closer to the defender as he goes past him, turning his back slightly toward the defender so that the defender has a limited chance to bump the receiver's chest as the receiver goes by.

EXECUTING THE BREAK

As the receiver escapes from the line of scrimmage, he must avoid being forced into a lateral path by the defender. The receiver should lean back into the defender, quickly achieve a vertical path and get back in his lane as if he were a car passing another car on the highway. This action will ensure that the receiver can run his route to the proper depth before making a break or a cut.

At the break point, if the defender is playing tight, the receiver might have to push the defender off, using the forearm or elbow closer to the defender, not the open hand. Or, if the defender is slightly behind the receiver, the receiver can fake a hard step away from the direction of his route before breaking to his route. This hard fake step, called a stick fake, should cause the defender to react in the wrong direction and result in good separation for the receiver from the defender on the final route.

Common Errors

You may run into several common errors when teaching your athletes how to release.

Error	Error correction
Receiver plays too high.	Some receivers simply try to release from the line without making any moves. In doing so, they stand up and become easy targets for the defender's hands. Emphasize to receivers that they must sink the hips and dip the shoulders to reduce the hitting area that the defender can attack.
Receiver ends up on the wrong side.	The best release will be useless if the receiver ends up on the wrong side, because he will have to get past the defender again to finish his route. The receiver must plan the release!
Receiver fails to use his hands effectively.	Receivers often do a good job with their fakes but don't use their hands well. Do drills with the receivers standing still and practicing the various hand movements like the rip and swim.
Receiver's fakes are ineffective.	Explain to receivers that faking is like acting on stage—to be effective, they must exaggerate all movements! What a receiver thinks is a great fake may be too subtle to influence the defender.

Drive Block

When blocking at the point of attack, an offensive lineman or tight end uses the drive, or base, block, the most common block in football. The primary goal of the drive block is to get movement on the defender. Schematically, the drive block is one of the simplest skills in football. The offensive lineman or the tight end (hereafter called the blocker) is not trying to overtake the defender's gap, and he does not have to go anywhere to get to his assignment because the defender whom he has to block is the defensive lineman who is lined up right over him. The drive block is a contest of physical power, strength and technique, one blocker against one defender, each trying to move the other out of the way. See examples of plays where the drive block is used in Appendix B, "Gap Plays Versus 5-Man Line," on page 357.

CREATING A BASE OF POWER

The blocker must focus on his weight distribution to maintain balance, the key to the power he will incur on the drive block. He must keep his weight down and at the center of the body, with most of his weight on the insteps of his feet, to distribute the weight evenly. To maintain this base of power throughout the entire block, he should avoid leaning in one direction or the other.

PROPER FOOTWORK

At the snap of the ball, the blocker should take his first step with the foot closer to the defender whom he is going to block (see figure 3.37a). This first step is short, approximately 6 inches, and is directed toward the near number on the defender's jersey. The blocker then takes a short second step, just long enough to form a good base (see figure 3.37b).

The blocker should not cross over on the second step he will take on the drive block. He should try to keep as many cleats on the ground as possible. If a blocker crosses over, he loses his base of power. The urge to cross over is strong, because the blocker believes that by doing so he can get to his contact point quicker. He also is tempted to cross over when he is engaged and the defensive player starts to slip off the block. In both cases, however, the blocker will experience more success if he resists this temptation, keeps a solid, wide base and continues to take short, quick steps to initiate or sustain his block.

Overstriding on these steps can also cause loss of balance and subsequent loss of power. The blocker should focus on taking short, 6-inch steps that keep the feet under the shoulders at all times. These steps will also be quicker than longer strides would be, allowing the blocker to keep his feet on the ground more and maintain a strong, solid base.

(continued)

a   b

Figure 3.37 *(a-b)* **Proper footwork for the drive block.**

Figure 3.38 Blocker contacting the defender on a drive block.

CONTACTING THE DEFENDER AT THE LANDMARK

The blocker's landmark, or aiming point, for the drive block is down the middle of the two numbers on the defender's jersey. The first contact with the defender should be an aggressive punching blow with the hands at the landmark, followed by contact with the nose of the helmet (see figure 3.38). The objective of this punch should be to stop the opponent's charge and establish a base of contact with him.

Offensive blockers are always taught that low pads win, because the lower player controls the leverage and can sustain his balance. The blocker must be careful to achieve this low pad level by bending at the knees, not the waist. Although the blocker may feel that he is playing low by bending at the waist, he will be off balance and ineffective.

FOLLOW-THROUGH

The finish, or follow-through, of the block is the most difficult part to master. After making contact, the blocker should work his hands inside to the defender's chest and battle to sustain control inside the defender's hands and arms for the duration of the block. The blocker must explode through the defender on contact, using short, powerful steps. The blocker cannot get up on his toes; he must maintain a wide base and work to lock out, as if he were pushing a stalled car. Finally, he uses his legs and hips to drive high and hard through the defender to finish the block.

At a Glance

The following parts of the text offer additional information on the drive block.

Stance and Start for Offense	p. 22
Reach Block	p. 64
Cutoff Block	p. 67
Down Block	p. 70
Pulling	p. 82
Defending Basic Run Blocks	p. 96

Common Errors

You may run into several common errors when teaching your athletes how to drive block.

Error	Error correction
Blocker stops moving feet on contact.	Blockers must keep the feet going, even after striking the initial blow. Have them practice driving a sled or teammate holding a bag, keeping the feet driving at all times.
Blocker grabs the defender's shoulders with his hands.	The urge is to grab the defender to stop him, but doing so can become a bad habit and result in holding calls. Require your linemen to maintain inside hand position and keep their feet moving to sustain every block.
Defender gets past the blocker.	Usually, the blocker is playing with his pads too high if the defender eludes him. If the pads are high, the lineman is standing too tall, limiting his ability to move laterally and causing him to lose his balance or lunge at the defender. Have players work on starts with a low pad level (including work in a chute). Stress to blockers the need to play with their pads below the defender's pads.
Blocker crosses over with the second step.	The second step was too big. Linemen must work on getting the second step back on the ground quickly. In practice, have linemen take 10 steps in blocking position without crossing over.
Blocker falls forward.	The blocker has too much weight forward on his toes. When a defender moves, the lineman who has too much weight forward will have difficulty keeping his balance.

Reach Block

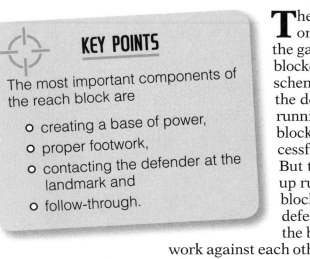

KEY POINTS

The most important components of the reach block are

- creating a base of power,
- proper footwork,
- contacting the defender at the landmark and
- follow-through.

The reach block is an effort by an offensive lineman or tight end (hereafter called the blocker) to overtake the gap that the defender aligned on him is playing. If the blocker is successful in reaching the defender, the defensive scheme is immediately compromised because the gap that the defender was supposed to protect is now open and a running lane should be available for the offense. The reach block is a difficult assignment and will not always be successful, especially against well-coached defensive players. But the attempt to reach block a defender can also open up running room for the offense in a second way. As the blocker tries to reach, or get outside, the defender, the defender has to work laterally to the outside to prevent the blocker from being successful. As the two opponents work against each other and fight to get outside, the next gap inside tends to become wider and more open (see "Running to Daylight" on page 191 for more information), giving the ball carrier an opportunity to run inside the reach block. See examples of plays where the reach block is used in Appendix C on page 361.

CREATING A BASE OF POWER

The blocker must focus on his weight distribution to maintain balance, the key to power. He must keep his weight in the center of the body, with most of his weight on his insteps, to distribute the weight evenly. To maintain this base of power, he should avoid leaning either way.

PROPER FOOTWORK

At the snap of the ball, the blocker takes his first step with the foot nearer the defender whom he is trying to reach. This first step varies depending on the alignment of the defender because the blocker is going to step toward an aiming point on the outside number of the defender. If the defender is lined up in a tight shade (close to the blocker), the step will be fairly short, about 12 inches, and the foot will land on or slightly in front of the line of scrimmage (see figure 3.39a). If the defender is lined up in a loose shade (farther from the blocker), the first step may have to be a drop step, in which the blocker takes a longer stride, about 18 inches in length, and places the foot slightly behind the line of scrimmage (see figure 3.39b).

The blocker must get his second step on the ground quickly to establish his base of power. The blocker should not cross over on the second step and should try to keep as many cleats on the ground as possible. If a blocker crosses over, he loses his base of power. The urge to cross over is strong, because the blocker believes that by doing so he can get to his contact point quicker. He also is tempted to cross over when he is engaged and the defensive player starts to slip off the block. In both cases, however, the blocker will experience more success if he resists this temptation, keeps a solid, wide base and continues to take short, quick steps to initiate or sustain his block.

Overstriding can also cause loss of balance and subsequent loss of power. After the first step on the reach block, the blocker should focus on taking short, 6-inch steps that keep the feet under the shoulders at all times. These steps will also be quicker than longer

a   b

Figure 3.39   **Blocker's first step against a defender in a** *(a)* **tight shade and** *(b)* **loose shade.**

strides would be, allowing the blocker to keep his feet on the ground more and maintain a strong, solid base.

CONTACTING THE DEFENDER AT THE LANDMARK

The landmark, or aiming point, for the reach block is the outside number of the defender, with the blocker attempting to get his head and both hands to that number (see figure 3.40). The blocker must threaten a point outside the defender to cause him to widen his position in an effort to keep his outside arm free. After establishing contact, the blocker should try to lock, or straighten, the outside arm to turn the defender and either hook him or stretch out the hole.

Offensive blockers are always taught that low pads win, because the lower player controls the leverage and can sustain his balance. The blocker must be careful to achieve this low pad level by

Figure 3.40   **Blocker positions his head and hands at his landmark (defender's outside number).**

(continued)

At a Glance

The following parts of the text offer additional information on the reach block.

Stance and Start for Offense	p. 22
Drive Block	p. 61
Cutoff Block	p. 67
Down Block	p. 70
Pulling	p. 82
Defending Basic Run Blocks	p. 96

bending at the knees, not the waist. Although the blocker may feel that he is playing low by bending at the waist, he will be off balance and ineffective.

FOLLOW-THROUGH

The blocker must finish the reach block by continuing to attack the outside half of the defender, forcing the defender to continue to work down the line of scrimmage toward the sideline to keep his outside arm free.

Common Errors

You may run into several common errors when teaching your athletes how to reach block.

Error	Error correction
Blocker's first step is too far downfield.	The first step on the reach block must point toward the outside number of the defender. The wider the defender is aligned, the deeper the step should be. Blockers frequently take a first step that is not lateral enough to point them toward their target. Have them watch videotape of themselves doing this technique in practice and concentrate on placement of the first step.
Blocker stops moving feet on contact.	Blockers must keep the feet going, even after striking the initial blow. Have them practice driving a sled or teammate holding a bag, keeping the feet driving at all times.
Blocker grabs the defender's shoulders with his hands.	The urge is to grab an opponent to stop him. The blocker must work the hands to the proper position and use the legs to drive the defender.
Blocker "wheels" in the hole.	Some blockers turn their shoulders too far toward the sideline in attempting a reach block. Although still trying to work the defender toward the outside, they are no longer in position to reach the defender because they have turned their back into the hole and are in essence working on the defender's inside half instead of the outside half. Although they want to stretch the defender toward the sideline, they cannot turn and face the sideline on this block; they attack the defender's outside arm and try to gain leverage outside the defender.
Blocker crosses over with the second step.	The second step was too big. Linemen must work on getting the second step back on the ground quickly. In practice, have linemen take 10 steps in blocking position without crossing over.
Blocker falls forward.	The blocker has too much weight forward on his toes. When a defender moves, the lineman who has too much weight forward will have difficulty keeping his balance.

Cutoff Block

The cutoff block is a backside block used by offensive linemen or tight ends (hereafter called blockers) to prevent a defender from pursuing to a play being run to the other side of the formation. The cutoff block has two variations, depending on the shade, or alignment, of the defender. First, if the defender is shaded away from the play (for example, the play is going to the right and the defender who is going to be blocked is shaded on the blocker's left), the cutoff block is similar to a drive block. The blocker already has the defender outflanked and he simply needs to work to prevent the defender from flowing to the play (see "Drive Block" on page 61 for more information). Second, in a more challenging maneuver, if the defender is shaded toward the direction of the play (for example, the play is going to the right and the defender who is going to be blocked is shaded on the blocker's right), the execution of the cutoff block is similar to a reach block (see "Reach Block" on page 64 for more information). See examples of plays where the cutoff block is used in Appendix B on page 357 and Appendix C, "Off-Tackle Zone," on page 361.

CREATING A BASE OF POWER

The blocker must focus on his weight distribution to maintain balance, the key to power. He must keep his weight in the center of the body, with most of the weight on the insteps, to keep the weight evenly distributed. To maintain this base of power, he should avoid leaning either way.

PROPER FOOTWORK

If the defender is shaded away from the play, the blocker's first step at the snap of the ball will be with the foot closer to the defender, to prevent penetration. The blocker takes a 6-inch step toward the near number of the defender. He then takes a short second step, just long enough to form a good base. An example of this is shown in figure 3.37 on page 62.

If the defender is shaded in the direction of the play, the blocker's first step at the snap of the ball will be with the foot closer to the defender. This step will be a flat, or drop, step. The second step must get on the ground quickly to establish a solid base. An example of this is shown in figure 3.39 on page 65.

In both instances, the blocker should avoid the temptation to cross over on this second step. If a blocker crosses over, he loses his base of power. The urge to cross over is strong, because the blocker believes that by doing so he can get to his contact point quicker. He also is tempted to cross over when he is engaged and the defensive player starts to slip off the block. In both cases, however, the blocker will experience more success if he resists this temptation, keeps a solid, wide base and continues to take short, quick steps to initiate or sustain his block.

(continued)

Overstriding can also cause loss of balance and subsequent loss of power. The blocker should focus on taking short, 6-inch steps that keep the feet under the shoulders at all times. These steps will also be quicker than longer strides would be, allowing the blocker to keep his feet on the ground more and maintain a strong, solid base.

CONTACTING THE DEFENDER AT THE LANDMARK

If the defender is shaded away from the play, the landmark, or aiming point, is the inside number of the defender. The first contact with the defender should be an aggressive punching blow with the hands, followed by contact with the nose of the helmet. This punch should stop the opponent's charge and establish a base of contact with him. At this point, the blocker should work his hands inside to the defender's chest and battle to sustain control inside the defender's hands (arms) for the duration of the block.

If the defender is shaded in the direction of the play, the landmark, or aiming point, is the far number of the defender. The blocker should strike at the defender with both hands attempting to get to that number. After establishing contact, the blocker should try to lock out, or straighten out, the outside arm to turn the defender and either hook him or stretch out the hole.

Frequently, the cutoff block is used by an offensive blocker against a linebacker who is playing off the line of scrimmage. The same landmarks apply, as we learned previously, based on the linebacker's initial alignment. However, the blocker must sprint out of his stance to a point that is a few feet in front of where the linebacker started, because at the snap, the linebacker will move toward the play when contact is made. The usual coaching points for footwork and follow-through (as will be discussed in "Follow-Through") apply, but if the blocker does not take the proper initial course, anticipating linebacker movement, he will never reach the correct landmark for his block.

Additionally, offensive blockers are always taught that low pads win, because the lower player controls the leverage and can sustain his balance. The blocker must be careful to achieve this low pad level by bending at the knees, not the waist. Although the blocker may feel that he is playing low by bending at the waist, he will be off balance and ineffective.

At a Glance

The following parts of the text offer additional information on the cutoff block.

Stance and Start for Offense	p. 22
Drive Block	p. 61
Reach Block	p. 64
Down Block	p. 70
Pulling	p. 82
Defending Basic Run Blocks	p. 96

FOLLOW-THROUGH

The blocker must keep a wide base and maintain contact without leaning too far forward. The blocker does not have to work for movement; a stalemate in this situation is a victory for the blocker. The blocker must keep his head up and control any movement by the defender to try to get away or disrupt the play.

Common Errors

You may run into several common errors when teaching your athletes the cutoff block.

Error	Error correction
Blocker takes improper first step.	If the defender is shaded away from the play, the blocker tends to step with the foot away from the defender because the play is going that way. But the defender must be neutralized immediately, so the first step must be with the foot nearest the defender. If the defender is aligned toward the play, the first step on the block must point toward the far number of the defender. The wider the defender is aligned, the deeper the step must be.
Blocker stops moving feet on contact.	Blockers must keep the feet going, even after striking the initial blow. Have them practice driving a sled or teammate holding a bag, keeping the feet driving at all times.
Blocker grabs the defender's shoulders with his hands.	The urge is to grab the defender to stop him, but doing so can become a bad habit and result in holding calls. Require your linemen to maintain inside hand position and keep their feet moving to sustain every block.
Blocker lunges.	Many blockers worry about penetration upfield by the defender, so they lunge at the defender and fail to make good contact. They need to focus on a good first and second step.
Blocker crosses over with the second step.	The second step was too big. Linemen must work on getting the second step back on the ground quickly. In practice, have linemen take 10 steps in blocking position without crossing over.
Blocker falls forward.	The blocker has too much weight forward on his toes. When a defender moves, the lineman who has too much weight forward will have difficulty keeping his balance.

Down Block

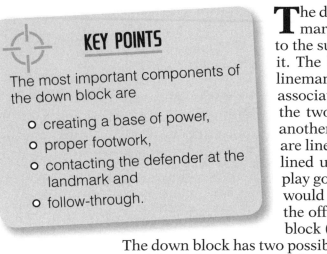

KEY POINTS

The most important components of the down block are

- creating a base of power,
- proper footwork,
- contacting the defender at the landmark and
- follow-through.

The down, or back, block takes place away from the primary point of attack on a running play, but it is crucial to the success of the play. A lineman or tight end executes it. The blocker does not pull for this block; he blocks a lineman adjacent to him. The down block is frequently associated with pulling (see "Pulling" on page 82) because the two blocks are often used in conjunction with one another. For example, assume that two offensive blockers are lined up next to each other, with a defensive lineman lined up in the gap between them. On a trap or power play going to the right, the offensive lineman on the right would down block the defender in the gap (to his left) and the offensive lineman on the left would pull behind that block (going to the right) to block another defender.

The down block has two possible purposes, depending on the reactions and techniques of the defenders. First, the down block prevents penetration across the line of scrimmage by a defender who is charging upfield and trying to disrupt pulling linemen (see more about this in "Pulling" on page 82). Second, the down block prevents flow laterally down the line of scrimmage by a defender who is trying to chase a play that is going away from him. The down block is intended to seal the backside of a running play, keeping defenders who are not lined up at the point of attack from being able to help defend a running play. This block is primarily used as part of the blocking scheme on gap running plays such as the trap, the counter and the power (see "Running to the Gap" on page 187 for more information). See examples of gap plays in Appendix B on page 357.

CREATING A BASE OF POWER

The blocker must focus on his weight distribution to maintain balance, the key to power. He must keep his weight in the center of the body, with most of his weight on his insteps, to distribute the weight evenly. To maintain this base of power, he should avoid leaning either way.

PROPER FOOTWORK

At the snap of the ball, the blocker takes his first step with his backside foot, the foot closer to the defender whom he is going to block. This first step is a drop step, about 12 inches in length, laterally toward the sideline, down the line of scrimmage (see figure 3.41a). This step may have to be slightly backward if the defender is quick and aggressive upfield. The second step must gain ground slightly downfield, as shown in figure 3.41b, to prevent the defender from "crossing face" down the line of scrimmage.

The blocker should not cross over on the second step. He should try to keep as many cleats on the ground as possible. If a blocker crosses over, he loses his base of power. The urge to cross over is strong, because the blocker believes that by doing so he can get to his contact point quicker. He also is tempted to cross over when he is engaged and the defensive player starts to slip off the block. In both cases, however, the blocker will experience more success if he resists this temptation, keeps a solid, wide base and continues to take short, quick steps to initiate or sustain his block.

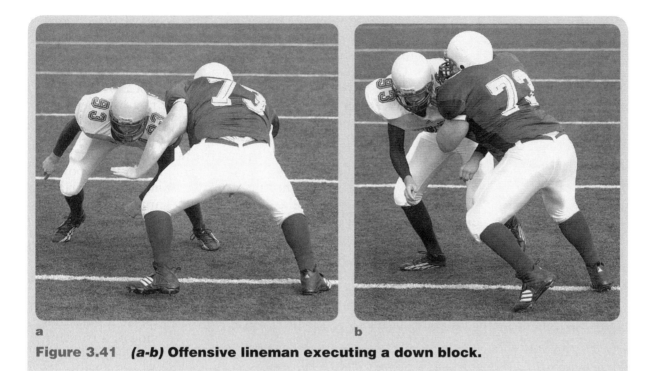

a
b

Figure 3.41 *(a-b)* **Offensive lineman executing a down block.**

Overstriding can also cause loss of balance and subsequent loss of power. The blocker should focus on taking short, 6-inch steps that keep the feet under the shoulders at all times. These steps will also be quicker than longer strides would be, allowing the blocker to keep his feet on the ground more and maintain a strong, solid base.

CONTACTING THE DEFENDER AT THE LANDMARK

The landmark, or aiming point, for the down block is the near hip of the defender. The block must split the defender so that he can neither penetrate upfield nor cross the blocker's face laterally down the line of scrimmage.

The blow must occur on the second step. The blocker tries to get the backside hand, the one nearer the defender, to the near side of the defender's chest, and the playside hand under the defender's shoulder pads just behind his shoulder (see figure 3.42). In other words, the blocker is trying to get one hand on each

Figure 3.42 **Blocker's hand position when contacting the defender on the down block.**

(continued)

side of the blocker's near arm. This hand position gives the blocker optimum control of the defender in two directions—up the field and down the line of scrimmage.

Offensive blockers are always taught that low pads win, because the lower player controls the leverage and can sustain his balance. The blocker must be careful to achieve this low pad level by bending at the knees, not the waist. Although the blocker may feel that he is playing low by bending at the waist, he will be off balance and ineffective.

FOLLOW-THROUGH

The blocker must keep a wide base and maintain contact without leaning too far forward. The blocker does not have to work for movement; a stalemate in this situation is a victory for the blocker. The blocker must keep his head up and control any movement by the defender to try to get away or disrupt the play.

Common Errors

You may run into several common errors when teaching your athletes how to down block.

Error	Error correction
First step doesn't open.	The most common error on the back block is a poor first step. The first step cannot be downfield; the blocker must drop and gain width so that he can turn his body toward the near-hip landmark.
Blocker stops moving feet on contact.	Blockers must keep the feet going, even after striking the initial blow. Have them practice driving a sled or teammate holding a bag, keeping the feet driving at all times.
Blocker grabs the defender's shoulders with his hands.	The urge is to grab the defender to stop him, but doing so can become a bad habit and result in holding calls. Require your linemen to maintain inside hand position and keep their feet moving to sustain every block.
Blocker lunges.	Many blockers worry about penetration upfield by the defender, so they lunge at the defender and fail to make good contact. They need to focus on a good first and second step.
Blocker crosses over with the second step.	The second step was too big. Linemen must work on getting the second step back on the ground quickly. In practice, have linemen take 10 steps in blocking position without crossing over.
Blocker falls forward.	The blocker has too much weight forward on his toes. When a defender moves, the lineman who has too much weight forward will have difficulty keeping his balance.

Double-Team Block

KEY POINTS

The most important components of the double-team block are

o identifying the defender,
o proper footwork,
o creating movement,
o preventing the split, and
o finishing the block.

A double-team block involves two offensive linemen blocking one down defender. The double team is used most often at the point of attack of a power play such as the trap, the isolation, the counter or the off-tackle power. The double-team block, with its two-to-one advantage for the offense, has the potential to create movement on the down defender, pushing him off the line of scrimmage and opening a running lane for the ball carrier. The disadvantage of the double-team block is that when two blockers focus on one defender, another defender is unblocked and the defense might be able to outnumber the offense elsewhere on the play. See examples of plays where theh double-team block is used in Appendix B on page 357.

IDENTIFYING THE DEFENDER

Based on the play call and the defensive alignment, blocking schemes for any offensive play can vary. The defender who is going to be double-teamed may be aligned between a center and a guard, between a guard and a tackle, or between a tackle and a tight end. The offensive blockers must communicate accurately on the line of scrimmage to identify the defender who is going to be doubled and, of course, who is going to be involved in the double team itself.

PROPER FOOTWORK

When the ball is snapped, the two blockers who are going to be involved in the double team must both take the correct initial step. They each must take their first step with the foot that is closer to the defender, meaning that the blocker on the left takes his first step with his right foot and the blocker on the right takes his first step with his left foot, as shown in figure 3.43a. Each blocker's landmark is the near number on the defender's jersey, and the blocker should aim his nearer hand, arm and shoulder pad at that target. The blockers follow the first step and delivery of the blow with a short second step that should bring each blocker into a position to block half a man—obviously, the half nearer the blocker (see figure 3.43b).

CREATING MOVEMENT

As the blockers initiate contact on the double team, they must be positioned shoulder to shoulder and lower than the defender (see figure 3.44). Although they have a two-to-one advantage, the blockers will not be successful in moving or controlling the defender unless they keep a solid, low base throughout the entire block. They must remember to take short steps, not cross over and keep both feet on the ground as much as possible.

(continued)

a   b

Figure 3.43 *(a-b)* **Blockers executing a double-team block.**

Figure 3.44 Blockers' positioning when contacting the defender in a double-team block.

Using their numerical advantage, the two blockers must force the defender backward, off the line of scrimmage, and remember that their responsibility is to control the down defender. The blockers cannot lose focus on the defender or leave to block another defender. They must stay on the down defender, move him off the line and force him away from the path of the ball carrier.

PREVENTING THE SPLIT

The defender who is being doubled-teamed has most likely been taught to try to split the double team by going between the two blockers. The blockers must work to prevent the split by maintaining their shoulder-to-shoulder positioning. To stay in this position, each blocker should press to the inside by driving his helmet into the defender's armpit area and clamping his outside arm on the defender's outside hip.

FINISHING THE BLOCK

To finish the double team, the two blockers must follow through by continuing to drive the feet while maintaining a lower pad level than the defender. Some defenders may try to spin out of the double team. The blocker on that side should try to prevent the spin by using pressure against the defender with his helmet and outside arm. Other defenders may fall to the ground and try to make a pile that will clog the running lane. When that happens, the blockers must stay on their feet, avoid falling down and continue to try to push the defender backward. They should keep blocking until the whistle blows!

At a Glance

The following parts of the text offer additional information on the double-team block.

Drive Block	p. 61
Reach Block	p. 64
Cutoff Block	p. 67
Down Block	p. 70
Pulling	p. 82
Defending the Double-Team Block	p. 100

Common Errors

You may run into several common errors when teaching your athletes how to double-team block.

Error	Error correction
Down defender splits the double team.	The blockers did not get shoulder to shoulder as they started the double team. In two-on-one drills, emphasize control of the down defender with each blocker's inside shoulder.
Double team does not create movement.	The blockers' pad level is too high, or one of the blockers bumped the other off the double team, losing the two-to-one advantage.
One of the blockers loses his footing.	Although the blockers are pushing forward aggressively, they must always keep their feet underneath them, not getting too much weight on their toes, so that if the defender moves they don't fall down. If one of the blockers falls down, the double team loses its two-to-one advantage.

Mirror Block

KEY POINTS

The most important components of the mirror block are

o reaction,

o breaking down and

o engaging the defender.

Although wide receivers specialize in the art of catching passes and focus on pass receiving as their primary job on the field, their blocking ability can add many yards to the offensive production and turn a big play into a touchdown because they are blocking defensive backs, the opponent's last line of defense. The type of block that a wide receiver most often uses is the mirror block. On the mirror block, the receiver simply positions himself between a defender and the ball carrier and then mirrors the defender's movements until the defender tries to get past him to make a tackle. At that point, the receiver physically engages the defender and keeps him away from the ball carrier. The mirror block requires quickness, good footwork and patience before contact with the defender. At contact, the block requires strength, persistence and tenacity. See example of a running play where the mirror block is used in Appendix C, "Outside Zone," on page 361.

REACTION

The receiver should explode off the line of scrimmage, forcing the defender to backpedal and play the threat of a pass. The objective for the receiver is to get the defender as far from the line of scrimmage as possible before initiating the mirror block. Therefore, as long as the defender continues to backpedal, the receiver should run at him, being careful not to get too close. When the defender reads the play and realizes that it is a run, he will stop his backpedal, plant and react to the play. When the defender reacts, the receiver must also react and immediately break down to get ready to block. The receiver must be sure, as he reacts, that he establishes a position inside the defender, between the defender and the ball.

Note here that if the defender is playing man coverage and turns his back to the line of scrimmage as the receiver comes off the line, the receiver has the option simply to keep running down the field, taking the defender farther and farther away from the running play. For this tactic to be successful, however, the receiver will have to run hard to make the play look like a pass.

BREAKING DOWN

When getting ready to mirror block, the receiver breaks down by coming to a stop in a balanced set with his feet shoulder-width apart. The receiver should maintain a balanced stance that includes a good base with the knees bent, hips down, head up and back straight.

He must also break down early enough to position himself 3 to 4 yards from the defender. This space, known as a cushion, allows the receiver to react to the path that the defender will eventually take to get to the ball carrier. As the defender approaches, the receiver must focus on the defender's midsection to prevent the defender from faking him out of position. The receiver must take short lateral steps, mirroring the defender's movements and maintaining inside position, not letting him get past.

ENGAGING THE DEFENDER

When the defender finally tries to get by the receiver, the receiver should whip his hands up to the chest of the defender and widen the elbows to broaden the blocking surface (see figure 3.45a). Operating from a good, low stance, the receiver should then uncoil the hips and use the legs to deliver a powerful blow, stopping the defender's charge and neutralizing his momentum (see figure 3.45b). The receiver must be sure not to overextend himself by trying to be too physical. After the initial contact, the receiver must recoil, get his feet moving into a good stable position again and repeat the blocking contact as often as necessary.

If the receiver loses a balanced blocking position and the defender tries to get away, the receiver should get his opposite ear across the defender's numbers and run him to that side, keeping the elbow on that side high to prevent the defender from spinning out. The receiver should try to hold the block as long as possible and continue to block with tenacity until the whistle blows.

At a Glance

The following parts of the text offer additional information on the mirror block.

Lead Block	p. 79
Pass Protection	p. 85
Defending Against the Bullets	p. 153

Figure 3.45 *(a-b)* **Receiver positioning when the defender tries to get past.**

(continued)

Common Errors

You may run into several common errors when teaching your athletes how to mirror block.

Error	Error correction
Defender quickly dodges the receiver.	The receiver didn't keep a big enough cushion, which probably means that he didn't break down quickly enough. Remind the receiver to stop and settle into a blocking stance at least 3 or 4 yards from the defender.
Receiver pushes the defender from the side.	The receiver tried to block with his hands instead of his feet. The feet must move laterally as the receiver begins to strike a blow; otherwise the defender's momentum will carry him right by the receiver–blocker.
Receiver gets pushed straight back.	The receiver is playing too high. He must get a low base, with knees bent, and dig in with the balls of the feet, using leg strength to hold the position against the onrushing defender.
Receiver makes contact but does not sustain the block.	The receiver probably lunged at the defender, bending forward at the waist and reaching forward with his hands instead of bringing his feet to the block. Teach receivers to keep their backs straight on contact, taking several quick steps to get into position for blow delivery with the hands.

When leading the way for a teammate who is carrying the ball on a running play, a running back executes a lead block. The two most common plays that use a lead block are the isolation play, in which the lead back blocks an inside linebacker, and the off-tackle power play, in which the lead back blocks a defensive end or outside linebacker. On the isolation play, the lead back can block the inside linebacker with either shoulder, and the running back behind him must read the block and break away from the linebacker. On the off-tackle power play, the lead back must kick out the defender, so he must take an inside-out course and execute the block with his outside shoulder. Lead blocks are a key element of the running game, and fullbacks, who are big, strong and typically known for their blocking ability, usually execute them. See examples of plays where the lead block is used in Appendix B on page 357.

TAKING THE PROPER COURSE

When the ball is snapped, the running back who will be executing the lead block must explode out of his stance and attack the line of scrimmage in the direction of the defender whom he is assigned to block. On most isolation plays and on all power plays, the running back will be using his outside shoulder to block the defender, so he must be sure to take an inside-out course toward the block as he approaches the defender.

On an isolation play block, the running back must run almost straight ahead, directly toward the center–guard gap on the side of the play and then veer slightly to the outside as he approaches the linebacker who will be stepping up into the hole (see figure 3.46a). On a power play block, the running back angles toward the tackle–tight

Figure 3.46   Running back making an *(a)* isolation play block and *(b)* a power play block.

(continued)

end gap, but he must be sure to run toward the line of scrimmage enough so that, by the time he reaches the off-tackle area where the block will occur, his course is more toward the sideline than it is toward the line of scrimmage (see figure 3.46b). On both blocks, if the running back starts out on a course that is too wide, he will never be able to reroute and get his outside shoulder on the inside half of the defender for proper execution of the block.

FOCUSING ON THE TARGET

The lead blocker must remember that the defender whom he is blocking is a moving target. Therefore, after locating the defender whom he is supposed to block, the blocker must keep his eyes up and continuously focus on that defender so that he can track the defender's movement and maintain his proper inside-out leverage before the block. If the linebacker on the isolation play scrapes outside or if the defensive end on the power play runs upfield, the blocker must change course, staying inside out but adjusting his path so that he can successfully contact the defender. This adjustment by the blocker in reaction to the defender's course is especially important if the defender is assigned to spill the lead block (see "Spilling Blocks" on page 103) because in that case, the defender will be trying to get under, or inside, the lead block and he will move inside as the blocker approaches. On the isolation play, the blocker must react to the linebacker's inside movement by adjusting which shoulder will lead the block, meaning that the blocker will now take on the linebacker with his inside shoulder instead of his outside shoulder. On the power play, however, the assignment to kick out the defender does not change, so the blocker must see the defender's inside movement and adjust his course to stay inside for the block, still taking it on with his outside shoulder. (Note that both players, the lead blocker trying to kick out the defender and the defender assigned to spill the block, have the assignment to get under, or inside, their opponent. If they both use proper technique, it will be difficult for either to execute his assignment well.)

CONTACTING THE DEFENDER

Just before contact with the defender, the lead blocker must lower his shoulder pads below the shoulder pads of the defender. The blocker should dip, sinking his hips, and then hit on the rise, driving up through the defender.

Offensive blockers are always taught that low pads win, because the lower player controls the leverage and can sustain his balance. The blocker must be careful to achieve this low pad level by bending at the knees, not the waist. Although the blocker may feel that he is playing low by bending at the waist, he will be off balance and ineffective.

After he makes contact, the blocker should also work his hands inside to the defender's chest and battle to sustain control inside the defender's hands and arms for the duration of the block. The blocker also should keep his elbows in, almost against his sides, for additional power and leverage against the defender. If the blocker's hands and elbows get too wide, the blocker cannot use the power of his arms to push the defender backward and he runs the risk of being called for holding.

FOLLOW-THROUGH

Immediately after contact, the blocker must drive his legs forward and his hips upward, keeping his feet moving and his legs driving for the duration of the block. His feet must be at proper width at this point. If the feet are too close together, the blocker will lose his balance; if the feet are too far apart, he will lose power on his leg drive.

The collision at the point of impact might initially stop the blocker's forward momentum, but if the blocker has kept his pads low and has stayed on balance with proper foot position, he should be able to drive his legs and move the defender backward. The defender will also be taught to stay low and drive his legs, so the player who wins this matchup will be the one who uses the best technique and has spent the most time in the weight room developing strong hips and legs.

At a Glance

The following parts of the text offer additional information on the lead block.

Drive Block	p. 61
Mirror Block	p. 76
Spilling Blocks	p. 103
Squeezing Blocks	p. 107
Reacting When Unblocked	p. 232

Common Errors

You may run into several common errors when teaching your athletes how to lead block.

Error	Error correction
Blocker makes contact with the wrong shoulder.	First, be sure that the blocker understands his assignments and knows that power plays require him to block using his outside shoulder. If the player knows his assignment and still fails to make contact with the proper shoulder, he probably is taking a poor course toward the block.
Blocker fails to get inside the defender on the kickout block.	Many young players take a course that is too wide as they approach the defender, allowing the defender to establish position underneath the blocker and making it impossible for the blocker to hit the block with the outside shoulder. Be sure that the blockers are taking an inside-out course to the block, moving forward first, then working outside toward the defender.
Blocker is driven backward.	Typically, the problem is that the blocker is playing too high, meaning that he is not bending his knees and lowering his pads. Blockers should practice lowering their pad level as they block sleds or bags in practice.
Blocker whiffs on the block.	If the defender sidesteps the blocker or the blocker simply misses the defender, then the blocker is probably not keeping his eyes on the target. (He might even be closing his eyes as he approaches the moment of impact!) Teach the blocker to keep his head up so that he can keep his eyes up and see his work.
Blocker falls forward as he makes contact.	The blocker must bend at the knees, not at the waist. If the blocker drops his head before impact or bends forward at the waist before impact, he will not be able to keep his balance and sustain the block. Be sure that players are developing strength and flexibility in their hips so that they can play low with proper technique.

Pulling

KEY POINTS

The most important components of pulling are

o movement on the snap,

o contacting the defender and

o follow-through.

A blocker is said to be pulling when he leaves his area and works down the line of scrimmage, crossing behind one or more of his teammates on the offensive line before reaching the defender whom he is assigned to block. Pulling provides a blocker with some momentum to clear an area for the ball carrier, and it allows the blocker to attack a defender who is not aligned directly over him. If the pulling lineman blocks an inside defender such as a defensive tackle, the block is called a trap. If the pulling lineman blocks a defensive end or outside linebacker, the block is called a kickout. See examples of plays where pulling is used in Appendix B on page 357.

MOVEMENT ON THE SNAP

The blocker who is pulling must be in a good stance before the snap, not leaning left or right or backward, so that he does not tip off the defense to the fact that he is going to pull. At the snap, the blocker must whip the playside arm back forcefully to start the turn of the body in the direction of the pull (see figure 3.47a). He then takes a drop step with the playside foot, pointing his toes toward the sideline, to clear the adjacent offensive lineman (see figure 3.47b). His second step, unlike the steps that he uses in most other blocks, is a crossover step (see figure 3.747c).

As soon as the blocker gets his body turned to pull, he must get his head up and his eyes focused in the direction that he is pulling so that he can find the defender whom he is assigned to block. He runs parallel to the line of scrimmage, never losing ground and angling slightly upfield when that course is available. His body must remain low so that he can move quickly and be prepared to block forcefully, but he must be able to sift through the confusion of other blockers around him and find the defender whom he is going to trap or kick out.

a   b   c

Figure 3.47 *(a-c)* **Blocker's initial movements when pulling.**

CONTACTING THE DEFENDER

The pulling lineman must take a downhill course toward the defender to get his helmet on the downfield side of the defender (inside out) and make the block with the upfield shoulder (see figure 3.51), which would be the right shoulder if he is moving to his right and the left shoulder if he is moving to his left. The aiming point for a trap or kickout is the defender's inside number.

On his course to the defender, the blocker can run using normal footwork instead of the short, wide steps that he use in base, drive or reach blocks. He needs to get to his assigned defender quickly, giving the defender a limited time to recognize that he is being trapped or kicked out.

Figure 3.48 **Blocker contacting the defender in a trap or kickout.**

Offensive blockers are always taught that low pads win, because the lower player controls the leverage and can sustain his balance. The blocker must be careful to achieve this low pad level by bending at the knees, not the waist. Although the blocker may feel that he is playing low by bending at the waist, he will be off balance and ineffective.

FOLLOW-THROUGH

The blocker must keep a good, wide base and maintain contact without leaning too far forward. The blocker does not have to work for movement; a stalemate in this situation is a victory for the blocker. The blocker must keep his head up and control any movement by the defender to try to get away or disrupt the play.

(continued)

Common Errors

You may run into several common errors when teaching your athletes how to pull.

Error	Error correction
Blocker collides with adjacent lineman.	The blocker took a poor first step. The first step must be a drop step, not a step straight down the line of scrimmage. Although the lineman is excited about the opportunity to pull and trap or kick out a defender, he cannot be in such a hurry that he fails to execute a proper drop step. Remind him that he will get there slower if he collides with a teammate!
Blocker fails to move the defender.	The blocker is playing too high. Some linemen stand too tall when they pull, so when they get to the defender, they have no base of power in the lower body and cannot move the defender even though they have some momentum. Work the linemen in a chute where they have to stay low when they pull.
Defender spills the block.	On this play, the player who gets his helmet downfield best will win. Defenders are often taught to spill a trap or kickout block by getting the helmet inside and taking on the block with the outside shoulder. Conversely, the pulling lineman is taught to get his helmet downfield and execute the block with his play-side shoulder. To trap a defender who is going to try to spill the block, the offensive lineman must attack the defender on a downhill course, getting far enough inside the defender that he cannot get underneath the blocker and spill the play.
Blocker stops moving feet on contact.	Blockers must keep the feet going, even after striking the initial blow. Have them practice driving a sled or teammate holding a bag, keeping the feet driving at all times.
Blocker falls forward.	The blocker has too much weight forward on his toes. When a defender moves, the lineman who has too much weight forward will have difficulty keeping his balance.

Pass Protection

Pass protection describes the efforts by the five offensive linemen (plus, occasionally, a running back or two and even a tight end in some schemes) to keep onrushing defenders on a drop-back pass play away from the quarterback long enough for him to deliver the pass. Pass protection, however, also literally refers to protecting the quarterback from being knocked down and possibly injured by being hit when looking downfield and throwing the ball—a time when he is unable to protect himself. To achieve this protection, the five offensive linemen (hereafter called blockers) may each have to initiate pass protection when a pass play is called.

Pass protection is a difficult challenge for offensive linemen. Patience, poise and the ability to be physical at the appropriate time without losing balance and position are the attributes of an effective pass blocker. Unlike in run blocks, pure aggressiveness is not especially helpful, especially in the first few moments of this technique. Overaggressive blockers are vulnerable to quick, evasive moves and run a high risk of losing the defender at the beginning of the play. Instead, the blocker must set up properly, read the defender's actions and react to stay between him and the quarterback.

Note: This skill specifically addresses the protection techniques for pass plays in which the quarterback takes a five-step drop. On three-step passes, the pass protectors can be somewhat more aggressive, since the pass will be delivered more quickly.

BALANCED STANCE

The blocker's initial stance, before the start of the play, is important to effective pass protection. The stance must be balanced, with the weight equally distributed between the two feet and the down hand (see figure 3.49). Having too much weight forward will not allow the blocker to set back off the line of scrimmage, but putting too much weight on the feet and having no pressure on the hand will tip off the defensive linemen. The stance, therefore, should be the same on all plays—both runs and passes.

POP AND SET

The initial pass set for the blocker is crucial. He must get out of the stance quickly, snapping the head and shoulders back to a position in which his nose is behind his knees, as shown in figure

Figure 3.49 Blocker's initial stance for pass blocking.

3.50. Simultaneously, the hands pop up into a ready position with the hands above the elbows, ready to deliver a blow. The knees should be flexed, the feet shoulder-width

(continued)

Figure 3.50   Blocker achieving the initial pass-set position.

apart and the back straight. The player should practice this pass set repeatedly until he can quickly achieve a balanced, ready pass-blocking position.

Figure 3.51   Proper body positioning for pass protection.

BODY POSITIONING AND FOOTWORK

The blocker must keep the shoulders parallel to the line of scrimmage at all times, as shown in figure 3.51, staying on the inside half of the defender to protect against an inside move. Unlike in run blocking, the blocker must keep the head back, out of the block, to maintain balance and not lean too far forward.

The blocker should never bring his feet together; he must keep a wide base for better balance. The blocker should take short steps, never crossing over and trying to keep as many cleats in the ground as possible. Specifically, the initial footwork should be a step-and-slide move—a

RUNNING BACK PASS PROTECTION

Running backs will sometimes have to block on pass protection, picking up a blitzing linebacker or blocking a defensive end if the offensive line runs a gap, or slide, protection in which they each block a gap to one side and the running back takes the outside rusher. The techniques used by the running back are similar to those used by the offensive linemen in many respects, but a significant difference is that the running back sets up in the backfield and has more time than the offensive linemen does to locate the defender whom he is supposed to block. In this case, then, the running back does not have to pop and set as an offensive lineman does.

After he identifies the onrushing defender whom he is supposed to block, the running back must concentrate on his footwork and body positioning. He must quickly move to a position inside the defender, using short, quick steps to adjust his position and stay inside while staying under control and not attacking the defender with too much forward momentum. Then, at the moment of impact, the running back must accelerate his feet forward into the defender with short, choppy steps while simultaneously striking an aggressive, two-hand blow to the defender's chest. Keeping the elbows in for leverage and power while at the same time keeping the feet wide enough for a solid base of power, the running back should drive his feet and push the defender out away from the center of the pocket where the quarterback is setting up to throw. As he drives the defender, the running back adjusts his hand position and helmet position so that the helmet is on the outside half of the defender, the outside hand is down and the inside hand is up. (In adjusting the helmet and hands, the blocker should feel as if he is driving a car with his hands on a steering wheel. If the defender is on the blocker's left, the blocker's right hand would be at one o'clock on the steering wheel, his left hand would be at seven o'clock and the helmet would be at eleven o'clock. If the defender is on the blocker's right, the left hand would be at eleven o'clock on the steering wheel, the right hand would be at five o'clock and the helmet would be at one o'clock.) The blocker continues to drive the defender by driving his legs, keeping a good base for balance at all times and forcing the defender outside and past the quarterback's position in the pocket.

step back, a quick slide step to regain his base, another step back and then another quick slide to regain his base—until he encounters the defender. Quick feet are essential to establishing proper body position against the defender's pass rush moves. The blocker should also attempt to keep his weight down the center of the body, with the weight on the insteps at all times.

PUNCH

As the pass rusher approaches, the blocker delivers a punch (see figure 3.52). The hands should be up with thumbs together and palms forward, about 12 inches away from his

Figure 3.52   Blocker delivering a punch.

(continued)

At a Glance

The following parts of the text offer additional information on pass protection.

Stance and Start for Offense	p. 22
Mirror Block	p. 76
Lead Block	p. 79
Pass Rush	p. 110
Pass Protection on the Edge	p. 222
Taking the Inside Rush	p. 229
Punt Protection	p. 281

own chest. The actual punch should be a 6-inch jab, timed to reach the defender's numbers or chest just before the arms lock out. After the punch, the blocker needs to reset his hands quickly and be prepared to punch again. While punching, the blocker must be sure not to overextend and get his weight over his toes, because he would be likely to lose his balance and be unable to stay in position between the rusher and the quarterback.

Common Errors

You may run into several common errors when teaching your athletes how to pass protect.

Error	Error correction
Blocker grabs or reaches instead of punching.	The lineman must learn that he can't stop the defender by grabbing him! He must develop a firm punch that he can use repeatedly to stop the defender. He must be sure that the hands don't stay in contact with the defender longer than for the brief moment of contact; he then retracts the hands and prepares to punch again.
Blocker gets beat to the inside.	The lineman must stay square to the line of scrimmage, being sure to set up inside the defender, not too far to the outside.
Blocker gets pushed to one side or the other.	To avoid losing his balance, the lineman must keep his head back, keep his feet apart in a wide base and continuously take short lateral steps.
Blocker gets run over or pushed backward.	The lineman is too passive. His weight is too far back, he is too conscious of the set and he does not place enough emphasis on the punch.
Blocker lunges.	The lineman must not overextend or overemphasize the punch. He must be patient, keeping the body weight back and the head up throughout the block.
Blocker gets beat off the ball.	The offensive lineman knows the snap count and must use it to his advantage. He must have confidence in his pass set and beat the defender to the spot where they will meet.

chapter 4

Defensive Technical Skills

This chapter covers the defensive technical skills that you and your players must know to be successful. In this chapter, you will find the following skills:

Stance and Start for Defense

KEY POINTS

The most important components of stance and start for defense are

- o choosing the appropriate stance,
- o eliminating false steps and
- o moving out of the stance.

Players improve their execution of every technique in football if they begin the play with the correct stance and an efficient start. Defensive players use a variety of stances depending on the position they play, but they all need to be ready to move at the snap of the ball in the proper direction, without false steps.

CHOOSING THE APPROPRIATE STANCE

Defensive linemen usually choose a stance with at least one hand on the ground, using either a three-point (one hand) or four-point (two hands) stance. In the three-point stance, as shown in figure 4.1, the feet will be staggered, with the outside foot back and the hand on that side on the ground. In the four-point stance, as shown in figure 4.2, the feet are set evenly, with neither foot ahead of the other and both hands on the ground. The back should be flat and the shoulders parallel to the line of scrimmage. The head should be up and the eyes focused on the ball. Linemen generally use the three-point stance on regular down-and-distance plays (first and second downs and third down with medium or long yardage to go). They generally use the four-point stance in short-yardage situations—such as third and short, fourth and short, and goal-line plays with short yards to go—because they play lower, or closer to the ground.

Linebackers and defensive backs use a two-point stance, but their stances differ (see figure 4.3, *a-b*). Linebackers use a squared stance, keeping their feet even at shoulder-width, whereas defensive backs align in a staggered stance, with the outside foot placed slightly ahead of the inside foot. Safeties, however, may want to use more of a linebacker's two-point stance if their pass assignment is shallow and their run assignment is primary force. All defensive players in a two-point stance should dangle their arms in a relaxed manner.

Figure 4.1 Defensive lineman in a three-point stance.

Figure 4.2 Defensive lineman in a four-point stance.

a   b

Figure 4.3 Two-point stance for *(a)* linebackers and *(b)* for defensive backs.

ELIMINATING FALSE STEPS

When the ball is snapped, all defensive players must react and move without wasted steps. Linemen should keep most of their weight on their down hand (60:40 ratio).

(continued)

They should be positioned on the balls of their feet but have enough weight on the inside foot so that the initial step is with the outside foot only and the inside foot does not false-step. Linebackers must keep their weight on the balls of their feet, without favoring either foot, so that they can take an initial step in either direction without using a drop step. Defensive backs, using their staggered two-point stance, should keep most of their weight on the front foot so that they can begin their backpedal by pushing off the front foot and reaching back with the back foot.

At a Glance

The following parts of the text offer additional information on stance and start for defense.

MOVING OUT OF THE STANCE

All defensive players need to burst out of the stance at the instant the ball is snapped, with a low pad level and no wasted steps. They should focus their eyes on the key so that they can read the play as they move. These two actions, moving and diagnosing the play, must be simultaneous. Neither should slow performance of the other. Consequently, the stance and start must become natural and instinctive, so that players can do it without conscious thought. They can then concentrate on reading the play.

Common Errors

You may run into several common errors when teaching your athletes the proper stance and start for defense.

Error	Error correction
Defender hesitates at the snap.	The defender is probably trying to read the play and is not yet sure what the play is; therefore, he doesn't move anywhere. Defensive players must read on the run and use an explosive start on every snap and learn to read on the run. You must drill reads every day and demand a good start as players execute the read.
Defender takes false steps.	Emphasize weight distribution before the snap. Linebackers can point their feet inward somewhat to ensure that their weight is on the inside front part of the foot. Drill the first step or two for every player in both directions to eliminate false steps; then add reads.
Defender plays too high.	Defenders must learn to read the play while in good football position, not while standing up and looking over the line to see what is happening!
Defender's initial step is too big.	Emphasize that the first step should be no more than 6 inches in length. Any step larger than that will not allow a quick second step and a fast start in the appropriate direction.

Tackling

Tackling is the single most important defensive skill in the game of football. Every player on the defensive team must be able to tackle consistently and must be able to do it well. No defensive scheme or concept will ever stop a play unless the offensive man is tackled. Thus, tackling is one of the few skills in football that is critically important on nearly every play of the game.

Tackling can also be dangerous if it is not executed properly. Tacklers must remember never to drive their helmet or facemask into the opponent as the initial point of contact. In particular, head-down contact (initiating contact with the top, or crown, of the helmet), also known as spearing, greatly increases the risk of injury.

COMING TO BALANCE

As he approaches the ball carrier, the tackler must come to balance, meaning that he must shorten his stride, widen the placement of his feet and lower his hips by bending his knees (see figure 4.4). A balanced position with low pad level is critical for leverage, power and stability in the tackle and will help prevent the tackler from missing or being pushed backward by the ball carrier.

SQUARING UP

At the final ready position before contact, the tackler should keep his back straight and his head up with his eyes on the chest of the ball carrier or, for a better focus, with his eyes on the ball. As in catching a football, the eyes lead the tackler to the end result, and if the eyes stray from the target (if the tackler ducks his head, for example) or if they close, the tackler may miss his mark and miss the tackle.

Figure 4.4 Balanced position as the tackler approaches the ball carrier.

CONTACTING THE DEFENDER

At the moment of impact, the tackler should explode off the foot that is on the side of the shoulder that will be making contact. When executing a head-on tackle, the

(continued)

Figure 4.5 Tackler head and body positioning for a *(a)* head-on tackle and *(b)* an angle tackle.

Figure 4.6 Securing the tackle.

player can explode off either foot, but for an angle tackle, he must explode off the foot and shoulder nearer the ball carrier. The tackler should make contact with the shoulder pad, not the helmet, and drive the shoulder pad up through the ball carrier's chest, keeping the helmet to the side for a head-on tackle (see figure 4.5*a*) and in front of the ball carrier for an angle tackle (see figure 4.5*b*). For both, the hips and legs must explode upward through the ball carrier.

WRAPPING THE ARMS

After the initial contact and leg drive, the tackler must

wrap his arms to secure the tackle (see figure 4.6). He should use both arms to wrap up the runner and grab the cloth on the back of the opponent's jersey if possible. As the legs continue to drive, the tackler lifts the ball carrier and drives him to the ground.

At a Glance

The following parts of the text offer additional information on tackling.

Ball Security	p. 29
Open-Field Tackling	p. 168
Evading Tacklers	p. 194
Finishing Plays in Man Pass Coverage	p. 244
Pursuit Angles	p. 254

Common Errors

You may run into several common errors when teaching your athletes how to tackle.

Error	Error correction
Defender ducks his head.	Many young players flinch at the oncoming contact and instinctively duck their heads, causing them to lose sight of the ball carrier and increasing the risk of injury. Do drills at a slower pace with minimal contact, teaching proper head position and initial shoulder contact so that young players get the feel of the tackle and learn the proper form before going full speed with full contact.
Defender has his pads too high.	Ball carriers will fall forward and gain extra yards every time, and break tackles some of the time, if defensive players play too high. Spend time on the blocking sled or with stand-up bags, teaching players how to bend their knees with the back straight and play lower than the opponent.
Ball carrier breaks an arm tackle.	The dreaded arm tackle results from failure to make contact with the shoulder pad or failure to wrap both arms aggressively around the ball carrier. The tackler probably wasn't close enough to the ball carrier when he tried to make the tackle.
Defender has his eyes closed.	Many missed tackles occur because defenders shut their eyes just before contact. Stress to defenders that they must see their work and concentrate on keeping their eyes open.
Defender leaves his feet.	When defenders have to leave their feet to make a tackle, they were probably not in proper position before contact. Before tackling, the defender must be close enough to the ball carrier to step on his toes. Tell players to get their feet to the runner before they use their arms. In addition, teach defenders to keep their feet running through the tackle. They must never dive at the ball carrier or leave their feet intentionally because the ball carrier can easily make them miss if they do that.

Defending Basic Run Blocks

Before the start of a play, defensive players must understand the possible threat of run blocks and react accordingly. Effective defense requires each defensive player to defend himself from offensive blocks so that he can stay on his feet and eventually pursue the play. Defensive players must also defend blocks with the positioning and leverage called for by the defensive scheme so that the defense remains gap sound, with one player in each gap, to minimize running lanes for the opponent.

Here, we will discuss the techniques that defenders use in taking on the drive, reach and down blocks—the basic run blocks that they will encounter. Although the exact technique of defending these various run blocks varies, the basic principles are always the same—stay gap sound, stay on the feet and continue to pursue until the whistle blows. See examples of basic run plays and blocks used in these plays in Appendix B on page 357 and Appendix C on page 361.

RECOGNIZING THE BLOCK

Each defensive player who plays in the nucleus of the defensive alignment (defensive linemen and linebackers lined up over the center, guard, tackle and tight end if there is one) is positioned in, or assigned to, a specific gap between two offensive blockers on the line of scrimmage. On any given running play, these players have five basic blocking scenarios to consider:

1. One blocker might try to drive block the defender away from his gap and open up a running lane inside.
2. One blocker might try to reach block the defender and overtake his gap.
3. One blocker might try to down block the defender and open up a lane outside.
4. Two blockers might try to double-team the defender (see "Defending the Double-Team Block" on page 100).
5. Two blockers might both block other defenders, leaving the defender unblocked and essentially giving him two gaps, one on either side of the next blocker's body, to defend. In this case, the defender has to know whether he should squeeze the next block—that is, take it on with his inside shoulder and turn the play inside—or spill the block, that is, take on the block with his outside shoulder and make the play go outside (see "Spilling Blocks" on page 103 and "Squeezing Blocks" on page 107).

BODY POSITION

At the start of each play, then, the defender must recognize who is going to block him and what that blocker is trying to accomplish. When a defensive lineman or linebacker takes on a drive block, as shown in figure 4.7a, he must widen his base slightly, take short, quick steps, lower his pad level below the blocker's pads, adjust his head to his gap responsibility and stop the blocker's momentum. When a defender takes on a reach block, as shown in figure 4.7*b*, the defender must see the lateral movement of the blocker and take short, strong steps in the same direction to keep from getting reached, being sure to work over the top of the blocker. Against the down block, as shown in figure 4.7*c*, the defender must sink his hips low and hold his ground, hitting the blocker with the shoulder pad on the side of the block and leaning into the blocker to avoid giving up any ground.

Figure 4.7 **Defending (a) a drive block, (b) a reach block and (c) a down block.**

(continued)

a

b

Figure 4.8 Defender *(a)* establishing leverage against a drive or reach block or *(b)* compressing the blocker backward against a down block.

ESTABLISHING LEVERAGE

After recognizing the block and establishing solid initial body position, the defender must use his hands, arms and legs to gain leverage and thereby establish control over the blocker. Against drive blocks and reach blocks, the defender should work his hands inside the blocker's hands to a position on the blocker's breast plates and then extend his arms, pressing the blocker away with his hands and keeping his body and legs free from the blocker (see figure 4.8a). He must keep his head up while he establishes control of his gap and drive his legs in an effort to bubble the blocker backward and cause a pile that might disrupt the ball carrier's running lane. Against the down block, the defender should use his forearm on the side of the block to stop the blocker. He should then lower his pad level and use his legs and hips to squeeze the blocker backward, compressing the running lane (see figure 4.8b). Again, he should keep his head up to find the ball.

NEUTRALIZING AND SEPARATING

The process of establishing leverage against the blocker, as described previously, gives the defender a chance to neutralize the blocker. The defender can neutralize the blocker only by keeping his pad level low, keeping his feet moving, maintaining a wide base to stay balanced and driving with his hips and legs to cancel the blocker's momentum. As the defender reads the play, he has to make sure that his gap responsibility is not threatened before he disengages from the blocker. When his gap is no longer threatened, he should separate from the blocker, shedding him with aggressive hand action, and then find the football and run to it.

At a Glance

The following parts of the text offer additional information on defending basic run blocks.

Drive Block	p. 61
Reach Block	p. 64
Cutoff Block	p. 67
Down Block	p. 70
Defending the Double-Team Block	p. 100

Common Errors

You may run into several common errors when teaching your athletes how to defend basic run blocks.

Error	Error correction
Defender peeks in the backfield.	The offensive blocker will succeed every time if the defender peeks in the backfield to find the ball and does not see what type of block is coming. The defender must key the blockers and recognize his threat first, concentrating on defeating the block before running to the football.
Defender's hands go stagnant.	Although movement of the feet and overall pad level are crucial, hand action eventually separates the defender from the blocker. Defenders should constantly practice using their hands on blocking bags and sleds to ensure that the hands remain active when the play starts.
Defender plays too high.	Many defensive players are so eager to find the ball that they stand up and look over the blocker into the backfield to see what is happening. Drill defenders to play low and stay low so that they can neutralize blocks, sustain their gap responsibility and hold their ground.
Defender plays with his head down.	Defenders cannot be successful if they play with the head down. Defenders must play with low pad level and a solid base but keep the head and eyes up so that they can find the ball carrier.

Defending the Double-Team Block

Perhaps the toughest assignment for a defensive line-man is the double-team block, in which two offensive blockers attack one down defender. Sometimes, the offensive blockers sustain the double-team block throughout the play. At other times, the double team is just the first phase of a combination block, in which one of the blockers will eventually leave the double team and block a linebacker. In either case, the down defender who is double-teamed has two primary tasks. First, although he is up against two blockers, he must not allow them to drive him off the line. He must give up ground grudgingly and try to make a pile that will slow the ball carrier. Second, he must work to prevent being reached, even though one blocker is pinning him as the other blocker is overtaking him. Additionally, although the odds are daunting, the defender must try to retain his gap responsibility in spite of the fact that the reach blocker is getting help from a teammate.

RECOGNIZING THE BLOCK

At the outset of the play, if two players attack one defender, the defender must determine if the scheme is a true two-on-one double team or the beginning of a two-on-two combination block. Generally, if both players attack the defender and neither attempts to get his head across the face of the defender, the block is a true double team. If one of the blockers tries to "helmet adjust" across the defender so that both blockers will be on the same side, then the block is a combination block. Also, double teams (two-on-one) are more likely to be used on gap plays that rely on power, such as the trap, the isolation play and the off-tackle power play. Combination blocks (two-on-two) are more likely to be used on zone plays that rely more on finesse. Through scouting and game-day observation, the defender should be able to recognize the type of play, and therefore the blocking scheme, that he is encountering.

NEUTRALIZING THE BLOCK

If the block is a true double team, the defender should lower his center of gravity by bending his knees and sinking his hips so that he can hold his position (see figure 4.9a). As the two blockers attempt to move him, the defender should continue to stay low and on his feet. He should then make himself skinny and try to split the defenders, working between them and driving upfield, as shown in figure 4.9b. If this effort is unsuccessful, as a last resort the defender can grab cloth on one of the blockers and sink even lower, being willing to drop to the ground if he starts to lose his position on the field. If he goes to the ground, his primary goal is to create a pile at or near the running lane so that the ball carrier will have to slow down or bounce the play outside. Although he is being double-teamed, the defender should focus on defeating just one of the blockers, preferably the lineman whom he shaded, or lined up on, at the beginning of the play.

Figure 4.9 *(a-b)* Defender reacting to a double-team block.

(continued)

At a Glance

The following parts of the text offer additional information on defending the double-team block.

SPLITTING THE BLOCK

In a combination block, after the initial double team, one of the blockers will try to reach the defender as the other blocker leaves to block the linebacker. After recognizing this scheme, the defender needs to work hard to avoid getting reached, working laterally with short, powerful steps and using his arms as he would against a one-on-one reach block to keep his outside arm free and his gap defended. The outside blocker will make lateral movement difficult, but the defender needs to work aggressively against that blocker to maintain his position so that when that blocker leaves, the defender is in position to defeat the reach block of the second opponent. In this case, the defender must stay on his feet and keep working laterally for outside leverage. If he falls to the ground, he will have surrendered his gap.

Common Errors

You may run into several common errors when teaching your athletes how to defend the double-team block.

Error	Error correction
Defender peeks in the backfield.	The offensive blocker will succeed every time if the defender peeks in the backfield to find the ball and does not see what type of block is coming. The defender must key the blockers and recognize his threat first, concentrating on defeating the block before running to the football.
Defender goes for a ride.	The player has the pads too high and fights the block with hands instead of dropping down, giving up the feet-on-the-ground position and creating a pile.
Defender's hands go stagnant.	Although movement of the feet and overall pad level are crucial, hand action eventually separates the defender from the blocker. Defenders should constantly practice using their hands on blocking bags and sleds to ensure that the hands remain active when the play starts.

KEY POINTS

The most important components of spilling blocks are

o recognizing the scheme,

o engaging the blocker and

o completing the spill.

Spilling, or wrong shouldering, is a call that a defense uses to tell an unblocked defender to take on the next blocker (usually a fullback or a pulling lineman) with his outside shoulder. This technique places the defender underneath the blocker and eliminates the gap inside that blocker, thus spilling the play to the outside. Spilling is a defensive strategy. If unblocked by the offensive linemen on a play, each defensive player decides, based on the defense that is called and the offensive blocking scheme that unfolds, whether to spill the next blocker. Here, we will focus on the process of spilling blocks—a technique that requires quick reactions and aggressive movements. This technique is effective in neutralizing traps and kickout plays like powers and counters. For more about the decision-making process for defenders who are unblocked, see, for defensive linemen, "Reacting When Unblocked" on page 232 and, for linebackers, "Choosing to Spill or Squeeze" on page 241.

RECOGNIZING THE SCHEME

Two previous skills ("Defending Basic Run Blocks" on page 96 and "Defending the Double-Team Block" on page 100) explained how defenders should react to blocks from the offensive linemen who line up across from them. On some offensive plays, however, neither of those offensive linemen blocks the defender; instead, the offensive linemen block other defenders, and the offensive blocking scheme calls for a running back or pulling lineman to block the defender. When that happens, the offense has, in effect, created an extra gap for the defense to defend, one gap on each side of the running back or pulling lineman. See figure 4.10 for an example of an extra gap created by the offense on an isolation play.

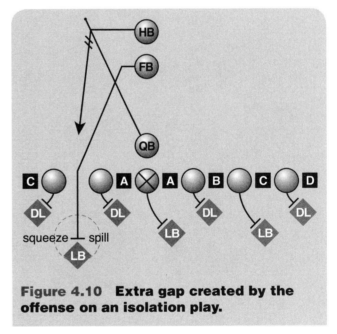

Figure 4.10 Extra gap created by the offense on an isolation play.

If a defensive lineman is not blocked by the man over him and the defensive strategy for that play requires the defensive lineman to spill any subsequent block, his immediate reaction must be to look inside as he halts his progress up the field. He must then find his next threat, probably a guard or a fullback, and prepare to take on the block with his outside shoulder. The key to a successful spill against a blocker is quick recognition of the blocking scheme. If the defensive lineman does not recognize the threat early enough, he could get too far up the field to be able to get back underneath the blocker.

Linebackers must also recognize the blocking scheme. The linebacker must quickly determine whether the blocker approaching him is a lineman who was lined up in front of him, a running back (on a isolation play, for example) or a pulling lineman

(continued)

(on a counter or power play, for example). If the blocker is a running back or pulling lineman and the linebacker's assignment is to spill that type of block, he must be sure not to overrun the play, getting himself too far outside to be able to get his outside shoulder underneath the blocker.

ENGAGING THE BLOCKER

After a defensive lineman who has an assignment to spill a block recognizes the offensive blocking scheme and finds the blocker who is his threat, he must plant his feet, stop his own upfield progress and turn back down the line of scrimmage with his shoulders and hips perpendicular to the line of scrimmage, as shown in figure 4.11a. He then must rip his outside arm underneath the onrushing blocker while stepping with his outside foot inside the onrushing blocker, as shown in figure 4.11b, to establish inside position and avoid being kicked out or trapped.

a   b

Figure 4.11 *(a-b)* **Defensive lineman engaging the blocker on the spill.**

A linebacker who has a spill assignment operates 1 or 2 yards behind the defensive linemen, so the path that his blocking threat takes will usually be more perpendicular to the line of scrimmage than the path that a blocker takes to block a defensive lineman (more parallel to the line of scrimmage). The linebacker, after recognizing the blocking scheme, must slow his outside pursuit, find his blocking threat and then attack the inside shoulder of the blocker with his outside arm and foot, working underneath the blocker (see figure 4.12).

Figure 4.12 Linebacker engaging the blocker on the spill when the ball is on his right.

COMPLETING THE SPILL

After the defender (either the defensive lineman or the linebacker) has engaged the blocker, the play is not over. The defender cannot just run inside the blocker and leave a big opening outside the block. He must physically challenge the blocker and slow him down. Then, as he works underneath the blocker, the defender must slow his own inside momentum and continue to rip through the blocker, dipping his shoulder (see figure 4.13a) and trying to run a tight circle behind the blocker. A defensive lineman will have to flip his hips around so that he is parallel to the line of scrimmage again (see figure 4.13b), whereas a

a   b

Figure 4.13 *(a-b)* Completing the spill.

(continued)

At a Glance

The following parts of the text offer additional information on spilling blocks.

linebacker might still have his hips parallel to the line of scrimmage as he meets a more head-on block. In both cases, the defender should try to force the blocker backward, causing a bubble that the ball carrier or any other pulling blockers will have to work around. When the defender executes the spill properly, the ball carrier will be forced to bounce the play laterally and will be slowed down. All this gives the spilling defender time to pursue to the ball.

Common Errors

You may run into several common errors when teaching your athletes how to spill blocks.

Error	Error correction
Defender gets kicked out.	The defender might have gotten excited when he was initially unblocked and he forgot that another blocker is on the way. He can't get too far upfield and be duped. Defenders should think about traps and kickouts every time they line up for a play (unless the defense makes a pass rush call). Drill recognition of these plays constantly.
Defender runs down the line.	The job is only half over when the defender gets underneath the blocker. He must work back upfield and restrict the running lane outside.
Defender is driven backward.	If the blocker drives the defender backward, the foot that the defender planted on the ground was probably opposite the shoulder that is making contact. The foot on the ground should be on the same side as the shoulder that makes contact. So, when the defender spills a blocker with his right shoulder, his right foot should be on the ground (and the blocker attacked him from the left).

Squeezing Blocks

The most important components of squeezing blocks are

o recognizing the scheme and
o attacking the block.

Squeezing is a call that a defense uses to tell an unblocked defender to take on the next blocker (usually a fullback or a pulling lineman) with his inside shoulder, keeping his outside arm free. This technique places the defender outside the blocker and eliminates the gap outside that blocker, thus squeezing the play back inside.

Squeezing is a defensive strategy. If he is unblocked by the offensive linemen on a play, the defensive player has an assignment, based on the defense that is called and the offensive blocking scheme that unfolds, that tells him to squeeze the next blocker. Here, we will focus on the process of squeezing blocks, a technique that requires quick reactions and powerful, aggressive contact with the offensive player. For more about the decision-making process for defenders who are unblocked, see, for defensive linemen, "Reacting When Unblocked" on page 232 and, for linebackers, "Choosing to Spill or Squeeze" on page 241.

RECOGNIZING THE SCHEME

Two previous skills ("Defending Basic Run Blocks" on page 96 and "Defending the Double-Team Block" on page 100) explained how defenders should react to blocks from the offensive linemen who line up across from them. On some offensive plays, however, none of the offensive linemen block the defender; instead, the offensive linemen block other defenders, and the offensive blocking scheme calls for a running back or pulling lineman to block the defender. When that happens, the offense has, in effect, created an extra gap for the defense to defend, one gap on each side of the running back or pulling lineman, as shown in figure 4.10 on page 103.

If a defensive lineman is not blocked by the man over him and the defensive strategy for that play requires the defensive lineman to squeeze any subsequent block, his immediate reaction must be to look inside as he halts his progress up the field. He must then find his next threat, probably a guard or a fullback, and prepare to take on the block with his inside shoulder.

Linebackers must also recognize the blocking scheme. The linebacker must quickly determine whether the blocker approaching him is a lineman who was lined up in front of him, a running back (on a isolation play, for example) or a pulling lineman (on a counter or power play, for example). If the blocker is a running back or pulling lineman and the linebacker's assignment is to squeeze that type of block, he must be sure not to be caught inside the blocker. He must attack the block at an angle that will allow him to take on the block with his inside shoulder.

The key to squeezing a block is for the defender to recognize the threat early. The defender must read the run, understand the developing blocking scheme and see the course of the blockers. The defender's footwork must be patient on the first two steps as he reads the blocking scheme. Then the defender must become aggressive so that he can establish leverage and position on the blocker who is attacking him.

(continued)

ATTACKING THE BLOCK

Figure 4.14 *(a-b)* **Defensive lineman attacking the blocker on the squeeze.**

After recognizing the blocking threat, the defender cannot hesitate. A defensive lineman must plant his feet, stop his upfield progress and square his shoulders so that they are parallel to the line of scrimmage (see figure 4.14*a*). He lowers his center of gravity by sinking his hips and then shuffles powerfully toward the blocker (see figure 4.14*b*).

A linebacker who has a squeeze assignment, after recognizing the blocking scheme, must attack the threat downhill toward the line of scrimmage, with the location and path of the blocker determining the angle of his approach to the line. If the blocker is approaching directly toward the defender and the ball carrier is directly behind the blocker, the defender will attack straight ahead with the objective of meeting the blocker at or near the line of scrimmage. If the blocker is angling or pulling laterally and trying to establish a position outside the defender, the defender must be sure to attack the blocker on an angle that will cross the face of the blocker and attack the outside half of that blocker with the inside shoulder and forearm.

When the defender attacks the blocker, he must keep his outside arm free. This means that any contact with the blocker must be with the inside arm and shoulder. When making contact with the blocker, the defender delivers a forearm blow with the inside arm and simultaneously lowers his inside shoulder and delivers a blow with the shoulder pad on that side to neutralize the blocker's momentum (see figure 4.15). The defender's objective is to keep his legs and outside arm free from the blocker, but he also must engage the blocker with enough contact to stop him and squeeze the running lane as much as possible.

At a Glance

The following parts of the text offer additional information on squeezing blocks.

Pulling	p. 82
Defending Basic Run Blocks	p. 96
Spilling Blocks	p. 103
Reacting When Unblocked	p. 232
Choosing to Spill or Squeeze	p. 241

Figure 4.15 Defender attacking the blocker while keeping his outside arm free.

Common Errors

You may run into several common errors when teaching your athletes how to squeeze blocks.

Error	Error correction
Defender takes false steps.	Work the read steps for linebackers every day. Teach them to be patient at the beginning of every play, because they will have a better chance to defeat the block if they read the play correctly and don't take unnecessary steps or steps in the wrong direction.
Defender's pad level is too high.	The defender may be peaking in the backfield, or he may be bending at the waist, not at the knees. Be sure that the defenders are using low leg and hip action as well as hand and arm action to defeat blocks.
Defender gets tied up with the blocker.	Usually this problem occurs when the defender focuses on the ball carrier too early in the play. The defender must concentrate on defeating the block before he takes on the ball carrier.
Defender gets reached (outside arm is not free).	The defender probably took a poor angle toward the blocker and got outflanked. Drill linebackers on reading the path of the blocker and adjusting their course to a wider angle as the blocker moves laterally.

Rushing the passer is the best form of pass defense. The obvious goal is to sack the quarterback, but a fierce pass rush can also disrupt the passing game by knocking down passes, forcing the quarterback to shorten his passing motion by squeezing the pocket, narrowing the quarterback's field of vision by compressing the throwing lanes, causing the quarterback to hurry his pass and perhaps causing the quarterback to scramble out of the pocket and not throw at all.

Defenders must understand that rushing the passer produces infrequent rewards. One or two sacks in a game would be an excellent performance, and the quarterback may have attempted 30 or even 40 passes. The defender must rush tenaciously. With great desire and hustle, he will occasionally win the battle. Determination is one of the pass rusher's most valuable attributes.

RECOGNIZING PASS PROTECTION

A great pass rusher has already planned his move before the next pass play happens. He knows how he will attack, once he reads pass, and he can execute his pass rush aggressively and authoritatively without hesitating. At the snap of the ball, if the offensive lineman pops up out of his three-point stance, the read is pass and the defender assigned to rush the quarterback must spring into action. The quarterback will not hold the ball for long; thus the defender doesn't have much time to make his move.

In some high-tendency passing situations, such as third down and long yardage to go, some coaches may turn loose their pass rushers, telling them to start their pass rush on the snap of the ball instead of waiting to read the offensive blocker, a tactic that should give them a good head start on their pass rush moves. This ploy may weaken the ability of the defense to stop a run, but if the offense chooses to run the ball on long yardage, the hope is that the linebackers and safeties can make the tackle short of a first down.

STAYING IN THE LANE

Defenders who are rushing the passer are assigned pass rush lanes that define, generally, the path that their defensive coaches want them to take on their way to the quarterback. Two rushers are always designated as contain rushers, meaning that they are supposed to stay outside the last pass protector in the pocket of the offense, where the quarterback is located. Although they are still trying to get pressure on the quarterback, their primary job is to be sure that the quarterback cannot scramble out of the pocket toward either sideline. The other two rushers in a traditional four-man pass rush are assigned a lane between the quarterback and the contain rusher on their side. Again, they are trying to put pressure on the quarterback, but they must each rush on their side of the ball, keeping the quarterback on the inside shoulder so that the quarterback cannot find a way out of the pocket. The contain rushers, within certain guidelines, can occasionally take an inside rush to keep the pass blockers honest (see "Taking the Inside Rush" on page 229 for more information), but if they do choose to go inside, their coaches will tell them that they better be sure to sack the quarterback!

USING THE RIP AND THE SWIM

The two most common pass rush moves are the rip technique and the swim technique. Both moves attack one side of the blocker and use aggressive hand action to evade the blocker's pass protection. A pass rusher should use the rip or the swim when he is matched up one-on-one with a pass blocker who begins to favor one side or the other on his pass setup and pass blocking. The pass rusher should threaten the side that the pass blocker favors, possibly using a head fake or hard step in that direction, and then use the rip or swim move to get past the blocker on his opposite side.

   As an example, let's say that the blocker is favoring the inside rush and the defender decides to try to beat him outside with the rip or swim move. In either case, the defender sets up the move with a fake and then takes a quick step to the outside with the outside foot (see figure 4.16a), followed by a long second step with the inside foot (see figure 4.16b). The outside arm of the defender then drives down hard on the outside arm of the blocker, pushing that arm into his body. The defender drives his inside arm under the blocker's outside arm on the rip (see figure 4.17a) or over the blocker's outside arm on the swim (see figure 4.17b). As this hand action takes place, the defender drives his inside leg past the outside leg of the blocker, driving his hips and his inside shoulder aggressively through any contact. Great quickness and hand actions make these moves extremely effective.

a   b

Figure 4.16 *(a-b)* **Defender's footwork for the rip and swim techniques.**

(continued)

Figure 4.17 **Defender's arm movement for (a) the rip technique and (b) the swim technique.**

At a Glance

The following parts of the text offer additional information on the pass rush.

USING OTHER MOVES

The pass rusher cannot be effective if he always rushes on the same side of the blocker or uses only the rip or swim. He should occasionally vary his approach and use a head-on bull rush, in which he attacks the blocker straight ahead and just tries to force him back into the quarterback's lap. This occasional bull rush forces the blocker to set up more inside and more firmly than he would if all he had to do was block the pass rusher on an outside rush. The pass rusher also can use a push-pull move in which he grabs the jersey of the pass blocker, pushes him backward a bit and then pulls him forward forcefully, hoping to cause him to lose his balance enough for the rusher to get by. The pass rusher should use these alternative moves often enough each game that the blocker has to think about them on every pass but not so often that he can anticipate when they are coming.

Common Errors

You may run into several common errors when teaching your athletes how to pass rush.

Error	Error correction
Defender is leaning and bull rushing every time.	The defender must develop a plan. He must think about the move that he wants to use for the upcoming play and try different strategies to get to the passer.
Defender has dead hands.	The defender should practice various hand moves without actually rushing the passer, working on having active hands, getting the blocker's hands off the chest and disengaging from the blocker's grip.
Defender lacks effort.	Pass rushing takes a lot of effort and does not always result in a sack. The defender must take pride in hurries, deflections and knockdowns (of the quarterback), not just sacks. He must be relentless on every play and let the quarterback know that he is close, even if he doesn't get there.
Defender rushes to the middle of the blocker.	If the pass rusher attacks directly to the middle of the blocker, he has little chance to get around on either side. He has not made the blocker adjust his set left or right, and he is right in the path of the blocker's most powerful punch. Instead, the rusher should attack one shoulder of the blocker, making him move laterally so that he must reach out to punch.
Defender is not clearing the hips.	If the pass rusher manages to work past the hands of the blocker and get even with him, he must clear his hips, meaning that he must get the hip that is closer to the blocker past the blocker's near hip, freeing his legs to run around the blocker to the quarterback. Pass rushers need to do drills in which they run in a tight circle to simulate the clearing of the hips and taking the tight corner around to the quarterback.

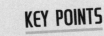

KEY POINTS

The most important components of feathering are

○ recognizing the play,

○ body positioning,

○ focusing on the quarterback and

○ reacting to the quarterback.

When the offense runs a typical lead option or speed option play, the quarterback comes down the line of scrimmage with a running back trailing him in pitch relationship. The quarterback attacks the first unblocked defender and has the option to keep the ball or pitch it to the back. The best technique for the unblocked defender to use in this situation is feathering the option. The technique is known as feathering because it is nonaggressive and requires light, quick footwork and lots of patience on the part of the defender. The defender's assignment is to create confusion in the mind of the quarterback about whether, or when, he should pitch the ball. The longer the quarterback waits to make up his mind on the option, the more time other defenders have to get off their blocks and get to the play. For further discussion on the decision-making process of feathering the option, see "Defending the Option" on page 235.

RECOGNIZING THE PLAY

As soon as the defender realizes that he is unblocked, he must look inside and find his next threat (see "Reacting When Unblocked" on page 232 for more information). If no blocker is threatening him, but the quarterback is approaching with the ball, the defender must immediately recognize the play is an option and stop his initial charge across the line of scrimmage. The sooner the defender recognizes the option, the more successful he will be in playing the feather technique, because he must react and begin to feather before the quarterback has a chance to get to him.

BODY POSITIONING

When the defender recognizes that the play is an option and stops his forward progress, he drops his outside foot and shoulder back to the line of scrimmage so that his shoulders are parallel to the line of scrimmage. He turns his head to look at the quarterback but does not turn his body to face the quarterback. The defender assumes a low, balanced athletic position so that he can shuffle down the line of scrimmage ahead of the quarterback, playing between the quarterback and the pitch back in a position where he can either tackle the quarterback if he keeps the ball or help tackle the pitch back if the quarterback pitches it back to him. The defender also must be able to move in either direction—toward the quarterback or toward the pitch back, depending on the option taken—with equal quickness. His weight should be on the balls of his feet, his knees must be bent, his arms should be dangling in front of him and he should not be leaning in either direction (see figure 4.18).

FOCUSING ON THE QUARTERBACK

As the defender levels off and shuffles toward the sideline, he should focus solely on the quarterback's midsection. His most important assignment is to tackle the quarterback

Figure 4.18 Defender's body positioning when feathering the option.

if the quarterback keeps the football, so the defender has to focus on the quarterback intensely and be ready to react back to him if he turns up the field. The defender should never attempt to make a play on the ball, such as trying to deflect the pitch, because if he starts reacting to ball movement, the quarterback could fake a pitch to get him out of position, turn up the field and gain good yardage.

REACTING TO THE QUARTERBACK

The defender shuffles laterally down the line slightly ahead of the quarterback, staying in front of him but not so far in front that he opens up a big gap for the quarterback to turn upfield and run with the ball. If the quarterback chooses to run with the ball, the defender must plant his outside foot, drive his next few steps back to the inside and securely tackle the quarterback. If the defender sees the ball leave the quarterback's hands on a pitch to the trailing back, he can flip his hips and sprint flat down the line of scrimmage, trying to help out on the tackle of the pitch back. He must, however, be sure that the ball is pitched before he starts to turn and run!

At a Glance

The following parts of the text offer additional information on feathering.

Option Pitch Mechanics	p. 33
Option Pitch Read	p. 177
Reacting When Unblocked	p. 232
Defending the Option	p. 235

(continued)

Common Errors

You may run into several common errors when teaching your athletes how to feather.

Error	Error correction
Defender gets too far upfield.	If the defender gets too far upfield, the quarterback can cut underneath him and make a big play. Teach the defender to stop his charge upfield immediately when he is unblocked and sees option.
Defender faces the quarterback.	The defender must not turn toward the quarterback; doing so gives the quarterback an easy pitch read, and the defender has no chance to turn all the way around and run down the line to help on the pitch player.
Defender falls for a fake.	Never encourage the defender to try to make a play on the ball. His job is to stall the quarterback and tackle him, not deflect the ball. He need not concentrate on the ball; he will know where it is.
Defender allows the quarterback too many yards.	Drill the defender to be patient in his shuffle; if he gets too far ahead of the quarterback, a lane will open up for the quarterback to run for good yardage.
Defender hits the quarterback after the pitch.	Many defenders sell out to their responsibility to take the quarterback and consequently hit the quarterback on every play, even after he pitches. This tendency makes an easy read for the quarterback and could result in a penalty if the hit is late or cheap. Moreover, that defender cannot help on the tackle of the actual ball carrier. Teach the defender to turn and run so that he can help on the tackle of the pitch back.

Zone Pass Drops

KEY POINTS

The most important components of zone pass drops are

o understanding the coverage,

o getting to the zone and

o leveling off in the zone.

Effective zone pass coverage begins with good pass drops by all defenders who are not rushing the quarterback. A pass drop is a retreat by a defender into the area of the field that he is assigned to defend. Pass drops vary somewhat by position—defensive backs use a straight backpedal to retreat into their zones, whereas linebackers turn and run at an angle toward their zones while keeping their eyes on the quarterback. The purpose of every defender's pass drop, however, is the same—to put himself in position where he can defend the deepest threat to his zone while still being able to react up and make a play on the ball or the receiver on a shallow route in his zone (for a detailed discussion on how to make these plays, see "Reads and Reactions in Zone Pass Coverage" on page 248).

UNDERSTANDING THE COVERAGE

Before the snap, every defender must know and understand what his assignment is going to be if the offense runs a pass play. Then, at the snap, if the play is a pass, each defender who is not assigned to rush the quarterback must drop to his assigned area in the zone coverage. Some defenders will be assigned to deep zones, and some will be assigned to underneath zones. Deep defenders must gain enough depth on their drops to defend a deep ball in their assigned areas and then react to help defend on a pass to an intermediate route. Underneath defenders must gain enough depth on their drops to take away throwing lanes to the intermediate routes in their assigned areas and then react to help defend on a pass to a shallow route.

GETTING TO THE ZONE

The technique on zone drops varies by the defender's position and assignment. Deep defenders should execute the backpedal, running backward comfortably with the same arm action that they use with a forward run, leaning slightly forward (chest over the toes) to prevent the pad level from getting too high and to prevent losing balance backward, and keeping the eyes up to read the quarterback and receivers, as shown in figure 4.19a. Their angle on the backpedal should take them to the center of the zone that they are defending. Underneath defenders also keep their eyes on the quarterback and the receivers, but they do not backpedal. These defenders turn their shoulders and use crossover steps to run to their zones, as shown in figure 4.19b.

As underneath defenders drop to their zones, they should make every effort to impede or disrupt the path of any receiver who is running vertically through that defender's area on his way toward a deeper zone. As long as they don't lose sight of the other receivers who might be threatening the underneath areas, the underneath defender can provide valuable assistance to his teammates who are defending deeper zones by slowing down or re-routing receivers.

(continued)

Figure 4.19 *(a)* **Deep defender and** *(b)* **underneath defender running to their zones.**

At a Glance

The following parts of the text offer additional information on zone pass drops.

LEVELING OFF IN THE ZONE

Players defending underneath zones should gauge their depth within their zones by the quarterback's drop. As long as the quarterback continues to drop back, the underneath defenders should continue to gain depth within their zones. When the quarterback sets up in the pocket, however, the underneath defenders must stop gaining depth, level off by taking short lateral steps and read the quarterback's eyes for the direction of the throw.

Players defending deep zones should continue to backpedal as long as the quarterback has the ball. These players cannot settle and level off when the quarterback sets up in the pocket; they must continue to drop and be sure that they are deeper than the deepest receiver in their areas. Because they will be defending deep passes, the ball will be in the air for a long time, so they should have time to react to the throw. They should read the quarterback's eyes and arm motion but know where the receivers are and keep them in front. They should focus on the quarterback and see the receivers through peripheral vision.

Common Errors

You may run into several common errors when teaching your athletes zone pass drops.

Error	Error correction
Defender looks at receivers instead of going to his zone first.	Drill zone defenders on dropping to their areas of responsibility without any receivers to defend, so that they understand the techniques of zone drops and the areas that they need to defend. Require them to use these techniques initially on every pass play with that coverage.
Defender bites on an underneath route.	Work underneath defenders against two receivers in the area (curl–flat, dig–drag). Teach them to ignore the shallow route, to hang under the deeper route until the ball is thrown short and only then to react to the ball. They should force the quarterback to throw to the shorter route.
Defender leans on one receiver in a deep zone.	Work deep defenders against two receivers in the area. Teach them to stay in the center of the area, to avoid leaning on one receiver or the other and to key the quarterback's eyes for clues about which receiver to favor, if any.

Man Pass Coverage

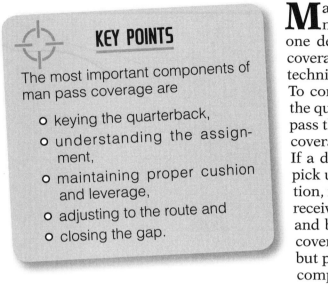
Man-to-man pass coverage is a classic, one-on-one match-up—one pass receiver running a route against one defender assigned to cover him. Man-to-man pass coverage can be effective if the defender plays with good technique and is able to stay close to his assigned man. To complete a pass against tight man-to-man coverage, the quarterback must throw a quicker and more accurate pass than he would to complete a pass against most zone coverages. Man-to-man pass coverage also has its risks. If a defender makes a mistake on coverage and fails to pick up his man, the receiver will be wide open. In addition, if a defender is mismatched against a fast or elusive receiver, the receiver might break away from that defender and be open. For that reason, many defenses play man coverage with a free safety who is not assigned to a man but plays deep as an extra defender to help prevent long completions.

KEYING THE QUARTERBACK

Defensive backs in man-to-man coverage should key the quarterback on the first two steps of their backpedal so that they can break on short, three-step-drop passes. If the quarterback stops his drop after only three steps, the defensive backs must settle their feet, interrupting their backpedal, and recognize the receiver's route. After recognizing the route, the defensive back must break to the interception point and try to get there just as the ball arrives. If the quarterback's drop goes beyond three steps, the defensive back turns his attention to the receiver and settles into the techniques described in the following sections.

UNDERSTANDING THE ASSIGNMENT

Defenders covering tight ends, slots, wingbacks or running backs must first know for sure which man they are covering. Then, at the snap, they must focus their total attention on that player's release. If he runs a pass route, regardless of any other keys or indicators of what the offensive play might be, the defender must cover the offensive player, assuming that the play is a pass.

MAINTAINING PROPER CUSHION AND LEVERAGE

When covering a player who releases to run a pass route, the defender must settle into a comfortable backpedal, maintaining a forward lean with the shoulders over the toes and taking short, quick steps backward (as shown in figure 4.19a on page118). For as long as possible, the defender should try to maintain at least a 3-yard cushion between himself and the receiver while at the same time angling his backpedal to give himself proper leverage (inside or outside position) on the receiver. The defender should maintain inside leverage position against the receiver unless he has help from the free safety to the inside, in which case he should maintain outside leverage.

ADJUSTING TO THE ROUTE

If the receiver tries to run a deep route, the defender must rotate his hips toward the receiver, turning to run with him. The defender must execute this turn before the receiver eliminates the 3-yard cushion. The defender must keep his center of gravity and his hips low on the turn, driving the elbow that is closer to the receiver and punching the opposite knee into a tight, quick turn—commonly called a "man turn"—at the angle of the route that the receiver is running (see figure 4.20).

If the receiver breaks off a short route, the defender must plant his back foot (see figure 4.21a), point his front foot (see figure 4.21b) and drive immediately downhill to the route. The defender must waste no movement and take no extra steps; his footwork must always be plant, point and drive.

Figure 4.20 **Defender executing a "man turn" against a deep route.**

a　　　　　　　　　　　　　b

Figure 4.21 *(a-b)* **Defender's footwork against a short route.**

(continued)

CLOSING THE GAP

After recognizing the route, the defender must concentrate on closing the gap to the receiver before trying to find and play the ball. Against deep routes, the defender should establish inside leverage position at the receiver's hip, running smoothly with him and being sure that he does not fade away and gain separation. Against intermediate and shallow routes, the defender must break to the receiver's upfield shoulder, closing any separation and making any play on the ball *through* the receiver, not in front of him (for a detailed discussion of the man defender's reactions when the pass is thrown, see "Finishing Plays in Man Pass Coverage" on page 244).

As the defender closes the gap, he should key the receiver's hands and eyes to learn whether the ball is on the way. Only then should the defender look in the direction of the throw to make a play on the ball.

Common Errors

You may run into several common errors when teaching your athletes man pass coverage.

Error	Error correction
Defender misses his assignment.	The greatest danger of man defense is having one defender miss an assignment and leave a player wide open. This usually happens when the defender plays run first, not keying his receiver.
Defender loses sight of the receiver.	If the defender keeps his eyes on the quarterback too long at the beginning of the play, or if he looks back for the ball too early, he could lose sight of the receiver and lose his man. Emphasize the importance of always knowing where the receiver is and, if he does get away, finding him and establishing close contact with him before looking for the ball.
Defender goes for the interception (wrong hand).	The defender must play through the upfield shoulder and go for the knockdown with the inside hand; the outside hand must remain behind the receiver's back to assist with the tackle if he catches the ball.

Speed Turn

Pass defenders are taught to open their hips toward the receiver's intended route when defending in man-to-man coverage. But if the receiver makes a good fake in one direction, causing the defender to open his hips that way, and then breaks his route in the opposite direction, the defender will have opened his hips in the wrong direction. When reacting to the receiver's second cut, the defender must make an exception to his normal rule of turning toward his receiver. Trying to match the receiver's turn will take too long, allowing the receiver to achieve considerable separation. The quickest way for the defender to recover is to use a maneuver called the speed turn.

REACTING TO A WRONG TURN

The defender will obviously prefer to keep a cushion on the receiver and break to the receiver's route by facing him (see figure 4.22a). But if the receiver turns him the wrong way, the defender must immediately realize what has happened and whip his head around, away from the receiver, and then, keeping his center of gravity low, bring his hips and lower body around (see figure 4.22b).

After the defender whips his head around, the arms must immediately follow in the same direction to make the turn as quick as possible. The defender must drive his outside arm, the arm farther from the receiver, backward forcefully, keeping the elbow and arm close to the body. He brings the other arm around immediately afterward. The body will naturally follow the arms.

a   b

Figure 4.22 *(a-b)* **Speed turn.**

(continued)

At a Glance

The following parts of the text offer additional information on the speed turn.

Running Deep Routes	p. 55
Man Pass Coverage	p. 120
Finishing Plays in Man Pass Coverage	p. 244

FINDING THE RECEIVER

The major drawback to the speed turn is that the defender briefly turns his back to the receiver and therefore loses sight of him momentarily. So, as soon as the head whip and arm drive have initiated the speed turn, the defender must locate the receiver and sprint to his upfield shoulder. The defender should not look for the ball as he comes out of the speed turn; he should devote his total attention to finding the receiver and reestablishing his position on the shoulder of the receiver. If the defender finds the receiver, he will eventually find the ball because if the receiver is going to make a catch, the ball has to come to him. If the defender looks for the ball coming out of the turn, he will lose sight of the receiver and not be able to regain a position where he can deflect the pass or make the tackle.

Common Errors

You may run into several common errors when teaching your athletes how to execute the speed turn.

Error	Error correction
Defender gets too high to make a good turn.	As the defender makes the turn, he must sink his hips and lower his center of gravity. Have players practice the turns slowly in drills until it feels natural for them to stay low.
Defender looks back for the ball.	The natural instinct of a defender who is in trouble and has momentarily lost contact with his receiver is to look for the ball to see whether it is on its way to the receiver. But in the process of looking back, the defender cannot see where the receiver is going, and the receiver will gain more separation from the defender. The first objective after the speed turn is to locate and sprint to the receiver, getting back in position on his shoulder, before worrying about the ball.

In press man coverage, a defender is assigned to cover a receiver wherever he goes on the field, but instead of lining up with a cushion and backpedaling on the snap (as described previously in "Man Pass Coverage" on page 120), he aligns as close to the receiver as the rules will allow, taking a press position on the receiver's inside hip. The defender's main objective is to disrupt the receiver's release and destroy the timing between the quarterback and the receiver.

KEY POINTS

The most important components of press man coverage are

o keying the receiver's inside hip,

o proper footwork,

o disrupting the release and

o establishing hip-to-hip alignment.

KEYING THE RECEIVER'S INSIDE HIP

The defensive back aligns in a square stance with his outside foot on the inside foot of the receiver (see figure 4.23). The defender squeezes the line of scrimmage as much as possible without being offside, approximately one arm's length from the receiver if the receiver is on the line of scrimmage. The defender's focal point is the inside hip of the receiver.

PROPER FOOTWORK

The key to press man coverage is great footwork. The defender's hands must be active, especially against an inside release, but the feet must move first for the defender to maintain proper inside leverage. The defender should take short, quick steps laterally to match the receiver's release. These steps should be within the framework of the defender's body, never wider than shoulder-width. After the receiver starts downfield, the defender opens his hips at a 45-degree angle and runs with him.

Figure 4.23 **Defensive back in a square stance.**

(continued)

DISRUPTING THE RELEASE

Figure 4.24 **Disrupting a release *(a)* to the outside and *(b)* to the inside using a long-arm punch.**

The goal of press man coverage is to disrupt the pass timing and give the rush time to get to the quarterback, so the defender wants to slow the receiver's release by jamming him at the line of scrimmage with his hands.

If the receiver attempts to release outside, the defender punches the receiver's chest with his inside hand using a long-arm punch, as shown in figure 4.24*a*. Then, after maintaining contact with the receiver for as long as possible with his punch, the defender turns with the receiver, attempting to cut him off and slow him down. If the receiver attempts to release inside, the defender disrupts the receiver's release with an aggressive long-arm punch with the outside hand to the receiver's body (see figure 4.24*b*) and tries to flatten off the receiver's route along the line of scrimmage. In either case, the defender has to be patient and avoid lunging at the receiver.

ESTABLISHING HIP-TO-HIP ALIGNMENT

Regardless of the type of release that the receiver attempts, the defender must ultimately establish hip-to-hip alignment with the receiver, running with him and staying in contact, to continue to disrupt his route. The defender should not concern himself with the location of the ball until he has established this position; the receiver will let the defender know when the ball is on its way because he will look for it and extend his hands for it. Only then should the defender find the ball and make the play (for a more detailed discussion of how to make a play on the ball, see "Finishing Plays in Man Pass Coverage" on page 244).

At a Glance

The following parts of the text offer additional information on press man coverage.

Running Shallow or Intermediate Routes	p. 51
Releases	p. 58
Man Pass Coverage	p. 120
Speed Turn	p. 123
Press Man Route Adjustments	p. 210

Common Errors

You may run into several common errors when teaching your athletes press man coverage.

Error	Error correction
Defender spreads his feet.	If the defender takes steps that are too large as he attempts to disrupt the receiver's release, he will end up with a base that is too wide and will be unable to react to the receiver's route. He must work on keeping the feet close together with short, choppy steps.
Defender strikes with the hands first.	Defenders will have the urge to punch with their hands as soon as the receiver makes a move. This error causes the defender to lunge and may cause him to lose his leverage on the receiver. The defender's feet must move first, in response to the receiver's attempted release, and the hand punch follows the movement of the feet.
Defender opens the gate.	If the defender overreacts to a fake, the receiver can make a clean release at the line of scrimmage and make it difficult for the defender to recover. The defender must focus on the inside hip to reduce his vulnerability to a fake.
Defender looks back for the ball.	The defender should not concern himself with the location of the ball at all until he has established position on the receiver's inside hip; the receiver will let the defender know when the ball is on its way because he will look for it and extend his hands for it. Only then should the defender find the ball and make the play.

A blitz is a defensive call in which one or more defenders who usually play off the ball (linebackers or defensive backs) attack the line of scrimmage. If the offense has called a pass play, the blitz adds pass rushers and puts more pressure on the quarterback but reduces the number of defenders available to cover receivers. If the offense has called a run play, the blitz gives the defense a chance to run through a gap and destroy the offensive blocking scheme, but it also reduces the number of defenders available to pursue the ball carrier if he breaks into the open field. As a result, blitzing is an exciting component of football—a high-risk, high-reward strategy that can produce a great defensive play or a big offensive play, depending on assignments, execution and calling the right blitz to the right place at the right time!

An entire book could be written on the Xs and Os of blitzing. Defenses can blitz one, two, three or even four defenders at once, through all sorts of gaps and gap combinations; they can play man coverage behind the blitz or use a zone blitz concept in which they blitz a linebacker and vacate the underneath zone that he usually plays in zone coverage; they can blitz frequently or seldom; they can blitz in any situation on the field or only in long-yardage situations.

For blitzing to be effective, however, each defender who is blitzing must execute the skill with great technique, reading the play on the run and reacting correctly to the block that he encounters.

ELEMENT OF SURPRISE

One of the most important aspects of a successful blitz is the element of surprise. Any defensive player who is going to blitz should remain poised, with the weight of his feet evenly distributed on the balls of his feet, and wait to blitz until the moment the ball is snapped. This player can take an alignment closer to the line of scrimmage than usual so that he can hit the blitz more quickly, as long as he does not take such a shallow alignment that the offense becomes suspicious of his intentions.

Many players become excited about the opportunity to blitz, so they become agitated and jumpy before the snap. They take false steps toward the line of scrimmage, lean forward so far that they lose their balance and otherwise seem considerably more animated before the snap than they are on other plays. These changes in body position and stance tip the offense that the blitz is on the way and allow them to be better prepared than they would be otherwise.

ATTACKING THE CORRECT GAP

The blitz is an exciting, aggressive defensive play, but it is not without rules and assignments. Each player who blitzes through one of the inside gaps is assigned to a particular gap, and he has to defend that gap. He also has rules for squeezing or spilling blocks, so he knows which arm to keep free if he encounters blockers on a run play (see "Spilling Blocks" on page 103 and "Squeezing Blocks" on page 107). Additionally, he has a pass rush lane that he must adhere to if the play is a pass (see "Pass Rush" on page 110). Each outermost defender who blitzes becomes the force player (for more information, see "Force" on page 251). He must squeeze all blocks and keep the ball inside him if he encounters a run play as he blitzes, and he becomes the contain rush player if the play is a pass. In short, defenders who blitz cannot just blindly run into the offensive formation; they must blitz to the correct gap and keep the correct arm free, based on how the defensive call matches up with the play that is occurring.

At a Glance

The following parts of the text offer additional information on blitzing.

Defending Basic Run Blocks	p. 96
Picking Up the Blitz	p. 197
Choosing to Spill or Squeeze	p. 241
Force	p. 251

REACTING TO THE PLAY

To accomplish the assignments of gap responsibility listed in the previous section, the blitzing defender must be able to read the blocking scheme as he attacks the line of scrimmage. First, he must see the pad level of the offensive linemen to determine whether the play is a run (low pads) or pass (high pads). Second, he must be able to discern which direction the play is going or whether the play is a drop-back pass. To do this, he must keep his eyes up, see the quarterback and ball carriers through the blocking scheme and adjust his course to the play. Finally, he must read the blocking scheme to ascertain which offensive blocker is assigned to him and will therefore become his next threat.

TAKING ON A BLOCKER

When a blitzing defender penetrates the line of scrimmage on a pass play, either an offensive lineman or a running back will pick him up and attempt to block him. The blitzing defender must adjust his course to attack one side of the blocker or the other. He can then work his technique for shedding blocks, ripping his arm and shoulder underneath and through the blocker on the side that he has chosen to attack (see "Defending Basic Run Blocks" on page 96, "Spilling Blocks" on page 103 and "Squeezing Blocks" on page 107).

The "attack half the man" concept is key for the blitzing defender. Too often, the blitzing defender is going so fast that he runs directly into the blocker and is an easy target to stop. The blitzing defender must remember to attack under control enough so that he can fake, plant and break and attack only one side of the blocker.

(continued)

Common Errors

You may run into several common errors when teaching your athletes how to blitz.

Error	Error correction
Defender gives away the blitz.	Being overeager to blitz can cause the defender to take false steps, fall forward, or otherwise let the offense know that he is about to blitz. Patience during the snap count is crucial; a low, balanced stance with the weight on the balls of the feet will give the defender a great start on the snap. Have defenders practice blitzing against varying snap counts to drill the concept of reacting, not guessing.
Defender runs directly into the blocker.	Blitzing defenders often attack the blocker assigned to them by running directly into the middle of his body. The effort is admirable, but the defender will rarely get past the blocker and threaten the quarterback. Blitzing defenders must learn to pick one side of the blocker or the other, and attack that side, working a move with the hands and arms to avoid the blocker.
Defender fails to see the play.	Blitzing defenders sometimes get so caught up with the blitz that they forget to keep the head and eyes up to see what play is being run and where the ball is going. They still have gap responsibilities and rules for taking on blocks, so they have to see the blocking scheme, the type of play and the play direction. A good drill is to run the same blitz several times in a row, changing the offensive play each time so that the blitzing defenders see all the different reactions that they might have to make on one blitz.

chapter 5

Special Teams Technical Skills

This chapter covers the special teams technical skills that you and your players must know to be successful. In this chapter, you will find the following skills:

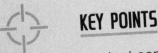

KEY POINTS

The most important components of the kickoff are

- consistent alignment,
- approaching the ball,
- planting the foot,
- contacting the ball and
- follow-through.

The kickoff is the first play of every game, and it affects the initial field position for the game and the starting field position for every possession that follows a score. Statistics show that offensive teams score far less frequently when the start drives deep in their own territory, so the kickoff play is critical in every game. To allow consistent, effective coverage, the kicker has to place the kick accurately, with maximum distance and the best possible hang time. This seemingly simple skill is actually extremely challenging, requiring both precision and great physical exertion from the kicker.

Most kickers today use a modified version of a soccer-style kick, in which the kicker contacts the ball with the top of the instep, as opposed to the original, straight-ahead kick, in which the kicker contacts the ball with his toe. We will describe only the modified soccer-style kick in this skill.

CONSISTENT ALIGNMENT

Each kicker will have his own preferences for alignment. Basic parameters for alignment before the approach is a spot 8 to 12 yards from the ball and four to six steps laterally, in the direction away from the kicker's dominant foot. Kickers should experiment with alignment until they discover the spot that allows them to approach the ball with accuracy and consistency.

Figure 5.1 **Proper positioning of the plant foot for the kickoff.**

APPROACHING THE BALL

The kicker's first steps should be slow and measured, covering the same distance and course every time. Gradually, the kicker should increase the speed and length of his steps as he approaches the ball. Some kickers take more steps than others do in the approach, but every kicker should arrive at a key point, before his last three steps, that is always the same yardage from the ball. For the last three steps, the kicker should accelerate to about 75 percent of his maximum speed.

PLANTING THE FOOT

The plant foot should land even with, or slightly ahead of, the ball, and just slightly to the side of the ball (see figure 5.1). The toe of the plant foot should point in the direction of the target. Consistent and accurate placement of the plant foot is one of the most important factors in executing the kickoff.

CONTACTING THE BALL

The kicking leg should be fully flexed behind the kicker at the moment the plant foot hits the ground. Initiating movement with the hips, the kicker powerfully swings the leg toward the ball, turning both the hips and the shoulders toward the target.

The contact point should be just above the arch on the top of the kicker's foot, making contact on the bottom half of the ball (see figure 5.2a). As the foot makes contact, the leg and foot lock at the knee and ankle joints, respectively, while the plant leg locks at the knee and ankle and the plant foot pushes off hard (see figure 5.2b).

FOLLOW-THROUGH

After impact, the kicking leg extends forcefully upward. Next, the plant foot comes off the ground, momentum carries the kicker forward and he lands on his kicking leg first. The kicker must keep his head down, watching the spot where the ball was placed on the tee, throughout the entire follow-through process, to be sure that he does not peek downfield before contacting the ball.

Figure 5.2 *(a-b)* **Contacting the ball on the kickoff.**

At a Glance

The following parts of the text offer additional information on the kickoff.

(continued)

Common Errors

You may run into several common errors when teaching your athletes how to kick off.

Error	Error correction
Kick is not high enough.	The plant foot is probably too far behind the ball. The kicker should work on his steps with several dry-run approaches until he achieves consistency. He also must be sure that his point of contact with the football is below its vertical midpoint.
Kick goes right or left of the target.	The plant foot may be pointed away from the target. Videotape the kicker's approach and study the alignment of the plant foot relative to the direction of the kick. Also emphasize that the kicker should keep his head down, looking at the ball, until the kick is away.
Kick does not go far enough.	The kicker may not be pushing off his plant foot hard enough to generate speed on the kicking leg. He also may need to focus on driving his hips through the kick. Finally, he should be sure to achieve lockout at the point of impact, so that the legs do not give at contact.
Kicks are erratic.	The kicker is probably looking downfield too early, taking his eyes off the ball before making contact. He must focus on keeping his head down throughout the follow-through to eliminate the chance that he will peek downfield early.

KEY POINTS

The most important components of the onside kick are

- adjusting alignment,
- approaching the ball,
- planting the foot,
- contacting the ball and
- follow-through.

An onside kick is an attempt by the kickoff team to take advantage of the rule in football that makes the ball live on a free kick, eligible to be recovered by the kicking team, after it travels 10 yards from the kickoff line. Teams use the onside kick in two situations: first, when the kicking team is behind and needs to get the ball back quickly to try to score again, and second, when the kicking team senses a weakness in the receiving team's deployment or movements after the kick, a circumstance that gives them a good opportunity to surprise the receiving team and recover a short kick. In this skill, we will be discussing the first scenario, an onside kick that both teams know is coming.

A good onside kick has two essential elements. First, it must hit the ground in the 10-yard neutral zone, so that it is live to be recovered by either team after it goes 10 yards (if it does not hit the ground, the receiving team has the opportunity to fair catch the ball uncontested). Second, the ball must take a high hop, or big bounce, just before it goes 10 yards, so that the receiving team has to jump up and reach in the air to make the recovery, just as the kicking team's players are arriving to contest that recovery. Although rarely used, the onside kick can be a critical part of a close game. Therefore, teams usually spend many hours of practice time to learn how to execute this kick even though they may use it only a couple of times in an entire season.

ADJUSTING ALIGNMENT

The kicker's alignment for an onside kick is totally different from his alignment for a regular kickoff. The kicker should be only a couple yards behind the kickoff line, whereas on a normal kick he would be 10 or 12 yards behind the kickoff line. He should be only 7 or 8 yards from the ball, a position much closer to the ball than he would be on a normal kickoff. In addition, he lines up facing more toward the sideline than down the field, which is opposite from his alignment for a normal kickoff. Additionally, the ball should be placed slightly more upright than normal, possibly with a slight forward lean, as shown in figure 5.3. The laces of the ball should face toward the sideline instead of down the field.

Figure 5.3 Ball placement for an onside kick.

(continued)

Figure 5.4   Proper positioning of the plant foot for the onside kick.

APPROACHING THE BALL

Before starting his approach, the kicker should pick out an aiming point on the sideline about 12 yards downfield from the kickoff line. He then should visualize a straight line from that aiming point through the ball to his position. As he approaches the ball, he should try to stay on that imaginary line, taking a direct, straight-line approach to the ball. The kicker also approaches the ball much more slowly than he does on a normal kickoff, so that he can stay perfectly aligned and concentrate on contacting the top one-third of the ball (as opposed to the contact point on the bottom half of the ball for a regular kickoff).

PLANTING THE FOOT

The plant foot should land slightly behind the ball and just enough to the side so that the kicking leg can swing cleanly in the direction of the kick (see figure 5.4). The toes of the plant foot should point in the direction of the kick.

CONTACTING THE BALL

The kicker makes contact with the ball farther forward on his foot than he does on a regular kickoff. He should contact the ball on top of the foot above the big toe for the onside kick, as opposed to contacting it on top of the foot above the arch for a regular kick. The contact point should be near the top one-third of the ball, on or near the stripe, so that the ball will roll end over end toward the aiming point.

At a Glance

The following parts of the text offer additional information on the onside kick.

FOLLOW-THROUGH

The onside kick has to be kicked forcefully to produce a big hop, or high bounce, that will give the kickoff team time to contest the recovery (for more information, see "Recovering the Onside Kick" on page 275). Therefore, the kicker has to follow through fully, swinging upward, finishing high (but not quite as high as he does on a regular kick), accelerating aggressively through the contact point, landing on his kicking foot and keeping his head down even after the contact, to be sure that he does not peek downfield at the moment of impact.

Common Errors

You may run into several common errors when teaching your athletes the onside kick.

Error	Error correction
Kick fails to roll end over end.	Check to see where the toe hits the ball. If the ball pops up or knuckles in a line drive, the contact point probably was too low.
Ball does not go 10 yards.	Make sure that the kicker's aiming point is far enough downfield that the ball will travel 10 yards down the field before going out of bounds. Many young kickers cut the angle too close, trying to help their teammates recover the ball by keeping it close to the 10-yard distance. But if the ball fails to travel the required 10 yards, the play is an immediate failure. The kicker must take an aiming point far enough down the field and kick the ball hard enough that it will travel the required 10 yards.
Ball fails to take a big hop.	The ball needs more rotation. The kicker must make sharp contact with the ball at a spot on or near the stripe, being sure to swing the leg upward and through the ball to produce the required rotation.

Catching the Kickoff

KEY POINTS

The most important components of catching the kickoff are

o judging the flight of the ball,

o arm positioning and

o securing the ball.

The kickoff return can be an exciting part of a football game, but the key part of the return is catching the kickoff. If the return man executes the catch properly, he will have good forward momentum going into his return and room to run before encountering the first defenders. Conversely, if he bobbles or drops the kick, the result will usually be a poor return.

JUDGING THE FLIGHT OF THE BALL

One of the most important parts of making a successful catch is accurate judgment of the ball in flight. Players should study the flight of the ball before moving in any direction. They should factor in the direction and strength of the wind; high kicks will hang if kicked into the wind and sail if kicked with the wind. They should watch the spin of the ball. If the ball is angled left at the top of its spin, it will go left and vice versa. Players should not try to guess; they should practice reading the flight of the ball.

When the ball is in flight, the return man must resist the temptation to move forward. If the kick is short, he will have time to recover because he can move faster forward than he can backward if he has misjudged the ball. He must always stay farther back than he thinks he needs to, knowing that he can adjust forward at the last minute. He should plan to catch the ball low, at the chest or lower, instead of high, at the shoulders or higher, because doing so will help him keep his forward momentum. He should catch the ball moving slightly forward, or at least with the weight on the balls of the feet. He must avoid catching a kick and then taking a gathering, or balance, step backward; doing so will waste valuable time in starting the return.

Figure 5.5 Return man catching the kick.

ARM POSITIONING

As the return man makes the catch, he should hold the arms so that the elbows are down, into the belly with a slight bend (see figure 5.5). The palms should be up with the hands open. The elbows are in, so that the ball cannot slip between the arms. The return man should cushion the catch with a slight bend of the knees and waist so that the ball does not bounce off the chest.

The return man should look at the ball as it touches his arms. Even if the ball arrives so quickly that he cannot actually see the catch, the idea of watching the ball hit his hands will keep his eyes on the ball long enough that he will be in proper position to make the catch. As the ball enters his midsection, he should squeeze the ball with his arms.

SECURING THE BALL

After he makes the catch, the return man should shift the ball to a secure position under one arm, with the hand covering the front point of the ball and the elbow squeezing the back point of the ball, as shown in "Ball Security" in figure 3.9 on page 30. As the return man begins to run, he should initially run vertically upfield, covering as many yards as possible before adjusting his course to the return that has been planned.

At a Glance

The following parts of the text offer additional information on catching the kickoff.

Ball Security	p. 29
Catching	p. 48
Catching the Punt	p. 148
Wedge Return	p. 294

Common Errors

You may run into several common errors when teaching your athletes how to catch the kickoff.

Error	Error correction
Return man judges the ball poorly.	The return men should practice catching kicks in a variety of conditions, including wind. The only solution for poor ball judgment is repeated practice, over several days and weeks. Use a jugs machine if not enough kickers are available to kick balls to the return men.
Return man takes backward steps after the catch.	Do not let the return man take a backward step in practice after any catch. Insist that he catch the ball with forward momentum. Reward forward momentum even if the return man drops the ball; criticize backward steps even if he catches it. No return can be successful if the return man takes a backward step after the catch!
Ball goes between the arms of the return man.	If the ball slips between the arms and falls on the ground, one of two errors must have occurred: The return man either looked up too soon to see how close the coverage players were or had his elbows too far apart, allowing a hole in his midsection where the ball could fall through. Emphasize the eyes and the elbows.

KEY POINTS

The most important components of the punt are

- leg alignment,
- balanced stance,
- making the catch,
- hand positioning for the drop,
- punt approach,
- contacting the ball and
- follow-through.

On fourth down, the offense has three choices. They can run an offensive play and try to make a first down; attempt a field goal, in which the ball is kicked off the ground; or punt the ball, in which the ball is kicked before it touches the ground. Failed tries on offensive plays and field goals give the ball to the other team at the spot where the play ends, but a properly executed punt gives the other team the ball 30 to 40 yards down the field. The punt is by far the most common play, and the prudent, fourth-down choice except when the distance to gain a first down is very short or when the offense has the ball deep in the opposing team's territory.

The best punts combine distance and hang time because the goal is to send the ball the maximum number of yards down the field while keeping it in the air long enough for the coverage people to get there and make the tackle, minimizing the number of yards gained on the return. The punt must also be executed quickly and consistently, in the face of the opponent's rush. Therefore, the punter must possess good hands, lateral agility, above-average reaction time, flexibility, self-control and a solid technique that does not vary under pressure.

LEG ALIGNMENT

The punter should align himself with his kicking leg directly behind the center, as opposed to lining up with the middle of his body behind the snapper. The depth of his alignment varies by formation, but the standard depth would be about 13 or 14 yards from the line of scrimmage.

BALANCED STANCE

The punter should take a comfortable, balanced stance with his feet shoulder-width apart and the punting foot slightly behind the plant foot (see figure 5.6). The punter's knees are slightly flexed, his head is up looking at the ball and his hands are hanging loosely at his sides. This balanced stance allows the punter to adjust to a snap that is off line, high or low, and the placement of the feet ensures that his first step will be with his punting foot, giving him the proper footwork for good operation time on his punt.

Figure 5.6 Punter in a balanced stance.

MAKING THE CATCH

The punter must look the ball into his hands and catch it cleanly. He should keep his feet in the same position—punt foot back, shoulder-width apart—on the catch as they were before the snap when he was in his balanced stance. After securing the catch, the punter should rotate the ball so that the laces are facing upward. If the laces are down and the punter contacts them when he punts the ball, the punt may come off his foot erratically.

HAND POSITIONING FOR THE DROP

The drop hand is the hand on the side of the punt leg. The punter holds the ball with the drop hand in a handshake position. The hand is on the outside portion of the ball, and the top seam is between the thumb and index finger (see figure 5.7). The guide hand is on the front third of the ball, with the index finger along the first seam below the laces. This hand position must be consistent so that punter can drop the ball in exactly the same manner for every punt.

Figure 5.7 Proper punter hand positioning for the drop.

PUNT APPROACH

As he is catching the ball, the punter must shift his weight onto his plant foot. His first step must be a short, balancing step with the punt leg (see figure 5.8a), and his second step will be a full stride with the other leg (see figure 5.8b). He cannot afford to take a preliminary step with his plant foot before he takes his first step with the punting leg because doing so will lengthen his operation time and increase the risk of having the punt blocked. The key is to adjust the feet while the ball is in the

a   b

Figure 5.8 (a-b) Punter taking a two-step approach to the punt.

(continued)

air on the snap, get the feet in the proper position and distribute the weight properly before the catch.

CONTACTING THE BALL

Just before the plant foot hits the ground and the punting leg starts its swing toward the ball, the punter drops the ball. When dropped, the ball should be positioned over the punting leg with the elbow just outside the hip and the forearm tilted slightly upward (see figure 5.9). The punter should drop the ball from a height between his chest and waist in the same vertical plane as the kicking leg. He must drop the ball so that it is perfectly horizontal as it falls.

As the foot comes forward, the punter's leg speed increases aggressively and the knee locks on impact at a point below the punter's waist but above his knees. The plant leg also locks, and the punter forcefully pushes his hips forward. The punter's weight shifts to the toes of his plant foot, and he explodes his foot into the ball. The toe points down. The punter should make contact on the ball with outside of the foot above the toes and below the arch (see figure 5.10).

Figure 5.9   Proper positioning for the ball drop.

Figure 5.10   Proper positioning for the punt at contact with the ball.

FOLLOW-THROUGH

The punter must be sure to follow through with his punting leg high above his head and his plant foot coming off the ground. Without proper follow-through, the punter runs the risk of stopping, or slowing, his leg swing at impact instead of accelerating the leg swing through impact. The punter has to feel as though his leg is swinging through the ball, not just to the ball.

At a Glance

The following parts of the text offer additional information on punting.

Sky Punt	p. 144
Corner Punt	p. 146
Long Snap	p. 155
Punt Protection	p. 281
Punt Coverage	p. 284
Punting Inside the 40-Yard Line	p. 288

Common Errors

You may run into several common errors when teaching your athletes how to punt.

Error	Error correction
Punt has inconsistent direction and height.	The most important factor in a good punt is the ball drop, so this is the first correction to consider. Have the punter first practice the ball drop without punting the ball, to be sure that it lands on the ground horizontally and on a line even with the punter's foot. Then study the punter's drop as he punts the ball. If the drop is consistent, check the alignment of the punter's steps. Both of his approach steps and his leg swing must be in a straight line toward his target. Have the punter practice his steps on a yard line, going across the field and punting half speed, to be sure that he lines up his steps correctly.
Punter takes too many steps before the punt.	Toss the ball underhanded to the punter and be sure that he adjusts his feet to the proper position every time he catches the ball. Work on the snapper–punter combination and develop the punter's ability to focus. Use a drill that forces the punter to catch poor snaps while still keeping proper foot alignment.
Punt is not high enough.	The release point of the drop is too low or the ball is dropped too far in front. Have the punter hold the ball slightly higher in front of his body before he drops it to elevate the contact point. Alternatively, have him hold his hands slightly closer to his body before he drops the ball to bring the contact point back somewhat.

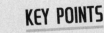

KEY POINTS

The most important components of the sky punt are

o maintaining normal approach mechanics,

o contacting the ball,

o emphasizing hang time and

o aiming for the 10-yard line.

The sky punt is used when the distance between the line of scrimmage and the 10-yard line is inside the effective range of the punter. The punter kicks the ball higher than normal so that the punt coverage players can get to the return man before the ball gets there, forcing the return man to make a fair catch and thus eliminating any return. If the ball is not caught, the bullets (see "Bullets" on page 150), or initial coverage players, should sprint ahead of the ball to the goal line, turn around with their backs to the end zone and try to prevent the ball from rolling into the end zone for a touchback.

MAINTAINING NORMAL APPROACH MECHANICS

Although he is going to kick the ball shorter and higher than normal, the punter must not change any of his mechanics on the approach. His alignment, foot position, catching concentration, rotation of the ball, drop and approach steps should all be the same as they would be for punts in normal down-and-distance situations (as discussed previously in "Punt" on page 140) until he makes contact with the ball.

Figure 5.11 Punter's foot position on contact for a sky punt.

CONTACTING THE BALL

The punter's first change in mechanics for the sky punt is his foot position on contact. Instead of pointing the toes downfield and contacting the ball with a flat foot, the punter should point his toe more in the air and direct the ball into a higher arc (see figure 5.11). The ball contacts the punter's foot on top of the arch, as it would on a normal punt, but the angle of the toes changes the release of the ball into a more elevated trajectory.

The second change is the elevation of the ball at the contact point. The punter should lift his drop slightly so that the point of contact is slightly higher than it would be on a normal punt. This adjustment will help direct the ball into a higher arc.

EMPHASIZING HANG TIME

The punter should try to kick the ball very high, hoping for a long hang time, which is the length of time that the ball is in the air on a punt. With longer hang time, the punt coverage players will have more time to get to the ball and down it before it goes into the end zone. Evaluation of this play is based not on the length of the punt but on the position, or yard line, where the ball is downed.

AIMING FOR THE 10-YARD LINE

The punter should try to land the ball at the 10-yard line. Most teams will fair catch a punt at the 10-yard line, which is a fine outcome for the punting team on this play. Any punt not caught by the punt return man that lands at the 10 or just inside the 10 can take a bounce or two toward the goal line, and the coverage team has time to get into position and down the ball before it crosses the goal line. Many punters get greedy and try to land the ball on or near the goal line. Unfortunately, most of those punts either go into the end zone on the fly or bounce once near the goal line and ricochet immediately into the end zone, giving the opponent the ball at the 20-yard line.

At a Glance

The following parts of the text offer additional information on the sky punt.

Punt	p. 140
Corner Punt	p. 146
Catching the Punt	p. 148
Bullets	p. 150
Punt Protection	p. 281
Punt Coverage	p. 284
Punting Inside the 40-Yard Line	p. 288

Common Errors

You may run into several common errors when teaching your athletes how to execute the sky punt.

Error	Error correction
Ball goes into the end zone.	In terms of mechanics, the punter probably needs to pull his kicking toe back toward his body or move his point of contact with the ball up slightly. Another factor is that when punters relax and try to punt the ball easy, they may make better contact than usual and sail the ball into the end zone. If that happens, have the punter practice his normal punts with the relaxed motion that he used on his sky punts to see whether his distance improves. In practice, have the punter stand on the 45-yard line and attempt to land his punts on a cone placed on the 10-yard line.
Punt is too short or doesn't travel very far.	The punter might be backing off too much on the velocity of his swing. The sky punt is achieved with a full leg swing, not an abbreviated one.

Corner Punt

The most important components of the corner punt are

o maintaining normal punting mechanics,

o turning toward the target,

o maintaining a straight-line approach and

o aiming for the 10-yard line.

The corner punt is an alternative to the sky punt when the punting team is trying to down the ball inside the 20-yard line. The corner punt is used when the punter feels more confident about executing an angling punt toward the sideline rather than the high-arching, straight-ahead sky punt, discussed in "Sky Punt" on page 144. Some punters work on both punts, and other punters choose one or the other so that they don't have to divide their practice time between the two. On the corner punt, the punter turns after catching the snap so that he is aiming at a point where the 10-yard line meets the sideline. The object is to kick the ball out of bounds so that the return team cannot make a return and will have to start the subsequent possession in poor field position.

Figure 5.12 **Adjusted aiming point for the corner punt.**

MAINTAINING NORMAL PUNTING MECHANICS

The corner punt is a variation of the normal punt, in terms of the target, but the punter should not change the mechanics of the approach. He should maintain all his normal fundamentals so that he punts the ball consistently and accurately.

TURNING TOWARD THE TARGET

When attempting the corner punt, the punter must physically turn his body to the aiming point, where the 10-yard line meets the sideline (see figure 5.12). He should make the turn just as he is catching the ball from the snapper, so that he has completed the turn when he catches the ball and does not have to take additional steps before taking his normal steps for the punt.

MAINTAINING A STRAIGHT-LINE APPROACH

The punter should visualize a straight line extending from his position on the field to the target, or aiming point, on the sideline. This imaginary straight line will cross the yard lines at an angle, so the punter has to maintain excellent concentration to keep his approach lined up properly. To have the best chance to execute an accurate punt, the punter should be sure that the steps, drop and leg swing all take place on the imaginary straight line.

AIMING FOR THE 10-YARD LINE

Punters attempting the corner punt usually hope to execute the crowd-pleasing kick that goes out of bounds inside the 1-yard line. Aiming at the 1-yard line, however, will cause some kicks that are just slightly off target to go into the end zone. Therefore, the punter should aim at the 10-yard line to give himself some margin for error between the 10-yard line and the goal line. A ball that goes out at the 10-yard line is still 10 yards better than where the ball would be spotted on a touchback, at the 20-yard line. Ten yards of field position in a football game is important!

At a Glance

The following parts of the text offer additional information on the corner punt.

Punt	p. 140
Sky Punt	p. 144
Catching the Punt	p. 148
Bullets	p. 150
Punt Protection	p. 281
Punt Coverage	p. 284
Punting Inside the 40-Yard Line	p. 288

Common Errors

You may run into several common errors when teaching your athletes how to execute the corner punt.

Error	Error correction
Punter kicks the ball into the end zone.	Be sure that the punter is aiming for the 10-yard line, not the goal line, so that he has some room for error. Check his body position at the catch to be sure he has turned fully toward the target. Check his steps and leg swing to be sure that they are following a straight line toward the target.
Punter shanks the punt.	Some punters are so eager to see the result of the corner punt that they look up toward the target before they contact the ball, and consequently they miss it slightly. Be sure that the punter is not looking up too soon! In addition, some punters try to direct the ball toward the sideline with a sideways swing of the punting leg, which frequently results in a mis-hit and a shanked punt. Be sure that the body is turned and the leg swing is straight toward the target.

Catching the Punt

The most important components of catching the punt are

o judging the flight of the ball,
o making the catch and
o evading tacklers.

Catching a punt in a football game is one of the most exciting and terrifying skills in sports. Punts are difficult to judge and catch, adding an element of suspense to the skill. Worse yet, coverage players, eager to deliver a big hit and knock the ball loose, are frequently reaching the vicinity of the return man just as he is attempting to make the catch. This skill takes great courage and concentration. As a coach, be sure to assign this task to a player who will catch the ball consistently, even if he is not the fastest or best return man on the team. A dropped or muffed punt can be an extremely costly mistake. Do not sacrifice ball security for the chance of a big return.

JUDGING THE FLIGHT OF THE BALL

The return man must see the ball leave the punter's foot. The top of the ball will tell him where the ball is headed. If it stays up, the ball will be short. If the point of the ball turns over, it will be going deeper. The lateral tilt of the ball will indicate direction to the right or left. If the return man is uncertain about the distance that the punt will travel, he should hang back a bit deeper because when he figures out the final path of the punt he will be able to react faster when moving forward than when retreating.

MAKING THE CATCH

Before the catch, the return man should hold his arms so that the elbows are down, into the belly, with a slight bend (see figure 5.13). The return man should overemphasize the feeling of having his elbows together, because they will usually be farther apart than he realizes and having them together is a somewhat unnatural position. The palms should be up with the hands open.

As the ball comes down, the return man should stay back a little farther than his instinct might tell him so that he doesn't have to catch the ball at chest level or higher. He must focus on

Figure 5.13 Arm positioning before catching the punt.

Figure 5.14 Arm positioning when catching the punt.

the ball, tracking it with his eyes until it settles into his arms. As the ball enters the breadbasket formed by his hands and torso, he squeezes the ball with his elbows and covers the points of the ball with his hands (see figure 5.14).

The catch is always more important than the return. The punt return man must resist the temptation to look up, find or avoid the onrushing defenders until after he makes the catch and secures the ball. He must always be aware of the importance of maintaining possession of the ball; the other team is giving it away, and he must secure it for his team before trying to gain any yards.

EVADING TACKLERS

After catching and securing the ball (as shown in "Ball Security" in figure 3.9 on page 30), the return man looks up and quickly locates the nearest defender. Often, because of the speed and aggressiveness of the first defenders down the field, the punt return man can make the first defender miss by taking a quick lateral step or by faking a step one way and then taking a step in the opposite direction (see "Evading Tacklers" on page 194 for more information).

At a Glance

The following parts of the text offer additional information on catching the punt.

Ball Security	p. 29
Catching the Kickoff	p. 138
Bullets	p. 150
Defending Against the Bullets	p. 153
Punt Coverage	p. 284
Wall Return	p. 291

Common Errors

You may run into several common errors when teaching your athletes how to catch the punt.

Error	Error correction
Return man judges the ball poorly.	The punt return man must catch hundreds of punts, working almost daily with the punters, to get a feel for the trajectory and ultimate landing point of the ball.
Ball goes through the arms to the ground.	The return man must concentrate on keeping his elbows together every time he attempts to catch a punt.
Return man catches the ball higher than chest level.	If the return man gets too close to the ball as it comes down, he sometimes has to catch it with his fingers up and thumbs together, above chest level. This type of catch is inconsistent and insecure. The correction is for the return man to stay back a bit farther than he thinks he needs to and then react with a forward step or two just before the catch, after he has tracked the final path of the ball. This final forward adjustment is easy and does not interfere with making a secure catch. Have the return men work on this technique with easy, 20-yard underhand spiral tosses to each other until they understand how it feels to stay back.
Ball bounces off the chest.	If the return man gets too eager to run with the ball, he may take his eyes off the ball and misjudge it or move forward too early and literally bounce the ball out of his hands with his own chest. Stress the importance of ball security and making the catch before the run!

KEY POINTS

The most important components of bullets are

- assuming a comfortable stance,
- releasing against the defender,
- finding the return man and
- breaking down.

One advantage of the spread punt formation is that the two split ends, known as bullets, do not have protection responsibilities, so they are free to release immediately downfield to cover the punt (see "Punt Protection" on page 281 and "Punt Coverage" on page 284 for more information). Each bullet must understand that at least one opponent, and sometimes two, will be defending him on every punt play. These opponents are determined to stop the bullets or at least slow them down as they try to move down the field to cover the punt (see "Defending Against the Bullets" on page 153 for more information). The bullets must work together, using speed, agility and strength to defeat the defenders, and they must be able to make an open-field tackle if the punt return man catches the punt and tries to advance the ball upfield.

Figure 5.15　Initial stance for bullets.

ASSUMING A COMFORTABLE STANCE

Prior to the snap, the bullet should assume a comfortable two-point stance with his outside leg forward and his head looking inside so that he can see the snap of the football and get a good takeoff from the line (see figure 5.15). Peripherally, he must strive to see the alignment of the defender or defenders assigned to him.

RELEASING AGAINST THE DEFENDER

Bullets can't be so eager to get downfield that they simply try a straight-ahead sprinter's start. The bullet must have a release plan to avoid the defender or defenders assigned to him. If a defender is pressed up close to him, the bullet must use a rip, swim or series of fakes, similar to a wide receiver's release moves, to get away (see "Releases" on page 58 for more information). If the defender is off but playing with leverage inside, the bullet must attack that leverage, forcing the defender to adjust his position even farther inside, and then burst by the defender to the outside. The bullet should always plan his release move in advance of the snap, so that he does not waste time hesitating at the snap.

The bullet's assignment is to gain separation from the defender, but he cannot allow himself to be forced inside. If the bullet tries a series of fakes, he should ultimately finish with an inside fake and an outside release. After a good release move, the bullet should work to accelerate past the defender while widening slightly to the outside. If the bullet's only recourse is to release inside, he cannot allow the defender to force him farther inside. Instead, the bullet must immediately get vertical, running straight down the field and then gradually regaining outside leverage.

FINDING THE RETURN MAN

The bullets must continue to sprint downfield as the ball is in the air while keeping track of the position of the return man and the ball. They should continually adjust their course to the location of the return man, keeping the return man on the inside shoulder so that he is always between the two bullets. Ideally, one of the bullets will make the tackle on the return man. If a bullet is not close enough to make the tackle, his job is to force the return man toward the other bullet. If the return man gets outside one bullet, the effort of the other bullet will be wasted.

BREAKING DOWN

After releasing from the line and sprinting downfield, the bullet must ultimately decelerate and break down as he reaches the return man. This process must happen a few yards in front of the return man, not on top of him, because if the bullet is too close he will be called for a penalty (interfering with the catch) or will fly past the return man and miss the tackle. The bullet must begin to slow down as he approaches the return man, continue to fight off any persistent blocker and still maintain his outside leverage. He then assumes a balanced athletic position so that he can move laterally, mirror the return man and get in on the tackle (see "Open-Field Tackling" on page 168).

Most players in the role of the bullet have a vision of that role—sprinting down the field and making a bone-crushing, crowd-pleasing hit on the return man just moments after he catches the punt. Unfortunately, that play by a bullet is rare, very difficult to accomplish and is simply not a "percentage play" because the over-aggressive bullet will miss too many tackles. To be truly effective, the bullet must put that vision out of his mind, train himself to break down at the proper point and consistently trap the return man between himself and other bullet.

At a Glance

The following parts of the text offer additional information on the bullets.

Releases	p. 58
Tackling	p. 93
Press Man Coverage	p. 125
Defending Against the Bullets	p. 153
Open-Field Tackling	p. 168
Punt Protection	p. 281

(continued)

Common Errors

You may run into several common errors when teaching your athletes how to assume the role of a bullet.

Error	Error correction
Bullet is being held up by the defender.	The bullet needs to think about, rehearse and use release moves. First, be sure that he is trying a release move of some kind. Second, teach him to fake first and then use his hands and arms aggressively on his release move. Third, be sure that he stays low coming off the line. If he rises and exposes his chest to the defender, he becomes an easy target and the defender will hold him up.
Bullet is unable to get off the block downfield.	If the bullet can't get away downfield, he probably has a speed disadvantage. In that case, teach him to change speeds, weave and fake inside cuts to gain separation. Place the bullet with his inside hip next to the outside hip of a defender and have them race to a point 15 to 30 yards downfield.
Bullet overruns the ball.	The toughest part of the bullet's assignment is to go as fast as possible down the field and then stop quickly to defend and try to tackle the return man. Have the bullet work on breaking down, using short, choppy steps, with at least 5 yards of cushion in front of the return man. Waiting too long to start slowing down usually causes the bullet to run past the return man.
Bullet is getting blocked while breaking down.	When the bullet does slow down, he becomes vulnerable to being blocked by the player who has been chasing him. Teach the bullet to block out the chasing defender with his back, using the basketball player's technique of establishing rebounding position, while maintaining his outside leverage position on the return man. If the blocker gets in front of the bullet, between him and the return man, the bullet must maintain his focus on the return man and not let him get outside. This action should force the return man back to the other bullet who, ideally, will be unblocked.

Defending Against the Bullets

The bullets, typically the split ends who are the first defenders downfield in a spread punt formation, can play havoc with a punt return team. The players assigned to block the bullets and slow them down must have the same physical skills as the bullets do—speed, agility and tenacity. In addition, they must be able to react to the bullets' various escape moves, maintaining contact as the two bullets work downfield.

KEY POINTS

The most important components of defending against the bullets are

- adjusting to the bullets' abilities,
- disrupting the inside release,
- maintaining inside leverage and
- reestablishing the block.

ADJUSTING TO THE BULLETS' ABILITIES

Typically, the defender assumes a good two-point stance with his weight on the balls of his feet. He aligns to the inside of the bullet and 1 to 2 yards off the ball. But if scouting or game experience indicates that the bullet is extremely fast or elusive, the defender should deepen his alignment while maintaining inside leverage. This head start must be enough to allow the defender to get to the punt return man at the same time or before the bullet does. The defender will not be able to slow down the bullet from this position, but if the defender aligns too close to the bullet and then immediately loses contact, he will have no chance to protect his return man from that bullet.

DISRUPTING THE INSIDE RELEASE

The defender aligns inside the bullet so that the bullet cannot release inside and take a straight-line path to the punt return man. If the bullet attempts to release inside, the defender must deliver a punch to the bullet's chest or inside shoulder, preventing the inside release.

If the bullet tries to escape to the inside by faking out the defender, the defender must have the patience and poise to react minimally to all fakes and maintain inside position. His rule must be to contest the inside release with contact and run with the outside release.

MAINTAINING INSIDE LEVERAGE

If the bullet attempts to outrun the defender on an outside release (with or without a release move or a collision), the defender should attempt to keep in close contact by sprinting full speed to a point slightly inside and slightly behind the bullet. This hip-trail position allows the defender to continue to wall off inside moves by the bullet and force the bullet to run wider than he wishes. If the bullet is too fast for the defender, the defender should leave the bullet, sprint at a direct angle to the punt return man and try to get there before the bullet does.

(continued)

At a Glance

The following parts of the text offer additional information on defending against the bullets.

Releases	p. 58
Tackling	p. 93
Press Man Coverage	p. 125
Bullets	p. 150
Open-Field Tackling	p. 168

REESTABLISHING THE BLOCK

Eventually, the bullet will have to slow his sprint, break down to contain the return man and make a tackle. When the defender sees the bullet lower his hips and begin to break down, he should quickly establish inside position against the bullet, placing himself between the bullet and the return man. After he establishes this position, the defender drops his hips, balances his weight and takes on any blows from the bullet as he screens off the bullet from the return man.

Common Errors

You may run into several common errors when teaching your athletes how to defend against the bullets.

Error	Error correction
Defender loses contact with the bullet.	If the bullet immediately loses the defender, then the defender was aligned too close to the bullet and got beat off the ball by a faster man. The defender must deepen his alignment against a fast bullet. The defender may also be too aggressive at the line, lunging at the bullet and missing him or overreacting to fakes and allowing the bullet to elude him. Have the defender practice going nowhere on the snap and reacting patiently to the bullet's moves while maintaining inside leverage and being prepared to establish a position in contact with the bullet down the field.
Defender fails to disrupt the inside release.	The defender must maintain inside position and not be too eager to start the chase downfield. He must be balanced and poised, ready for contact, so that if the bullet attempts the inside release, a collision will occur. Have bullets and defenders work against each other repeatedly, going only from the line of scrimmage about 10 yards downfield, emphasizing initial release possibilities.
Defender is unable to maintain leverage.	Align a defender so that he trails a bullet by a few yards. Then, on your signal, both players run toward a cone that represents the punt return man. The defender must use a burst of speed and take an appropriate angle to catch up and get inside the bullet by the time the bullet gets to the return man.
Defender fails to reacquire the block.	The defender can never give up hope that he can eventually defeat the bullet. Regardless of how the first part of the coverage goes, the defender will almost always get a second chance when the bullet slows down for the punt return man's catch. Teach defenders to hustle to the end of every play and get back inside the bullet when he breaks down.

Long Snap

KEY POINTS

The most important components of the long snap are

- assuming a comfortable stance,
- proper hand positioning,
- releasing the ball and
- follow-through.

A long snap is the underhand pass from the center (hereafter called the snapper) to the punter. The long snap typically travels anywhere from 12 and 15 yards, depending on the alignment of the punter. This snap is called the long snap to differentiate it from the short snap from the center to the holder on points after touchdown (PATs) and field goals, which generally travel only 7 yards (see "Short Snap" on page 158 for more information). The long snap is an important skill that goes unnoticed when it is good but can change the course of the game if it is errant and causes the punter to muff the ball or allows the opposing team to block the punt. Finding and developing a good long snap is well worth the time because a good snap makes it almost impossible for the opponent to block a punt.

The long snapper does not have to be a center, or even a lineman, on regular down-and-distance plays in the game; sometimes the best long snappers are linebackers or skill-position players like wide receivers or defensive backs.

While snapping the ball accurately and quickly is the long snapper's highest priority, he also may be required to block a man or an area after snapping the ball. Furthermore, after snapping and blocking, he becomes part of the coverage unit, running down the field to help fiind and tackle the punt return man (see "Punt Protection" on page 281 and "Punt Coverage" on page 284 for more information).

ASSUMING A COMFORTABLE STANCE

The snapper must experiment until he finds a solid, comfortable stance. His feet should be wider than shoulder-width, knees bent, hips slightly higher than the shoulders, weight on the balls of his feet and hands slightly in front of the head (see figure 5.16). His head should be down, looking back through his legs to establish the location of his target, the punter.

Figure 5.16 Snapper assuming proper stance before the snap.

(continued)

Figure 5.17 **Proper hand positioning for the long snap.**

PROPER HAND POSITIONING

When the snapper approaches the line of scrimmage for this play, the ball will be lying on the ground. The rules allow the snapper to rotate the ball to place his hands in the proper positions on the ball, but he cannot lift the ball off the ground while rotating it. The snapper should place his throwing hand on the ball with two fingers across the laces as if he is going to throw a pass (see figure 5.17). He rotates the laces and the throwing hand so that the laces are almost underneath the ball, on the ground. The guide hand is over the top of the ball with fingers spread. The nose of the ball should be tilted upward.

RELEASING THE BALL

As the arms pull the football through the legs with a sweeping motion along the ground, the hips rotate down and through for added momentum. The arms extend as far backward as possible, and the elbows lock out. The elbows will hit the snapper's thighs.

The ball should leave the snapper's hands at a point only a few inches above the ground. The snapper's hips must stay low, not rising into the air at the release. The trajectory of the snap should be low and almost parallel to the ground, although it will rise slightly as it travels to the punter. The target of the long snap is the hip of the punter's kicking leg.

Figure 5.18 **Snapper's hand and arm positioning on the follow-through for the long snap.**

FOLLOW-THROUGH

As the snapper's elbows hit against his thighs, the fingers should point toward the punter's hip with palms extended outward (see figure 5.18). Meanwhile, the knees lock out and the head stays down to keep the ball down. The follow-through must be low to keep the ball from arriving at the punter above his waist or, worse, over his head. The snapper must feel as though he is following through at ground level, although his hands and arms will be rising slightly as they finish the motion.

At a Glance

The following parts of the text offer additional information on the long snap.

Punt	p. 140
Short Snap	p. 158
Punt Protection	p. 281

Common Errors

You may run into several common errors when teaching your athletes the long snap.

Error	Error correction
Snap is too high.	The snapper's hips may have lifted upward at the release or the hands and arms may have traveled upward on the release. The snapper should not feel as though he has to elevate the ball on the long snap; he should feel as though he is skimming the ball along the ground, straight back to the punter. The natural arc of the long-snapping action will give the ball all the lift it needs.
Snap is off to either side.	Unequal pressure on the ball by the hands will cause the snap to go off to the side. Have the snapper hold the ball in proper position over his head while standing upright and throwing two-handed overhand passes to a partner. This drill isolates the hand movements and allows the snapper to see and feel the cooperative actions of his hands.
Snap is too slow.	The snapper should increase the angle of the wrist on the throwing hand before the snap; that is, move the ball slightly farther forward in front of his head and tilt the ball more by angling the wrist more. Another tactic might be to coach the snapper to increase the extension of his arms as he completes the snap. The snapper can also work on thrusting his hips down and through on the snap. But as he increases his hip action, he must be sure not to lift his hips upward on the snap because then the snap will be high.

A short snap is the underhand pass from the center (hereafter called the snapper) to the holder on PATs and field goals. The short snap typically travels a distance of 7 yards. This snap is called the short snap to differentiate it from the long snap to the punter on punting plays, which generally travel 12 to 15 yards (see "Long Snap" on page 155 for more information).

The short snap for a PAT or field goal is critical to the success of the kick. The short snapper must be able to snap the ball each time to an exact position that allows the holder to place the ball properly. The snap must also have as much velocity as possible, while still being accurate, because the overall operation time of the snap, hold and kick must be short to prevent kicks from being blocked. Usually a larger player is preferred for this role because of the protection responsibilities after the snap (see "PAT and FG Protection" on page 297 for more information).

ASSUMING A COMFORTABLE STANCE

As with the stance for the long snap, the snapper must experiment until he finds a solid, comfortable stance. Again, his feet should be wider than shoulder-width, knees bent, hips slightly higher than the shoulders, weight on the balls of his feet and hands slightly in front of the head, as shown in figure 5.17 on page 155. His head should be down, looking back through his legs to establish the location of his target, the hands of the holder.

HAND POSITIONING

Hand positioning for the short snap is the same as it is for the long snap. When the snapper approaches the line of scrimmage for this play, the ball will be on the ground. The rules allow the snapper to rotate the ball to place his hands in the proper positions on the ball, but he cannot lift the ball off the ground while rotating it. The snapper should place his throwing hand on the ball with two fingers across the laces as if he is going to throw a pass, as shown in figure 5.18 on page 156. He rotates the laces and the throwing hand so that the laces are almost underneath the ball, on the ground. The guide hand is over the top of the ball with fingers spread. The nose of the ball should be tilted upward.

RELEASING THE BALL

As the arms pull the football through the legs with a sweeping motion along the ground, the hips also rotate down and through for added momentum. The arms extend as far backward as possible, and the elbows lock out. The elbows will hit the snapper's thighs. The ball should leave the snapper's hands just a few inches above and nearly parallel to the ground. The target for the short snap is 12 to 18 inches off the ground at the holder's target hand.

If possible, the snap should arrive at the holder with the laces up, on top of the ball, so that when the holder lowers the ball to the ground for the kick, the laces are away from the kicker, facing the goal posts, and the kicker will not have to kick the laces (see "Holding for the Place Kick" on page 160 for more information).

FOLLOW-THROUGH

As the elbows hit against the thighs, the fingers point at the target with palms outward. Meanwhile, the knees lock out and the head stays down to keep the ball down. The follow-through must be low, so that the holder can catch the ball without having to raise his hands higher than the target of 12 to 18 inches off the ground. Catching the ball higher than the target height slows the operation time of the kick and disrupts the timing of the kicker's approach to the ball. The snapper must feel as though he is following through at ground level, although his hands and arms will be rising slightly as they finish the motion.

At a Glance

The following parts of the text offer additional information on the short snap.

Long Snap	p. 155
Holding for the Place Kick	p. 160
Place Kick	p. 162
PAT and FG Protection	p. 297

Common Errors

You may run into several common errors when teaching your athletes the short snap.

Error	Error correction
Snap is too high.	The hips of the snapper may have lifted upward at the release or the hands and arms may have traveled upward on the release.
Snap is off to either side.	Unequal pressure on the ball by the hands will cause the snap to go off to the side. Have the snapper hold the ball in proper position over his head while standing upright and throwing two-handed overhand passes to a partner. This drill isolates the hand movements and allows the snapper to see and feel the cooperative actions of his hands.
Snap is too slow.	The snapper should increase the angle of the wrist on the throwing hand before the snap; that is, move the ball slightly farther forward in front of his head and tilt the ball more by angling the wrist more. Another tactic might be to coach the snapper to increase the extension of his arms as he completes the snap.
Laces are in the wrong place.	The easiest solution to this problem is to move the holder forward half a yard or backward half a yard. Changing the holder's spot changes the number of times the ball will rotate from the snapper to the holder. If the snapper is somewhat consistent, experimentation with the holder's spot should result in the laces coming up in the holder's hands.

KEY POINTS

The most important components of holding for the place kick are

o assuming the stance,

o providing a target and

o making the catch.

The seemingly simple task of holding for a place kick (PAT or field goal) actually requires great precision and is critical to the success of the kick. The holder must place the ball on the tee or ground in exactly the right spot and at exactly the right angle for the kicker's steps to work out correctly and for contact with the ball to be accurate.

Figure 5.19 **Holder's stance when waiting for the snap.**

ASSUMING THE STANCE

The holder should place his front knee on the ground and his back knee up, as shown in figure 5.19, even though this stance may seem awkward. If the front knee is on the ground, it will not get in the way of the arms as the holder moves to catch the snap.

PROVIDING A TARGET

After the kicker identifies the spot on the ground where he wants the ball (or the tee) to be placed, the holder places the fingers of his front hand on that spot. He places the back elbow against the thigh of the left leg. When the kicker is ready, the holder raises his front hand 12 to 18 inches off the ground immediately in front of the spot and opens that hand, signaling to the snapper that he may now snap the ball (see figure 5.20). The holder may also flex his hand to give the snapper a visual count for the snap. Alternatively, the holder may keep his hand open and still, and the snapper is free to snap the ball when he is comfortable and ready.

MAKING THE CATCH

The most important part of the hold is the catch. If the holder is too eager to spin the ball or place it on the tee, he may lose focus and muff the catch. The holder must be poised and patient, concentrating on the ball and using both hands to make the catch while seeing the ball hit his hands.

Figure 5.20 **Holder's hand positioning to signal to the snapper that the kicker is ready.**

Figure 5.21 Holder's hand positioning after making the catch.

After he catches the ball, the holder feels for the laces and spins the ball so that the laces are facing away from the kicker. Using the back leg as a stop for the left elbow, he lowers the ball to the spot. He removes the front hand from the ball and places the index finger of the back hand on top to keep the ball in the proper position (see figure 5.21). A fraction of a second after the holder removes the front hand, the kicker contacts the ball.

At a Glance

The following parts of the text offer additional information on holding for place kicks.

Catching	p. 48
Short Snap	p. 158
Place Kick	p. 162
PAT and FG Protection	p. 297

Common Errors

You may run into several common errors when teaching your athletes how to hold for the place kick.

Error	Error correction
Holder mishandles the snap.	The holder must first concentrate on the catch. Every day, he should practice catches without a kicker so that he can isolate the skills of catching the ball without the pressure of placing it on the tee. The holder should do these drills with the snapper who will be playing in the game so that they can get used to working with each other.
Holder fails to find the tee.	The holder must again work on his eyes. After the catch, he must immediately turn his head to the spot for the kick and focus on the task of placing the ball on that spot.
Ball leans incorrectly.	If the ball is tilted incorrectly, the kick will sail left or right. The holder must work repeatedly with the kicker to determine exactly what angle of tilt the kicker prefers and then strive to place the ball in exactly that position every time.
Laces are positioned improperly.	If the kicker contacts the laces when he kicks the ball, the trajectory of the kick could be adversely affected. The holder must rotate the laces away from the kicker as he places the ball on the tee. Working with the short snapper, the holder should find a distance where he can line up (start at 7 yards behind the line of scrimmage and adjust forward or backward half a yard) that will usually result in the laces being on top of the ball when he makes the catch.

Place Kick

KEY POINTS

The most important components of the place kick are

- o determining the alignment,
- o assuming a comfortable stance,
- o approaching the ball,
- o contacting the ball and
- o follow-through.

The place kick is a kick executed by one player while a teammate controls the ball on the ground during a scrimmage-down situation. This type of kick can be used for either a field goal (FG) or a point after touchdown (PAT). This skill requires consistent, repeated practice and great attention to fundamentals. Small variations in technique will result in major deviations from the intended path of the ball, especially on longer kicks. The kicker must seek the proper balance of elevation, distance and accuracy.

Two variables that affect the accuracy and consistency of this kick are the snap (see "Short Snap" on page 158) and the hold (see "Holding for the Place Kick" on page 160). A bad snap or bad hold can cause a kick to go awry even if the kicker's steps are perfect, as discussed in previous skills. Another factor that affects the success of place kicks is operation time. The opposing team is rushing the kick with the intention of blocking it, and the blockers on the protection unit can keep those rushers at bay for about only two seconds (see "PAT and FG Protection" on page 297 for more information). Therefore, the snap, hold and kick must be accomplished in less than two seconds to ensure that the kick is not blocked.

Figure 5.22 **Kicker's initial stance for a place kick.**

DETERMINING THE ALIGNMENT

Although the exact location of the kicker's initial alignment will vary based on the length of his strides, the most common alignment is 3 yards directly behind the spot where the ball will be placed on the ground and then two lateral steps directly to the side away from the kicker's dominant, or kicking, foot. The kicker has some freedom to determine his prekick alignment, but after he finds a location that produces the most accurate and consistent results, he must return to that spot every time he kicks in practices or games.

ASSUMING A COMFORTABLE STANCE

Before the kick, the kicker should assume a comfortable, athletic stance with his nonkicking leg in front (see figure 5.22). His shoulders should be over his knees, with his arms dangling comfortably at his sides. His body weight should be distributed slightly heavier on his kicking foot, because that foot will be the push-off foot when he begins his approach to the ball and he does not want to take a false step with that foot.

APPROACHING THE BALL

The snap must have good velocity, the hold has to be quick and decisive, and the kicker must start his approach to the ball when the holder makes the catch, not after the holder places the ball on the tee (use a stopwatch to take operation times on a regular basis when the team is practicing place kicks).

The kicker should take three steps (and no more, for the sake of the all-important operation time) on the approach to the ball, beginning with a short step by the non-kicking foot (see figure 5.23*a*). The second step is a longer drive step with the kicking leg (see figure 5.23*b*), designed to increase the kicker's speed toward the ball. The third step is a short, solid plant step with the nonkicking leg (see figure 5.23*c*).

a

b

Figure 5.23 *(a-c)* **Kicker's approach to the ball on a place kick.**

(continued)

c

Figure 5.23 (continued)

The kicker must place the plant foot in exactly the same position, relative to the ball, every time he makes his approach. Finding the initial alignment and stride length that will result in consistent plant foot placement requires a lot of practice time. When the plant step is completed, the toes of the plant foot should point at the target, 6 to 12 inches laterally from the ball and on a line directly even with the ball placement.

Figure 5.24 **Proper positioning of kicking leg on impact.**

CONTACTING THE BALL

As the kicking leg swings toward the ball, the leg gradually straightens out. Just before the downward movement is completed, the kicking leg must lock out to transmit maximum force to the ball on impact (see figure 5.24). The kicker's shoulders and hips rotate to face the target, and the upper body leans slightly away from the ball.

The aiming point for the kicking foot to contact the ball is 2 inches below the midpoint of the ball and 2 inches to the outside. The foot should contact the ball just above the arch on the top inside portion of the foot.

FOLLOW-THROUGH

As the leg swings through the ball, the kicker should feel as though the path of the leg is a straight line beginning about 12 inches before contact and continuing about 12 inches after contact. This straight-line swing through the ball ensures solid contact and enhances the accuracy of the kick. After contact, the kicker should follow through completely, rising off the ground and then landing on the kicking foot first.

At a Glance

The following parts of the text offer additional information on the place kick.

Common Errors

You may run into several common errors when teaching your athletes how to place kick.

Error	Error correction
Kick is wide left.	If the kick goes to the left, the plant foot is usually too close to the ball or is pointed to the left of the target.
Kick is wide right.	If the kick goes to the right, the plant foot is usually too far from the ball or is pointed to the right of the target.
Kick is too low.	If the kick is too low, the plant foot is usually too far behind the ball or the contact point is too high on the ball.
Kick is too high.	If the kick is too high and therefore does not have enough distance, the plant foot usually is too far in front of the ball or the contact point is too low on the football.

One of the most exciting and momentum-producing plays in football is the blocked kick. A blocked punt immediately gains the receiving team at least 40 yards of field position, and a blocked PAT or field goal prevents the opponent from putting points on the board. Blocked kicks, however, do not happen by accident. A good blocking scheme must be devised to put a player in position to make the block, and the individual player must put forth great effort and superior technique to get the job done.

EXPLODING OFF THE LINE

Good timing and speed off the snap is critical to blocking a kick. The kick blocker must watch the snapper and explode off the line on his first movement. The kick blocker must remain poised and avoid being distracted by snap counts, protection calls or movement by the protectors. He must stay low and drive up the field vertically for two or three steps to get the protector on his heels before making any moves.

AVOIDING PROTECTORS

When engaging a protector, the kick blocker must use quick, aggressive hand movement to knock down the protector's hands. He must simultaneously attack the gap between two protectors, instead of attacking a single protector. He must keep his pads low and his shoulders turned so that his back is toward the closest protector and he is giving that protector the least possible surface to contact.

AIMING FOR THE BLOCK POINT

The focal point for the kick blocker is not the punter or kicker. They both move forward and contact the football well in front of their original alignment. Therefore, the kick blocker must focus on an imaginary spot approximately 2 yards in front of the punter's foot or about 1 yard in front of the holder for a place kick. This point, called the block point, is crucial for kick blocking for two reasons: First, this forward aiming point gives the kick blocker a better chance to get his hands on the ball than an aiming point on the punter's or kicker's leg, and, second, this aiming point reduces or eliminates the chance that the kick blocker will run into the kicker and cause a penalty.

MAKING THE BLOCK

As he approaches the block point, the kick blocker should put his hands together so that the thumbs and index fingers form a triangle (see figure 5.25). If his hands are touching in this fashion, the ball cannot escape through his hands and the combined surface area of his two hands gives him a better chance to contact the ball.

With his hands together, the kick blocker should reach out and take the ball off the kicker's foot—a phrase that reminds him not to reach up or jump. His best chance to make the block is to run through the block point, keeping his hands low and together, contacting the ball soon after the kicker's foot hits it. Blockers on a PAT or field goal should have the same thought process regarding their hands but will probably have to dive in front of the kicker to have a chance to block a kick.

SCOOPING THE BALL

After the ball has been blocked, all defenders should look for it. If the ball has not crossed the line of scrimmage, the nearest player should approach the ball with hands together, palms up and low to the ground. He scoops up the ball and runs toward his goal line. He has nothing to lose in this effort, because if he muffs the recovery, his team will retain possession regardless of who recovers the kick, as long as the ball remains behind the line of scrimmage. His teammates should be sure that no player on the kicking team can recover the ball and carry it for a first down. After the blocking team scoops up the ball, teammates should look for the nearest opponent to block.

Figure 5.25 Kick blocker's hand positioning when approaching the block point.

At a Glance

The following parts of the text offer additional information on blocking the kick.

Releases	p. 58
Pass Rush	p. 110
Punt Protection	p. 281
PAT and FG Protection	p. 297

Common Errors

You may run into several common errors when teaching your athletes how to block kicks.

Error	Error correction
Defender hits the kicker.	Drill defenders on finding the block point by using a cone as an aiming point. They must stay on their feet.
Defender misses the ball.	The hands are apart or are too high. Defenders must take the ball off the kicker's foot.
Defender is tripped on the line.	Place stepover bags between blockers so that defenders learn to pick up their feet as they go through the line.

Open-Field Tackling

The special teams tackle usually occurs in the open field where the return man has some room to maneuver. The tackler should strive to use the tackling techniques that every defensive player learns. On special teams plays, however, several players may have to be involved to accomplish the tackle. Therefore, the first player to reach the ball carrier must be sure to slow him down and give other tacklers time to arrive.

Tackling can also be dangerous if it is not executed properly. Tacklers must remember never to drive their helmet or facemask into the opponent as the initial point of contact. In particular, head-down contact (initiating contact with the top, or crown, of the helmet), also known as spearing, greatly increases the risk of injury.

MAINTAINING LEVERAGE

As he approaches the ball carrier, the tackler must keep leverage on his opponent by maintaining a position to one side of the ball. He must never allow the ball carrier to gain a head-up alignment, running directly at the tackler. The leverage of an appropriate approach gives the ball carrier only one direction to run, greatly limiting his options.

BREAKING DOWN

At a point at least 5 yards, but not more than 8 yards, from the ball carrier, the tackler must get his body under control. Slowing down, he drops his hips, widens his feet and shortens his stride into short, choppy steps. He must be able to react to any move that the ball carrier makes, but he cannot move laterally if he is still moving rapidly forward, so he must slow down and get under control.

In order to gain body control, the tackler must come to balance, meaning that he must shorten his stride, and widen the placement of his feet and lower his hips by bending his knees. A balanced position with low pad level is critical for leverage, power and stability in the tackle and will help prevent the tackler from missing or being pushed backward by the ball carrier.

CONTACTING THE BALL CARRIER

At the moment of impact with the ball carrier, the tackler should attempt to use all the fundamental elements of tackling as discussed in "Tackling" on page 93. The main points of tackling are getting under the ball carrier, squaring up with the eyes on the ball, initiating contact with the shoulder, exploding up through the hips and wrapping the arms.

FINISHING THE TACKLE

As the collision is taking place, the tackler grabs hold of the ball carrier's jersey or any other part of the uniform that he can reach. The tackler continues to drive his feet on contact and keeps his arms wrapped around the ball carrier, trying to change the momentum of the return man from forward to backward. Although the solo tackle is desired and impressive, it is also difficult to carry out and rare in special teams situations, so the tackler who makes first contact should focus on slowing the runner to allow teammates to arrive and take the runner to the ground. The first tackler cannot be thinking about the big hit; he must be thinking about making contact, especially in the open field.

At a Glance

The following parts of the text offer additional information on open-field tackling.

Tackling	p. 93
Bullets	p. 150
Defending Against the Bullets	p. 153
Evading Tacklers	p. 194

Common Errors

You may run into several common errors when teaching your athletes how to make open-field tackles.

Error	Error correction
Player whiffs, or misses the tackle.	Coverage players often become too excited as the moment of impact approaches, and they continue to sprint at full speed until they cannot possibly change direction and make contact. This overeager approach results in a whiff, or missed tackle. Constantly drill the importance of the breakdown technique by having players sprint 20 to 25 yards, one at a time, and then break down and react to a simulated ball carrier who tries to make them miss.
Player is in good position, but only gets an arm on the return man.	The player may be lowering his head and taking his eyes off the target just before contact. Emphasize keeping the head and eyes up.
Player has trouble finishing the tackle.	The player is probably failing to keep his feet moving throughout the tackle. Use sleds or blocking dummies to drill foot movement on contact.
Return man breaks away from the tackler.	The tackler is probably not wrapping his arms around the return man, or perhaps he is not "grabbing cloth" on the return man's uniform. Practice half-speed tackling with the emphasis on wrapping arms and grabbing cloth.

PART III

Teaching Tactical Skills

Tactical skills get at the heart of football. Without proper understanding and execution of tactical skills, your players will often commit basic errors in game situations. You can empower your athletes by teaching them how to read situations, apply the appropriate knowledge and make the correct decisions.

This part focuses on the basic and intermediate tactical skills in football, showing you how to teach your athletes to make good decisions. These skills include offensive tactical skills such as the progression of receivers, the pass–run option and curl route adjustments and defensive tactical skills such as when to take the inside rush, linebacker reads, force and pursuit angles. This part also covers the special teams tactical skills, such as the onside kick and the wall return.

THINKING TACTICALLY

Throughout the presentation of tactical skills, you will see references to athletes needing to know what is called the game situation. As described in Rainer Martens' *Successful Coaching, Third Edition,* the game situation includes the down and distance, the score, and the time remaining in the quarter and game. In other words, your players need to know specific information when your team faces a specific situation. For example, in a third-and-3 situation when leading late in a game, you may ask yourself, *How important is it that we maintain possession of the ball? Has our run game been able to move the ball consistently? Can we risk a pass here?*

You and your team must know what key information you need to make the best decision. Following are a few questions that you and your team must keep in mind when facing tactical situations during a game:

- What is your strategy?
- How does your game plan affect your strategy?
- How does the game situation (the score, the strengths and weaknesses of the players involved at that particular time, the physical playing conditions and so on) affect your game plan?

For each skill, we first present an overview that paints a picture or puts you and your athletes into a specific scenario in the game in which you would be likely to use the particular tactical skill. The "Watch Out!" element highlights the distractions that may affect your athletes' ability to make appropriate decisions and provides insight on what to look for. The "Reading the Situation" element offers important cues that your athletes need to be able to read so that they can make the appropriate decisions for the situation. The next section, called "Acquiring the Appropriate Knowledge," provides the information that your athletes need to understand in order to make the proper decision and successfully execute the skill, as presented in the overview. Finally, as in the technical skill chapters, the "At a Glance" section refers you to the other important tools in the book that will help you teach the skill.

chapter 6

Offensive Tactical Skills

This chapter covers the offensive tactical skills that you and your players must know to be successful. In this chapter, you will find the following skills:

The quarterback generally identifies the best available receiver by following a progression in which he checks a primary defender, then checks a secondary defender and, if no passing lanes are available, checks the ball down to his outlet receiver. For example, assume that the quarterback drops back to pass. He knows the routes that his receivers are running, and he knows what progression to use to check those receivers. He scans the field, finds the defensive player who is his primary read and decides whether that defender is in the throwing lane to his first receiver, taking away his first throw. If the first possible throw is defended, the quarterback finds the second read and makes the same kind of choice. If his first two alternatives are covered, the quarterback checks down, meaning that he finds his third and final target, his outlet receiver, and delivers the ball to him.

⚠ WATCH OUT!

The following circumstances may distract your quarterback:

- o Focusing on his receivers. The quarterback must learn to trust his receivers and know the spot to which they will be running so that he can direct his undivided attention to the defenders.

- o Letting the pass rush distract his vision. He can't look at the onrushing linemen; he must "feel" the pressure but "see" downfield.

- o Having tunnel vision and seeing only one defender. The quarterback must keep a wide field of vision, scanning both sides of the primary defender for other defenders.

READING THE SITUATION

What factors can you and your quarterback use to give you the best chance to deliver the ball to the appropriate receiver? Teach your quarterback to do the following:

- Locate the primary defender before the snap without making it obvious.

- Know where his receivers are, and where they are going, without looking specifically at them.

- Look for pre-snap clues indicating a defender's potential to defend the pass.

- At the snap, find the primary defender again and watch his pass drop to see how fast and wide he is dropping and what receiver seems to have his attention.

- Decide within the first three steps of the drop whether the primary defender is in position to take away the pass to the first receiver.

- See the open space around the defenders.

ACQUIRING THE APPROPRIATE KNOWLEDGE

To use modifications in the progression of receivers, you and your quarterback must know about the following:

Rules

You and your quarterback need to know several main rules when determining which receiver to throw to after the snap:

- o Defenders cannot continue to bump or hold receivers on their routes after the ball is in the air, if the pass is thrown downfield past the line of scrimmage. If the quarterback sees a defender holding a receiver, he can deliver the ball and may get a pass interference penalty called.

- On a screen or swing pass, a defender can legally collide with a receiver while the ball is in the air, so the quarterback can deliver the ball to this location only if no defenders are nearby.

Physical Playing Conditions

The physical playing conditions significantly affect the game. Thus, you and your quarterback must pay attention to the following physical conditions when determining which receiver to throw to after the snap:

- If the ball is wet and difficult to throw, the short pass to the check-down receiver might be the best option even if one of the other receivers is open, because the short pass will be much easier to complete.
- If the wind is strong, the quarterback must consider that any intermediate pass against the wind will be held up or possibly blown off target. Again, the short check-down pass might be more effective.
- When throwing the ball with the wind, the quarterback might want to take a chance on a deep or intermediate pass because the ball will travel farther with more velocity than it normally would.

> **REMINDER!**
>
> You and your quarterback must understand the team strategy and game plan and assess the progression of receivers based on those plans and the situation at hand. Make sure that you and your players consider the questions on page 172.

Strengths and Weaknesses of Opponents

You and your quarterback must account for your opponent's strengths and weaknesses to know how to deliver the ball to the appropriate receiver. Consider the following about your opponents:

- How fast is the defense? Defenders with great speed can close on the ball more quickly than those who are slower.
- Do blitzes occur frequently? The blitz often causes the offense to forego the progression of receivers because the quarterback may not have enough time to read all his defenders. The offense then often goes to plays called blitz beaters, which are quick, timing throws to an isolated receiver. These plays involve a more technical set of skills: one receiver trying to beat one defender and the quarterback trying to get him the ball in a hurry.
- Are the opponent's linebackers and safeties big, strong and good run defenders? If so, they might not be as good at pass drops. The tactic of drop-back passing and attacking underneath the defenders can be effective if these defenders don't have great range.
- Is the defensive pass rush blockable? If so, the quarterback will have time to drop back, find the defenders and deliver the ball.

Self-Knowledge

Besides being aware of your opponent's abilities, you and your quarterback need to know about your own team's strengths and weaknesses. When considering which receiver to throw to after the snap, you and your quarterback should be aware of the following:

- Do you have an outstanding receiver? If so, the quarterback can deliver the ball even if the defender is fairly close, knowing that the receiver will run a good route, come back for the ball and catch the ball in a crowd.
- Do you play aggressively? The more aggressively your team plays, the more times the quarterback should deliver the ball to the primary or secondary receiver. A high-octane passing team wants its quarterback to take a few chances, whereas a team that runs the ball and wants to play field position at all costs will coach the quarterback to take far fewer chances and throw the ball downfield only if the receiver is wide open.

(continued)

o Do your receivers run good routes? If the quarterback can depend on his receivers to be in the correct place on every pass play, he can confidently focus his attention on the defenders, choose the appropriate throwing lane and deliver the ball to a location where he knows the receiver will be.

o Does your team have good pass protection? When the quarterback drops back to pass, he will be able to read the defense with confidence if he is not worried about dodging and evading pass rushers. The offensive line should be able to give the quarterback up to four seconds of solid protection so that he can take his five-step drop, locate the defenders and get rid of the ball.

o Does your quarterback have good vision, coupled with good, quick decision-making skills? Watch your quarterback's eyes and feet when he drops back to pass in a team situation compared with his mechanics when he is throwing in drills without a rush. He may rush his steps more under the pressure of a pass rush, or he may not be able to read the defense as well when he must pass over the action on the line. He also may be indecisive, holding the ball too long before delivering it and allowing the pass rushers to close in on him. The effective quarterback has to be able to see the defenders and make decisions just as effectively when performing in team situations as in drills.

Never judge a quarterback on drills alone; good vision and decision-making skills are revealed only when playing 11-on-11.

Decision-Making Guidelines

When deciding how to gain the best advantage in delivering the ball to the appropriate receiver, you and your quarterback should consider the previous information as well as the following guidelines:

o Successful passes require precise timing between the quarterback and receivers. Although the read by the quarterback is crucial, it will be meaningless if the quarterback does not deliver the ball on time to the receiver in a location where he can catch it. Devote a segment of every practice to route timing, a drill in which the quarterback simply drops back and throws the ball to an uncovered receiver, working on timing, route depth, speed and trajectory of the pass for every route in the offense.

o Insist that the quarterback take the correct number of steps for every pass in the offense. Precise timing between the quarterback and the receivers is impossible if the quarterback takes too many or too few steps.

o Under pressure, some quarterbacks throw the ball with a more rushed or more abbreviated delivery than normal. You must evaluate every throw in practice and games to ensure that your quarterback's mechanics are not breaking down in critical situations.

o All the work in practice on reading receivers will be ineffective if the receiver drops the ball. Devote a segment of every practice to drills for proper technique in catching the ball.

o In designing pass plays, you must construct route combinations that stretch the defense either horizontally or vertically, attacking specific defenders. Pass plays cannot be effective if the defense can stop them simply by making the right call. Every pass play must have options that the quarterback can use, including an outlet, or check-down, receiver, if defenders are positioned in the primary passing lanes.

Option Pitch Read

On an option pitch play the final ball carrier is not determined in the huddle. Instead, the quarterback reads the defense and then decides whether to keep the ball or pitch it to a trailing back. As the option play unfolds, the quarterback attacks down the line of scrimmage with his running back in pitch relationship. The offensive blocking scheme also intentionally leaves a defensive end or outside linebacker unblocked for the quarterback to attack with the option. The quarterback reads the unblocked defensive player to determine whether to keep the ball or pitch to the back.

⚠ WATCH OUT!

The following circumstances may distract your quarterback:

- A player who breaks through the line of scrimmage before the quarterback gets to the pitch read. The quarterback should not make the pitch. He should keep the ball and get as much yardage as possible, because the blocking scheme has been compromised.

- Operating very close to the line of scrimmage. Quarterbacks naturally tend to drift away from the blocks occurring on the line of scrimmage, but the effectiveness of the play diminishes if the quarterback gets too far off the line. He must focus on the unblocked man whom he is going to read and ignore the commotion next to him on the line.

READING THE SITUATION

How do you and your quarterback best execute the option pitch? Teach your quarterback to do the following:

- Immediately seek the defensive player who is the pitch read and focus only on him.

- Attack the upfield, or inside, shoulder of the defensive player to see which way he will commit. If he turns toward the quarterback or attacks, the quarterback should execute the underhand pitch to the running back. If he stays wide or crosses the line of scrimmage to take the pitch back, the quarterback must turn upfield and keep the ball.

ACQUIRING THE APPROPRIATE KNOWLEDGE

To use modifications when reading the option pitch, you and your quarterback must know about the following:

Rules

You and your players need to know several main rules when reading the option pitch:

- The quarterback must make sure that the pitch is a lateral (away from the line of scrimmage) so that he does not have to worry about when he crosses the line of scrimmage before pitching. If the pitch is lateral, the quarterback cannot be penalized for making an illegal forward pass from beyond the line of scrimmage.

- A pitch dropped on the ground is a live ball, and the team who recovers it will have possession, so the quarterback and running back must chase all loose balls!

Physical Playing Conditions

The physical playing conditions significantly affect the game. Thus, you and your quarterback must pay attention to the following physical conditions when reading the option pitch:

- If the ball is wet, the quarterback must be careful not to throw an errant pitch. He may want to consider pitching a little earlier than usual so that he can take a bit more time executing the pitch, and for added ball security he may want to consider using a two-handed pitch instead of the usual one-handed pitch.

(continued)

REMINDER!

You and your quarterback must understand the team strategy and game plan and assess the option pitch based on those plans and the situation at hand. Make sure that you and your quarterback consider the questions on page 172.

○ If the field is wet or slippery, the quarterback must shorten his strides and use quick, choppy steps to turn upfield if he chooses to keep the ball. If he plants too aggressively on his turn upfield, he will likely fall down, ending the play.

Strengths and Weaknesses of Opponents

You and your quarterback must account for your opponent's strengths and weaknesses to know how to read the option pitch. Consider the following about your opponents:

○ Will the defensive end use a feather technique to play the option? The toughest read for the quarterback is a feathering end who does not commit to either the quarterback or the pitch back but stays right on the line of scrimmage and strings out the play. This tactic, when played correctly by the defense, slows the quarterback's read and allows the interior and secondary defensive players to react to the play.

○ Will the defensive end attack the quarterback on the speed option? If the defensive end quickly and aggressively tackles the quarterback, the speed option has a good chance to be effective. The quarterback, with no uncertainty about his choice of action, simply needs to be prepared to pitch early in the play and then protect himself from a big hit by turning his head and shoulders away from the onrushing end. The pitch back will get the ball to the perimeter quickly, outflanking the defense.

○ What type of pass coverage does your opponent play? Defensive teams that play solid zone pass defense usually defend the option relatively well, because the defenders are facing the offense and can react quickly to the play when they see the quarterback running down the line of scrimmage. Defensive teams that blitz a lot and play man-to-man coverage can be vulnerable to the option because the pass defenders turn their backs to the play as they cover their men and thus are unable to react quickly to the running play. Blitzes also can be ineffective because the blocking scheme on the speed option is a simple gap scheme that protects every seam in the line, so the blitzers should have no room to penetrate the line and get to the quarterback as he quickly attacks the perimeter.

Self-Knowledge

Besides being aware of your opponent's abilities, you and your quarterback need to know about your own team's strengths and weaknesses. When considering the option pitch, you and your team should be aware of the following:

○ Is the quarterback quick and decisive? An option quarterback must be able to make an instantaneous decision on the run and have enough speed to beat the defenders to the perimeter. Even if he pitches the ball, if he causes the defensive end to make an early read, the pitch back has a better chance to outflank the rest of the defenders.

○ Can this play be effective with a slower quarterback? Although the pitch option is designed for a quick quarterback, a slower athlete can be effective if he plays with good technique, stays on the line of scrimmage and makes good reads. If he keeps the ball, he should try to get vertical to gain a few yards because he knows that he may not be able to outrun the defenders toward the sideline.

○ Do you have to commit to being an option team to run the speed option? The answer is no. Teams that run a lot of power plays or throw a lot of passes can practice this one option play and learn to run it effectively. In addition, making your upcoming opponent's defense practice option assignments all week puts pressure on them because they will have less time to practice defending everything else in your offense.

Decision-Making Guidelines

When deciding how to gain the best advantage when using the option pitch, you and your quarterback should consider the previous information as well as the following guidelines:

- The quarterback should watch the defensive player's far shoulder. If that shoulder stays back, parallel to the line of scrimmage, the quarterback should keep attacking because the defensive player is trying to feather, or string out, the option. If that shoulder turns toward the quarterback, the read will probably be to pitch the ball, because the defender cannot turn back around fast enough to make a play on the pitch back.

- The speed option is a good way to outnumber the defense because the quarterback is a legitimate running threat and someone in the defensive scheme must be assigned to take him.

- The speed option is an effective play against man-to-man coverage teams because the offense can run off the secondary players with their wide receivers and run the ball outside.

- The speed option is also good against the blitz because the offensive blockers can protect all the gaps in the line, allowing the quarterback to get the ball to the outside quickly. The blitzing linebackers have little chance of penetrating quickly enough to get to the quarterback or flowing laterally to the ball carrier after they blitz.

- The speed option, however, is a high-risk play because the ball carrier is not predetermined and the quarterback may have to pitch the ball under duress. Offensive teams that run the option must be prepared to suffer some turnovers in the effort to make big plays.

At a Glance

The following parts of the text offer additional information on using the pitch read option.

Option Pitch Mechanics	p. 33
Catching	p. 48
Feathering	p. 114
Reacting When Unblocked	p. 232
Feathering the Option	p. 235

Pass–Run Option

The pass–run option is a sprintout or bootleg after a play fake in which the quarterback attacks the perimeter of the defense, with the option to throw a pass or run with the ball. As soon as the quarterback gets outside the pocket, past his tackle's original alignment, he looks to find his primary receiver, who would usually be running some kind of flat route. If that receiver is open, the quarterback delivers the ball to him promptly (known as throwing on time) before any defenders have time to react to the play. If a defender is in the throwing lane to the primary receiver (see "Progression of Receivers" on page 174 for more information), the quarterback checks the area where his secondary receiver should be, usually some kind of curl route or possibly a deep flag route. If that pass is also well defended, the quarterback secures the ball and runs.

⚠ WATCH OUT!

The following circumstances may distract your quarterback:

- Slowing down to throw the ball or read the defense. Don't forget that the defensive linemen and backside linebackers are pursuing the quarterback. If he slows down, he is going to be caught from behind!

- Focusing on just the receiver or just one defender. The quarterback can't stay with one receiver too long. He must check out the pass to the first receiver, make a decision and either throw on time or move his eyes to the throwing lane for the secondary receiver.

- Looking back at chasing defenders. The quarterback should never look back. He must assume that the inside defenders are on the way. He should keep running hard, be decisive and make some positive yards.

- Looking back into the middle of the field to try to find a receiver. The quarterback should never attempt to throw the ball back across his body to a receiver in the middle of the field, even if the receiver is open. The quarterback cannot see all defenders, and the chances for a tipped ball or an interception are high.

READING THE SITUATION

How do you and your quarterback gain the best advantage when using the pass–run option? Teach your quarterback to do the following:

- Know that the primary receiver is most likely to be open early in this play, before the defenders have time to react to the direction of the quarterback's sprint. He must quickly find the defender nearest the throwing lane to the primary receiver and deliver the ball if the defender is out of position.

- If the primary receiver is not open, the quarterback must quickly check the defender or defenders near his secondary receiver to see whether that throw is available, knowing that additional defenders are closing in on the play.

- If the pass options are covered, the quarterback tucks the ball away and runs for positive yardage, attacking toward the sideline to keep away from as many chasing defenders as possible.

ACQUIRING THE APPROPRIATE KNOWLEDGE

To use modifications when using the pass–run option, you and your quarterback must know about the following:

Rules

You and your players need to know about several main rules when using the pass–run option:

REMINDER!

You and your players must understand the team strategy and game plan and assess the pass–run option based on those plans and the situation at hand. Make sure that you and your players consider the questions on page 172.

- The quarterback must have a sense of where the line of scrimmage is because he cannot throw the ball forward unless he is behind the line. The longer he delays before throwing the ball, the closer he will probably be to the line of scrimmage, which is why he must think pass first on any pass–run option.

- Defenders cannot hold or grab receivers when the ball is in the air. If the quarterback sees that a defender who is out of position is in contact with a receiver, he should immediately pass the ball to that receiver to draw a pass interference or holding penalty on the defense.

- All the flow on this play is in the same direction toward one of the sidelines. The quarterback who chooses to run should continue to run in that direction because if he tries to cut back, he will put his teammates in a position where they might illegally block a defender in the back.

- Receivers cannot block downfield on a pass play. Receivers on this type of play must learn to use restraint before blocking. They must be sure that the quarterback is not going to throw the ball to a teammate before they start to block anyone downfield. The quarterback can help prevent this penalty by being decisive by throwing early and on time or not at all.

Physical Playing Conditions

The physical playing conditions significantly affect the game. Thus, you and your players must pay attention to the following physical conditions when using the pass–run option:

- On a wet or slippery field, the quarterback has to be cautious with his footwork as he starts this play, because if he slips and falls trying to get out of the pocket quickly, the play will be over before it even starts!

- If the ball is wet and difficult to handle, the quarterback might choose the option of running with the ball more often than he would if the ball were dry.

- If the wind is blowing hard from behind him, the quarterback must understand that its force, combined with his momentum as he runs, will push the ball away from the receiver. Conversely, if the wind is blowing toward the quarterback, he will have to lead his receiver to the outside.

Strengths and Weaknesses of Opponents

You and your quarterback must account for your opponent's strengths and weaknesses to know how to use the pass–run option properly. Consider the following about your opponents:

- How good are the opponent's contain players (usually the defensive ends)? A defense that has a great player at defensive end or a scheme in which the defensive end plays very wide and moves laterally quickly will make it difficult for the quarterback to get to the perimeter, in effect stopping the play before it starts.

(continued)

- How often does the opponent blitz from the outside? When an opponent frequently uses a blitz off the edge (from outside the defensive end toward the pocket), the pass–run option is a dangerous play to call. Use scouting reports and game-day charts to identify when the blitz is least likely and call this play only in those situations.

- How good is the opponent's pass rush? If your opponent has an outstanding front four (the two defensive tackles and the two defensive ends) or if they frequently blitz the inside linebackers up the middle in passing situations, drop-back passing might be difficult. Attacking the perimeter with the pass–run option is a good way to get the passer away from the rush and give him a chance to be successful passing the ball.

- What kind of coverage does the opponent play? When an opponent plays a zone defense and the players are disciplined to stay home—that is, stay in the portion of the field that they are assigned to defend—they are tougher to attack with this type of play because play fakes do not pull them out of position and sprintouts cannot outflank them. But if the opponent plays man-to-man defense, the offense can clear an area for a sprintout or bootleg by running a receiver on that side down or across the field as a decoy, knowing that his defender will chase him. Furthermore, if a defender takes his eyes off his man for just a moment at the beginning of the play and watches the play fake, the receiver he's assigned to cover can often get good separation from that defender and get open.

- How quick and aggressive is the opponent's defense? Teams that react quickly to the first thing that they see on offense are vulnerable to misdirection plays that start with a play fake one way and end up with the quarterback attacking the perimeter in the other direction.

Self-Knowledge

Besides being aware of your opponent's abilities, you and your quarterback need to know about your own team's strength and weaknesses. When considering using the pass–run option, you and your team should be aware of the following:

- What kind of athlete is your quarterback? If your quarterback is quick and versatile, you will want to use those skills by designing plays in which he can attack the perimeter and incorporate the threat of the run with the passing game. He must have enough speed to outrun the inside defenders, be able to throw the ball on the run to both the left and the right, be able to find defenders and make good decisions while on the run, and be able to protect the ball when he carries it and gain enough yards as a runner to hurt the defense.

- How solid is your pass protection? If the offensive line is undersized or inexperienced, protecting the quarterback in a drop-back passing game may be difficult. In those situations, a perimeter attack with sprintouts and bootlegs would be a good strategy. On the other hand, if the offensive line does a good job of pass protection in the drop-back passing game, the quarterback can throw more passes from the pocket, which allows you to attack the entire field with your passing game instead of limiting yourself to half the field with the perimeter passing game.

- Can your running backs block the defensive ends? On both the sprintout and the bootleg, a key block is the running back against the defensive end. The play has a slim chance to be successful unless the running back can outflank the defensive end and pin him inside, allowing the quarterback to break contain and attack the perimeter. A good play-action fake by the other running back can help the blocking back carry out his assignment, and you can help the blocker by putting him in motion or aligning him in an offset position where he has a better chance to establish outside position.

Decision-Making Guidelines

When deciding how to gain the best advantage when using the pass–run option, you and your quarterback should consider the previous information and the following guidelines:

- The quarterback should never attempt to throw the ball back across his body to a receiver, even if the receiver is open. This pass is too dangerous because the quarterback cannot see all the potential defenders and cannot throw the ball with enough velocity or accuracy to ensure that it will arrive safely.

- If the first two receivers are not open, the quarterback must resist the temptation to ad lib, trying to find a third or fourth receiver coming in his direction from the other side of the formation. Throwing back into the middle of the field while running toward the sideline is extremely difficult, and the chances for a tipped ball or an interception are high. The best choice is to run for a few yards, huddle up and call the next play!

- Play-action bootlegs and sprintout passes are good calls in short-yardage situations when the defense is packed in with many defenders close to the nucleus and up on the line of scrimmage, because the quarterback has a good chance of getting outside.

- Offensive players must understand that on pass–run option plays, the pass game attacks only one-half or one-third of the field. The play has to be quick and decisive because the longer the play lasts, the more crowded the field becomes in the area where the quarterback needs to throw the ball.

At a Glance

The following parts of the text offer additional information on the pass–run option.

Scramble

The scramble is an ad lib situation in which the offensive skill players are trying to make something out of nothing by completing a pass when exact timing and precise routes are no longer available. In reality, the rules for a scramble situation are just general guidelines that can help offensive players see each other, anticipate where to go and connect on the pass. For example, assume that the quarterback has dropped back to pass, the receivers have run their assigned routes but the protection breaks down. The quarterback must scramble out of the pocket and begins running left or right away from the pursuing defenders.

⚠ WATCH OUT!

The following circumstances may distract your quarterback:

- Looking at the chasing defenders who initially were the pass rushers. The quarterback must keep his eyes downfield looking for possible receivers.

- Reversing direction after he has escaped the pocket. After the quarterback gets out of the pocket, he should sprint toward the sideline and never turn back. He can't see all the pursuing defenders, so when he reverses direction he is at risk of taking a blindside hit and he stands a good chance of losing more yardage on the play if he gives ground.

READING THE SITUATION

How do you and your players gain the best advantage when faced with a scramble? Teach your players to do the following:

- The quarterback should always look deep first to see if a defensive player has lost track of his receiver. Next, he should look at the intermediate level for a receiver running parallel to him. Finally, he should look to the sideline for a player waiting for a short escape or check-down type of pass.

- Receivers should initially stay at the level of their route and run parallel to the line of scrimmage in the direction that the quarterback is running.

- Any receiver who is near the sideline or who gets close to the sideline after running parallel to the quarterback across the field should turn upfield and see if a defender stays with him.

- If the defenders stay with every receiver as those receivers reach the sideline and turn upfield, the quarterback should tuck the ball and run.

- Trying to make too big a play. The scramble situation is a broken play, and the quarterback must realize that any yards gained are a bonus, considering the situation. His primary focus should be to get the ball back to the original line of scrimmage, even if that means throwing the ball away for an incomplete pass or tucking the ball and running it.

ACQUIRING THE APPROPRIATE KNOWLEDGE

To use modifications when faced with a scramble, you and your players must know about the following:

Rules

You and your players need to know several main rules when facing the scramble:

- The quarterback needs to keep a sense of where the line of scrimmage is because he will incur a significant penalty if he throws a forward pass after he crosses that line. He is better off to take a sack or a short gain, or throw the ball away, than to throw a forward pass when he is past the line of scrimmage.

- Defenders cannot hold or grab receivers when the ball is in the air. If the quarterback sees that a defender who is out of position is in contact with a receiver, he should immediately pass the ball to that receiver to draw a pass interference or holding penalty on the defense.

REMINDER!

You and your players must understand the team strategy and game plan and assess the scramble based on those plans and the situation at hand. Make sure that you and your players consider the questions on page 172.

- All the flow on this play is in the same direction toward one of the sidelines. The quarterback who chooses to run should continue to run in that direction because if he tries to cut back he will put his teammates in a position where they might illegally block a defender in the back.

- Receivers cannot block downfield on a pass play. Receivers on this type of play must learn to use restraint before blocking. They must be sure that the quarterback is not going to throw the ball to a teammate before they start to block anyone downfield. The quarterback can help prevent this penalty by being decisive by throwing early and on time or not at all.

Physical Playing Conditions

The physical playing conditions significantly affect the game. Thus, you and your players must pay attention to the following physical conditions when facing a scramble:

- On a wet or slippery field, the quarterback has to be cautious with his footwork as he starts to scramble, because if he slips and falls trying to get out of the pocket quickly, the play will be over before it even starts!

- If the ball is wet and difficult to handle, the quarterback might choose the option of running with the ball more often than he would if the ball were dry.

- If the wind is blowing hard from behind him, the quarterback must understand that its force, combined with his momentum as he runs, will push the ball away from the receiver. Conversely, if the wind is blowing toward the quarterback, he will have to lead his receiver to the outside.

Strengths and Weaknesses of Opponents

You and your players must account for your opponent's strengths and weaknesses to know how to react in a scramble situation. Consider the following about your opponents:

- How disciplined is the opponent's pass rush? Some opponents work consistently to keep the quarterback in the pocket, requiring their defensive ends to play wide and their defensive tackles to rush in their lanes with one on each side of the center. Although this type of opponent might record fewer sacks, they rarely allow the quarterback to scramble and make a big play.

- How aggressive is the opponent's defense? Some overaggressive opponents focus almost solely on hitting the quarterback. Often, these defenses leave a lane open for the quarterback to get out of the pocket and scramble to find receivers. Your team must be prepared to make good plays in this ad lib situation by practicing the scramble.

- How do the defensive backs react when the quarterback scrambles? At times, you may face defensive backs who are not disciplined when the quarterback leaves the pocket.

(continued)

When this type of defensive back sees the quarterback run, he forgets about his receiver and reacts toward the quarterback to tackle him, even when the quarterback is still behind the line of scrimmage. This reaction is dangerous for the defense, because the receiver assigned to that defensive back, or to his zone area, can drift down the field and be wide open. And, if the quarterback scrambles properly, he will find him.

Self-Knowledge

Besides being aware of your opponent's abilities, you and your players need to know about your own team's strengths and weaknesses. When considering the scramble, you and your team should be aware of the following:

- What kind of athlete is your quarterback? If the quarterback runs well, the scramble can be an effective play because he can use his athletic ability. If the quarterback is slow or not athletic, he should stay in the pocket longer, perhaps looking to pass to a check-down receiver instead of taking off on a scramble.

- How good is your pass protection? If the pass protection has a tendency to break down from time to time, have the offense rehearse the scramble situation frequently so that they know how to react. If the pass protection is consistent and solid, you may not have to practice the scramble situation as often.

Decision-Making Guidelines

When deciding how to gain the best advantage when facing a scramble situation, you and your players should consider the previous information as well as the following guidelines:

- Any team that passes frequently will face the scramble situation a few times each game. Having set rules for the quarterback and receivers to follow will help the offense make a few plays in this situation during the season. Script this situation into practice a few times each week so that all players can rehearse their reactions when the quarterback really does have to scramble. Set up the situation by telling only the quarterback about the play. Don't tell the receivers or defensive players what is coming. Even if the quarterback has pass protection, he escapes the pocket and initiates a scramble situation. With repetition, the scramble can become a good play! (In addition, your defense will learn how to react and stop big plays in scramble situations.)

- Set up rules for the quarterback in the scramble situation, such as the following: Never throw into a crowd, never throw back into the middle of the field, don't take a chance on the deep throw if a run can produce positive yardage (especially in third-and-short or third and medium situations!), never stop running and keep two hands on the football as long and as often as possible.

- Work with the receivers so that they become more visible to the quarterback. You have to coach backside receivers to hustle in the scramble situation, to help them believe that a broken play can have a good outcome. They must sprint across the field to get into the quarterback's field of vision. Teach frontside receivers who reach the sideline to raise a hand into the air when they turn to go deep, so that the quarterback can see them and know that they are going deep.

Running to the Gap

Running plays in football are of two basic types—gap plays and zone plays. On gap plays, the blocking scheme is designed to open a hole at a specific gap in the defense and the ball carrier's only chance for positive yardage is to run to the gap because unblocked defenders will be on both sides of that gap (zone plays will be discussed in the following skill, "Running to Daylight," on page 191). Gap running plays are vital for teams that want to play power football, with a strong running game that minimizes turnovers and allows the offense to keep the ball away from the opposing team. The most common gap plays are, from inside out, trap, isolation, off-tackle or power, and counter (see examples of these plays in Appendix B on page 357).

⚠ WATCH OUT!

The following circumstances may distract your players:

- Many players on both sides of the ball will be in front of the runner. The ball carrier must learn to ignore players, on both offense and defense, who are not the key blockers for the play.

- The line play may become so congested as the play starts that the runner may not believe that any running room will be available at the assigned gap. He must ignore the inclination to bounce the play outside or to cut back on the play. He must trust that the blocking scheme will open up a hole for him by the time he gets there.

- The linemen must understand that they also have no option to ad lib on these plays. If the lineman's assignment is to down block, or to kick out, he must execute that block to the best of his ability regardless of the technique or skills of the defender. The lineman must block aggressively, with power and great technique, knowing that the ball carrier is depending on him to open up a hole.

READING THE SITUATION

How do you and your players gain the best advantage when running to the gap? Teach your running back to do the following:

- Learn who the key blocker(s) is on each gap play, find him and get in position to follow his block through the hole.

- Take time to use proper footwork, secure the ball and hit the hole immediately after the key blocker(s) execute their blocks. At the same time, the runner cannot be late because his timing must be in sync with his blocker(s).

- Understand that sometimes the hole through the assigned gap may not be large, especially in short-yardage and goal-line situations. The ball carrier must lower his pads, place two hands on the ball and cram it into the correct gap, running with power and determination not looking for a new place to run but trying to gain as much yardage as possible at the assigned gap.

ACQUIRING THE APPROPRIATE KNOWLEDGE

To use modifications when running to the gap, you and your players must know about the following:

Rules

You and your players need to know several main rules when running to the gap:

- If a ball carrier does not run to the correct gap, he may set up his teammates for a penalty such as holding. For example, if the ball carrier bounces a gap play outside a kickout

(continued)

REMINDER!

You and your players must understand the team strategy and game plan and assess running to the gap based on those plans and the situation at hand. Make sure that you and your players consider the questions on page 172.

block, the defender being kicked out is now in position to run freely to the ball carrier, and the blocker might be tempted to stop him by grabbing him.

o Players sometimes have a tendency to tense up before gap plays, especially in crucial short-yardage and goal-line situations, because they know that the block and the run will require terrific effort, great power and a huge collision. Consequently, players may be more likely to jump offside or false start on these plays. Teach the quarterback to use a short cadence or the same snap count every time in these situations to minimize the risk of a penalty.

Physical Playing Conditions

The physical playing conditions affect the game significantly. Thus, you and your players must pay attention to the following physical conditions when running to the gap:

o Gap plays are a good strategy when the field is wet or slippery because defenders have difficulty holding their position on a sloppy field.

o Gap plays are also a good strategy when the ball is wet because the ball handling on these plays is simple and safe (no options, no pitches, no passes).

o Gap plays are unaffected by high winds, bright sun or other weather considerations.

Strengths and Weaknesses of Opponents

You and your players must account for your opponent's strengths and weaknesses to know how to run to the gap properly. Consider the following about your opponents:

o How strong are the opponent's line and linebackers? Big, strong defenders can make gap plays tough to run. Offensive blockers cannot move these defenders much, and sometimes the hole to run through is not large. Smaller, quicker defenders sometimes have trouble stacking up and stopping correctly run gap plays. If the offense is big and strong and the defense is small and quick, use the gap attack.

o How do the defensive linemen play trap blocks and kickout blocks? Opponents who defend gap plays by spilling or wrong shouldering the blockers (see "Reacting When Unblocked" on page 232 and "Choosing to Spill or Squeeze" on page 241 for more information) can close the gap successfully and virtually force the running back to bounce the play, contrary to all his teaching, because there just isn't any place to run. You must scout your opponents on this important point and consider running fewer gap plays against teams who effectively teach the spill technique.

o Do opponents extensively use the squeeze technique? Opponents who squeeze traps, powers and counters by taking on blockers with the inside shoulder and keeping the outside arm free are vulnerable to gap plays because the player squeezing the play has a tough assignment trying to close the gap completely. Coaches who see their opponent using this technique should schedule frequent use of gap plays in the game plan.

o How often does the opponent blitz their linebackers or run line games (slants and angles) with their defensive line? Gap plays can be very effective against blitzing, slanting and moving defenses because the blockers simply block an area, or gap, and they can adjust to most defensive movement.

Self-Knowledge

Besides being aware of your opponent's abilities, you and your players need to know about your own team's strengths and weaknesses. When considering running to the gap, you and your team should be aware of the following:

o How powerful is the offensive line? For gap plays to be effective, offensive blockers have to be strong and physical on their down blocks and on the traps and kickouts. Notice that the key words here are *strong, physical* and *powerful*, not *big*. The line does not have to be big if they play with low pad level, great aggressiveness and good technique on the blocks. Sometimes big linemen are not powerful blockers if they have sluggish feet or play with their pad level too high.

o How powerful are the primary running backs? For an offense to be effective in running to the gap, the ball carriers have to be disciplined, strong and powerful. They must be able to run hard through a tight space and resist the urge to bounce or cut back. Again, the back does not necessarily have to be big to be a good gap runner. If he is determined, understands the concept and runs with power, he'll be effective.

o Is power the only factor to consider in running a gap play? Although power is still the most important element for success on gap plays, you should assess your linemen and running backs in the areas of timing and finesse as well. Great gap running backs learn to set up the kickout block by initially threatening a wider course, causing the defender to loosen his position slightly, before the kickout block occurs and the ball carrier runs through the resulting gap. Linemen and tight ends who execute down blocks with excellent technique, pinning their defenders inside and not allowing any penetration across the line of scrimmage, give the gap play a good chance for success by setting a solid inside wall. Guards who pull on a good course and get the head inside the defender on traps and kickouts make trap plays and counters effective.

o Are wide receivers useless on gap plays? The defender who usually makes the tackle on a well-executed gap play is the safety because the blocking scheme should have accounted for all defensive linemen and linebackers. You should design blocking assignments for the wide receivers to block the safeties on gap plays, using motion or short splits to get them in better position to make those blocks.

Decision-Making Guidelines

When deciding how to gain the best advantage when running to the gap, you and your players should consider the previous information as well as the following guidelines:

o The gap running play fits perfectly with a conservative strategy in short-yardage and goal-line situations. The plan is to execute a power running play against a defense that probably anticipates that running play, but with great execution and attention to detail, the offense can be successful. The offense is trying to win with execution, not trick the defense. The back has to fit into this concept by cramming the ball into the correct gap even if the play is well defended.

o If a running back bounces or cuts back a gap play, he stands a good chance of losing yardage or gaining nothing, a result that seriously hampers the conservative offense's chances to sustain the drive. This type of offense needs to average 3 or 4 yards per play and can't afford to have negative-yardage or zero-yardage plays.

o Ball security is crucial. Offenses that use gap plays want to keep the ball away from the other team's offense for extended periods. One lost fumble in a game for this kind of offense would be too many fumbles, because, of course, the drive would be over and the

(continued)

At a Glance

The following parts of the text offer additional information on running to the gap.

other team would immediately get the ball. Gap runners are always running in traffic with lots of hands trying to pry the ball loose. You must insist on proper hand and elbow position (see "Ball Security" on page 29) to minimize the chances for fumbles.

○ You must constantly assess the defensive alignment to every formation because if the defense outnumbers the offense, the gap plays will have limited success over the entire game. Consider the number of blockers available on offense and the number of defenders in the nucleus of the defensive alignment. If the defense has more players than the offense does, the offense needs to do something to loosen up the defense, such as throwing some play-action passes over the heads of the safeties, spreading out the formation with three or four wide receivers or calling a bootleg or sprintout play. After the defense expands to cover those types of plays, the gap running game has a better chance to be successful.

Running to Daylight

The two basic types of running plays in football are gap plays and zone plays. As we learned, "Running to the Gap" on page 187, on gap plays the blocking scheme is designed to open a hole at a specific gap in the defense. The ball carrier's only chance for positive yardage is to run to the gap because unblocked defenders will be on both sides of that gap. On zone plays, however, all the offensive linemen block in the same direction, trying to get the defense moving laterally. The ball carrier has the freedom to run to daylight wherever he can find a seam.

Zone running plays take advantage of a running back who is quick, decisive and instinctive. When running to daylight, he takes the handoff and initially runs toward a specific gap in the defense (called his aiming point), but unlike with a gap play, he does not have to take the ball through that gap. If the gap at his aiming point is open (called a "cram"), he can run there, of course, but he is allowed, and encouraged, either to bounce the play outside if the defense is not reacting quickly down the line or to cut back behind the original aiming point if the defense is flowing quickly down the line. See examples of zone plays in Appendix C on page 361.

⚠ WATCH OUT!

The following circumstances may distract your players:

- Focusing on the entire line and all the blocks. The running back must focus on the block at his aiming point only, ignoring all other blocks, to decide whether he should run straight through his gap, bounce outside, or cut back.

- Looking at the quarterback, who is handing him the ball. The running back must keep his eyes on the blocks at his aiming point at all times or he will be unable to make a good read. He must have confidence that the quarterback will get him the ball!

READING THE SITUATION

How do you and your players gain the best advantage when running to daylight? Teach your players to do the following:

- Focus initially on the block at the point of attack. Every zone play has an aiming point and an initial block to read.

- After the initial read, rely more on instinct than on a focused read of a specific block. After the ball carrier chooses to bounce or cut back, the play happens too quickly for him to pick up a specific second block. Instead, he has to sense where the daylight is and quickly decide how far to bounce, or how far to cut back, before he gets vertical and takes the ball directly down the field.

- Be patient. The great zone running backs don't run at top speed from the moment the ball is snapped. They exercise restraint and don't cut back or bounce too early, stretching the play and reading the flow of the defense. Once the ball carrier attacks the line of scrimmage, he should still keep his options open for his cuts until he gets to the heels of the offensive linemen.

ACQUIRING THE APPROPRIATE KNOWLEDGE

To use modifications when running to daylight, you and your players must know about the following:

Rules

You and your players need to know several main rules when running to daylight:

(continued)

REMINDER!

You and your players must understand the team strategy and game plan and assess running to daylight based on those plans and the situation at hand. Make sure that you and your players consider the questions on page 172.

- The ball carrier should never bounce a zone play outside an attempted reach block if the defender has not been reached. If the ball carrier goes outside in this situation, the unreached defender will be free to work down the line to make the tackle, and the blocker may be tempted to grab him or hold him to prevent him from making the play.

- The ball carrier must be decisive. If he hesitates in the backfield, the offensive linemen might lose contact on their blocks and resort to grabbing or holding to prevent the defenders from making a play. The ball carrier must make his read, make his decision and then go for it with no second thoughts!

- Because combination blocks are frequently used on zone running plays, players must understand the rules prohibiting chop blocks (high–low contact by two offensive players on one defender).

Physical Playing Conditions

The physical playing conditions significantly affect the game. Thus, you and your players must pay attention to the following physical conditions when running to daylight:

- Wet or slippery field conditions do not favor the running back, because he would like to make a dramatic cutback or bounce on a zone play. On a slippery field, running backs must take shorter, more controlled steps on their cuts to avoid slipping to the ground and ending the play prematurely.

- A wet football is always more likely to be fumbled than a dry one. The quarterback must be focused and cautious on his handoff, and the running back should take extra caution to secure the ball, especially as he approaches the line of scrimmage.

Strengths and Weaknesses of Opponents

You and your players must account for your opponent's strengths and weaknesses to know how to run to daylight properly. Consider the following about your opponents:

- How well does the opponent play against the reach block? Opponents who are quick and disciplined in defending reach blocks make zone plays difficult. If every defensive player maintains his gap responsibility (for example, no one gets reached), the ball carrier may end up being flattened off after cutting back and might not find much daylight.

- How does the number of offensive blockers compare to the number of defenders in the nucleus? Opponents who overload against the run can fill all the gaps and make it tough for the ball carrier to find daylight. The offense must then use play-action passes, spread formations or perimeter attack plays like sprintouts to loosen up the defense and give the running game a chance to be successful.

- Are any gaps undefended? Opponents that deploy to stop the pass sometimes end up with five defenders to cover six gaps, or seven defenders to cover eight gaps, which means that one of them is going to have the task of defending two gaps. A well-executed zone play has the flexibility that allows the running back to see where the open gap is after the play starts.

- Is the opponent gap sound when deploying line movement or stunts? Opponents who are aggressive and use line games and stunts are not always gap sound (one player in each gap) on defense. This circumstance gives the offense an opportunity for a big play. Your team won't always know before the snap which gap the defense is going to leave open, but by giving the ball carrier the option to run to daylight, he can bounce or cut back to find the open gap after the play starts. In contrast, when the ball carrier is running to the gap, as described on page 187, a gap may be open but the ball carrier may never get there because he has to run to a predetermined gap.

Self-Knowledge

Besides being aware of your opponent's abilities, you and your players need to know about your own team's strengths and weaknesses. You and your team should be aware of the following when running to daylight:

○ How good are the linemen at executing reach blocks and combination blocks?

○ Is the ball carrier able to read the initial block, or does he appear to be guessing? Studying tapes from practice and games shot from behind the backfield, called a tight shot or an end zone shot, will help both you and the player answer this question.

○ Can the ball carrier be patient and let the play develop before making his cut? Patience is key for the ball carrier. He should continue to run at his aiming point until he is almost on the heels of his blocker there before deciding whether to bounce, stay on course or cut back.

○ Is the ball carrier decisive, accelerating with a burst of speed when he makes his cut?

At a Glance

The following parts of the text offer additional information on running to daylight.

Ball Security	p. 29
Reach Block	p. 64
Cutoff Block	p. 67
Double-Team Block	p. 73
Running to the Gap	p. 187
Evading Tacklers	p. 194

Decision-Making Guidelines

When deciding how to gain the best advantage when running to daylight, you and your players should consider the previous information as well as the following guidelines:

○ The game plan relies on players who are flexible and patient. Sometimes the running back will make a wrong decision and be stopped, but a good player who gets enough opportunities will turn some of the plays into big gainers.

○ Zone running plays are not as effective as power or gap plays in short-yardage and goal-line situations because the defense stacks its alignment in those situations. They put a player in every gap, and the ball carrier doesn't have much daylight. At times, your team will need to use power instead of finesse to gain those tough yards.

○ The ball carrier must focus on the blocker at his aiming point to make that first crucial decision on whether to take the ball through that gap. If the blocker at the aiming point has successfully reached (see "Reach Block" on page 64) his defender, the ball carrier should bounce the play outside. If the defender has avoided being reached, he has probably worked laterally down the line toward the outside, and the running back should either stay on course ("cram") or cut back, depending on the flow of the backside defenders. (The instinctive part of the play ensues here. The ball carrier might cut back one or two or three gaps, depending on the defensive reactions and whether the backside cutoff blocks by the offensive line were successful.)

○ The ball carrier should never cut back or bounce too early. For a cutback to work, the defenders must have flowed laterally down the line, working to defeat reach blocks and prevent the play from bouncing outside. If the ball carrier cuts back too early, the defense will not have flowed far and they will be able to react to the cutback. Before cutting back, the ball carrier must threaten the bounce and the path through the initial aiming point on every zone play to get the defense moving laterally.

○ When in doubt, the ball carrier should run north and south instead of toward the sideline. He should end every play with the effort to get vertical and gain positive yards.

Any running back should be able to run through a gaping hole to gain yards, but the best running backs can evade tacklers. This skill, also known as making someone miss, may involve running through an arm tackle, faking a cut and breaking away in the opposite direction, or it may simply entail lowering the pads and fighting for positive yards (see "Understanding Plus Yards" on page 195). Assume that the ball carrier has taken the handoff, executed his basic read and found some room to run. A defender approaches. In this one-on-one situation between the running back and the defender, can the running back make him miss?

 **WATCH OUT!**

The following circumstances may distract your players:

- Slowing down or allowing the defender to administer all the contact. The running back must attack the tackler with contact (low pads, high knees) or deception (fakes, false steps).

- Focusing on players chasing the play. The running back should focus on the primary threat, the opponent who is going to get to him first!

- Thinking too much. Evading a tackler in a live situation must be an instinctive play that has been rehearsed in drills and practice but can't be planned when it happens.

READING THE SITUATION

How do you and your players gain the best advantage when evading tacklers? Teach your running backs to do the following:

- Focus attention on the first possible tackler.
- Be aware that ball security is always paramount. Keep the ball in the outside arm, away from the tackler.
- Accurately judge the tackler's angle and speed. If he is gaining and has the angle to make contact, make a move. Slow down and then speed up again, or plant and try to cut behind him.
- Lower the pads if the tackler is closing fast and contact is imminent.
- Pump the legs and drive the knees hard at contact.
- Take on half a man by using the free arm and shoulder away from the ball to rip a forearm blow through the near shoulder of the tackler or to straight-arm the tackler to keep him away.

ACQUIRING THE APPROPRIATE KNOWLEDGE

To use modifications when evading tacklers, you and your players must know about the following:

Rules

You and your players need to know several main rules when eluding tacklers:

- The ball carrier cannot hurdle, or attempt to jump over, a defender who is on his feet. The ball carrier can jump over prone defenders but not a defender who is in position to attempt a tackle.
- Neither the ball carrier nor the tackler can grab the facemask.

- The tackler cannot trip the ball carrier to bring him down.

Physical Playing Conditions

The physical playing conditions significantly affect the game. Thus, you and your players must pay attention to the following physical conditions when eluding tacklers:

- Sharp cuts and fakes are difficult on a wet or slippery field because the ball carrier is likely to lose his footing and fall down.

- Maintaining ball security is more difficult with a wet ball. If the ball is wet, the ball carrier must concentrate on wrapping two arms around the football when contact is imminent.

REMINDER!

You and your players must understand the team strategy and game plan and assess the players' abilities to evade tacklers based on those plans and the situation at hand. Make sure that you and your players consider the questions on page 172.

Strengths and Weaknesses of Opponents

You and your players must account for your opponent's strengths and weaknesses to know how to evade tacklers properly. Consider the following about your opponents:

- How sound is your opponent's tackling technique? Some opponents have great tacklers. If your opponent dominates in the open field, run more power plays and don't rely so much on the running back to make the big play. If your opponent misses open-field tackles frequently, use short passes and run-to-daylight plays to give your running back as many one-on-one opportunities as possible.

- How aggressive are the defenders? If they are looking for the big hit with overaggressive play, the running back can use a stop-and-go or stutter step to make them miss.

- How fast are the linebackers and defensive backs? If they are too fast to outrun, the running back can use power (low pads and leg drive) and the stiff arm to make them miss.

Self-Knowledge

Besides being aware of your opponent's abilities, you and your players need to know about your own team's strengths and weaknesses. You and your team should be aware of the following when evading tacklers:

- How powerful are the running backs in short-yardage situations? Use backs who play with low pad level and great leg drive to gain yards on these plays.

- Can the running backs evade tacklers while running at full speed and maintaining ball security? Be sure that the ball carrier continues to squeeze the elbow on the ball, keeping it in contact with his side, when he is near any potential tackler.

UNDERSTANDING PLUS YARDS

Emphasize the concept of positive, or plus yards, in evaluating running backs. Plus yards are all those yards that the running back gains after he encounters the first possible tackler. If a running back breaks through a gaping hole and runs 30 yards uncontested for a touchdown, he would get 0 plus yards on that play. If he encounters a safety 3 yards down the field after breaking through a hole, runs over him and drags him for a 7-yard gain on the play, he would have 4 plus yards. If he breaks outside, fakes out the cornerback and goes 80 yards for a touchdown, he would have 80 plus yards. This concept separates the better running backs from the others. It also recognizes that running backs use different styles to make defenders miss. You can easily calculate plus yards from game and scrimmage tapes.

(continued)

- Do the running backs use a variety of techniques to evade tacklers, or do they use the same technique all the time?

Decision-Making Guidelines

When deciding how to gain the best advantage when evading tacklers, you and your players should consider the previous information as well as the following guidelines:

- Running backs should work on an arsenal of moves but not plan which one to use. They must be instinctive.
- Breaking a tackle is as good as faking someone out and happens more often. Running backs should learn to play with low pads and high knees, and use the free arm effectively.
- They should accelerate, not decelerate, at the moment of contact.
- Coaches should create situations to give elusive running backs opportunities to get into the open field where they can make defenders miss and make a big play. The offensive team may make more yards on a swing pass or screen pass that travels just a few yards than on a long pass that travels far downfield if the running back who catches the short pass can make defenders miss.
- Remind players that they are carrying the most important object on the field: the ball. They should be sure that they have it in their possession when the play ends.

Picking Up the Blitz

In many pass protection schemes, a running back is assigned to block a specific defender, usually a linebacker, if that defender blitzes (rushes the quarterback). The running back picks up the blitz by stepping up and blocking his assigned defender when that defender rushes the quarterback. (Occasionally other players, such as an uncovered lineman or a tight end, could have the assignment of picking up a blitz. Tight ends may also pick up a blitzing defender in some pass protection schemes, even though the tight end is also an eligible receiver). If the assigned defender drops into pass coverage, however, the running back releases out of the backfield and runs a pass route. This release is called a check release because the running back checks the defender first and then releases if that defender does not blitz. Essentially, the running back must understand that he will be either a blocker or a pass receiver on the play, depending on the defense's action.

Note: A pass protection scheme may sometimes ask a running back to check two defenders before releasing, but in this chapter, we will describe an assignment in which he has just one defender to check.

⚠ WATCH OUT!

The following circumstances may distract your running back:

o Watching defensive players other than the one assigned to him. The running back is responsible for blocking only one specific defensive player. Other offensive players have assignments to block the other defensive players who rush the quarterback, so the running back doesn't have to worry about them. He must look past those players, find the man assigned to him and determine whether he is blitzing.

o Getting in the way of the quarterback. If the running back is lined up directly behind the center, he must step out of the path of the quarterback who is dropping back while at the same time finding and reading his defender.

o Finding his way out of the backfield. By the time the running back checks his defender and decides that he can release out of the backfield, the linemen will be blocking their defenders. The running back must find an opening, almost as he would if he were running with the ball, and get out of the backfield without interfering with the pass protection of the linemen.

o Being in a hurry to run the pass route. The running back must remember his priorities—block first, then get out of the backfield to run his route. If he starts to run the route and then sees his defender blitzing, the steps he has already taken might prevent him from being able to get in position to block the blitz.

READING THE SITUATION

How do you and your players gain the best advantage when picking up the blitz? Teach your players to do the following:

- Always know which defender is assigned to them.

- Find the assigned defender before the play starts to make it easier to locate that defender once the play begins.

- Assume that the assigned defender will rush the passer. Your players must be prepared for the pass block every time; the blitz must never surprise them.

- Step up in the pocket to clear out the area where the quarterback needs to be to drop back and throw the ball.

(continued)

REMINDER!

You and your players must understand the team strategy and game plan and assess picking up the blitz based on those plans and the situation at hand. Make sure that you and your players consider the questions on page 172.

ACQUIRING THE APPROPRIATE KNOWLEDGE

To use modifications when picking up the blitz, you and your players must know about the following:

Rules

You and your players need to know several main rules when picking up the blitz:

- Pass blockers cannot grab pass rushers. Pass blockers must keep the hands inside the frame of the pass rusher's body.
- Depending on the rules in various states, blocking the blitzing defender below the waist (or chop blocking him) may be illegal. Check with your local state high school football association about this rule.

Physical Playing Conditions

The physical playing conditions significantly affect the game. Thus, you and your players must pay attention to the following physical conditions when picking up the blitz:

- If the field is wet and slippery, players must use short, choppy steps to navigate out of the backfield.

Strengths and Weaknesses of Opponents

You and your players must account for your opponent's strengths and weaknesses to know how to pick up the blitz properly. Consider the following about your opponents:

- What kind of matchup does the pass protection scheme create? Be careful not to match your running back against a much bigger defender.
- How often will you lose your back from your pass game? If your opponent blitzes often, your running back may have few chances to check release into his pass routes. If the opponent blitzes infrequently, however, the check release is a safe and effective way to protect the quarterback and still get five receivers out into the pass patterns.
- How deceptive are the opponent's blitzes? If the linebackers move around a lot and blitz from several different alignments, the scheme of assigning one of them to the running back is a good tactic because the running back is set off the line and will have time to find and block his linebacker if he does blitz.
- How fast are the defensive ends, and how do they match up with your tackles? If an offensive tackle can't block a quick defensive end, you could assign the running back to that defensive end. The running back would not have many chances to check release, but he might be able to block the pass rush from his backfield position.

Self-Knowledge

Besides being aware of your opponent's abilities, you and your players must know about your own team's strengths and weaknesses. When considering picking up the blitz, you and your team should be aware of the following:

○ How effective are the running backs as blockers? A running back must have physical strength and aggressiveness to stand up against a defender approaching at full speed on a blitz.

○ How quickly will the running back be able to react to an elusive maneuver by the blitzing defender?

○ Is this assignment too complex for the running back to master?

○ Does the passing game benefit from getting all five receivers out in the patterns? If not, you could eliminate the check release and keep the running back in the backfield on every pass play to help with pass protection.

At a Glance

The following parts of the text offer additional information on picking up the blitz.

Pass Protection	p. 85
Pass Rush	p. 110
Blitzing	p. 128
Playing the Long-Yardage Situation	p. 260

Decision-Making Guidelines

When deciding how to gain the best advantage when picking up a blitz, you and your players should consider the previous information as well as the following guidelines:

○ Players should locate the assigned defender early and assume that he is going to blitz.

○ Players should step up and attack the defender when he blitzes.

○ Players should make a quick decision and find their way out of the backfield into the route so that they can be part of the passing game if the defender does not blitz.

○ Players must stay out of the quarterback's way!

Crossing Route Adjustments

On a play that calls for the receiver to run a crossing route, such as a shallow cross (5 to 7 yards) or a dig (15 to 17 yards), the receiver runs the stem of his route while at the same time observing the defense to see whether the coverage is man or zone. If a defender picks up the receiver using man coverage, the receiver reaches the break point for the route, starts across the field and keeps running to get open. If the defense drops back into zone coverage, the receiver reaches the break point for the route, starts across the field and finds an opening at the appropriate depth and location on the field, between two defenders, where he stops and faces the quarterback, or "sits down," with his hands in position to catch the ball. In short, your receiver must be able to determine whether the coverage on the crossing route is man or zone and react accordingly.

⚠ WATCH OUT!

The following circumstances may distract your receivers:

- Focusing only on the defender over him. After checking the initial steps of the defender over him, the receiver must scan the secondary quickly to get an early indication of the coverage. Are defenders chasing other receivers, or are they dropping to areas?

- Cutting the route depth too short. Sometimes receivers are so eager to get across the field that they start crossing before they get far enough downfield. Receivers must run every route at the correct, prescribed depth!

- Looking back at the quarterback too soon. The receiver should not look back until he is sure about the coverage and is prepared to keep running or has decided where to sit down in his route.

READING THE SITUATION

How do you and your players gain the best advantage when adjusting crossing routes based on the defensive coverage being played? Teach your receivers to do the following:

- As the play starts, the receiver should look at the nearest defender or two who are in pass coverage and observe their initial steps. If one of those defenders directs his attention to the receiver, the coverage is man-to-man. If the defenders backpedal at the snap with eyes on the quarterback, the receiver can initially assume that the coverage is zone.

- The receiver should quickly check to see whether inside underneath defenders are dropping to areas (zone coverage) or chasing individual receivers (man coverage).

- The receiver should continue to observe the defenders during the stem of the route because the defenders might be playing a soft man coverage. The receiver won't know for sure until he breaks across the field and sees whether the defender chases him.

ACQUIRING THE APPROPRIATE KNOWLEDGE

To use modifications when adjusting crossing routes to the coverage, you and your players must know about the following:

Rules

You and your players need to know several main rules when determining the coverage being used on a crossing route:

- Defenders cannot hold receivers, but if a defender grabs a little cloth to slow down the receiver, the receiver must knock the defender's hands away. The receiver cannot expect the official to solve his problem for him.

- Offensive players cannot set a pick on a defensive player to free up a receiver from man coverage. But if a defensive player runs into an offensive player who is running a legitimate pass route, the contact is deemed incidental and there is no foul. Offensive players whose paths cross need to run legitimate routes, passing as close together as possible, and hope that the defensive player has trouble staying with his man. Do not teach offensive players to run into a defensive player who is covering another receiver because that tactic is a pick and should be called a foul.

- Defenders dropping into zones can collide with receivers and knock them off their routes as long as the ball has not yet been thrown. After the ball is thrown, such collisions are deemed pass interference.

- Defenders can never chop a receiver (cut his legs out from under him with a block) as he runs his route.

Physical Playing Conditions

The physical playing conditions significantly affect the game. Thus, you and your players must pay attention to the following physical conditions when adjusting crossing routes to the coverage:

- Wet and slippery field conditions require short, choppy steps instead of dramatic cuts.

- Trying to stop in an open area against a zone defense will also require a series of short, choppy steps if the field is wet and slippery.

- The receiver may have to catch a wet ball against his body.

Strengths and Weaknesses of Opponents

You and your players must account for your opponent's strengths and weaknesses to adjust crossing routes based on the coverage. Consider the following about your opponents:

- Does the opponent give away the coverage by alignment? A team that plays with a pressed look when they are playing man and aligns with a soft (deep) secondary when using zone gives the offense an easy read regarding the coverage. Both the quarterback and the receiver know before the snap whether the route will be a running route or a sit-down route, which should improve the chances for a completion.

- How well does the opponent play man coverage? Teams that have quick, agile man defenders can be effective against crossing routes because they don't allow the receivers to gain much separation even if the receiver keeps running across the field. These defenders also can be in position to bat down even well-thrown passes.

> **REMINDER!**
>
> You and your players must understand the team strategy and game plan and assess the coverage of the crossing route based on those plans and the situation at hand. Make sure that you and your players consider the questions on page 172.

(continued)

o Do the underneath zone defenders look to disrupt crossing routes? Crossing routes are not effective if the defense disrupts the routes with collisions.

o How tall are the defensive linemen compared with the quarterback? Crossing routes are tough to throw if the quarterback is short and the defensive linemen are tall. Conversely, a tall quarterback working over a shorter line should be able to see and throw crossing routes well.

o How well do the underneath defenders react? Crossing routes are tough to complete if the underneath defenders are quick with good anticipation and good ability to read where the quarterback is going to throw the ball.

o What should the offense do if the defense runs a combination coverage (part man, part zone), such as a zone blitz or man-free coverage? Combination coverages confuse this read for the offense and might cause the offense to shy away from calling crossing routes. When facing a team that runs combination coverages, the receiver should always choose to sit down as if the coverage were a zone concept, because the most dangerous outcome of misreading the coverage would be to keep running on a crossing route toward a free defender who could deliver a crushing collision to the receiver.

Self-Knowledge

Besides being aware of your opponent's abilities, you and your players must know about your own team's strengths and weaknesses. When adjusting crossing routes based on the coverage, you and your team should be aware of the following:

o How consistently do the receivers run their routes? Regardless of the route (shallow cross, dig or other crossing route), be sure that the receiver reaches the proper depth and does not drift any deeper than that as he runs across the field against man coverage or sits down against a zone.

o Can the receivers gain separation from man defenders? Against man coverage, the receiver must use speed, elusiveness and craftiness to get open if the defender is close to him when he makes his break across the field.

o How well do the receivers establish their positions against the zone defense? Against zone coverage, the receiver must be able to sense the best place to sit down on his route, where he can shield the nearest defender with his back and maintain enough space in front of him to catch the ball before another defender can close and make a play.

o How well do the receivers and quarterback communicate on whether the receiver will keep running or sit down? Ideally, they see the same coverage and come to the same conclusion!

Decision-Making Guidelines

When deciding how to gain the best advantage when adjusting crossing routes to the coverage, you and your players should consider the previous information as well as the following guidelines:

o If the defense varies the coverage between man and zone, the offensive team must be able to adjust the crossing routes. Crossing patterns in which the receiver keeps running against zone defensive schemes is ineffective and dangerous for the receiver, because zone defenders can wait for the receiver to come to them and be in position to deliver a crushing hit on the running receiver when the ball arrives. Running crossing routes against man-to-man coverage is effective, however, because covering a moving target is much more difficult for the defender than covering a receiver who sits down and becomes stationary.

- If the offense can identify a defender who is slower than one of the receivers, they can try to arrange that matchup. When the defense plays man coverage, the receiver should win on the running crossing route because of his greater speed. This throw is easier to complete than a deep pass matching up the same two players because the throw is shorter.

- If the defensive players are supposed to drop into zones, but they chase receivers who are crossing through their areas, the vacated area should be available for a different receiver to catch the ball.

- If the receiver starts across the field against man coverage and the defender manages to stay right with him, the receiver should try a stair-step move, faking an upfield cut and then leveling off across the field again at a slightly deeper yardage. This path should make it difficult for the chasing defender to maintain his tight coverage. The receiver can also look for a teammate running a crossing route and try to run close enough to that teammate to cause the chasing defender to slow down or alter his course.

- When the coverage is man, the receivers do not have to worry about a defender getting a good hit from outside in after making the catch. In man coverage, all other defenders should be busy running with other receivers, so none of them should be free to make contact from the other side of the field.

- When the coverage is zone, the receiver needs to understand that continuing to run across the field is extremely dangerous (either before or after the catch) because a defender on the other side of the field could be waiting to deliver a crushing blow. The receiver must sit down on his route to be safe and to have the best chance for a completion and positive yardage. Furthermore, after the catch he should immediately turn 180 degrees and run vertically (north or south) away from the quarterback so that no zone defender on either side of him can deliver a direct hit.

- On all crossing routes, the receiver must establish inside position, either by stemming the route inside against a soft corner or using a release move to get inside a pressed corner. Whether the coverage is man or zone, the receiver will have a better chance to run the route at the proper depth and get into a good position to catch the ball if he starts working the route inside from the beginning of the play.

Curl Route Adjustments

The curl route resembles a fishhook, with a smooth arc coming back to the inside. In reality, however, the route might look much different. For example, if as the receiver turns inside, he sees an underneath defender working quickly to the outside to the curl area, the receiver must adjust his route back to the inside to find a throwing lane inside that curl defender. Conversely, if the receiver sees an underneath defender dropping to the inside but not rapidly gaining width, he has to adjust his route more to the outside so that he doesn't curl back inside toward that defender. Adjusting the curl route in this manner is essential for an effective passing game because if the receiver goes to the same spot on the field every time he runs a curl, the underneath defenders will have no trouble running to that spot and denying the throw.

⚠ WATCH OUT!

The following circumstances may distract your players:

- Thinking about the route or the possible catch and forgetting to key the underneath defender.

- Failing to ignore pass rushers and pass protection blockers. Both the quarterback and the receiver have to ignore the pass rushers and the pass protection blockers. They must see each other right through those players, as if they weren't there.

- Failing to ignore the deep defender. The quarterback must ignore the deep defender and assume that the receiver will win against him. The quarterback must keep the throw under the receiver's chin, but he should rely on the receiver to come back for the ball and make the catch.

READING THE SITUATION

How do you and your players gain the best advantage when adjusting the curl route? Teach your players to do the following:

- Both the quarterback and the receiver must identify the underneath defender responsible for the curl area, usually a strong safety or outside linebacker playing in the alley between the offensive formation and the wide receiver. That player's drop will be the key read for offensive players in making their adjustments.

- Both the quarterback and the receiver must see the same open area in the defense, either inside or outside the curl defender, based on the depth and width of the defender's drop. The quarterback does not throw to the receiver; he throws to the open area. The receiver adjusts his route to get to the open area and arrives there just as the ball does.

- The receiver has to feel how close the deep defender is and have a sense of how fast he is closing. The closer he is, the farther the receiver must come back toward the quarterback and the ball.

ACQUIRING THE APPROPRIATE KNOWLEDGE

To use modifications when running the curl route, you and your athletes should understand the following:

REMINDER!

When making adjustments to the curl route, you and your players must understand the team strategy and game plan. Don't forget to consider the questions on page 172.

Rules

You and your players need to know several main rules when adjusting the curl route:

- Defenders are not allowed to hold receivers or collide with them when the ball is in the air. If the quarterback sees that an underneath defender has collided with the receiver as the receiver was adjusting his curl route, one option is to throw the ball in that direction and hope for the pass interference call.

Physical Playing Conditions

The physical playing conditions significantly affect the game. Thus, you and your players must pay attention to the following physical conditions when adjusting the curl route:

- In wet and slippery field conditions, the receiver must reduce the length of his strides and use short, choppy steps to keep his footing. He won't be able to adjust the curl route as significantly on this type of surface as he would on a dry surface.

- If the ball is wet, the receiver will have to adjust his route so that he can come back farther toward the quarterback because the quarterback will probably not be able to put as much velocity on the ball.

Strengths and Weaknesses of Opponents

You and your players must account for your opponent's strengths and weaknesses to know how to make adjustments to the curl route. Consider the following about your opponents:

- If the opponent blitzes, how do you adjust the curl route? When opponents blitz frequently and play a lot of man coverage, the receiver doesn't need to adjust his route because the underneath defender has either blitzed or is covering another receiver man to man. The curl receiver simply has to beat his defender and come back for the ball.

- Why not just run the curl to a predetermined spot? Wouldn't the timing and the throw be more consistent? The throw and catch on the curl route that is never adjusted will be consistent in drills. But in games, when facing an opponent who plays solid zone coverage, the underneath defender will easily get to the curl area. Without the ability to adjust the curl route, the play will be unsuccessful.

- Does the defensive coverage always require a route adjustment? On some occasions in every game, the underneath defender will take a deep drop and leave the curl route open at the traditional spot 12 yards deep over the original alignment of the wide receiver.

- How difficult is it to teach receivers to adjust the curl route? If you set up practice so that the quarterback and receiver have a defender to read when they are working on this throw, the adjustments will become natural and the concept of throwing to the open area will become instinctive.

(continued)

At a Glance

The following parts of the text offer additional information on adjusting the curl route.

Self-Knowledge

Besides being aware of your opponent's strengths and weaknesses, you and your players need to know about your own team's ability. Teach your players to be aware of the following when adjusting the curl route:

○ What are the main points for a receiver in adjusting the curl route? The receiver cannot hesitate or second-guess himself. He must be decisive and believe in himself.

○ What are the main points for a quarterback in adjusting the curl route? The quarterback must be able to see through the linemen and find the curl defender. The taller he is, the more effective he will generally be at this skill.

○ How fast is the wide receiver? If the wide receiver has excellent speed and can threaten to beat the cornerback on a deep route, the cornerback will have to play with greater depth and a quicker backpedal, which should allow the wide receiver to get open in front of him on the curl. If the cornerback does not feel threatened deep by the wide receiver, he will sit on the curl route and be in position to defend the throw no matter how well the receiver adjusts and comes back to the ball. Work on a curl and go, in which the wide receiver shows a curl break at curl yardage but instead of breaking inside, bursts past the outside shoulder of the cornerback, avoiding contact and trying to win on the deep route.

Decision-Making Guidelines

When deciding how to gain the best advantage when adjusting the curl route, you and your players should consider the previous information as well as the following guidelines:

○ The quarterback should not look at the receiver initially. He looks for the curl defender and throws away from him to the open area.

○ Remember that the ball does not have to go to the wide receiver every time the curl route is called. If the design of the play includes a check-down receiver and the underneath defender is defending the curl well, the quarterback can throw to the check-down receiver (see "Progression of Receivers" on page 174) instead of forcing the ball to the curl receiver. Often, after a couple completions to the check-down receiver, the underneath defender will start to focus on the route of the check-down player. When the defender reacts too much to that route, the curl will be open for the throw and the completion.

○ If the cornerback backpedals on the snap (known as playing a soft corner technique), then the wide receiver can curl in front of him and read the underneath defender or defenders for his route adjustments. If the corner shuffles laterally or moves forward toward the receiver at the snap (known as playing a hard corner technique), then the curl route should be aborted completely and the receiver should adjust to a fade or void route (see "Hard Corner Route Adjustments" on page 207 and an example of a hard corner route adjustment in Appendix A on page 355).

Hard Corner Route Adjustments

The pass play calls for a curl route or a comeback route for the wide receiver. He begins his route, but the cornerback doesn't backpedal. Instead, he rolls up toward the receiver, trying to collide with him and force him inside. The cornerback is using what is called a hard corner technique, in which he plays the flat and the safety behind him plays any deep route on that side of the field. The hard corner technique can also be called a funnel technique, because the cornerback's assignment is to funnel the receiver inside to the safety. The receiver must recognize that the defense has added another player to the underneath coverage to take away the curl and the comeback and adjust his route to go to the void area 15 to 20 yards deep near the sideline, behind the corner and away from the safety who is playing deep coverage behind the corner. See an example of a hard corner route adjustment in Appendix A on page 355.

⚠ WATCH OUT!

The following circumstances may distract your receiver:

- Assuming that the cornerback will play soft.
- Falling into the corner's trap.
- Fearing the half-field safety closing in as the ball approaches.

ACQUIRING THE APPROPRIATE KNOWLEDGE

To use modifications when adjusting routes to a hard corner, you and your athletes should understand the following:

READING THE SITUATION

How do you and your players gain the best advantage when adjusting routes against the hard corner technique? Teach your receiver to do the following:

- Recognize when to run a void route by checking the contour of the safety and corner before the snap. If the safety is deep, on the hash marks, and the corner is not as deep, the receiver might be able to anticipate the hard corner.
- Key the cornerback from the beginning of the play, watching his first steps to determine the adjustments that might be necessary.
- Always attack the outside shoulder of the defender if there is any chance that he might roll up. Working back inside and running a normal curl route if the defender backpedals is much easier than starting with a vertical stem and then trying to react outside when the defender rolls up. The corner who is rolling up has to widen his position drastically to honor the receiver's threat to go outside, and that movement opens up more space that the receiver can use to avoid the funnel.

Rules

You and your athletes need to know several main rules when adjusting routes against a hard corner:

- Although the receiver has to attack the corner to the outside, he cannot allow the cornerback to force him out of bounds. If the receiver goes out of bounds, he cannot come back inbounds and make a reception.
- Defenders cannot hold receivers or grab their jerseys. They also cannot be in contact with the receiver when the ball is in the air. If the quarterback sees that the cornerback is holding or is in contact with the receiver as the receiver is adjusting his route to the void, he should get the ball in the air in that direction in the hope of drawing a penalty.

(continued)

> **REMINDER!**
>
> When adjusting routes to a hard corner, you and your players must understand the team strategy and game plan. Don't forget to consider the questions on page 172.

Physical Playing Conditions

The physical playing conditions significantly affect the game. Thus, you and your players must pay attention to the following physical conditions when adjusting routes against a hard corner:

- Wet and slippery field conditions require short, choppy steps instead of dramatic cuts.
- The receiver may have to catch a wet ball against his body.

Strengths and Weaknesses of Opponents

You and your players must account for your opponent's strengths and weaknesses to know how to adjust routes against a hard corner. Consider the following about your opponents:

- How often does the opponent blitz? Opponents who blitz frequently and play a lot of man coverages usually don't give the offense many hard corner opportunities, so the receivers will not have many chances to convert curl routes to the void area.
- Does the opponent play man coverage in the underneath zones? Some opponents play a two-deep coverage in which the five underneath players each cover a receiver instead of playing in five underneath zones. Your outside receiver may read this coverage as a soft corner instead of a hard corner because the underneath defender over him is playing man to man.
- Do the opponent's corners sink back? When the corners sink back under the void route after playing the hard corner, throwing the ball to that area will be tough. If neither the #2 nor the #3 receiver runs a route to the flat, the corner can sink and make the throw to the void area extremely difficult. Conversely, opponents whose corners never sink back make it easier for the offense to throw the ball to that area. If the corner stays at 5 or 6 yards deep in the flat after playing the hard corner technique, the throw to the void area is easy.
- Are the opponent's coverages easy to recognize? Opponents who line up pre-snap in their coverage are vulnerable to this route adjustment because the offense has little uncertainty about what to do and where to go.
- Do the opponent's safeties stay on the hash mark? Safeties who stay right on the hash mark in two-deep coverage have a lot of territory to cover to get to the sideline and will have difficulty trying to stop the void pattern.

Self-Knowledge

Besides being aware of your opponent's strengths and weaknesses, you and your players must know about your own team's ability. Teach your players to be aware of the following when adjusting routes against a hard corner:

- Do you want the passing game to be a significant part of your offense? If so, your players must learn to adjust routes. The hard corner coverage (called cover 2 because it has two deep safeties, each playing half the field in the deep zones) places five players in underneath zones and can effectively stop curls and comebacks. This coverage, however, is vulnerable in the deep level on the outside and in the hole between the two safeties. If the offense learns to read the coverage and adjust the route, the offense always has the right play called.

Decision-Making Guidelines

When deciding how to gain the best advantage when running a void route, you and your players should consider the previous information as well as the following guidelines:

- o Remember, if the cornerback backpedals on the snap, playing a soft corner technique, the wide receiver curls in front of him and reads the underneath defender or defenders for his route adjustments. But if the cornerback shuffles laterally or moves toward the receiver at the snap, the receiver changes his route from the curl to the void, or fade. The receiver's first priority is to recognize the cornerback's intent and decide whether to adjust to the void.

- o When the corner rolls up to play the hard corner technique, he wants to force the receiver to go inside toward the safety playing on the hash mark. The receiver must understand what is happening and try to go outside the corner toward the sideline. If the corner widens considerably to deny the receiver's attempt to go outside, the receiver should be able to slip underneath the corner without being funneled because the corner had to widen out so far.

- o After your receiver has passed the cornerback, he must quickly widen his route to the spot 15 to 20 yards deep near the sideline, away from the safety playing deep coverage.

- o If the ball comes to the receiver on the void (fade) route, the safety will try to come off the hash and defend that throw. If the receiver has avoided being funneled, he should have established a position near the sideline on his route and therefore should be able to devote his entire attention to making the catch safely, avoiding a big hit from the approaching safety. The quarterback can help by not leading the receiver too far downfield with the throw.

At a Glance

The following parts of the text offer additional information on adjusting routes to a hard corner.

Catching	p. 48
Running Shallow and Intermediate Routes	p. 51
Running Deep Routes	p. 55
Releases	p. 58
Curl Route Adjustments	p. 204

The pass play calls for a curl, comeback, hitch or some other short or intermediate route. Before the snap, the defender moves up close to the receiver and aligns on the receiver's inside shoulder, preparing to play press man coverage (see "Press Man Coverage" on page 125). Press man is a tough, physical form of man pass coverage that requires the receiver to make significant route adjustments to get open. Instead of running a smooth, uncontested stem on his route, the receiver must execute a release move against the corner, adjust the path of his route and use decisive, deceptive moves to gain separation (see "Releases" on page 58). Unless the receiver can make these adjustments, the defense can eliminate him from the game with only one defender, leaving more defenders available to stop the run and the other receivers.

READING THE SITUATION

How do you and your players gain the best advantage when adjusting the route for press man coverage? Teach your receivers to do the following:

- Recognize not only the defender's alignment, but also his intentions. Some defenders will show a press alignment, then "bail" out to play a soft corner technique.
- Match the release with the route called. For inside breaking routes like a post or dig, work on inside release. For outside breaking routes like a streak or comeback, work on outside release.
- Adjust all hitch routes to fades.

⚠ WATCH OUT!

The following circumstances may distract your receivers:

- Failure to pay attention to the corner's alignment. The receiver must scan the field and be alert for the corner sneaking up on him to get in press alignment.

- Thinking of the route instead of the release. If the corner presses, the receiver has to focus on getting off the line of scrimmage before he can begin to think about running his route.

- Getting in a hurry to look for the ball. Many receivers turn and look for the ball far too soon when pressed by a defender. Receivers must remember that they have a good three to four seconds to operate, and they must use all that time to gain separation before looking back.

- Allowing the corner to force him wide. Just because the corner lines up inside doesn't mean that the receiver has to run for the sideline at the snap to get away. Too much lateral movement reduces the field available to the receiver to run his route.

ACQUIRING THE APPROPRIATE KNOWLEDGE

To use modifications when adjusting routes for press man coverage, you and your players must know about the following:

Rules

You and your athletes need to know several main rules when adjusting routes for press man coverage:

- The receiver must align on or behind the line of scrimmage and must be set for one count before the snap if he is not in motion. When faced with a defender playing press technique, some receivers forget these obvious, simple rules. They fail to double-check their alignment, or they get excited and jump offside!

- Defensive backs cannot hold the receiver, but they can collide with the receiver. The defender's hands will be in contact with the receiver. The receiver has to use his hands and arms to knock away the defender's hands.
- Defensive backs cannot be in contact with the intended receiver when the ball is in the air, so the quarterback may at times want to throw the ball to his receiver when the defender is contacting him, hoping for the pass interference call.

> **REMINDER!**
>
> When adjusting routes for press man coverage, you and your players must understand the team strategy and game plan. Don't forget to consider the questions on page 172.

Physical Playing Conditions

The physical playing conditions significantly affect the game. Thus, you and your players must pay attention to the following physical conditions when adjusting routes for press man coverage:

- In wet or slippery field conditions, the receiver will not be able to make dramatic moves against the pressed corner. The corner will have to deal with unsure footing as well. Receivers should cut down the length of their strides and keep their feet under them as they try to execute their releases.
- If the offense has a strong wind at their backs, they should challenge the pressed corner down the field on a takeoff or fade route because the wind will help the ball go the required distance. If a strong wind is in the face of the offense, however, the downfield throw against a pressed defender will be risky.

Strengths and Weaknesses of Opponents

You and your players must account for your opponent's strengths and weaknesses to know how to adjust routes for press man coverage. Consider the following about your opponents:

- How physical are the corners? A physical, aggressive defender can eliminate a receiver at the line of scrimmage if he can make solid contact and destroy the timing of the route. Receivers who face physical corners must use deceptive releases to minimize contact at the line.
- How tall are the corners? A tall defender playing press can be tough because he can play heavy inside, force the offense to throw the ball outside down the field and then use his height and reach to break up the play.
- How fast are the corners? The speed matchup between the corner and the receiver is crucial. If the receiver is faster, he can challenge the corner down the field when the corner plays press technique. Then, later in the game, the receiver can threaten him down the field to a depth of 10 to 12 yards before breaking off a curl or comeback.
- How often do the corners use the press man? If they use the press frequently, the offense should not call as many intermediate routes, such as curls and comebacks, because they are difficult to adjust and complete against press technique. Instead, the offense should call routes that are more effective against the press, such as the shallow cross, the flag (to the #2 receiver) and the fade.

Self-Knowledge

Besides being aware of your opponent's strengths and weaknesses, you and your players need to know about your own team's ability. Teach your players to be aware of the following when adjusting routes for press man coverage:

- Can your team win deep? The best answer to the press technique is to complete a deep fade route over the corner's head for a long gain or touchdown. Offenses must work on

(continued)

the timing and accuracy of this throw and seek the best possible matchup for their receiver against the defender.

- Will you have time to throw? Defenses often use the press in conjunction with blitzes. The press takes away most quick, short routes such as the hitch and the slant, forcing the quarterback, who is being pressured, to throw a deeper, more difficult pass such as a fade or flag. Offenses must work on picking up the blitz (see "Picking Up the Blitz" on page 197) so that the quarterback has at least enough time to take a five-step drop (see "Quarterback Drops" on page 58) and deliver the ball.

- How do the receivers match up on releases? The receivers must work daily on release moves, especially if the scouting report shows that the opponent might play some press technique (see "Releases" on page 58). If the receivers cannot escape at the line of scrimmage, the opponent will have a big advantage in the game.

Decision-Making Guidelines

When deciding how to gain the best advantage when adjusting routes for press man coverage, you and your players should consider the previous information as well as the following guidelines:

- Understand that the defense usually combines the press with a blitz. Your receiver should scan the linebackers nearest him and see whether they are showing signs of blitzing such as creeping up to the line of scrimmage and leaning forward on their toes before the snap count so that he can be prepared to work against the press and will know that his quarterback won't have all day to throw.

- Receivers should learn and use several different releases. To escape from the press at the line of scrimmage, the receiver must keep the cornerback guessing. He must mix powerful, aggressive releases with releases that begin with fakes. He must not give the aggressive corner a big target to hit.

- If the corners are big or physical but not faster than the receivers, consider adjusting all routes against the press to the fade. One or two big completions might convince the opponent to give up on the press, which would then allow the offense to run all its normal routes, such as curls, comebacks, hitches and so on.

- If the offense does not want to convert all routes to fades, then the receiver must at least threaten the defender down the field. After the release, the receiver should always put on a burst of speed, trying to sell the cornerback that he is going deep, and then plant and try to win on the intermediate route (such as a curl or comeback).

- The corner may choose to come up and press late in the snap count, or he might show a press alignment and then bail out at the last second to play a softer technique. Receivers must key the corner until the ball is snapped and keep an open mind about what technique he is finally going to use.

- If the receiver's assignment is an inside-breaking route, such as a curl or a dig, his release must take him inside the defender. If his assignment is an outside-breaking route, such as a comeback or a flag, his release must take him outside the defender.

- The hitch is dead against the press technique, so the receiver must adjust that route to a fade, using a good outside release at the snap, getting vertical immediately and looking for the ball to be thrown over his outside shoulder down the field.

The reach block is a man-to-man blocking scheme used with many zone running plays and some off-tackle plays in which the offensive lineman tries to gain outside position against a defender who is aligned on his outside shoulder. If the reach block is successful, the defensive front has an undefended gap that the offense can run through for a big play. Defenses can counter the reach block by playing a looser, or more outside, shade against the offensive lineman, but doing so makes them vulnerable to inside runs. Alternatively, defenses can counter the reach block by occasionally slanting one or more defenders inside and having a linebacker scrape outside to cover the gap being vacated by the slanting defender. This concept of defensive movement is difficult, but essential, for offenses to block.

With this kind of defensive movement, the offensive lineman must be aware that the defender he is trying to reach might occasionally slant to the inside, and if he does, the offensive lineman still has the responsibility to block him. The offensive lineman with a reach block assignment faces a dilemma. The bigger the step he takes to the outside, the better the chance he has to reach an outside defender, but the more vulnerable he is to the defender's slant inside.

⚠ WATCH OUT!

The following circumstances may distract your offensive linemen:

- Focusing on other defensive players. The lineman should focus only on the defender whom he is blocking.

- The defender's movements before the snap. The defender may move around, changing his shade, before the snap. Linemen should just take a solid first step and then react to the defender's movement.

READING THE SITUATION

How do you and your players gain the best advantage when reach blocking against defensive movement? Teach your offensive linemen to do the following:

- Evaluate the shade of the defender to get an early indication of what he might plan to do. A looser outside shade might mean that he is going to stay outside, whereas a tighter inside shade might be a tip that he is going to slant inside.

- Remember that the length of the first step is the key to a successful block. Match the first step to the shade of the defender.

- Evaluate other characteristics of the defender's stance. For example, if he is tilted inside or agitated before the snap, he might be trying to get a quick start for the attempt to slant inside.

- Pay attention to defensive calls that might be signals to the down linemen to slant inside. Work with teammates throughout the game to try to discern a pattern.

- Know the offensive snap count and get an aggressive start.

- React with the second step to the defender's first move, whether inside or outside.

(continued)

REMINDER!

When reach blocking against defensive movement, you and your players must understand the team strategy and game plan. Don't forget to consider the questions on page 172.

ACQUIRING THE APPROPRIATE KNOWLEDGE

When reach blocking against defensive movement, you and your players must know about the following:

Rules

You and your athletes need to know several main rules when reach blocking against defensive movement:

o Obviously, offense can't move before the snap, but a great takeoff on the snap is crucial.

o Offensive players can't hold. Lineman should not grab cloth; instead, they must work their feet.

Physical Playing Conditions

The physical playing conditions significantly affect the game. Thus, you and your players must pay attention to the following physical conditions when reach blocking against defensive movement:

o In wet and slippery field conditions, a big step is ill advised even if the block seems to require one. Lineman must take shorter, more controlled steps so that they stay on their feet.

o In wet and slippery conditions, the defender might not be able to get as quick a takeoff on the slant move, so the offensive lineman can afford to take a shorter, more controlled step.

Strengths and Weaknesses of Opponents

You and your players must account for your opponent's strengths and weaknesses to know how to reach block properly against defensive movement. Consider the following about your opponents:

o How quick is the defensive lineman? A quick defender can be difficult to block man-to-man when he slants. Combination blocks or a gap scheme might have to be used to neutralize him.

o Can the defender be reached? A defender may be big and powerful, but if he is slow off the ball or has slow reactions, he can be reached, and then the defense will not be gap sound.

o What kind of shade does the defensive lineman typically play? If he always aligns head up or in a tight shade, the reach block is manageable and should be effective, even if the defender is a good player, because the offensive lineman should be able to overtake him and gain outside leverage after one or two well-executed reach steps.

o Do the defenders change their shades when they slant? If the defenders clearly tighten down their shades when they are slanting and keep loose shades when they are not slanting, the reach block will be effective because the offensive lineman can be confident and aggressive on his first few steps.

Self-Knowledge

Besides being aware of your opponent's strengths and weaknesses, you and your players need to know about your own team's ability. Teach your players to be aware of the following when reach blocking against defensive movement:

- How quick are your offensive linemen? If your linemen have quick feet and are aggressive, they should be able to reach outside shaded defenders while still being able to react to slants inside.

- How powerful are your offensive linemen? Sometimes, a powerful offensive lineman can be an extremely effective blocker in these situations because he can drive the defender out of the way and down the field even if he does not always reach him and gain true outside position.

- How good is the lineman's first step? All the hours in the weight room and on the practice field are important, but they are less important than the lineman's first step. Use videotape study from behind the offensive line to critique and improve each lineman's first step.

At a Glance

The following parts of the text offer additional information on reach blocking against defensive movement.

Reach Block	p. 64
Defending Basic Run Blocks	p. 96
Controlling the Gap	p. 226

Decision-Making Guidelines

When deciding how to gain the best advantage when reach blocking against defensive movement, you and your linemen should consider the previous information as well as the following guidelines:

- Linemen should always gain a pre-snap key from the defender's alignment and adjust the first step accordingly. The offensive lineman should make the defender line up in a compromised shade (favoring neither the outside nor the inside) because he is concerned that the offensive lineman will be able to read his shades and know whether he is playing outside or slanting inside.

- Linemen must communicate with their fellow linemen. Sometimes, one of the players up front can discern a clue about the defensive call better than the others can. They should talk to each other about what they are learning about the defensive alignment and calls.

Combination Block

A combination block is a fluid concept in which two offensive linemen block one defensive lineman and one linebacker, but the blockers do not know, until after the play starts, which of them will be the one to come off and block the linebacker. Assume that two adjacent offensive linemen have the assignment of blocking the defensive lineman in the gap between them and the backside linebacker (two-on-two). After the snap, the two offensive linemen have to get both defenders blocked, regardless of how the defenders play the situation.

Initially, both blockers double-team the defensive lineman, keeping their eyes on the linebacker. After the linebacker reacts to the play, the offensive lineman on the side that he threatens leaves the double team and blocks him, while the other offensive lineman continues to block the defensive lineman. This concept of combination blocking helps neutralize defensive movement by stabilizing the defensive lineman and then reacting to the linebacker. Combination blocking also give the offense a better chance to reach a defender, because the outside offensive lineman knows that he has help to his inside if the defender slants inside. All he has to worry about is the reach block and the potential reaction to the linebacker. The disadvantage of the combination block is that it takes significant practice time and effort, because any two offensive blockers who might be involved in a combination block must learn to work together.

READING THE SITUATION

How can you and your players gain an advantage when using combination blocks? Teach your players to do the following:

- Always know the snap count and focus on a good first step on the snap of the ball.
- Check the shade of the defensive lineman to see which gap he is most likely to defend.
- Locate the assigned linebacker and see how far he is from the double team.
- Keep all eyes on the linebacker while blocking the defensive lineman!
- React to the linebacker's movement; do not guess where he is going to go.
- The blocker who remains on the defensive lineman must overtake and neutralize him after the other blocker leaves to block the linebacker.

 **WATCH OUT!**

The following circumstances may distract your athletes:

- Allowing distractions to affect getting off on the proper snap count. The snap count is still the offensive player's best advantage because it gives him a slight jump on the defender. The offensive player must use it to his advantage, getting a great start on the proper count by not letting defensive calls or movement cause him to false start or get a late start on the play.
- Identifying the wrong linebacker before the snap. If this happens, the offensive blockers will obviously come off to the wrong linebacker when the play starts and one of the other linebackers will be unblocked.
- Getting buried in the down defender. Many lineman glue their eyes to the down defender as the double team starts, and the linebacker runs by untouched to the ball carrier.

ACQUIRING THE APPROPRIATE KNOWLEDGE

When using combination blocks, you and your players should understand the following:

Rules

You and your players need to know several main rules when using combination blocks:

REMINDER!

When combination blocking, you and your players must understand the team strategy and game plan. Don't forget to consider the questions on page 172.

- Offensive linemen need to get a good start at the snap, but not a head start. Jumping offside is a 5-yard penalty that can jeopardize the success of the entire offensive series. Linemen must know the exact count and react at that precise moment in the cadence.
- When two blockers block one defender, the rules do not allow one blocker to block high and the other to block low. This dangerous tactic, called a chop block, has been prohibited in football. Both offensive blockers must stay high and maintain a good base, not lunging or reaching, so that neither of them slips off the double team and appears in any way to be blocking low.

Physical Playing Conditions

The physical playing conditions significantly affect the game. Thus, you and your players must pay attention to the following physical conditions when using combination blocks:

- In wet and slippery field conditions, lineman must take shorter, more controlled steps so that they stay on their feet.

Strengths and Weaknesses of Opponents

You and your players must account for your opponent's strengths and weaknesses to know how to use combination blocks properly. Consider the following about your opponents:

- How fast do the linebackers flow? If the linebackers are fast and flow quickly to the play, your blockers do not have much time to work on the double team before one of them has to come off and go for the linebacker. The two-on-one advantage is neutralized somewhat, and the linebackers are more difficult to cut off. But if the linebackers are somewhat slower, the offensive linemen have time to start with a double team, create some movement and still come off the double team and get position on the linebacker for a successful play.
- How powerful are the defensive tackles? If the matchup between any one of the offensive linemen and one or more of the defensive tackles favors the defender because he is especially powerful, then the offense should use combination blocking schemes that start with a double team on that defender, to try to get some movement on him and possibly get him reached.
- Do the linebackers like to run through open gaps? Some aggressive linebackers try to pursue running plays by running through an open gap, in effect chasing the play from behind instead of flowing laterally over the top of their defensive linemen to pursue the play. If your scouting report shows this tendency, use combination blocks because the backside offensive lineman in the combination can easily pick off the linebacker as he attempts to run through the gap.
- Does the defense use a lot of line games and stunts? Combination blocks give the offense flexibility to handle defensive line games and stunts. No matter which gap the down defender chooses to attack, and no matter where the linebacker chooses to run for the ball carrier, the offense should be able to react and block both defenders.
- Does the opponent line up in any fronts that cancel these blocks? Combination blocking is not possible if the defense aligns in a front that has a defensive lineman covering

(continued)

every offensive lineman ("Bear" front or goal-line front). If every offensive lineman is covered, no double teams are possible and running plays have to be blocked with man blocking instead of combination blocking.

Self-Knowledge

Besides being aware of your opponent's strengths and weaknesses, you and your players must know about your own team's ability. Teach your players to be aware of the following when using combination blocks:

○ How good is the teamwork between your offensive linemen? The two linemen working together on the combination block have to practice together and get a feel for each other, so that they have a good idea about when one of them is going to leave the double team.

○ How powerful are your offensive linemen? If your offensive line is not powerful enough to control the defensive linemen in one-on-one matchups, combination blocks will be helpful because the initial double team gives them at least a brief two-on-one advantage, allowing them to drive the defender off the line of scrimmage and create an opening for the ball carrier.

Decision-Making Guidelines

When deciding how to gain the best advantage when combination blocking, you and your players should consider the previous information as well as the following guidelines:

○ Before the snap, the offensive linemen must check the shade of the down lineman to see whether he is aligned in a position to cross the face of one of the offensive blockers. The down defender cannot be in position to get to all three possible gaps (outside one blocker, between them or outside the other blocker), so the offensive blockers can limit the possibilities to just two by evaluating his shade.

○ Before the snap, the offensive linemen must locate the linebacker who is the other defender whom they will block. The farther from the double team he is, the longer the blockers will be able to stay on the double team before one of them comes off to block him. If he aligns close to the double team or behind the down defender, the offensive blockers will have to make a quick decision about which one of them will be coming off for the linebacker.

○ On the initial double-team block, the offensive linemen must get shoulder to shoulder so that the defender cannot split the double team. As they are executing the double team, however, both blockers must keep their eyes on the linebacker. They must "feel" the double team and "see" the linebacker.

○ When the linebacker commits to a path toward the ball carrier, the blocker on that side will come off the down defender and attack the linebacker. Meanwhile, if the linebacker surges over the top of the double team, the backside blocker must "helmet adjust" and slide across the face of the down defender so that as his offensive teammate leaves, he overtakes the down defender and finishes the block by himself.

○ Blockers must communicate on the line. Linemen have to make calls at the line so that they know who is working with whom on combination blocks. If the guard is working a combination with the tackle, he can't work a combination with his center on the same play! But against certain fronts, the tackle will be working by himself on a block or working with the tight end on a combination, so the guard becomes available to work a combination with the center. The linemen must know their assignments and then be able to communicate to each other who is involved in combinations and who is not.

Pass Protection Against a Twist

On a pass play, two adjacent offensive linemen (a guard and a tackle, or a guard and the center) pop up on the snap for man pass protection against two defensive linemen. The two defenders execute a twist, in which one defender loops behind the other, so the two offensive linemen have to switch their blocking assignments to prevent the defenders from sacking the quarterback. The key is knowing when to give up one man and pick up the other. If one of the offensive blockers leaves his man too early, that man will get past the other offensive lineman and get to the quarterback. Conversely, if one of the blockers stays on his man too long, the other defender coming around on the twist will get past him for the sack.

Handling the twist in man pass protection is difficult. Zone, or area, pass protection schemes make it easier for the linemen to handle twists because each lineman stays in his area and the line basically builds a wall of pass blockers to protect the quarterback. The problem with zone pass protection is that the five offensive linemen have six gaps to protect, so a running back must be used in the protection scheme, meaning that he can't get out of the backfield to become a receiver. Furthermore, the defense frequently rushes only four players and the offense is committing six players for protection, again wasting the running back. Therefore, if the offensive linemen can learn to protect the quarterback in man pass protection, including handling the twist move, the offense can add the running back to the pass game and become more efficient and more effective.

READING THE SITUATION

How can you and your players gain an advantage when pass protecting against a twist? Teach your players to do the following:

- Focus on the snap count. Knowing the snap count is the offensive player's greatest advantage.

- Develop a quick, balanced pass set. A good pass set will give the offensive linemen the proper technique to start blocking the different types of pass rush schemes.

- Look for tips that a twist is coming, such as a tighter shade by a defensive end (more inside than usual) or a looser shade by the tackle (more outside than usual).

- Recognize a less aggressive pass rush than usual by one of the defenders. He's preparing to loop around on the twist move!

- Recognize when his pass rusher attacks the gap instead of attacking him. The pass rusher is trying to draw the blocker into the gap with him so that his partner can beat the blocker on the twist.

⚠ WATCH OUT!

The following circumstances may distract your players:

- Attempting to guess what the defense is going to do. Each lineman must cue his own defender, not guessing about whether a twist is coming but reacting to the pass rush course that he sees happening.

- Getting buried in the first defender. The offensive lineman cannot become preoccupied with the first defender whom he blocks, lower his head and lose sight of any potential second defender.

- Leaving the assigned defender for a blitzing linebacker. A blitz is different from a twist. An offensive lineman whose man assignment in pass protection is a down lineman would never give up that man to switch and block a blitzing linebacker, but he does switch with his adjacent teammate when two defensive linemen twist. So he must leave the linebackers alone and trust that one of his teammates will pick them up when they blitz.

(continued)

REMINDER!

When pass protecting against a twist, you and your players must understand the team strategy and game plan. Don't forget to consider the questions on page 172.

ACQUIRING THE APPROPRIATE KNOWLEDGE

When pass protecting against a twist, you and your players should understand the following:

Rules

You and your players need to know several main rules when pass protecting against a twist:

- A quick pass set on the snap count is crucial, but if the lineman tries to beat the count to give himself a head start on the defender, he runs the risk of a procedure penalty. Offensive linemen must know the snap count and execute a good pass set on time, not early!

- Offensive linemen cannot solve the problem of blocking a twist by grabbing the defenders; they must use good communication, excellent footwork and legal hand position to execute their blocks.

- Defensive linemen can use their hands, but they can't hold. Sometimes the first defender grabs the jersey of the offensive lineman who blocks him, so that the offensive lineman cannot get away to block the second, twisting, defender. This tactic is illegal and should be penalized, but offensive linemen know that the officials sometimes miss the infraction, so they must use their hands aggressively to disengage from any defender who tries to grab them.

Physical Playing Conditions

The physical playing conditions significantly affect the game. Thus, you and your players must pay attention to the following physical conditions when pass protecting against the twist:

- Wet and slippery field conditions may hurt the defenders more than the pass blockers, because the questionable surface will slow the twisting defender. Pass blockers still must concentrate on taking short, controlled steps and not overstriding on a wet surface.

Strengths and Weaknesses of Opponents

You and your players must account for your opponent's strengths and weaknesses to know how to pass protect against a twist. Consider the following about your opponents:

- How quick is the defensive line? If the defensive line is exceptionally quick and uses good technique when running their twists, the offensive blockers may have trouble blocking twists and other line games in man pass protection. The offense should mix in some sprintout passes to keep this defense honest because sprintouts are extremely effective against twists. On the other hand, slower defensive linemen are easier to block if they try to twist, so man protection is a good scheme against these types of players.

- How often does the opponent use the twist move? Scout your opponent for frequency of twists and situations when they use it. Call passing plays that use man protection in situations when your opponent is least likely to use the twist.

- Does the opponent do anything to tip off the fact that a twist is coming? Check for tighter shades, tilted stances and different angles on pass rush lanes when twists are used. Presnap cues can really help your offensive linemen react to the twist.

Self-Knowledge

Besides being aware of your opponent's strengths and weaknesses, you and your players need to know about your own team's ability. Teach your players to be aware of the following when pass protecting against a twist:

- How good is the communication between your offensive linemen? The two linemen involved in the switch have to communicate orally when the twist move starts. Teach them to be decisive, loud and repetitive with this call.
- How good are your linemen at their basic pass set? Picking up the twist is much easier when the blockers start each play with a quick, balanced pass set. When the head is back and the base is solid, the offensive lineman can see the defensive moves and react appropriately.

At a Glance

The following parts of the text offer additional information on pass protection against a twist.

Pass Protection	p. 85
Pass Rush	p. 110
Pass Protection on the Edge	p. 222
Taking the Inside Rush	p. 229

Decision-Making Guidelines

When deciding how to gain the best advantage when pass protecting against a twist, you and your players should consider the previous information as well as the following guidelines:

- On every twist move, one defender (called the penetrator) attacks the gap between two offensive linemen. A second defender (called the looper) fakes a normal upfield rush and then works around behind his teammate, trying to outflank the offensive lineman blocking the penetrator.
- The blocker who starts out blocking the looper will see the twist first. When his defender leaves, he should slide down to a position shoulder to shoulder with his teammate on the offensive line and yell, "Switch!" or "Twist!" to alert him that the looper is on the way. He then needs to pick up the penetrator and stop his charge by sliding his feet laterally into a position in front of that defender.
- The blocker who starts out blocking the penetrator also has to be suspicious that something new is happening, because his man is attacking a different pass rush lane than usual. The oral communication from his teammate that a looper is on the way will confirm his suspicions. He stays on the penetrator until he is shoulder to shoulder with the offensive lineman next to him. He then leaves the penetrator and slides laterally to pick up the looper.

221

An offensive tackle assigned to block the defensive end one-on-one in man pass protection has a difficult task. The offensive tackle has to set up with enough width and depth to stop a fast outside rush, but if he sets up too wide or otherwise overcommits to the outside, the defender can take the inside rush, going underneath and getting to the quarterback (see "Taking the Inside Rush" on page 229). Executing man pass protection on the edge of the pocket against the defensive end is vital for an effective passing game because passing schemes are most effective if all five eligible receivers can get out to run pass routes. This can happen consistently only if at least one offensive tackle can match up one-on-one in man pass protection against a defensive end (alternative blocking schemes that don't leave the tackle matched up one-on-one require a running back or tight end to help with pass protection instead of running a route).

⚠ WATCH OUT!

The following circumstances may distract your athletes:

o Becoming distracted by any noise, or calls, at the line of scrimmage. Players must listen only to the snap count and get off on the snap!

o Becoming distracted by other defensive players who are rushing the quarterback or faking blitzes. In man pass protection, the offensive tackle must block the defensive end only.

o Focusing on the head fakes or the waving hands of the defensive end as he rushes the quarterback. The offensive tackle should concentrate on the inside number of the end and stay in position just inside him.

o Turning outside on the pass set because the rusher is outside. Turning to face the rusher simply opens the door and shortens his path to the quarterback.

READING THE SITUATION

How can you and your players gain an advantage when pass protecting on the edge? Teach your players to do the following:

- Observe the defensive end's pre-snap stance. The wider he is, the more width will be required on the initial pass set.

- Know the snap count and get a good pass set on the proper count. Knowing the snap count is the offense's greatest advantage!

- Set up for pass protection with depth but don't turn to the outside. The offensive tackle must keep his body parallel to the line of scrimmage.

- Study the defensive end's inside number and remain poised to react to each of his possible moves.

ACQUIRING THE APPROPRIATE KNOWLEDGE

When pass protecting on the edge, you and your athletes should understand the following:

Rules

You and your athletes need to know several main rules when pass protecting on the edge:

REMINDER!

When pass protecting on the edge, you and your players must understand the team strategy and game plan. Don't forget to consider the questions on page 172.

- Obviously, the rules do not permit the offensive tackle to move into his pass set until the ball is snapped, but the threat of a quick outside rush from the defensive end often causes an anxious offensive tackle to jump offside. This mistake gives the defense 5 easy yards and does nothing to alleviate the threat of the outside pass rush. The offensive tackle must play with poise and get a quick pass set on the snap count, not before!

- Holding is not permitted. Offensive players should refrain from grabbing defenders, although it is tempting to do so if a fast rusher is on the outside or if the rusher fools the tackle and makes a good hard move inside. Offensive tackles must stop the rush with good footwork and good punch with the hands, not by grabbing and holding the defenders.

Physical Playing Conditions

The physical playing conditions significantly affect the game. Thus, you and your players must pay attention to the following physical conditions when pass protecting on the edge:

- In wet or slippery field conditions, the offensive tackle cannot take as deep or dramatic a first step on his pass set because he cannot afford to lose his footing.

- Poor field conditions will also slow the outside rusher, so the offensive tackle should have time to take a cautious set and still be able to get into position to block the rush.

Strengths and Weaknesses of Opponents

You and your players must account for your opponent's strengths and weaknesses to know how to pass protect on the edge properly. Consider the following about your opponents:

- How fast is the defensive end? The speed of the defensive end is the greatest concern for the offensive tackle. If the end has superior quickness, the assignment to block him both inside and outside is difficult for the tackle and he will have to concentrate on making a deep, quick pass set to be in position to protect the quarterback. If the end does not have explosive quickness, the offensive tackle can get by with a pass set that is slightly shallower and less difficult to attain.

- Does the defensive end have a good inside move? Through scouting and game-day observation, the offense should be able to ascertain the quality of the defensive end's inside move. If he has a good, quick move inside, the offensive tackle has to set slightly more inside, protecting against the inside move by alignment while shuffling backward to keep the outside rush away from the quarterback. If the defensive end does not have a good inside move, the offensive tackle can set more outside and take on the outside rush more firmly.

- Does the defensive end tip off his move? Some defensive ends align wider when they are rushing outside or come upfield less aggressively on the outside when they are planning to fake the outside rush and work underneath. Through scouting and game-day observation, the offense must evaluate the defensive end's alignment and his actions after the snap to try to discover clues about his intentions.

(continued)

○ How often does the defensive end rush inside? Through scouting and game-day observation, the offense should be able to calculate the percentage of times that the defensive end takes the inside rush. The offensive tackle can then play the percentages, setting up the same on every play but anticipating the inside move on a certain percentage of the plays.

Self-Knowledge

Besides being aware of your opponent's strengths and weaknesses, you and your players need to know about your own team's ability. Teach your players to be aware of the following when pass protecting on the edge:

○ How quickly can the offensive tackle set up for pass protection? Against a terrific outside rush, the offensive tackle must have a quick pass set to have a chance to be successful. If he does not have a quick pass set, the offense may have to consider rolling out the quarterback or calling play-action passes to slow the rush.

○ How good is the offensive tackle's pass protection technique? The most difficult aspect of pass protecting on the edge is convincing the tackle to set up facing the line of scrimmage instead of turning to face the outside rusher. The tackle must be poised and possess good footwork so that he can set up properly, backpedal from the line of scrimmage at an angle toward the outside and keep the outside rusher off the quarterback.

○ Does the quarterback throw the ball on time? Pass protection is difficult enough when the quarterback delivers the ball on time (in less than four seconds). But if the quarterback is indecisive and holds the ball too long, the offensive tackle will have to hold his block longer, making his job much more difficult.

Decision-Making Guidelines

When deciding how to gain the best advantage when pass protecting on the edge, you and your players should consider the previous information as well as the following guidelines:

○ A consistent, quick, stable pass set gives the tackle the best chance to be successful. He should gauge the alignment of the defensive end, set up inside his aiming point and then react.

○ If the defensive end continues to rush outside, the tackle should stay on his inside number. He should never try to overtake the outside rusher completely. The tackle should pedal backward and outside, pushing the defensive end up the field and making his circular path to the quarterback longer and longer.

○ If the defensive end bull rushes straight ahead, the offensive tackle should sink the hips and punch with the hands and forearms to stop the charge.

○ If the defensive end starts upfield and then attempts the underneath move, the offensive tackle should react with a quick step back downhill and punch his hands and arms to flatten him off, running him below (underneath) the quarterback.

○ If your team is committed to the pass game, at least one tackle will have to master this skill. To give the tackle some help, you can change pass protection schemes, such as doubling the end with the tackle and a back or using full zone protection in which the tackle would have to block only the outside rush while the guard inside him would block the inside move. But in both of those adjustments to pass protection, a running back would have to be used as a blocker and he would little chance, or possibly no chance, to get out of the backfield and run a pass route.

chapter 7

Defensive Tactical Skills

This chapter covers the defensive tactical skills that you and your players must know to be successful. In this chapter, you will find the following skills:

Controlling the Gap

Gap control is a key component to a good defense. Every defender in the nucleus of the defense (defensive linemen and linebackers) is responsible for a gap between two offensive blockers. For example, assume that the defensive lineman is poised at the line of scrimmage, ready for the offense to run a play. At the snap of the ball, the offensive lineman initiates a run block (either a reach block or a cutoff block), trying to take over the defensive lineman's gap. The defensive lineman must be able to read the block, determine that the play is a run and keep control of his gap. He has to keep his gap-side arm free without giving up too much ground laterally. If a defensive lineman loses control of his gap, either by being reached (when he is a playside defender) or by being cut off (when he is a backside defender), a seam opens up and the ball carrier will be able to run through to the safeties.

⚠ WATCH OUT!

The following circumstances may distract your athletes:

- The quarterback's cadence. The snap of the ball, not the sounds being made, keys the movement of the defensive line.

- Focusing on backfield action after the snap. Defenders must read and defend the block before they find the ball.

- Peeking into another gap and trying to make a play. Staying gap sound is crucial. If the ball goes to a teammate's gap, the defender must trust that his teammate will make the play.

READING THE SITUATION

How can you and your players gain the best advantage when controlling the gap? Teach your players to do the following:

- Check the offensive lineman's pre-snap stance to see whether he is leaning in a certain direction or has more or less weight on his front hand, which might tip off a run (more weight) or a pass (less weight).

- Key the ball, and the ball only, to get the best possible start out of the stance.

- Observe the offensive lineman's pad level to learn whether the play is a run. If the lineman's pads are low, it's a run. If the pads pop up in the air, it's a pass.

- Read the first step of the lineman and react in that direction. If the offensive lineman threatens a defender's gap, he must react and keep his head outside.

ACQUIRING THE APPROPRIATE KNOWLEDGE

When controlling the gap, you and your athletes should understand the following:

Rules

You and your athletes need to know several main rules when controlling the gap:

- Trying to get a jump on the snap will usually result in an offside penalty. Defenders must key the ball and react, not guess when the ball will be snapped.

- Offensive linemen aren't permitted to hold, but they will. Defenders must knock the blockers hands away and realize that the officials will not often call the hold.

Physical Playing Conditions

The physical playing conditions significantly affect the game. Thus, you and your players must pay attention to the following physical conditions when controlling the gap:

o   Wet or slippery field conditions might cause the defender to slip on his important first reaction step. He must narrow his stance and take shorter, quicker, more controlled steps to avoid slipping.

REMINDER!

When controlling the gap, you and your players must understand the team strategy and game plan. Don't forget to consider the questions on page 172.

Strengths and Weaknesses of Opponents

You and your players must account for your opponent's strengths and weaknesses to know how to control the gap properly. Consider the following about your opponents:

o   How quick are the offensive linemen? A quick offensive lineman is more likely to beat the defensive lineman on a reach or cutoff block than a slower offensive lineman is. Against the quicker blocker, the defender should take a looser shade, lining up a little bit wider to make the reach and cutoff blocks more difficult. Against a slower blocker, the defender can play a tighter shade.

o   Are the offensive linemen vulnerable to an inside move? Through scouting or experimentation early in the game, the defense should assess whether the offensive linemen can handle slant moves by the defensive line. The threat of an inside move can cause the offensive lineman to be less aggressive on his reach block. (The defense has to be sure, however, that the linebackers adjust to defend the gap vacated by the slanting defensive lineman.)

Self-Knowledge

Besides being aware of your opponent's strengths and weaknesses, you and your players need to know about your own team's ability. Teach your players to be aware of the following when controlling the gap:

o   How tight a shade can the defensive lineman play? A defensive lineman's first rule is: Don't get reached. The looser the shade he plays, the less likely it is that he will be reached. If he plays too loose a shade, however, the offensive blocker will have a clear release to block up on a linebacker or back on another defender. The defensive lineman must learn to play the tightest possible shade that he can without being reached. That way, he can collide with the offensive blocker when the blocker is not trying to reach him, and he can stay gap sound when the blocker attempts the reach block.

o   How well do your defensive linemen read offensive blocking schemes, and how quickly do they react? Through drills in practice and studying tapes of games, you must evaluate and train your defensive linemen on their ability to read and react. The better the defensive linemen do this, the more often and effectively the defense can play a base defensive scheme without having to use line games and stunts. If the defensive line is inconsistent at reading and reacting, the defense may have to rely on line games and stunts, which can be effective but carry a high risk of allowing a big play.

o   How physical and aggressive are the defensive linemen? A tough, physical, aggressive defensive lineman can make up for a slow read or a bad first step by tenaciously battling the offensive blocker throughout the play. This type of defender might initially appear to have been reached or cut off, but he might be able to fight back, counter the block and regain proper leverage.

(continued)

Decision-Making Guidelines

When deciding how to gain the best advantage when controlling the gap, you and your players should consider the previous information as well as the following guidelines:

- If the offensive lineman's initial steps threaten the defender's gap, the defender must counter that attack by moving his feet in that direction while repositioning his hands to the gap-side shoulder of the blocker.

- After neutralizing the blocker, the defender must see the path of the ball carrier and determine whether the ball is coming at him or going outside. If the ball carrier is threatening his gap, the defensive lineman must use aggressive hand action to shed the blocker and make a tackle. If the ball is going outside, he can focus on moving laterally in that direction, running away from his blocker and pursuing the play.

- The defender must be sure not to open the door to the next gap inside! He has to keep his outside arm free and his head outside, but if he gives up too much ground laterally to keep his outside position, the next gap inside will get larger and larger, making it difficult for the defender assigned to that gap to do his job. Defenders must fight the pressure of the reach block and give ground grudgingly while maintaining appropriate leverage.

Taking the Inside Rush

One of the time-tested adages of football goes something like this: The best pass defense is a great pass rush. If the front four on defense can put pressure on the quarterback while working against five offensive linemen, the seven remaining defenders have a numerical advantage over the five receivers and, better yet, the quarterback doesn't have much time to decide where to throw the ball. The defensive ends are the key to getting four-man pressure because they usually operate one-on-one against the offensive tackles, whereas the two defensive tackles are outnumbered three to two against the two guards and the center. Defensive ends generally have to stay outside the tackles on their pass rush, keeping the quarterback contained in the pocket. But occasionally the defensive end takes an inside rush, surprising the offensive tackle and making a big defensive play.

For example, assume that the defensive end sees the ball snapped and the play begins. The offensive tackle sets up for pass protection, and the quarterback begins to drop back. The defensive end begins his rush. The offensive tackle overcommits to the outside rush, the defensive end takes advantage and beats the tackle to the inside. This occasional inside rush not only produces a big play such as a sack but also forces the offensive tackle to be more cautious in his setup, thus giving the defensive end a better chance to win on the outside rush. Remember, however, that if the defensive end chooses the inside rush, he must get to the quarterback. If he goes inside and misses, the quarterback can escape from the pocket and buy more time to throw the ball.

READING THE SITUATION

How can you and your players gain an advantage when taking the inside rush? Teach your defensive ends to do the following:

- Key the ball. Get a great takeoff on every snap and create the threat of the quick outside rush on every play.
- See the lineman and read the block. When the offensive lineman's helmet pops up in the air on the snap, he is pass blocking and it's time to rush the quarterback! The defensive end can confirm the read when he sees the quarterback dropping back.
- Focus on the tackle's setup. If he turns to the outside or reaches or leans to the outside, he may be vulnerable to the inside move.
- Judge the final depth of the quarterback. If his pass setup is especially deep, considerably deeper than the pass protection set of the tackle, the inside rush is not a good choice.
- Only after beginning to threaten the outside rush should the defensive end locate the quarterback in the effort to see how deep his setup will be.

⚠ WATCH OUT!

The following circumstances may distract your athletes:

- Focusing on the quarterback's cadence. Movement is predicated on the snap of the ball, not on any sounds, and your defensive end should key only the ball before the snap.
- Focusing on the wrong cues. After the ball is snapped, the defensive end should ignore all cues except the offensive lineman's block.
- Visualizing a target that is too deep. Remember that the quarterback will step up in the pocket after he completes his drop-back steps. The defensive end should set his target 2 yards in front of the quarterback's deepest drop.

(continued)

REMINDER!

When taking the inside rush, you and your athletes must understand the team strategy and game plan. Don't forget to consider the questions on page 172.

ACQUIRING THE APPROPRIATE KNOWLEDGE

When taking the inside rush, you and your athletes should understand the following:

Rules

You and your athletes need to know several main rules when taking the inside rush:

o Defenders must never jump offside; they must key the ball.

o Offensive linemen aren't supposed to hold, but they will. Defensive ends must knock away the blockers' hands.

o Remember that the rules protect the quarterback. Although the defense wants to knock the quarterback down on every play, if the ball is out of his hand, defenders must avoid contact or the officials will call roughing the quarterback, a damaging penalty.

Physical Playing Conditions

The physical playing conditions significantly affect the game. Thus, you and your players must pay attention to the following physical conditions when taking the inside rush:

o In wet and slippery field conditions, sharp cuts are likely to result in slipping. Defensive ends must keep their feet under them and take shorter, more controlled steps.

Strengths and Weaknesses of Opponents

You and your players must account for your opponent's strengths and weaknesses to know how to take the inside rush properly. Consider the following about your opponents:

o How quick is the offensive tackle's pass set? Using scouting tapes and game-day assessments, evaluate the quickness of the offensive tackle's pass set. If he is slow getting up out of his stance, the outside pass rush should be the focus for the defensive end and the inside move probably won't be as important.

o Does the offensive tackle overcommit to the outside pass rush? An offensive tackle who overcommits to a fast outside rush is vulnerable to the inside move. The defensive end must set him up by rushing hard to the outside a few times and then look for signs, such as the shoulders or the feet turning toward the sideline, that the offensive tackle is overcommitted to the outside rush.

o How does the offensive tackle react to the inside move? A quick, agile offensive tackle who reacts well to the inside move and pins the defensive end down to the inside should cause the defensive end to use the inside move only occasionally. Instead, the defensive end should concentrate on a great outside pass rush and containing the quarterback.

Self-Knowledge

Besides being aware of your opponent's strengths and weaknesses, you and your players need to know about your own team's ability. Teach your players to be aware of the following when taking the inside rush:

o How good is the defensive end's get-off? If the defensive end has a quick and explosive start off the line of scrimmage (known as his get-off), he can put a great deal of pressure on the offensive tackle to protect against the fast outside rush. These kinds of defensive ends have the best chance to be successful at the occasional inside rush.

- How good is the defensive end's decision making? Every defender wants to sack the quarterback, and because the inside move can sometimes produce that result, some defensive ends use the inside move too often. The more times the defensive end uses the inside move, the better the offensive blocker will react to it. The defensive end should keep threatening, and using, the fast outside rush to set up the inside move.

- How well does the defensive end read and react to different blocking schemes? The hard-charging, outside-rushing defensive end can be vulnerable to traps, draws and counters unless he consistently reads the offensive tackle's block correctly. Defensive ends have to be able to initiate a pass rush on their first step or two every snap of the game, but they also must react correctly if the play turns out not to be a pass.

At a Glance

The following parts of the text offer additional information on taking the inside rush.

Quarterback Drops	p. 35
Pass Protection	p. 85
Pass Rush	p. 110
Pass Protection on the Edge	p. 222

Decision-Making Guidelines

When deciding how to gain the best advantage when taking the inside rush, you and your players should consider the previous information as well as the following guidelines:

- The defensive end should start every play as if it will be a pass and use a quick get-off. If the play ends up being a run, he must react quickly to that blocking scheme. But if he slows the get-off while reading the blocking scheme, his pass rush will not be successful.

- On every play, the defensive end should evaluate the offensive tackle's pass set. The defensive end should keep challenging the offensive tackle outside with speed and try to discern when he begins to overcommit to the outside rush.

- By observing the quarterback's drop, the defensive end will know how deep he usually sets up and can then decide if it is possible to get to him by beating the offensive tackle inside.

- The defensive end should avoid being greedy. He must use the inside move sparingly and only when the cues are right. As stated earlier, if he chooses to go inside, he must get to the quarterback.

Reacting When Unblocked

This skill is part of an assignment-based defense, in which rules of how to react govern each player's role on every play. For example, the defensive end sees the ball snapped and the play begins. The offensive tackle lined up across from the defensive end does not block the defensive end but instead blocks down on the defensive tackle or, in some situations, releases inside to block the linebacker. When this happens, the defensive end must locate his next threat both quickly and accurately and react to that threat with the proper assignment and technique. He might have to take on a kick-out block from either a fullback or a guard, defend an option play, chase a play going the other direction or defend a reverse or a bootleg coming back his direction.

All the parts of this defense fit together, and if each player does his job correctly, the defense should stop the play. For example, if the defensive end's assignment is to spill a kickout block, the linebacker's assignment would probably be to scrape outside and be in position to make the tackle when the ball carrier is forced to bounce the play. Likewise, if the defensive end takes the dive on the option, the next player will take the quarterback and another player will take the pitch.

Note: This skill describes the reactions for a defensive end when he is unblocked by the offensive tackle. Other defenders, such as defensive tackles or linebackers, might be unblocked by the linemen covering them on some plays and many of their cues and reactions could be similar to those presented in this skill.

READING THE SITUATION

How can you and your players gain an advantage when reacting when unblocked by the tackle? Teach your defensive ends to do the following:

- Know their assignments! They can react properly only if they are clear about what they should do in every situation.
- Key the ball so that they get a good takeoff on every snap.
- Read on the run. Defensive ends can't slow down to read the play. They must learn to react while attacking.
- Key the path of the tackle and recognize early that he is blocking another defender.
- Understand that there will always be a reason for not being blocked. They must be prepared for another type of play and recognize it quickly.
- When a defensive end is not blocked, he should check for the secondary threats in the following order: kickout, option, play away, reverse or bootleg coming back.

⚠ WATCH OUT!

The following circumstances may distract your athletes:

- Focusing on other cues. Defenders must ignore all sights and sounds, such as a hard count, motion or shifting, until the ball is snapped.
- Focusing on the wrong cues. After the snap, the defensive end should focus only on the offensive tackle's course until it is clear whom he is going to block.
- Looking for the ball before finding the first threat. When unblocked by the tackle, the defensive end's first reaction might be to go find the ball. But a blocker or an option play is probably coming, and he must react to those threats before trying to make a play on the ball.

ACQUIRING THE APPROPRIATE KNOWLEDGE

When reacting when unblocked by the tackle, you and your athletes should understand the following:

Rules

You and your athletes need to know several main rules when reacting when unblocked by the tackle:

- Obviously, the defensive end cannot break the plane of the line of scrimmage until the ball is snapped. He must key the ball and move across the line only when the ball moves.

Physical Playing Conditions

The physical playing conditions significantly affect the game. Thus, you and your players must pay attention to the following physical conditions when reacting when unblocked by the tackle:

- If the field is wet and slippery, the defensive end must adjust his takeoff on the snap to be a bit more deliberate so that he can keep his feet underneath him and not slip to the ground.

Strengths and Weaknesses of Opponents

You and your players must account for your opponent's strengths and weaknesses to know how to react properly when unblocked by the tackle. Consider the following about your opponents:

- How strong are the opponent's kickout blockers? If an opponent has an outstanding guard or fullback who is a great kickout blocker, the defensive end has the tough task of having to read his assignment first and then take on a quick, powerful blocker. If he hesitates, he can have difficulty taking on the block properly. He must read quickly and attack aggressively against a powerful blocker.

- How complex are the opponent's blocking schemes? If the offense has predictable blocking schemes (for example, using only the guard and never the fullback as the kickout blocker on the power play) the defensive end's read will be simpler because he has to look for only one threat. But if the offense has a variety of blocking schemes for each play (for example, using several different players as kickout blockers on the power play), the defensive end's read will be more difficult because his threats will be coming from different directions and angles.

- How many plays does the opponent run when the tackle does not block the defensive end? Through scouting and game-day observation, the defense should be able to ascertain how many different plays the defensive end will see if he is unblocked by the tackle. The fewer plays he has to worry about defending, the quicker and more aggressive his reactions can be.

Self-Knowledge

Besides being aware of your opponent's strengths and weaknesses, you and your players need to know about your own team's ability. Teach your players to be aware of the following when reacting if unblocked by the tackle:

- How quickly does the defensive end react? Some players play the game fast and aggressively when they know exactly what they are supposed to do before the snap, but they play slower and less confidently when they have to make a decision after the snap and

(continued)

> **REMINDER!**
>
> When reacting when unblocked by the tackle, you and your players must understand the team strategy and game plan. Don't forget to consider the questions on page 172.

then react. For a defensive end to be effective at this skill, he needs to be able to play at full speed while making a decision and reacting.

- How disciplined are the defensive players as a whole? The defensive ends who are reading and reacting will be more likely to play their assignments correctly if their defensive teammates are also disciplined in their assignments. The defensive end can take satisfaction in eliminating a blocker or an option threat even when he doesn't make a tackle on the play, as long as his teammates were in the right spot to stop the play. But if the teammates are inconsistent, eventually the defensive end may start trying to make plays on his own that are not part of his assigned reactions.

Decision-Making Guidelines

When deciding how to gain the best advantage when reacting when unblocked by the tackle, you and your players should consider the previous information as well as the following guidelines:

- The most dangerous threat is the kickout block from the fullback or the guard. Your defensive ends should immediately look inside to see whether the fullback or the guard is attacking them and, if so, prepare to wrong shoulder that blocker and spill the play outside. The first threat is the kickout block from the fullback. After checking for the fullback, the defensive end must check for the guard (see "Spilling Blocks" on page 103).

- If no kickout block is coming, the next possibility is an option coming down the line. This play could be a dive option, with the quarterback placing the ball in the belly of the running back, or a speed option, with the quarterback coming down the line with the ball and a back in pitch relationship. In either case, the defensive end's assignment is the first option threat coming at him, which would be the running back on a dive option and the quarterback on the speed option. Special techniques for playing the quarterback on the speed option are covered in "Defending the Option" on page 235.

- If no play is coming in his direction, the defensive end should stay square (shoulders parallel) to the line of scrimmage and squeeze down the line, looking to make a tackle on a running back who cuts back, but keeping an eye on the quarterback for a possible play-action bootleg. If the quarterback comes back, the defensive end must contain him (unless a blitz or other defensive call from the outside relieves him of this responsibility) by flowing back down the line of scrimmage.

- If the play goes away and the quarterback does not come back, the defensive end must check one more possibility. He should move down the line of scrimmage slowly, checking for a reverse coming back his direction. Only after the reverse threat is no longer possible can the defensive end turn and run down the field to pursue the play (see "Pursuit Angles" on page 264).

Defending the Option

The offense snaps the ball, and the quarterback attacks down the line of scrimmage with a back in pitch relationship. The offensive line has left the last man on the line of scrimmage unblocked so that the quarterback can option him, either turning upfield if the unblocked defender takes the pitch back or pitching the ball to the back if the defender takes the quarterback. The defender, however, does not commit to either the quarterback or the pitch back. He shuffles down the line of scrimmage ahead of the quarterback, maintaining a position where he can tackle the quarterback if he keeps the ball or turn and run toward the sideline to tackle the ball carrier if the quarterback pitches the ball. This technique of remaining uncommitted to either the quarterback or the pitch back is called feathering the option because it is a passive, unaggressive defensive technique. Nevertheless, it is an effective technique for defending the option because it creates confusion for the quarterback about whether he should keep the ball or pitch it. For a detailed discussion of the techniques involved in this skill, see "Feathering" on page 114.

Note: In this skill, we will only discuss the defensive end's reaction and decisions for defending option plays where he is facing a quarterback and a pitch back. Some dive, or veer, option plays require other reactions, but are not discussed in this skill.

⚠ WATCH OUT!

The following circumstances may distract your athletes:

o Focusing on the ball as the quarterback comes down the line. The defender must concentrate on the quarterback's midsection, not the ball. If the defender watches the ball, a pump fake of the pitch by the quarterback can fake him out.

o Focusing on the back. The defender must peripherally see the pitch back, but until the ball is actually pitched to him, the defender's primary assignment is the quarterback; he is the only defender with that assignment. He has to be in position to make the tackle if the quarterback chooses to run with the ball.

o Being in too much of a hurry to tackle the quarterback. Defensive players are used to being aggressive, and the sight of the quarterback carrying the ball makes them want to attack. However, the defender really needs to shuffle away from the quarterback initially, a very different reaction than he would have in almost any other situation.

READING THE SITUATION

How can you and your players gain an advantage when defending the option? Teach your players to do the following:

- Stop charging upfield when they realize that they are unblocked and look inside for the next read.
- When they see the option coming, they should turn their shoulders parallel to the line of scrimmage and not cross the line of scrimmage.
- Shuffle laterally down the line and stay slightly ahead of the quarterback, but not so far ahead that a big seam opens up for the quarterback to run up the field inside of them.
- Concentrate on the midsection of the quarterback's body as he comes down the line, watching for the quarterback to turn and attempt to run with the ball.

ACQUIRING THE APPROPRIATE KNOWLEDGE

You and your athletes should understand the following when defending the option:

(continued)

REMINDER!

You and your players must understand the team strategy and game plan when defending the option. Don't forget to consider the questions on page 172.

Rules

You and your athletes need to know several main rules when defending the option:

○ Muffed lateral passes are considered fumbles, so the defense can recover them. If an option pitch ends up on the ground, every defender must hustle to the ball and try to make the recovery.

○ Remember that the quarteback can still pitch the ball legally to the back after crossing the line of scrimmage, as long as the pitch is a backward pass or lateral. If the back is in pitch phase behind the quarterback anywhere on the field, he can legally receive a pitch from the quarterback and must be defended.

○ Many defenders sell out to their responsibility to take the quarterback and consequently hit the quarterback on every play, even after he pitches. This habit could result in a penalty against the defense if the hit is late or cheap.

Physical Playing Conditions

The physical playing conditions significantly affect the game. Thus, you and your players must pay attention to the following physical conditions when defending the option:

○ If the field is wet or slippery, the defender cannot get too far ahead of the quarterback on his shuffle down the line because he might slip when he reacts to the quarterback's attempt to run the ball.

○ In wet conditions, the option pitch is a dangerous play, so the defender should realize that the quarterback is more likely to keep the ball in those conditions.

Strengths and Weaknesses of Opponents

You and your players must account for your opponent's strengths and weaknesses to know how to defend the option properly. Consider the following about your opponents:

○ How fast and elusive is the quarterback? If the quarterback is elusive and quick, you may have to coach the defender to feather the quarterback only slightly, or not at all. The defender would still position himself parallel to the line of scrimmage but would not shuffle down the line as much, literally waiting for the quarterback to arrive and forcing him to pitch so that he can't end up running with the ball. Conversely, if the quarterback is not fast or elusive, the defender can shuffle further ahead of the quarterback, baiting him to run and then reacting to make the tackle.

○ Who is more dangerous with the ball: the quarterback or the pitch back? Evaluate which player you would rather see running the ball and then teach the defender to feather the option so that the less dangerous ball carrier is more likely to end up carrying the ball.

Self-Knowledge

Besides being aware of your opponent's abilities, you and your players need to know about your own team's ability. Teach your players to be aware of the following when defending the option:

○ How disciplined are the defensive ends? This technique requires great patience. Players who are undisciplined or overaggressive cannot perform it well.

- How fast are the defensive ends? If the ends are fast, they can play farther ahead of the quarterback and still be able to react back to him if he chooses to run. Playing farther ahead of the quarterback also gives the defender a better chance to react and run down the line to help tackle the ball carrier if the ball is pitched.

- How well does the rest of the defense respond to the option? The technique of feathering the option is crucial if the defense lacks team speed or has trouble defeating blocks and getting to the outside. Feathering slows down the quarterback, strings out the option and buys time for other defenders to react, defeat blocks and rally to the play.

At a Glance

The following parts of the text offer additional information on defending the option.

Option Pitch Mechanics	p. 33
Feathering	p. 114
Option Pitch Read	p. 177
Reactioning When Unblocked	p. 232

Decision-Making Guidelines

When deciding how to gain the best advantage when defending the option, you and your players should consider the previous information as well as the following guidelines:

- The key to defending the option effectively is the initial reaction by the defender. If the quarterback gets to the defender before the defender recognizes the play, turns his shoulders and levels off at the line of scrimmage, the quarterback will be able to pitch the ball quickly and the defender will be unable to help.

- Remember that the purpose of feathering the option is to slow down the quarterback, create indecision in his mind and buy time for other defenders to react and get to the play. The defender must be cagey and quick in playing this technique; he must not give the quarterback an easy decision!

- Remember that the defender who is feathering the option is assigned, by the defensive scheme, to tackle the quarterback if he keeps the ball. He should be ready to plant the outside foot, drive back at the quarterback and make the tackle at the line of scrimmage if the quarterback chooses to run.

- If the quarterback pitches the ball, the defender should drive his outside arm backward and quickly turn toward the sideline, running straight down the line of scrimmage to help tackle the ball carrier who has caught the pitch.

Linebacker Reads

The linebacker is in ready position, the ball is snapped, and the linebacker reads his keys. First, he studies the pad level of the offensive linemen in front of him—low pads mean run, and high pads mean pass. If the pads are low and blockers are approaching, the linebacker identifies his blocking threat and, looking through that threat to the backfield, sees the flow of the backs. He reacts to these keys and attacks the blocker with the correct shoulder so that he can "fit" into the gap he is assigned to defend. If the pads are high and the play is a pass, the linebacker either drops to his assigned area if his team is playing a zone pass coverage, or he finds his assigned receiver and immediately "melts" to him if his team is playing a man pass coverage. Accurate reads are the key to success as a linebacker. Early recognition of a play helps the linebacker get to his assignment quickly and gives him the best possible chance to beat the blocker on a run or get in position to defend a pass.

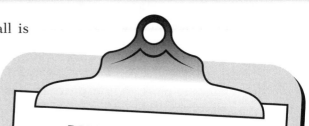

READING THE SITUATION

How can you and your players gain an advantage when making linebacker reads? Teach your players to do the following:

- Know the down and distance and the play-calling tendencies of the opponent to get a head start on what type of play might be most likely in each situation.

- Focus on the tops of the linemen's helmets and read the level. Generally, low pads mean run; high pads mean pass.

- Trust their instincts. See the blocking scheme and flow and explode out of their stance. React and then go full speed!

⚠ WATCH OUT!

The following circumstances may distract your athletes:

- Guessing the snap count. Linebackers must be poised and patient, not in a hurry to go anywhere until the ball is snapped and they make the read.

- Focusing on the quarterback, the ball or the backfield at the snap. Linebackers should pay total attention to the linemen for pass or run and blocking combination reads.

- Taking false steps. Linebackers must think about their feet and the first step or two. Their reaction to the play will be quicker if their first steps are correct and accurate.

ACQUIRING THE APPROPRIATE KNOWLEDGE

You and your athletes should understand the following about making linebacker reads:

REMINDER!

You and your players must understand the team strategy and game plan in making linebacker reads. Don't forget to consider the questions on page 172.

Rules

You and your athletes need to know several main rules when making linebacker reads:

- Linebackers (in fact, all defenders) are allowed to move around during the cadence and do not have to be set when the ball is snapped, as long as they have not crossed the line of scrimmage into the neutral zone. But making reads while moving is difficult and not recommended.

○ Offensive players cannot, by rule, grab or hold linebackers while blocking, but officials do not call all these penalties. Linebackers have to use aggressive hand and arm action to escape from blockers who hold, and they should not expect the umpire to come to the rescue by throwing a flag.

Physical Playing Conditions

The physical playing conditions significantly affect the game. Thus, you and your players must pay attention to the following physical conditions when using linebacker reads:

○ If the field is wet or slippery, the linebacker cannot rely on a dramatic plant step as he reacts to his initial read. He will have to shorten his stride and take smaller steps.

Strengths and Weaknesses of Opponents

You and your players must account for your opponent's strengths and weaknesses to know how to make linebacker reads properly. Consider the following about your opponents:

○ How complex is the opponent's blocking scheme? Teams that use standard blocking schemes for the run game and combine that with a traditional drop-back passing game are easier to read. Teams that employ a lot of misdirection can sometimes induce aggressive linebackers to overreact in an initial direction, putting them out of position for the play.

○ How quick are the offensive linemen? If the linemen are quick, the linebackers have to be decisive with their reads. The linebackers also could align slightly deeper to gain slightly more time to make the correct read.

○ How well does the opponent execute the play-action passing game? Play-action passes are difficult to read because they look like running plays initially, with the quarterback faking the handoff and then throwing a pass. Linebackers have to react to the run play every time, but they must remember to look at the pad level of the offensive linemen. If the play is really a run, the pads will be low. If the pads are high, linebackers can be suspicious of the run and look for the pass (see "Defending the Play-Action Pass" on page 254).

○ Does the offense run the draw play? The draw play is difficult to read because it looks like a pass, with high pad level by the offensive linemen and the quarterback dropping back, but it becomes a run when the quarterback hands off the ball to the waiting back. Linebackers have to react initially as if the play is going to be a pass, taking an open step, but if they see a running back waiting in the backfield they should not vacate their areas until the quarterback has dropped back past the back and can no longer give him the ball (see "Defending the Draw Play" on page 257).

Self-Knowledge

Besides being aware of your opponent's strengths and weaknesses, you and your players need to know about your own team's ability. Teach your players to be aware of the following when making linebacker reads:

○ Can the linebackers read effectively? Defenses that rely on reading can be effective if the linebackers learn to make their reads because they can flow quickly to every run and every pass and are never out of position. But if the linebackers cannot read for run or pass and for blocking schemes, the defense may not be able to use a reading defense. The defense would have to blitz linebackers to predetermined gaps, limiting the flow of the defense.

(continued)

○ How quick are the linebackers? If the linebackers are fast, they will be able to make their reads slightly more deliberately because they will be able to react quickly enough to defeat blocks and get to the play.

Decision-Making Guidelines

When deciding how to gain the best advantage when making linebacker reads, you and your players should consider the previous information as well as the following guidelines:

○ Some linebackers try to anticipate plays and end up guessing which direction they will go. These linebackers are frequently wrong and out of position. Linebackers have to keep an open mind and react, not guess.

○ If the linebackers are having problems reading plays, quiz them on where they are looking when the ball is snapped. Many linebackers have trouble resisting the temptation to look for the ball. They must watch the linemen.

○ Drill your linebackers repeatedly so that the first step is not a false drop step. Before the snap, the linebacker should have all his weight on the balls of his feet, evenly distributed, so that he is in a forward-leaning, balanced stance. The pushoff foot must stay on the ground, and the takeoff foot must step in the right direction (forward or back, left or right) with no wasted movement.

○ If the lineman's pads are low, the linebacker should watch the blocking combination unfold to reveal the direction of the play. He should see through the linemen to the backfield action for the flow of the backs (fast flow outside, inside or downhill action, split flow) and focus all attention on the oncoming blocker. He must know which gap he is assigned to defend and he must attack the blocker with the correct shoulder so that he is either squeezing the play back to the inside and attack with the inside shoulder and the outside arm free or spilling the play to the outside and attack with the outside shoulder and inside arm free (see "Spilling Blocks" on page 103 and "Squeezing Blocks" on page 107). The linebacker must attack the blocker properly and then defeat that blocker before he can move on to the task of tackling the ball carrier.

○ If the lineman's pads are high and the defense is playing a zone pass coverage, the linebacker should drop step and half turn to run toward his assigned area, keeping his eyes on the quarterback while beginning his drop. His technique and reads and reactions from that point on are discussed in "Zone Pass Drops" on page 117 and "Reads and Reactions in Zone Pass Coverage" on page 248.

○ If the lineman's pads are high and the defense is playing a man pass coverage, the linebacker locates the receiver he is assigned to defend and immediately "melts" to him as quickly as possible, ignoring all other receivers and cues. For more information on his technique from that point on, see "Man Pass Coverage" on page 244.

Choosing to Spill or Squeeze

The linebacker sees the ball snapped, and the play, a run play, begins. The offensive linemen in front of the linebacker block defensive linemen, giving the linebacker an open window into the backfield. The fullback or a pulling lineman approaches the linebacker as a lead blocker in front of the halfback, who takes the handoff on an isolation or power play. The linebacker has to fit the play properly, taking on the lead blocker with the correct shoulder so that he can either spill the play outside or squeeze the play back inside.

This skill requires that the linebacker know his teammates' positions so that he can execute his assignment. If the safety on his side is playing close to the line of scrimmage as a primary force player, the linebacker will spill the play to that safety, taking on the block with his outside shoulder, filling the inside gap and forcing the play outside. If the safety is off the line, playing deep as a secondary force player, the linebacker will squeeze the play, taking on the block with his inside shoulder, taking away the outside gap and forcing the play back to the next linebacker inside.

⚠ WATCH OUT!

The following circumstances may distract your athletes:

- Focusing on offensive maneuvers that don't dictate assignments. Motion, shifting, play fakes and other offensive movements can get in the way of a clean linebacker read.

- Paying too much attention, initially, to the ball carrier. The blocking scheme, not the ball carrier, should dictate the linebacker's course.

- Failure to find the first threat. The first threat is the primary blocker assigned to block the linebacker. The linebacker must find his first threat immediately after reading the initial flow and direction of the play. He must find that blocker and take him on with the correct shoulder.

- Getting too excited about contact! Linebackers must, by the requirements of their position, love contact. But when taking on a block, linebackers must remember their assignment regarding which shoulder to use, even if the impending collision is why they play the game.

READING THE SITUATION

How can you and your players gain an advantage when choosing to spill or squeeze? Teach your players to do the following:

- Focus on the key and read the running back action through the linemen.

- Understand which running back or pulling lineman is assigned to block the linebacker.

- Know and understand where teammates are positioned.

- Take on the lead blocker with physical force using the proper shoulder.

- Restrict the running lane by working throughout the blocker.

- Pursue to the ball carrier if your gap is not threatened.

ACQUIRING THE APPROPRIATE KNOWLEDGE

When choosing to spill or squeeze, you and your players should understand the following:

Rules

You and your athletes need to know several main rules when choosing to spill or squeeze:

REMINDER!

When choosing to spill or squeeze, you and your players must understand the team strategy and game plan. Don't forget to consider the questions on page 172.

(continued)

- According to most high school federation rules, the fullback or pulling lineman cannot chop the linebacker, so the linebacker can take on the block with his forearm and shoulder.

- The fullback or pulling lineman cannot, by rule, grab or hold the linebacker, but that doesn't mean he won't try to do so. The linebacker must aggressively use his hands and forearms to disengage from the lead blocker because he should not expect the holding penalty to be called.

Physical Playing Conditions

The physical playing conditions significantly affect the game. Thus, you and your players must pay attention to the following physical conditions when choosing to spill or squeeze:

- In wet or slippery field conditions, the linebackers should know that their base of footing may not be firm. They should shorten their stride and narrow their base to keep their legs underneath them in these conditions.

Strengths and Weaknesses of Opponents

You and your players must account for your opponent's strengths and weaknesses to know how to spill or squeeze blocks properly. Consider the following about your opponents:

- Does the opponent have a great passing game? If so, the safeties will have to play deeper in coverage or play man coverage behind blitzes. The linebackers, then, will have to squeeze all running plays.

- How fast is the lead blocker? If the lead blocker is fast, the linebacker will have to decide quickly whether to squeeze or to spill the block.

- Do the opponent's wide receivers crack block (come inside to block) the safeties? If so, the defense should make a call requiring the linebacker to squeeze blocks, because the safety might not be available to make the tackle.

- Does the opponent have an outstanding running back? If so, the defense might want to place the safeties closer to the line and ask the linebackers to spill more plays to the safeties. This tactic should also force the opponent's running back to run laterally instead of vertically down the field, which might slow him enough for the defensive pursuit to get to him.

- How powerful is the fullback or lead blocker? If the offense has a strong fullback or lead blocker who can overpower the linebacker, the choice to squeeze running plays might result in good gains for the offense because the blocker and running back can run more vertically (or north and south) up the field. The defense in this situation should consider making calls that ask the linebacker to spill more running plays, because spilling forces the ball carrier to flatten off his running course toward the sideline, making him run more laterally and therefore less powerfully.

Self-Knowledge

Besides being aware of your opponent's strengths and weaknesses, you and your players need to know about your own team's ability. Teach your players to be aware of the following when choosing to spill or squeeze:

- How well do the safeties tackle? If your safeties are solid, consistent tacklers, you should choose to spill plays to them. If they are inconsistent, you might be better off to squeeze plays back inside.

- How smart and disciplined are the linebackers? If the linebackers understand the concept of team defense and how their assignment fits that concept, they should be able to choose correctly whether to squeeze or spill. But if the linebackers have trouble grasping the overall concept, they will probably make mistakes, taking on blocks with the wrong shoulder.

- How do the corners match up against the wide receivers? If the corners can cover their wide receivers one-on-one, then the safeties can play closer to the line and the linebackers can spill plays. But if the wide receivers overmatch the corners, the safeties may have to play deeper to provide help for the corners, meaning that the linebackers will have to squeeze plays back inside.

Decision-Making Guidelines

When deciding how to gain the best advantage when choosing to spill or squeeze, you and your players should consider the previous information as well as the following guidelines:

- Understand that the coverage called in the huddle will dictate the safety's alignment and responsibilities, which in turn tells the linebacker whether to squeeze or spill when the offense runs a play with a lead blocker.

- Know which offensive player is coming to block him. Different blocking schemes by the offense require different reactions from the linebacker. He might spill a lead blocker but squeeze a frontside lineman. To know how to react, linebackers must recognize the blocker.

- Understand the offensive play being run. The combination of blocking scheme and backfield action also influences the linebacker's reaction. He might have the assignment to spill a play, but if the backfield action is fast flow (such as a toss play or option), he might have to play outside all blocks. To be correct, the linebacker must understand the concept of the offensive play.

- Be aggressive! Linebackers cannot become less aggressive or play in slow motion because they are trying to decide whether to squeeze or to spill. They must make a choice, right or wrong, and play hard.

- Get the correct foot on the ground before contact. After the linebacker has decided which shoulder to use to take on the block, he must get the foot on that side on the ground immediately before contact. This action will give him a firm base from which to attack the blocker and help him avoid being bent backward by the collision.

The defensive back is covering a receiver man-to-man. The receiver makes his move and gains a little separation from the defender. The quarterback delivers the ball. The defender must make a play, first to prevent a completion, but even more important, to prevent a run after the catch.

The defender must first close the gap between himself and the receiver as much and as quickly as possible. He then must decide whether he can locate the ball and deflect it away from the receiver or whether he is going to have to collide with the receiver when the ball arrives and try to knock it loose. If he can't break up the pass and the receiver makes the catch, the defender has to tackle him. Making the decision of whether to play the ball or the man, or trying to play the ball through the man, is the most challenging and critical aspect of man pass coverage.

⚠ WATCH OUT!

The following circumstances may distract your athletes:

- Losing sight of the assigned man at the snap. In man coverage, defenders must play pass first, checking to see whether their assigned man runs a pass route or blocks. Defenders must know where the receiver is and what he is doing when the ball is snapped.

- Looking back at the quarterback during the route. If the defender takes his eyes off the receiver, he will lose track of him and the receiver will gain good separation from the defender.

- Looking for the ball before the receiver does. The defender must stay focused on the receiver, without worrying about the ball, until the receiver looks for the ball and puts his hands up in preparation for a catch. Then the defender can turn and find the ball.

- Panicking after being faked out. If the receiver makes a great move and gains some separation, the defender should focus on recovering lost ground and closing the gap to the receiver before wondering whether the quarterback has thrown the ball or where the ball is located.

READING THE SITUATION

How can you and your players best learn how to finish plays in man pass coverage? Teach your players to do the following:

- Concentrate on eliminating any separation between themselves and the receiver. After the receiver makes his move, the defender must react using the proper footwork with no false steps and accelerate toward the receiver.

- Focus attention on the receiver's inside hip and stay with him, knowing where he is in every situation.

- Look for the ball when they see the receiver's eyes and hands react to the flight of the ball. The receiver's reactions are the defender's cue to locate the ball and decide whether he is in position to deflect it from the receiver.

- If the ball is out of reach, play through the man to the ball, timing the collision with the receiver so that it happens just as the ball arrives.

- If the ball gets to the receiver before the defender does, the defender must play through the receiver's upfield shoulder to make a sure tackle after the receiver makes the catch.

ACQUIRING THE APPROPRIATE KNOWLEDGE

When finishing plays in man pass coverage, you and your players should understand the following:

Rules

You and your athletes need to know several main rules when finishing plays in man pass coverage.

- The defender cannot grab or hold the receiver, which is often an instinctive reaction if the receiver makes a good move. The defender must use his feet to get in proper position, using his hands primarily to make plays on the ball.
- When the ball is in the air, the defender cannot collide with the receiver, grab or hold him or make more than incidental contact until the receiver touches the ball. At that point the defender can, and should, make contact with the receiver to try to knock the ball loose. Colliding with a receiver is legal (as long as the defender does not grab him) if the ball is not in the air. Defenders can use that tactic to disrupt the timing of the route.
- Face guarding where the defender puts his hand or hands over the face and eyes of the receiver so he can't see the ball is illegal and will consistently be penalized. Defenders must be sure that their hands go for the ball to avoid this penalty.

Physical Playing Conditions

The physical playing conditions significantly affect the game. Thus, you and your players must pay attention to the following physical conditions when finishing plays in man pass coverage:

- If the field is wet and slippery, the defender has to play with greater depth (more cushion) and make less dramatic cuts to be able to react to the receiver's routes without falling down or slipping and losing a lot of ground. Of course, the receiver will have to be more cautious in his footwork as well.
- If the ball is wet, the defender may have a little more time to react after the ball is thrown because the quarterback will likely not be able to throw it with as much velocity.
- If the wind is blowing hard, the defender has to play deeper and expect the ball to carry more when it is being thrown with the wind. Conversely, he has to play shorter and expect the ball to hang in the air when it is being thrown into a strong wind.

Strengths and Weaknesses of Opponents

You and your players must account for your opponent's strengths and weaknesses to know how to finish plays in man pass coverage. Consider the following about your opponents:

- How fast are the opponent's receivers? If the receivers are extremely fast, the man defender must play with greater depth (more cushion), respecting the deep route threat and reacting quickly to make tackles on intermediate or short routes. If the receivers are not as fast, the defender can tighten his cushion, play closer to his man and perhaps be in position to make more plays on the ball instead of the man, as long as he uses good technique.
- How accurate and skilled is the quarterback? If an opponent's quarterback throws with outstanding timing and accuracy, he can get the ball to his receiver even if that receiver is well covered. The defender may not be able to make plays on the ball, so he should

REMINDER!

When finishing plays in man pass coverage, you and your players must understand the team strategy and game plan. Don't forget to consider the questions on page 172.

(continued)

concentrate on making big collisions with the receivers after the ball arrives. If the quarterback is not as strong armed or accurate, or if his timing is slow, the defender may be able to make more plays on the ball, if he establishes good position against the receivers.

- How good is the opponent's pass protection? If an opponent's pass protection is excellent, the defenders may have to cover the receivers for a long time, giving the receivers a better chance to get open and putting pressure on the defenders to minimize separation between themselves and the receivers. If the protection is shaky, the defenders should play more aggressively, looking for opportunities to make plays on the ball if the quarterback throws early or throws less accurately in the face of a big pass rush.

- How well does the offense pick up blitzes? If the offense has difficulty, then a pressure pass rush with man coverage should put great stress on the quarterback and perhaps give the defenders some opportunities to make plays on the ball. If the offense does a good job, then the defenders in man coverage will be under pressure because they must be able to stay close to their receivers with no help from defensive teammates.

Self-Knowledge

Besides being aware of your opponent's strengths and weaknesses, you and your players need to know about your own team's ability. Teach your players to be aware of the following when finishing plays in man pass coverage:

- How do defenders match up against receivers? Man-to-man coverage is practical and tempting to use, because with only five eligible receivers, six defenders can rush the quarterback. But the defenders playing man-to-man coverage must not only be quick enough to stay with the receivers but also be adept at finding the ball and making plays on the ball when it is in the air. If the matchups favor the receivers, man coverage is risky.

- How disciplined are the defenders? Defenders must be aggressive at the right times, avoiding penalties for pass interference and holding when trying to finish the play and prevent the catch.

- How well do the defenders read their keys? One mistake in reading a key can leave a receiver wide open for a touchdown! Defenders can't finish the play properly unless they always identify and cover the receiver assigned to them in man coverage.

- Do the defenders understand when they can go for the ball? Defenders must learn to make plays on the ball only when they are certain that they can get two hands on it or get the downfield arm on the ball while keeping the upfield arm behind the receiver. If they are unsure, they should focus on hitting the receiver after the catch. If they try for the ball and miss, the receiver will get a big play or a touchdown.

- How well do your defenders tackle? Man defenders must be good tacklers because if they miss the tackle after a catch, the receiver will be free for a big play.

Decision-Making Guidelines

When deciding how to gain the best advantage when finishing plays in man pass coverage, you and your players should consider the previous information as well as the following guidelines:

- If the receiver breaks left or right, the defender has to plant, point and drive toward the receiver, staying in position behind the receiver's upfield shoulder.

- If the receiver runs a double route (stop and go, out and up), the defender has to collide with the receiver to throw off the timing of the second route. To be able to do this, the defender has to maintain a position over the outside shoulder of the receiver during the initial stages of any route.

- If the receiver tries to run a deep route, the defender must turn toward the receiver and run with him, trying to gain a position on the receiver's inside hip if the receiver is running down the sideline or over the receiver's outside hip if he is running an inside route such as a post pattern. The defender must not look for the ball until the receiver looks for it.

- If the receiver gets the defender to turn his hips the wrong way, the defender must use a speed turn, whipping his head and body around in the opposite direction, locating the receiver and sprinting toward his upfield shoulder to get back in position (see "Speed Turn" on page 123).

- When the ball arrives, the defender should go for it only if he can reach it with both hands and is sure that he can make a play on it. If he can't make a two-handed play on the ball, he should try to get his downfield hand on the ball while keeping the other hand behind the receiver. Alternatively, he could try to collide with the man just as the ball arrives, trying to jar the ball loose. When using either of these tactics, known as playing the ball through the man, the defender should always make sure he wraps his arms around the receiver after making contact so that he ends up tackling the receiver to the ground in case the receiver did, in fact, catch the ball.

- If the defender can't play the ball through the man, he must play the man. He should close the gap and make a sure tackle immediately after the receiver makes the catch.

At a Glance

The following parts of the text offer additional information on finishing plays in man pass coverage.

The quarterback drops back to pass. The defense has called for zone pass coverage, and the defenders begin to drop to the appropriate areas (see "Zone Pass Drops" on page 117). As the defenders complete their zone pass drops, they must master two skills to play effective zone pass defense. First, they must accurately read both the quarterback and the receivers to get in the best possible position to make a play. Second, they must react quickly and decisively to the throw to finish the play successfully.

⚠ WATCH OUT!

The following circumstances may distract your athletes:

- Reading the wrong key. All defenders must initially key the offensive line blocking and the quarterback's first few steps to determine run or pass. Defensive backs must resist the temptation to watch the receiver as the play starts, and linebackers must not watch the running backs as the play starts.

- Focusing too long on the quarterback. After reading pass and beginning their drops, the defenders must immediately turn their attention to the route combinations threatening their areas.

- Focusing on shallow routes in the zone. The defender should ignore the shallow routes and work to cover the deepest route in his area.

READING THE SITUATION

How can you and your players gain an advantage when reading and reacting in zone pass coverage? Teach your players to do the following:

- Keep receivers inside and in front. Defenders must never get outflanked or get beat deep.

- Know where the threats are. Defenders must see the patterns unfold and understand which receivers will be entering their areas to defend.

- Continue to track the receivers peripherally but find the quarterback and see where he is looking.

- Read the quarterback's hand position. When he takes his nonthrowing hand off the ball, delivery is imminent and the defender can get a jump on the ball.

- React decisively to the intended target and break up the play.

 ACQUIRING THE APPROPRIATE KNOWLEDGE

When reading and reacting in zone pass coverage, you and your players should understand the following:

Rules

You and your athletes need to know several main rules when reading and reacting in zone pass coverage:

- Defenders cannot grab or hold receivers.

- Defenders are allowed to collide with receivers if the ball has not yet been thrown. Underneath defenders should make contact with receivers who run through their zones, unless a deeper threat is also present in the zone.

- When the ball is in the air, the defender cannot grab, hold or collide with the receiver. The defender should try to make contact with the receiver just after the receiver touches the ball so that he can jar the ball loose.

Physical Playing Conditions

REMINDER!

When reading and reacting in zone pass coverage, you and your players must understand the team strategy and game plan. Don't forget to consider the questions on page 172.

The physical playing conditions significantly affect the game. Thus, you and your players must pay attention to the following physical conditions when reading and reacting in zone pass coverage:

- If the field is wet and slippery, zone pass defenders must play with greater depth and more caution so that they don't lose their footing and give up a big completion.
- In windy conditions, deep zone defenders must play with greater depth when the quarterback is throwing with the wind to guard against the ball being thrown over their heads.

Strengths and Weaknesses of Opponents

You and your players must account for your opponent's strengths and weaknesses to know how to read and react in zone pass coverage properly. Consider the following about your opponents:

- How accurate is the quarterback? An accurate, patient quarterback might pick apart a zone coverage with pinpoint shallow passes that produce first downs and move the ball steadily down the field.
- How patient is the quarterback? Impatient quarterbacks who want to throw deep too often may tend to throw interceptions against zone coverages.
- What type of receivers does the opponent feature? Bigger or slower receivers who play with good body position can have good success with possession catches against zone defenses.
- How good is the opponent's pass protection? Most zone coverages require seven droppers (linebackers and defensive backs) and only use a four-man rush. If the opponent's pass protection negates the four-man rush and the quarterback has lots of time to throw, he will eventually find some holes in the zone for completions.

Self-Knowledge

Besides being aware of your opponent's strengths and weaknesses, you and your players need to know about your own team's ability. Teach your players to be aware of the following when reading and reacting in zone pass coverage:

- How disciplined are the linebackers? Zone pass defense will be ineffective if the linebackers are inconsistent on their pass drops or are easily influenced by shallow routes in their areas. Linebackers must consistently play deep enough in their zones to be able to read the routes and the quarterback and react to stop both intermediate and short routes.
- How well do your defenders match up against the receivers? If the opponent's receivers are talented and fast, the defenders may be unable to stop them in man coverage. Zone coverage might be a safer strategy that allows fewer big plays because all defenders stay as deep as the deepest receiver in their areas and most of the passes end up being thrown to shallow receivers.

(continued)

○ How instinctive are your defenders? If your defenders react quickly to the ball even though they are not exceptionally fast or outstanding man coverage players, a zone coverage might be effective. Zone defenders primarily face the quarterback and are able to see the ball, whereas man defenders usually face away from the quarterback while they cover their receivers and are unable to see the ball as early in the play.

○ How good is your pass rush? The most frequently asked question regarding zone defense does not involve the actual pass defenders; it involves the front four defensive linemen: "Can we get four-man pressure?" If the front four can make the quarterback throw in a hurry, or at least on time (generally regarded as four seconds or less), zone coverage can be effective. The more time the quarterback has to throw, the more likely it is that he will find open areas in the zones.

Decision-Making Guidelines

When deciding how to gain the best advantage when reading and reacting in zone pass coverage, you and your players should consider the previous information as well as the following guidelines:

○ Read the route combinations. Defenders must stay off the shallow routes and drop deep in their zones.

○ Read the quarterback. The quarterback will eventually have to look at the target where he is throwing the ball, so the defenders should lean on (play a little closer to) the deepest route in the area where the quarterback is looking.

○ The quarterback has to take his nonthrowing hand off the football to release the ball. When he takes that hand off the football, the ball will be on its way and the defender should break in the direction of the throw.

○ Once the ball is thrown, the nearest defender must take an angle that will take him to the receiver's upfield shoulder. As in man coverage, the defender cannot afford to break in front of a receiver in an attempt to deflect a pass and miss, because he will give up a big play. Unless he is absolutely sure he can make a play on the ball, he will have to play the ball through the man.

Force

The force player is, horizontally, the outermost defensive player. He must force the ball carrier back to his teammates in the middle of the field. He must take on any blockers with his inside arm and shoulder, keeping his outside arm and leg free. Assume that the offense snaps the ball and runs an off-tackle or outside running play. One defender on the side that the offense is attacking is the force player for the defense. As the play comes toward him, he must be sure that the ball carrier goes inside. At the same time, the force player must not allow a gap so wide that the ball carrier can go inside and then get right back outside and run away from the rest of the defense.

Force players are important to an effective defense because they force the ball carrier back to the 10 pursuing defenders instead of letting him get outside and run away from the pursuit. By turning the play back inside and effectively reducing the width of the field, force players play an important role even though they probably won't make the tackle. Force players have one job: turn the play back inside.

READING THE SITUATION

How can you and your players gain an advantage using the force concept? Teach your players to do the following:

- Understand that no defensive strategy or game plan can be effective without solid, consistent force play.
- Know who the force players are on every play (one on each side of the defense, usually corners but possibly safeties, alley players or outside linebackers).
- Devote attention to potential blockers and keep them inside as the ball approaches.
- Know where the ball is, keeping it inside at all times.

⚠ WATCH OUT!

The following circumstances may distract your athletes:

- Reacting too hard to an inside move. If the ball carrier comes toward the force player and dips inside (faking a move upfield inside the force player), the force player should not react too quickly to the inside to get in on the tackle, because the ball carrier could potentially bounce the play back toward the sideline and get outside the force player.

- Going underneath a block. Sometimes the force player thinks that he can get to the ball carrier and does not see or disregards a potential blocker. If the force player goes underneath (inside) a block on the perimeter of the play, the ball carrier will be able to react and get outside the force player.

- Pursuing too quickly on plays away. If the ball initially goes away from the force player, he must be careful not to pursue too quickly. He must stay behind the ball in case the ball carrier cuts back (or the offense runs a reverse of some kind). If the ball comes back his way, the force player must be in position to turn the play back to the inside.

ACQUIRING THE APPROPRIATE KNOWLEDGE

When using the force concept, you and your players should understand the following:

Rules

You and your athletes need to know several main rules when using the force concept:

- By rule, blockers cannot grab or hold the force player. But they will sometimes try to pin the force player inside by grabbing his arms or jersey. The force player cannot expect the

(continued)

REMINDER!

When using the force concept, you and your players must understand the team strategy and game plan. Don't forget to consider the questions on page 172.

officials to make every holding call, so he must use aggressive arm and hand actions to escape from the blocker and maintain his outside leverage.

○ Blockers cannot chop (block below the waist) the force player, so the force player can attack any blocker aggressively, knowing that he will make solid contact with that blocker.

Physical Playing Conditions

The physical playing conditions significantly affect the game. Thus, you and your players must pay attention to the following physical conditions when using the force concept:

○ In wet and slippery field conditions, the force player has to be extra careful to establish solid footing and a balanced base before taking on blocks. He cannot afford to slip and fall because the other 10 players are relying on him to turn the play back to them.

Strengths and Weaknesses of Opponents

You and your players must account for your opponent's strengths and weaknesses to know how to use force properly. Consider the following about your opponents:

○ How fast are the opponent's running backs and receivers? Against a fast opponent, the force player will have to position himself wider on the field so that the ball carrier cannot outrun him to the sideline and get around the corner.

○ Do the opponent's ball carriers look for the cutback when they get in the open field? If the opponent has running backs or receivers who know how to cut back across the field when they get in the open, the force player who is backside will have to be cautious in his pursuit on every play to prevent the opponent from cutting underneath him and getting outside.

○ Does the opponent run the option? Force players have the pitch on all option plays and must stay outside any blocks, not react to take the quarterback. They must defend the pitch if the ball goes there.

○ Does the opponent run bootlegs and misdirection plays? Play-action passes and misdirection plays like counters and reverses have the potential to beat a backside force player if he reacts too quickly to the initial play direction away from him. Force players must be cautious on play action away because if the ball comes back, they must turn it back inside (contain it).

Self-Knowledge

Besides being aware of your opponent's strengths and weaknesses, you and your players need to know about your own team's ability. Teach your players to be aware of the following when using the force concept:

○ Are your force players strong enough to take on the opponent's kickout blocks? When taking on blockers, the force player must be physical and strong because his assignment is to restrict the running lane to the inside as much as possible. To prevent the matchup from favoring the offensive blocker too heavily, the force player must keep the pads low, use good leg strength and keep the outside arm and leg free.

- How aggressive is the force player? Some assignments and skills in football require tremendous aggressiveness, but the force technique requires patience and discipline. If the force player is too aggressive, he will either overreact to a play away or attack the ball carrier too vigorously on plays toward him, thus running the risk of getting beat to the outside.

- How much of a team player is the force player? Everyone on defense likes to make tackles, because then he hears his name on the loudspeaker or reads it in the paper the next day. But the force player must play for the team and understand that he will make fewer tackles than the players inside will.

At a Glance

The following parts of the text offer additional information on using force.

Open-Field Tackling	p. 168
Pursuit Angles	p. 264
Playing Force on Kick Coverage	p. 272

Decision-Making Guidelines

When deciding how to gain the best advantage when using the force concept, you and your players should consider the previous information as well as the following guidelines:

- Remember that although the primary job of a force player is to turn the play inside, he should avoid giving up a lot of ground laterally (toward the sideline) as he keeps his outside leverage so that he minimizes the running lane inside for the ball carrier. The force player must try to squeeze the field, give up ground grudgingly and turn the ball carrier inside as early as possible.

- Also, remember that although the force player must squeeze the field, he can never let the ball outside. He must balance physical play inside with patient, disciplined play outside.

- Every defensive scheme on every play must have a force player, but defenses can choose which players to designate as the force players, based on the speed of the offensive players and the type of attack that the offense is running. For example, some defenses like to play cover 2 against fast teams who run the option because the corners will roll up and become the force players, yet they play far enough outside that a speedy offense will have trouble outflanking them.

- If the play is option, the force player has the pitch man. The force player should ignore the quarterback and stay in position to tackle the pitch man if he gets the ball.

- If the force player blitzes from the outside, he still has the responsibility of preventing the play from getting outside. The force player blitzes to the quarterback, not the running back, to prevent bootlegs or keep plays, he blitzes to the pitch back on option plays, and he blitzes as a contain rusher outside the offensive tackle on drop-back pass plays.

Defending the Play-Action Pass

The offense snaps the ball, and the linemen come off low and hard. The quarterback takes the ball back toward the running back who is attacking the line of scrimmage. The quarterback extends the ball (or his open hand) to the back but does not give him the ball. Instead, he keeps it and either sets up to pass behind the fake or attempts to roll out or bootleg back with the ball, looking to pass. The offense has just executed a play-action pass, and the defense has to react. If the offense does a good job of faking the run, with low pad level and an aggressive takeoff, the defense will have to play run defense first, until the fake is made and receivers go out for passes. The defense has to look for cues that the play is not really a run, and react to those cues quickly to get back in position.

Defensive backs who are covering wide receivers, incidentally, always play pass first as long as the receiver is in position to run a route. Sometimes a wide receiver will fake a block on a play-action pass and then run his route. Again, the defender must look for cues that the play is not really a run and react quickly to the pass.

READING THE SITUATION

How can you and your players gain an advantage when defending the play-action pass? Teach your players to do the following:

- Play run first. Defenders must get off on the snap and stay gap sound against any blocking scheme that the offense shows in case the play is, in fact, a run.
- Look for high hats. Linemen do not stand up on real run plays. If the lineman's helmet goes up on the snap, he is setting up for pass protection.
- Key the eligible pass receivers. If any of the eligible receivers, especially tight ends who usually would be blocking on a run, burst off the line into a pass route, the play is a pass.
- Understand the situation. Play-action passes can be effective in true running situations, such as third and short yardage or fourth-and-short yardage. But if the offense shows run action on second and long or third and long, the defense must be suspicious and expect a play-action pass.

⚠ WATCH OUT!

The following circumstances may distract your players:

- Not seeing the whole picture. Defenders must grasp a general view of the entire offense as each play starts, looking for parts that do not fit the whole. On a real running play, every offensive player will attack the line of scrimmage, but on a play-action pass, some offensive players will be more passive. Their actions should alert some of the defenders that the play is not really a run.

- Focusing on the run fake instead of the linemen. Linemen will give away the play-action pass earlier than the backs will, because they have to protect the quarterback. Defenders must watch the linemen and ignore the play fake if the linemen are setting up for pass protection. Believe the linemen!

- Seeing the play action, not the football. If the quarterback fakes a handoff (play action) but is not close enough to the ball carrier to hand him the ball, or if he only extends an open hand to the ball carrier, the defenders must realize where the ball is—still in the quarterback's hands—and play pass defense.

ACQUIRING THE APPROPRIATE KNOWLEDGE

When defending the play-action pass, you and your athletes should understand the following:

REMINDER!

When defending the play-action pass, you and your players must understand the team strategy and game plan. Don't forget to consider the questions on page 172.

Rules

You and your athletes need to know several main rules when defending the play-action pass:

- Linemen cannot go downfield on a pass play. If an uncovered offensive lineman does not attack a linebacker in front of him, even as the play begins to look like a run, the play is probably a pass.
- Receivers cannot block downfield on a pass. Their path toward the defender in front of them will be less aggressive than it would be on a run play.

Physical Playing Conditions

The physical playing conditions significantly affect the game. Thus, you and your players must pay attention to the following physical conditions when defending the play-action pass:

- In windy conditions, expect the play-action pass only when the offense has the wind behind them. Most offenses will not take a chance on a play-action pass, especially a deep ball, if they are working into a strong wind.
- In wet or slippery conditions, defenders should not be in a hurry to make their reads because changing directions quickly after starting in the wrong direction could result in a fall. They should be deliberate to ensure better footing.

Strengths and Weaknesses of Opponents

You and your players must account for your opponent's strengths and weaknesses to know how to defend the play-action pass properly. Consider the following about your opponents:

- How well does the quarterback fake? Some quarterbacks are much better than others on play-action passes, usually because they are more patient and sell the run fake longer before they look to pass. Through scouting and game-day evaluation, assess the quarterback's execution of these plays and look for ways that he tips off the pass.
- What kind of release do the receivers make on play-action passes? When potential receivers on the play-action pass block first, or fake a block first, before going out to run their routes, the defense has a confusing read. Defenders must respect the initial run read, and they must watch their key players longer to be sure that they are not going to release on a route. On the other hand, if scouting and observation of the opponent reveals that the receivers immediately run a pass route on play-action passes, without first faking a block, then the linebackers and defensive backs should be able to get a definitive read early in the play by noting the release of the receivers.
- Do the linemen stand up on play-action passes? Offenses sometimes have difficulty executing a good play-action fake because the linemen tend to stand up immediately (or very soon after the snap) in pass protection. Teams who make this mistake give away the play and make it easier to defend.
- Do the running backs stop running as soon as the quarterback passes by? Because they do not have the ball, some running backs do not run hard after the quarterback gives them the play fake. They should attack the line of scrimmage convincingly, but most of them do not, which helps clarify the read for the defense.

(continued)

Self-Knowledge

Besides being aware of your opponent's strengths and weaknesses, you and your players need to know about your own team's ability. Teach your players to be aware of the following when defending the play-action pass:

○ How well does your defense read its keys? Reading defenses must react to what they see, and they must defend the run if the play initially looks like a run. But if they are well drilled in their reads, cues such as high hats and route running by the receivers will take them to the correct conclusion that the play is not a run.

○ Is your defense overaggressive? Defenses made up of players who are extremely intense and aggressive can be effective against base, or normal, offensive plays. But overaggressive defenders are susceptible to play fakes and play-action passes, and must learn to be sure about slowing down on their reads.

○ Are your safeties quick run defenders? When the safeties start making tackles near the line of scrimmage on running plays, the offense will likely consider a play-action pass to try to throw a deep ball one-on-one against the corner over the safety's head.

○ Can your corners run with the wide receivers? If the wide receivers are faster than your corners, the safeties must provide help for the corners on deep pass patterns. The safety (or safeties) assigned for deep help must never, never react toward the line of scrimmage on a play fake. They must be disciplined enough to stay deep and be sure the play is not a pass before they react to the run.

Decision-Making Guidelines

When deciding how to gain the best advantage when defending the play-action pass, you and your players should consider the previous information as well as the following guidelines:

○ Defenders must trust what they see their assigned receivers doing and ignore what is happening at the line of scrimmage. For example, if a tight end runs a pass route, the linebacker or safety assigned to him or his area must play pass defense and cover him even if a run play appears to be developing behind him. The same is true for cornerbacks who are keying wide receivers; if the receivers run a pass route, the defenders have to cover them, even if a run play appears to be happening behind them.

○ If the play-action pass causes trouble, defenders are probably not reading their keys properly. Teach the defensive backs, through drills in practice and structured play-action pass calls in scrimmages, to focus only on their initial key, to play pass first on every play and to avoid looking back into the backfield. (Remember that the defensive linemen and linebackers have to play run first because they are the primary run defenders.)

○ Uncovered offensive linemen often have trouble feigning a run block because they have no one to block. Likewise, the backside guard and tackle on offense have set up for pass protection quickly after the snap to protect the quarterback's blind side after he makes his fake. These linemen will likely get their hats high early in the play, thus revealing that a pass is coming.

○ The quarterback has to have the ball to pass. Defensive linemen who are chasing the feigned run play have to watch the quarterback carefully as he approaches the running back, find the ball and determine whether he places the ball in the running back's hands. If the linemen can see that the quarterback has not handed off the ball, they can abort the chase of the running back and immediately chase the quarterback.

Defending the Draw Play

The offense snaps the ball, and the quarterback drops back as if to pass. The defensive line sees pass sets from the offensive line and begins to rush the quarterback. The linebackers also see high hat sets from the line and begin their pass drops. But the running back is still in the backfield behind the quarterback, and when the quarterback gets to him, the running back receives the ball on a draw play.

The draw play, in which the offense shows pass but then runs the ball, is one of the most difficult run plays to stop because the reads for the defense are so challenging. The play also has the effect of making the defensive linemen and the linebackers hesitant about their reads, which makes them hesitant in playing both the run and the pass. To defend the draw play, both the defensive linemen and the linebackers must honor the initial pass keys but be alert for cues that indicate the offense's true intention, which is to run the football.

⚠ WATCH OUT!

The following circumstances may distract your players:

- Overreacting to the first cue they see. Although defensive linemen and linebackers must react quickly to the first cue they see, they must also be alert for secondary cues that might tip them off to deceptive offensive schemes.

- Failure to see the running back. Defensive linemen and linebackers must key linemen first, but they must also see through the line to the running back and read his steps and setup.

- Failure to read the quarterback. Most quarterbacks appear a little bit different on a draw play than they do on a true drop-back pass. Defenders must be alert for different ball handling, or a different drop, by the quarterback when the play is a draw.

READING THE SITUATION

How can you and your players gain an advantage when defending the draw play? Teach your defensive linemen and linebackers to do the following:

- Play pass first. Linemen must begin their pass rush, and linebackers must take their opening pass drop steps. Then, they find the running back and see where he sets up. The running back stays slightly deeper in the backfield and closer to the path of the quarterback's drop on a draw play than he does when he is involved in pass protection.

- Watch for cues from the offensive line that indicate run. If the offensive linemen give up too easily on pass protection, the defensive linemen must be suspicious of the play. If the offensive linemen release down the field toward the linebackers, the play cannot be a pass.

- Find the football. When the quarterback lowers the ball to hand it off to the running back, both the defensive linemen and linebackers must see that cue and immediately react toward the line of scrimmage to close in on the ball carrier.

ACQUIRING THE APPROPRIATE KNOWLEDGE

When defending the draw play, you and your players should understand the following:

Rules

You and your players need to know several main rules when you are defending the draw play:

REMINDER!

When defending the draw play, you and your players must understand the team strategy and game plan. Don't forget to consider the questions on page 172.

○ Offensive linemen are not allowed, by rule, to be downfield on a pass play, so if a linebacker sees an offensive lineman coming downfield at him, the play must be a run even if the quarterback is dropping back to pass. (If the quarterback *does* pass, the play will be called back.)

Physical Playing Conditions

The physical playing conditions significantly affect the game. Thus, you and your players must pay attention to the following physical conditions when defending the draw play:

○ If the field is wet and slippery, or if the ball is wet and difficult to handle, the offense might be more inclined to run the ball than to pass it, so the defense should be alert for cues that a draw play is coming.

○ If there is a strong wind in the face of the offense, the offense might be more inclined to run the ball than to pass it, so the defense should be alert for cues that a draw play is coming.

Strengths and Weaknesses of Opponents

You and your players must account for your opponent's strengths and weaknesses to know how to defend the draw play properly. Consider the following about your opponents:

○ How consistent is the quarterback's drop? Through scouting and game-day observation, the defense should be able to pick up some variations in the quarterback's drop when he is passing the ball compared with his drop when he is about to hand off the ball on a draw play.

○ Does the quarterback ever make a hand fake or ball fake to the running back on a pass play? If not, the defensive linemen and linebackers can react immediately and aggressively when the quarterback moves the ball toward the running back. But if the quarterback occasionally makes fakes, the defenders will have to react more cautiously to the quarterback's motions, waiting to see whether he hands off the ball before they commit to the run.

○ How well do the offensive linemen disguise the draw? Through scouting and game-day observation, the defense should be able to pick up some variations in the offensive linemen's pass sets when they are running the draw play compared with their pass sets on normal pass plays.

○ How well do the running backs disguise their pass sets? Do the running backs step more toward the line of scrimmage when they are pass blocking? Do they step more toward the quarterback when the play is a draw? They may even stay stationary on the snap on a draw play, whereas they go somewhere on every other play! Scouting and game-day observation should reveal some tendencies that can benefit the defense.

Self-Knowledge

Besides being aware of your opponent's strengths and weaknesses, you and your players need to know about your own team's ability. Teach your players to be aware of the following when defending the draw play:

○ How quickly do your defensive linemen read and react? Defensive linemen who are aggressive and read plays quickly can be vulnerable to offensive ploys like the draw play (as well as the play-action pass, screen pass and misdirection). You must drill these types of players to be alert for secondary cues and redirect if their first reaction is incorrect.

○ Can your linebackers be both patient and aggressive? Linebackers must play instinctively, but they also must see the big picture before they react and go. They must read the blocking scheme, the direction of the ball and the actions of the backfield, patiently but not slowly, and then believe what they see and fly to the football.

○ How can you stop the draw play if you are having trouble reading it? If your linebackers are frequently being fooled on the draw play, try using man coverage, in which a linebacker would be assigned to cover the running back. If the running back stays in the backfield, the linebacker should close toward, or melt to, him because of his coverage assignment. If the running back runs a route, the linebacker will be in position to pick him up. If the running back gets the ball on a draw play, the linebacker should also be in good position because he is already on his way toward the line of scrimmage.

At a Glance

The following parts of the text offer additional information on defending the draw play.

Faking	p. 45
Pass Protection	p. 85
Tackling	p. 93
Pass Rush	p. 110
Zone Pass Drops	p. 117
Linebacker Reads	p. 238

Decision-Making Guidelines

When deciding how to gain the best advantage when defending the draw play, you and your players should consider the previous information as well as the following guidelines:

○ Defensive linemen must be suspicious of a pass rush opportunity that is too good to be true. Offensive linemen setting up for a draw play sometimes intentionally open up their pass set more than usual and give the defender an open window to the quarterback, knowing that by the time the defensive linemen gets there, the quarterback will have handed off the ball to the running back.

○ Defensive linemen who see a cue for a draw play must retrace their steps. If the defensive lineman recognizes the draw play when he is 3 to 5 yards upfield, he will never have time to run laterally left or right to the ball carrier and make a play. His only chance to be involved in the tackle is to reverse direction 180 degrees and head back toward the line of scrimmage, where he might be able to catch the running back when he slows down to avoid a tackle or make a cut.

○ Linebackers may get a cue from an offensive lineman who is uncovered, because on the draw play these linemen usually give a pass set "on air" and then attack downfield to block the linebacker. If the offensive lineman is coming downfield, the play cannot be a pass, and the linebacker should react toward the offensive lineman, defeat his block and make the tackle.

○ In man coverage, the linebacker assigned to the running back cannot allow himself to be blocked on the draw play, because his teammates who are covering other receivers will be in poor position to help. He must find his running back and immediately close toward him when he reads pass, so that any potential blocker will have no time to get between him and the running back. (This movement is called melting to the running back.)

○ Do not allow opponents who are unskilled in the passing game to gain cheap yards by faking the pass, getting the line to rush hard upfield and the linebackers to drop out hard, and then handing off the ball on the draw play. Defensive linemen and linebackers should be especially alert for draw play cues from teams that do not pass the ball well!

○ Play the down-and-distance situation. If the situation is third and long (more than 10 yards), defensive linemen and linebackers can react to pass sets somewhat more aggressively and not be as concerned if the play turns out to be a draw, because they should still be able to react and tackle the ball carrier before he gets a first down. If the situation is second down or third and medium (6 yards or less), the defenders should be more alert to the draw because a gain of just 6 yards would be a clear positive for the offense.

Defensive teams must play long-yardage situations, especially on third downs, somewhat differently than they play normally. Assume that in the third quarter of a close game, it's third down and 12 yards to go. The offensive team has the ball deep in its own territory. As they approach the line of scrimmage, the defensive players check the first-down markers on the sideline to confirm the yardage needed by the offense, realizing that they could allow the offense to gain a few yards, as long as they don't gain enough yards for the first down. If the defense forces the offense to punt, they have accomplished their task. Their own offense will get the ball back in good field position. Defenders must understand their goal in this situation and adjust their alignment and reactions accordingly. They must line up deeper, read the play more deliberately, play sound football and tackle the ball carrier short of the first down.

⚠ WATCH OUT!

The following circumstances may distract your players:

- Being fooled by play fakes. The offense probably won't run a basic running play in this situation. Defenders should honor the run but be ready to react to the play-action pass.

- Selling out to the drop-back pass if a running back is still in the backfield. Defenders should check the running back's setup and anticipate the draw play or screen pass.

- Chasing shallow crossing routes. Linebackers dropping into coverage must ignore the shallow routes, get depth and stop the intermediate routes that would result in a first down.

READING THE SITUATION

How can you and your players gain an advantage when playing the long-yardage situation? Teach your players to do the following:

- Defensive linemen whose assignment is to rush the passer should anticipate a pass and prepare for a strong pass rush.

- Linebackers should line up 2 to 4 yards deeper than normal, depending on the yards to go, to make sure that intermediate routes do not get behind them.

- Linebackers should react deliberately to play fakes and misdirection, patiently find the ball and then go hard to make the tackle.

- Deep defenders should also align a couple of steps deeper than normal but anticipate routes that will break at the yardage needed for the first down.

ACQUIRING THE APPROPRIATE KNOWLEDGE

When playing the long-yardage situation, you and your players should understand the following:

Rules

You and your athletes need to know several main rules when playing the long-yardage situation:

- The offense has four tries to make a first down, so they will likely punt on fourth down. Third downs are therefore the most crucial downs of virtually every series in a football game. Teams must play these conversion downs with great concentration, intensity and intelligence.

o Pass interference and defensive holding result in automatic first downs for the offense, so the defense must be sure to play with good footwork and patience in these critical situations, perhaps allowing a short completion followed by a tackle rather than taking a chance on being called for a penalty by trying to break up the pass.

o Pass rushers must remember that roughing the quarterback results in an automatic first down. The pass rush must be intense and aggressive, but if the quarterback delivers the ball, the rusher has to peel off and avoid a possible late hit on the quarterback. The rusher has to trust that his teammates will stop the play short of the first down if he does not get to the quarterback in time to deflect the pass or sack the quarterback.

REMINDER!

When playing the long-yardage situation, you and your players must understand the team strategy and game plan. Don't forget to consider the questions on page 172.

Physical Playing Conditions

The physical playing conditions significantly affect the game. Thus, you and your players must pay attention to the following physical conditions when playing the long-yardage situation:

o In wet or slippery field conditions, the defenders must play cautiously in their initial footwork so that they don't fall down while reacting or changing direction and give up a big play for the first down.

o In windy conditions, pass defenders must allow more cushion and play with greater depth when the offense has the wind at their back to prevent the ball from getting behind them.

Strengths and Weaknesses of Opponents

You and your players must account for your opponent's strengths and weaknesses to know how to adjust to long-yardage situations properly. Consider the following about your opponents:

o Can you stop them in your base defense? The defense can play somewhat conservatively in third-and-long situations. A standard defensive call, with a four-man rush and zone coverage, will often be successful. But if the offense has a skilled quarterback and talented receivers, the base call might not be good enough. Defenses must play the third-and-long situation more aggressively against a talented passing team, using blitzes to put the pressure on the quarterback and varying their coverages to keep the receivers guessing.

o What style of team are you playing? Opponents who rely primarily on the running game and do not pass as much are more vulnerable in long-yardage situations. These offenses usually do not have a variety of intermediate pass plays and may instead resort to screens, draw plays and misdirection plays to try to convert. By playing the situation and reacting deliberately, the defense should be able to get the ball carrier stopped short of the first down.

o How good is the opponent's pass protection? Even the best pass coverage will be ineffective in long-yardage situations if the quarterback has lots of time to throw the ball. On the other hand, if the front four of the defense can get a good pass rush against the opponent's pass protection, the seven remaining defenders stand a good chance of stopping the play short of the first down. The better the pass protection, the tougher it will be for the defense to stop the offense.

o Can the check-down receivers make someone miss? If the defense plays the long-yardage situation properly, the quarterback will have to throw the check-down pass to his outlet

(continued)

receiver (see "Progression of Receivers" on page 174). This result should favor the defense unless the check-down back or receiver is an exceptional athlete who can break or avoid tackles. Against an opponent who features a player with these skills, the defense may have to play the long-yardage situation in a more traditional fashion, playing closer to all receivers and trying to limit the opportunities for the opponent's outstanding player to make plays.

Self-Knowledge

Besides being aware of your opponent's strengths and weaknesses, you and your players need to know about your own team's ability. Teach your players to be aware of the following when playing the long-yardage situation:

- Can a four-man rush put pressure on the quarterback? If the front four defenders are good enough on the pass rush to force the quarterback to throw early or at least on time, the defense has a decent chance to be successful in third-and-long situations because they will have seven players in pass coverage.

- How disciplined are your linebackers? If the linebackers do not overreact to play fakes and can lay off shallow pass routes in long-yardage situations, the defense has a good chance to be successful. Overaggressive linebackers will be vulnerable to play-action passes. Linebackers who chase the first read in their pass coverage areas will be susceptible to drop-back passes that send both a shallow receiver and an intermediate receiver into the same zone.

- Will your defensive backs be able to play with the right amount of cushion? By playing deeper and initiating the backpedal earlier, the defensive backs in long-yardage situations should be able to keep most intermediate pass routes (routes with a depth of 10 to 15 yards) in front of them. The key for these defensive backs is to play with enough cushion to be safe in case the receiver runs a deep route instead of an intermediate route, but not with so much cushion that the quarterback has an easy 10- to 15-yard completion for the first down.

- Can your defense match up with the opponent's offense? Defenses that are equal or slightly inferior to the opponent's offense in skill level and talent should not play the same coverage every time in long-yardage situations. By mixing up coverages and throwing in an occasional blitz, the defense may be able to stop the more talented opponent a fair number of times.

Decision-Making Guidelines

When deciding how to gain the best advantage when playing the long-yardage situation, you and your players should consider the previous information as well as the following guidelines:

- The defensive line must prepare for a good takeoff and pass rush maneuver. Linebackers must learn to lay off shallow routes such as drags, crossing routes or flat routes that are designed to pull them out of an area and open up a throwing lane to a receiver running an intermediate-level route. Linebackers should make the quarterback check down to those shallow routes and then rally to the ball carrier to make the tackle short of the first down. If the linebackers and defensive backs are fooled and the play is a run, they should be able to react and make a tackle before the ball carrier reaches the first-down marker.

- Linebackers should play pass first and react to the run. In long-yardage situations, the pass is more dangerous than the run. Linebackers should drop to their areas or assigned receivers if a pass is any threat at all, and then if the play turns out to be a run, they should have time to react and stop the play short of the first down.

- Defensive backs must anticipate routes that break at the yardage needed for the first down. Teams usually do not go for the home run on third and long. Defensive backs should maintain a deep cushion but hang at first-down yardage and make a play.

- Defenses should try to get the offense to throw to their check-down receiver. Occasionally, the defense should blitz in long-yardage situations and force the quarterback to throw quickly to a check-down receiver or a receiver running a short route. This receiver will usually catch the ball at a depth of about 5 yards, and the defense should be able to react to him and make the tackle before he gets a first down.

- Defenders should be sure to make solid tackles. They should keep their heads up, drive their legs and wrap their arms. A big hit is not essential here. Defenders must play under control, get the ball carrier down short of first-down yardage and force the offense to punt the ball.

At a Glance

The following parts of the text offer additional information on playing the long-yardage situation.

Pursuit Angles

On a running play or after a short pass completion, the ball carrier breaks into the open. The defense must react quickly to prevent a touchdown or hold the long gain to as few yards as possible.

No matter where a defensive player is located when the ball carrier breaks free, he has to turn and run as fast as he can at an angle that gives him an opportunity to cut off the ball carrier down the field. The outside defenders, usually cornerbacks but sometimes safeties, must be sure that the ball carrier never gets outside them toward the sideline. They must turn him back toward the middle of the field, toward the oncoming pursuit. Defenders pursuing from the back side of the play must sprint on an angle that will allow them to cut off the ball carrier, but they must be careful not to take such a deep or fast angle that the ball carrier can cut back across the field underneath them, getting outside and away from the other pursuing defenders.

⚠ WATCH OUT!

The following circumstances may distract your players:

- Getting tied up with offensive players. Defenders must break free and hustle down the field.

- Worrying about the damage that has already been done. Defenders can't become discouraged and fail to hustle after the ball. The key is to prevent a touchdown and force the offense to line up again before they score.

- Assuming that the player is too fast and can't be caught. Defenders should ignore the lead that the offensive player has. This chase is not a pure race; other defenders in the secondary might slow the ball carrier enough that he can be caught.

READING THE SITUATION

How can you and your players gain an advantage when using pursuit angles? Teach your players to do the following:

- Start running full speed down the field as soon as the ball carrier breaks free.

- Gauge the angle and direction of the ball carrier and set off on a course downfield that will intersect with the ball carrier if he is turned back inside or if he slows down to avoid a tackler.

- Remember that each player will take a different angle, based on location on the field and speed compared with the speed of the ball carrier.

- Be alert for offensive players who might be floating in the secondary, reacting to the play and looking for defenders to block.

- Be sure not to overpursue the play and allow the ball carrier to cut back to the inside. Cornerbacks and safeties, on the back side of the play must keep the ball carrier channeled toward the sideline and allow other pursuing defenders to continue on their angles.

ACQUIRING THE APPROPRIATE KNOWLEDGE

When using pursuit angles, you and your players should understand the following:

REMINDER!

When using pursuit angles, you and your players must understand the team strategy and game plan. Don't forget to consider the questions on page 172.

Rules

You and your athletes need to know several main rules when using pursuit angles:

- No blocks in the back or pushes in the side or back are allowed, so defenders can run hard downfield knowing that their only threats for being blocked will have to come from in front, in their field of vision.
- Sometimes defenders hit the ball carrier late, or out of bounds, after a big play, resulting in a personal foul penalty. Although the long gain can create some frustration, defenders must remain poised, make the tackle and get back in the huddle to prepare for the next play.

Physical Playing Conditions

The physical playing conditions significantly affect the game. Thus, you and your players must pay attention to the following physical conditions when using pursuit angles:

- In wet or slippery field conditions, defenders must be especially careful to take a deep pursuit angle because they will not be able to stop and change direction quickly if the ball carrier cuts back.
- In wet or slippery field conditions, defenders should pursue big plays with great hustle, knowing that the ball carrier might slip or slow down because of the conditions as he runs down the field.

Strengths and Weaknesses of Opponents

You and your players must account for your opponent's strengths and weaknesses to know how to use pursuit angles properly. Consider the following about your opponents:

- How fast are the opponent's breakaway players? Defenders must take deeper pursuit angles against fast opponents.
- How do the opponent's breakaway players try to evade tacklers? Through scouting and game-day observation, defenders must be aware whether their opponent will try to outrun them down the sideline, lower his head and shoulder and try to run over them or try to fake upfield and cut back underneath them (see "Evading Tacklers" on page 194). Based on this scouting report, defenders should adjust their pursuit angles accordingly.
- How securely do the opponents carry the football when running in the open field? Opponents who break away may either slow down a bit or relax their grip on the ball when they get in the open. Defensive hustle is important because the hustling defensive player may be able to catch the breakaway player and knock away the football from behind.
- How willingly, and how well, do the opponent's receivers block? Pursuit angles are relatively easy to judge and execute in the open field, but the presence of an opposing receiver who is trying to block the defender complicates the situation. The defender must focus on defeating the blocker first (including, perhaps, outrunning him) and then get back into his pursuit angle.

(continued)

Self-Knowledge

Besides being aware of your opponent's strengths and weaknesses, you and your players need to know about your own team's ability. Teach your players to be aware of the following when using pursuit angles:

- How fast are your defenders? Pursuit is one play on defense that is more mental than physical. Pursuit takes great effort and hustle in a discouraging situation, and defenders who are fast in pursuit situations are those who run at 100 percent speed, no matter how fast or slow they might run the 40-yard dash or how tired they are.

- How disciplined are your force players? If the force player lets the ball carrier get outside, the efforts of the other 10 defensive players will likely be wasted. If, conversely, the force player can turn the play back inside, then all his teammates have a chance to make a play (see "Force" on page 251).

Decision-Making Guidelines

When deciding how to gain the best advantage when using pursuit angles, you and your players should consider the previous information as well as the following guidelines:

- Practice pursuit drills frequently. Schedule team defensive drills on pursuit angles and practice them at full speed to develop the mentality that pursuit can limit big plays and prevent touchdowns.

- Use the sideline as an extra defender. If the ball carrier has escaped and is running down the sideline, the defender should be able to take a good pursuit angle, staying just behind the ball carrier to prevent the cutback and then using the sideline to force the ball carrier out of bounds.

chapter 8

Special Teams Tactical Skills

This chapter covers the special teams tactical skills that you and your players must know to be successful. In this chapter, you will find the following skills:

Kickoff Coverage

The kickoff coverage unit has an important responsibility to stop the opponents deep in their territory, forcing them to travel a long field to put any points on the board. The kick itself is important, of course, but the coverage unit must be fast, disciplined and sound for the unit to be consistently successful. Kickoff coverage can be broken down into three stages: first, avoiding the front wave of blockers; second, properly taking on the second wave of blockers; and third, making the tackle. The players on this unit must act in unison, taking on the blocks properly, with every player fitting correctly into his assigned spot. If any player goes the wrong way around the front wave, or takes on a second-wave block with the wrong shoulder, a big running lane could open up for the opponent's return man.

⚠ WATCH OUT!

The following circumstances may distract your players:

○ Letting the ball or the blockers pull the coverage man out of his lane. Each coverage player has a landmark on the field, called his lane, and he must initially stay in proximity to that lane no matter where the ball or blockers are.

○ Failing to keep the eyes up while sprinting. Kickoff coverage players have to run hard, but they also have to find their blocking threats. Right after the kickoff, the coverage players must find the front wave of blockers.

READING THE SITUATION

How can you and your players gain an advantage when covering kickoffs? Teach your players to do the following:

- Get a good takeoff but do not be offside. Work with the kicker on timing and getting that last step down just short of the kickoff line when the kicker strikes the ball.
- Know your landmarks and stay in your lane.
- Sprint hard with the eyes up. This play is full speed ahead from the very beginning.
- Go behind the blocks on the front wave.
- Attack the second-wave blockers with the outside arm free.
- Break down and gather momentum as the ball carrier approaches.
- Keep the eyes up and the hips low to prepare for the tackle.

○ Going directly to the football instead of behind the front-wave blocker. Coverage players must react to the front-wave blocks before they adjust to the football.

○ Reacting to the ball carrier instead of first taking on second-wave blockers properly. Coverage players must resist the temptation to head straight for the ball carrier; instead, they should first take on the second-wave blockers with their outside arm free and then react to the ball.

○ Trying for the big hit. Many kickoff coverage players dream of crashing into the ball carrier full speed to achieve the knockout collision. Such hits are rare and happen only if the coverage player does not get blocked and if the return man is not paying attention! Most return men can fake out a coverage man who is rushing down the field out of control.

ACQUIRING THE APPROPRIATE KNOWLEDGE

When covering kickoffs, you and your players should understand the following:

Rules

You and your athletes need to know several main rules when covering kickoffs:

REMINDER!

When covering kickoffs, you and your players must understand the team strategy and game plan. Don't forget to consider the questions on page 172.

- All players must be behind the kickoff line when the ball is kicked. Kickoff coverage units often violate this simple rule when the players are too eager to get downfield to make a play. The opponent gets a free play when this happens, and the kicker will have to kick again from 5 yards farther back, hurting field position. Players must not be offside!

- All blocks on kicking plays must be above the waist, so kickoff coverage players know that when an opponent approaches to block, he will have to stay high. Therefore, the coverage player can take on the block with his shoulder pads and forearm.

- If the ball goes out of bounds on the kickoff, the receiving team has the choice to take the ball 30 yards in front of the original kickoff line or have the kick replayed from 5 yards farther back. Neither of these scenarios is positive for the kickoff team; the kicker must keep the kick in the field of play.

- If the kick goes into the end zone (even if it is muffed; that is, touched but not controlled), the ball will come out to the 20-yard line. This result, making the opponent start their drive 80 yards from the end zone, is acceptable field position for the coverage team, so kicking the ball into the end zone is really the best kickoff coverage.

Physical Playing Conditions

The physical playing conditions significantly affect the game. Thus, you and your players must pay attention to the following physical conditions when covering kickoffs:

- In wet and slippery field conditions, kickoff coverage players must shorten their strides as they avoid blockers and try to keep their feet underneath them so that they do not slip and fall.

- If the kicker has a strong wind behind him, the ball may go in the end zone for a touchback, but the kickoff team should run full speed all the way to the goal line just to be sure.

- If the kicker is kicking into a strong wind, the kickoff team's job becomes more difficult because the kick won't go as deep. Coverage players must sprint extra hard while taking on blocks properly and try to make the tackle as deep as possible in the other team's territory.

Strengths and Weaknesses of Opponents

You and your players must account for your opponent's strengths and weaknesses to know how to cover kickoffs properly. Consider the following about your opponents:

- How fast and shifty is the return man? The better the return man, the faster the coverage unit will have to run downfield to get in position to make a tackle.

- What kind of scheme does the opponent use on kickoff return? If the opponent uses a wedge scheme (see "Wedge Return" on page 294), the kickoff coverage unit must designate three or four players who, after avoiding the front wave in the usual fashion, attack the wedge at the second level, with one player on each side of the wedge and one or two players hitting inside gaps in the wedge. If the opponent uses a man scheme, the rule of taking on second-level blocks with the outside arm free should work satisfactorily.

(continued)

o Do the opponents cross block? If the opponents use a cross-block scheme, in which a blocker or blockers come from the other side of the field to try to block a coverage player by surprise, you must train the kickoff team members to find those blockers and take them on with the outside arm free while not giving too much ground laterally.

Self-Knowledge

Besides being aware of your opponent's strengths and weaknesses, you and your players need to know about your own team's ability. Teach your players to be aware of the following when covering kickoffs:

o How talented and consistent is the kicker? If your kicker has a strong-enough leg to kick the ball in the end zone, have him kick away (as deep as he can kick it) every time. If he is weak or inconsistent on his depth, have him kick to a spot (such as deep left or deep right) and try to pin the opponents in a corner. If he is strong but wild left or right, have him kick less aggressively and try to teach him to kick to the spots (see previous point).

o How disciplined are your coverage players? Fast, aggressive coverage players will make plays on the kickoff unit, but if they are undisciplined, the opponents will eventually break off a big return. The players on the kickoff coverage unit should be disciplined athletes who will take on blocks properly and make sure tackles.

o How well do you make tackles? As in most defensive plays in the game, the bottom line is the percentage of tackles made versus tackles missed. Players on the kickoff coverage unit should be solid, sure-handed tacklers.

Decision-Making Guidelines

When deciding how to gain the best advantage when covering kickoffs, you and your players should consider the previous information as well as the following guidelines:

o The coverage players must work to perfect their timing with the kicker's approach to the kick. They can start slowly and accelerate with the kicker or wait longer and sprint full speed immediately when they start.

o Coverage players must sprint full speed immediately as the ball is kicked to force the front-wave blockers to retreat quickly. When the front wave is forced to retreat quickly, they have less time to get into position to set up their blocks, which forces them to show their blocking assignments early in the play.

o As the coverage players sprint forward, they must watch the front-wave blockers to see which way they are turning their shoulders and what kind of angle they are taking as they retreat. Each coverage player must continually scan the actions of the front-wave blockers to see which way they are setting up.

o As the front-wave blocker attempts to make his block, the coverage player attacks the back side of the blocker, going behind him and forcing the blocker to turn around. The coverage player should never try to avoid the blocker by going in front of him, unless he can undoubtedly get past the blocker without any contact.

o If the coverage player deviates from his lane as he avoids the front-wave blocker, he must immediately return to the vicinity of that lane after he passes the front wave. This practice ensures that the spacing between him and the other coverage players remains consistent.

- If the coverage player is reading the block correctly but getting hung up on the blocker, he needs to work on drills for releases, or escapes, from blocks. The player can practice hand and arm actions such as the underarm rip, the overarm swim or a club move with his outside arm to avoid the blockers as he goes past them.

- As the coverage player approaches the second wave of blockers, he must decelerate, get his body under control and prepare to move laterally, if necessary, to deliver a blow. Athletes cannot go two directions at once; if they are going forward, they cannot go sideways. They must break down, get settled into an athletic position and move laterally to stay outside the blocker and the ball.

- The coverage player must be able to see both the ball and the potential blockers. If the ball begins to move outside his lane, he must leave his lane and adjust laterally to keep the ball inside him, toward the middle of the field. He must also be aware of any blocker who is threatening him, and he must adjust laterally so that he can maintain his outside leverage against any block.

- The coverage players must understand the differences between taking on blocks at the front level and the second level. At the first level, the coverage players run behind blocks and then get back in their lanes. At the second level, the coverage players take on all blocks with the outside arm free and react to keep outside leverage on the ball (that is, keep the ball inside).

- In taking on a second-level block, the coverage player attacks the outside half of the blocker with a strong two-hand blow to the blocker's chest from a position with his knees bent and hips lowered. At the same time, he keeps the eyes up to continue to see the position of the football and maintain outside leverage on the ball.

At a Glance

The following parts of the text offer additional information on kickoff coverage.

Playing Force on Kick Coverage

On the two primary special teams kicking units, the kickoff team and the punt team, one player on each side of the coverage scheme will be assigned to act as the force player. This player is charged with the responsibility of turning the return man back inside if he comes his way and preventing any reverses or cutbacks if the return man goes toward the other side of the field. The force player must be disciplined and steady, adjusting his position on the field to the blocking scheme and the path of the ball carrier on the return. The force player can never let the ball get outside, but he cannot play so passively that he creates an opening for the return man to break a big gainer up inside. On plays away, he must be "slow to go," staying at the same level as the ball carrier and not compressing his distance radically across the field so that he doesn't open up a cutback lane or a lane for a reverse on the play. His role is to force every outside return and every cutback back toward the middle of the field, where all the other coverage players are, instead of letting the ball get outside where no defenders are located.

 **WATCH OUT!**

The following circumstances may distract your players:

- Looking for the big hit. The desire of the coverage player to go full speed down the field and make a huge, highlight-reel hit on the return man usually causes the coverage man to get faked out or miss a tackle, because he cannot change directions while flying down the field.

- Reacting too hard to an inside move. If the ball carrier comes toward the force player and dips inside (faking a move upfield inside the force player), the force player should not react too quickly to the inside to get in on the tackle because the ball carrier could potentially bounce the play back toward the sideline and get outside him.

- Going underneath a block. Sometimes the force player thinks that he can get to the ball carrier, not seeing or not paying attention to a potential blocker. If the force player goes underneath (inside) a block on the perimeter of the play, the ball carrier will be able to react and get outside him.

- Pursuing too quickly on plays away. If the ball initially goes away from the force player, he must be careful not to pursue too quickly. He should stay behind the ball in case the ball carrier cuts back (or the other team runs a reverse of some kind) so that he can force the play back to the inside.

READING THE SITUATION

How can you and your players gain an advantage when playing force on kick coverage? Teach your players to do the following:

- Understand that no special teams coverage scheme can be effective without solid, consistent force play.

- Devote attention to potential blockers and keep them inside as the ball approaches.

- Know where the ball is, always keeping it inside.

- Squeeze the field as much as possible, restricting the inside running lanes, without allowing the ball to bounce outside.

- Pursue plays away deliberately, being alert for cutbacks or reverses.

ACQUIRING THE APPROPRIATE KNOWLEDGE

When playing force on kick coverage, you and your players should understand the following:

REMINDER!

When playing force on kick coverage, you and your players must understand the team strategy and game plan. Don't forget to consider the questions on page 172.

Rules

You and your athletes need to know several main rules when playing force on kick coverage:

- By rule, blockers cannot grab or hold the force player. But they will sometimes try to pin the force player inside by grabbing his arms or jersey. The force player cannot expect the officials to make every holding call, so he must use aggressive arm and hand actions to escape from the blocker and maintain his outside leverage.
- Blockers cannot chop (block below the waist) the force player, so he can attack any blocker aggressively, knowing that he will make solid contact with that blocker.

Physical Playing Conditions

The physical playing conditions significantly affect the game. Thus, you and your players must pay attention to the following physical conditions when playing force on kick coverage:

- In wet and slippery field conditions, the force player has to be extra careful to establish solid footing and a balanced base before taking on blocks. He cannot afford to slip and fall because the other 10 players are relying on him to turn the play back to them.

Strengths and Weaknesses of Opponents

You and your players must account for your opponent's strengths and weaknesses to know how to play force on kick coverage. Consider the following about your opponents:

- How fast are the opponent's return men? Against a fast opponent, the force player will have to position himself wider on the field so that the return man cannot outrun him to the sideline and get around the corner.
- Do the opponent's return men look for the cutback when they get in the open field? If the opponent has kick or punt returners who know how to cut back across the field when they get in the open, the force player who is backside on every play will have to be extremely cautious.
- Do the opponents run outside returns? Force players will be sternly challenged by kickoff or punt returns that attack the outside and try to find a seam down the sideline. On these returns, the blocking scheme will assign at least one player, and often two players, to kick out the force player. The force player must recognize this blocking scheme, take on the blocker or blockers physically and restrict the running lane inside without letting the ball bounce outside.

Self-Knowledge

Besides being aware of your opponent's strengths and weaknesses, you and your players need to know about your own team's ability. Teach your players to be aware of the following when playing force on kick coverage:

- Are your force players strong enough to take on the opponent's kickout blocks? When taking on blockers, the force player must be physical and strong because his assignment is to restrict the running lane to the inside as much as possible. This task requires low

(continued)

pad level and good leg strength, as well as the discipline to keep the outside arm and leg free, so the force player must be able to match up with the offensive blocker.

○ How aggressive is the force player? Some assignments and skills in football require tremendous aggressiveness, but the force technique requires patience and discipline. If the force player is too aggressive, he will either over-react to a play away or attack the ball carrier too force-fully on plays toward him, thus running the risk of getting beat to the outside.

○ Is the force player a team player? All players on defense like to make tackles because they get to hear their names on the loudspeaker or read them in the paper the next day. But the force player must play for the team and understand that he will make fewer tackles doing his job than the players inside will.

Decision-Making Guidelines

When deciding how to gain the best advantage when playing force on kick coverage, you and your players should consider the previous information as well as the following guidelines:

○ If the return man attempts to outflank him, the force player must widen his position on the field to keep the return man on his inside shoulder and force him back to the inside.

○ Remember that although the primary job of a force player is to turn the play inside, if he gives up a lot of ground laterally (toward the sideline) as he keeps his outside lever-age, he will leave a big running lane inside for the opposing ball carrier. The force player must try to squeeze the field, give up ground grudgingly and turn the ball carrier inside as early as possible.

○ Also, remember that although the force player has to squeeze the field, he can never let the ball go outside. He must balance physical play inside with patient, disciplined play outside.

○ Every kickoff and punt coverage unit has to have a force player on each side, but that player does not have to line up on the outside at the beginning of the play. Many punt coverage units, for example, send their bullets, who are lined up outside, directly to the return man, and widen out their slot backs from the punt protection nucleus to be the force players. This tactic on punts allows the bullets to be more aggressive because they do not have the strict assignments given to force players, such as never letting the ball bounce outside. Many kickoff teams hide the force players somewhere in their original alignment and then loop them outside after the kick is in the air. This tactic on kickoffs helps protect the force players from being targeted for double-team blocks.

Recovering the Onside Kick

An onside kick is an attempt by the kickoff team to take advantage of the rule in football that makes the ball live on a free kick, eligible to be recovered by the kicking team, after it travels 10 yards from the kickoff line. Teams use onside kicks in two situations: first, when the kicking team is behind and needs to get the ball back quickly to try to score again, and second, when the kicking team senses a weakness in the receiving team's deployment or movements after the kick, a circumstance that gives them a good opportunity to surprise the receiving team and recover a short kick. For the purposes of this skill, we will call the first type an expected onside kick and the second type a surprise onside kick. A successful onside kick is the same as a turnover; it takes the ball away from the team that was expecting to be in possession (the receiving team) and gives it back to the team who just had it (the kicking team). Like all turnovers, this sudden change of possession can have a major effect in a game, changing field position, momentum, confidence and clock management.

⚠ WATCH OUT!

The following circumstances may distract your players:

- ○ Becoming so excited or anxious that they mistime their approach to the kickoff line. Any onside kick situation is exciting, but the kickoff team players must keep their composure, time their approach to the line with the kicker's approach to the ball and get a fast, legal takeoff that gives them a good chance to recover the ball.

- ○ Being so eager to recover the ball that they don't let it travel the required yardage. The ball is the object that everyone wants, but the kickoff team can't have it until it goes 10 yards. The kickoff team has to know where the 10-yard line is, not just where the ball is.

- ○ Overreacting to the first big hop. A great onside kick will hit the ground once and then take a big hop on the second bounce, allowing the kickoff team time to get to the spot where the ball is coming down just as the receiving team's player is making his attempt to catch it. But if all the kickoff team members run to that spot, none of them will be in position to recover a tipped or deflected ball. Some of the kickoff team members must look for tips and deflections.

READING THE SITUATION

How can you and your players gain an advantage when recovering the onside kick? Teach your players to do the following:

- Time up the approach. The kickoff team players should be taking their last legal step, just inches behind the kickoff line, when the kicker contacts the ball. If they are over the line, they'll be offside, but if they are farther back, they won't reach the recovery point as quickly.

- The kicker should work on his kick. Most kickers develop one good expected onside kick. Practice this kick to get used to the bounces that usually occur.

- The kicker should develop a good surprise onside kick. The kicker and one or two designated kickoff team members should practice a kick that can take advantage of an unsuspecting receiving team.

- Block any player who could recover the kick. After the ball has traveled 10 yards, the kicking team can legally block the receivers, and they should aggressively seek out and knock away players who might be in position to recover the kick.

- Look for deflections. Most onside kicks that are successfully recovered either bounce off a receiving team's player or are fumbled. Players on the kicking team should keep some spacing between each other and look for the fortuitous bounce to come their way.

(continued)

REMINDER!

When recovering the onside kick, you and your players must understand the team strategy and game plan. Don't forget to consider the questions on page 172.

ACQUIRING THE APPROPRIATE KNOWLEDGE

When recovering the onside kick, you and your players should understand the following:

Rules

You and your athletes need to know several main rules when recovering an onside kick:

- All players on the kicking team must stay behind the kickoff line until the ball is kicked; otherwise an offside penalty could be called and the receiving team would get a second try to recover the kick if the kicking team recovered the first one.

- The ball does not become live and legal for the kicking team to recover until it travels 10 yards from the kickoff line or touches someone on the receiving team. Teach members of the kicking team not to touch onside kick attempts that have not traveled the required 10 yards, because even if they later recover the ball, the receiving team will get the ball because the kicking team touched it prematurely.

- The kicking team cannot block members of the receiving team until the ball is live; that is, until it goes 10 yards or touches a member of the receiving team. Otherwise, a penalty will negate a recovery.

- If one or more players on either team touches the ball but no one gains possession of it and it then goes out of bounds, by rule the ball goes to the receiving team.

Physical Playing Conditions

The physical playing conditions significantly affect the game. Thus, you and your players must pay attention to the following physical conditions when attempting an onside kick:

- If the field is wet or slippery, the kicking team must realize that they will have difficulty stopping or changing directions as they try to chase the ball. They should shorten their strides, take smaller steps that are more under control and be sure to stay on their feet.

- A wet ball can easily slip out of anyone's hands on this play. Members of the kicking team should stay alive around the pile where the ball is and look for it to squirt out. In addition, if a member of the kicking team does recover the ball, he must instantly bring the ball into his body and cover it with two hands to ensure that it does not slip away.

Strengths and Weaknesses of Opponents

You and your players must account for your opponent's strengths and weaknesses to know how to recover an onside kick. Consider the following about your opponents:

- Does the opponent's regular receiving team have any holes in it? Scouting and game-day observation may indicate whether the receiving team is poorly aligned or weak in an area (for example, a front-line player may turn and retreat too fast, the front line may not be spaced out all the way to the sideline, or there may be a gap behind the front-line players by the sideline). If you observe a weakness, develop a surprise onside kick to attack that area.

- How will the opponent deploy their receiving team against an expected onside kick? If the opponent fails to put enough players on the line against an overloaded onside kick alignment, the kicking team should have an advantage.

- Will the opponent block your kickoff coverage players on an expected onside kick? Through scouting or game-day observation, try to ascertain whether the opponent's receiving team, on an expected onside kick, will assign front-line players to block oncoming kickoff team members. If not, the onside kick has a good chance to be successful, because those unblocked defenders will easily be able to get to the spot where the ball is being fielded.

At a Glance

The following parts of the text offer additional information on recovering the onside kick.

Kickoff	p. 132
Onside Kick	p. 135
Defending the Onside Kick	p. 278

○ Will the opponent match your expected onside kick team with a "hands team"? If you line up for an onside kick earlier in the game than usual, for example, with five or six minutes left in the game, the receiving team may not anticipate this move and may send their regular return unit onto the field instead of the hands team that usually defends against an onside kick. This scenario presents an unusual opportunity for the kickoff team—an expected onside kick against a normal return team. The opposite may also happen. The receiving team, anticipating an onside kick, may send their hands team on to the field, but the kicking team may not be executing an onside kick. Here, the kicking team has the unusual opportunity of kicking off deep against a hands team that is not used to running a normal return.

Self-Knowledge

Besides being aware of your opponent's strengths and weaknesses, you and your players need to know about your own team's ability. Teach your players to be aware of the following when attempting to recover the onside kick:

○ How skilled is your kicker at the onside kick? With practice, your kicker should consistently be able to send an expected onside kick the required 10 yards down the field, with a good angle toward the sideline where his kickoff coverage teammates will be arriving and with a high hop on the second or third bounce that will make the catch and recovery difficult for the receiving team.

○ Can your kicker develop a surprise onside kick? This kick is an exciting and deceptive weapon for your special teams, but not every kicker can execute a surprise onside kick using his regular approach to the ball. Of course, if his approach is different, the receiving team will notice the change and adjust to defend against the onside kick.

○ How fast and skilled are your coverage players? A great athlete who is exceptionally fast and aggressive can be an excellent target for a surprise onside kick toward the sidelines. The kicker can just pooch the ball over the front-line players of the unsuspecting return team, and the fast athlete can get to the ball before they do.

Decision-Making Guidelines

When deciding how to gain the best advantage when recovering the onside kick, you and your players should consider the previous information as well as the following guidelines:

○ Assess the odds for recovery of the surprise onside kick. Never try a surprise onside kick unless you have scouted the flaws in the alignment or movement of the receiving team and have confirmed them during one of the first free kicks of the game. Without a high probability of success (better than 50 percent), the normal deep kick is the best play because a failed onside kick gives the opponent great field position.

○ Assess the odds for recovery of the expected onside kick. Clearly, the expected onside kick is difficult to recover, and sometimes, even if not much time remains on the clock, the normal deep kick gives your team the best chance to win. Although more time will run off the clock, if you can stop your opponent and force a punt, you will get the ball in good field position. Always keep in mind that the onside kick recovered by the receiving team gives *them* great field position.

Defending the Onside Kick

Your opponent has just scored and is now behind by 8 points or less. They do not have enough time left in the game to kick off, stop your offense and force a punt. They must get the ball back immediately, so they decide to use an onside kick, in which they kick the ball only the 10 yards it needs to go to become a live ball and then try to recover it. You must have a plan to defend the onside kick using a specialized kickoff return unit called the hands team. The hands team consists of a select group of players whose ability to catch the football and excellent eye–hand coordination should enable them to react to a bouncing football and cover it. They also must be tenacious and tough, because the other team will be sending 10 of their best athletes charging at them to knock them out of the way and get the football back for themselves!

Note: The onside kick is likely at two other times other than in the very late stages of the game. First, when the kicking team is behind by 9 to 16 points with six minutes or less left in the game, they may try the onside kick because they have to score twice to win. Second, when the receiving team has been penalized 15 yards on the previous scoring play, the kicking team might try the onside kick because they are now kicking off from the 50-yard line instead of the 35-yard line and will not place the receiving team in great field position if the onside kick is unsuccessful.

READING THE SITUATION

How can you and your players gain an advantage when defending the onside kick? Teach your players to do the following:

- The hands team should deploy as a mirror to the kickoff team. If the kickoff team overloads one side of the field, the same number of hands team players should take positions in front of them, plus perhaps one extra player, just to be safe.

- The hands team should set up in two levels. Some players should be near the line where the ball becomes live (10 yards from the kick-off line), and some players should deploy 5 to 7 yards behind them, where they can look for the longer, higher bounces. One member of the hands team should be 20 to 25 yards behind the rest of the team, looking for a short, pop-over kick or an unexpected deep kick.

- Evaluate the way the kicker sets the ball on the tee to get an idea about which direction he will kick it. Players on the hands team should shift to that side of the field.

- Watch how the kicker lines up for his approach to get an idea about which direction he is going to kick the ball. Again, hands team players should shift in that direction.

WATCH OUT!

The following circumstances may distract your players:

- Watching the kicking team instead of the ball. After the kicker starts his approach to the ball, every hands team player must focus on the ball, not on the coverage players who are moving toward the kickoff line. The ball will take strange bounces, and the hands team has to be ready to react.

- Thinking about the score of the game or the crucial nature of the play. Although the onside kick is a vital play in the game and could determine which team wins and which team loses, the hands team must block those thoughts from their minds and focus solely on the football and the task at hand—recovering it!

o Being too anxious and therefore playing the ball too aggressively. After the onside kick is on its way, the hands team must not let the excitement of the situation and the impending collisions cause them to become too anxious. The hands team must stay in position, read the first or second bounce of the ball and then react to the ball instead of charging at the ball as it approaches, a technique that is likely to cause a misplay.

ACQUIRING THE APPROPRIATE KNOWLEDGE

REMINDER!

When defending the onside kick, you and your players must understand the team strategy and game plan. Don't forget to consider the questions on page 172.

When defending the onside kick, you and your players should understand the following:

Rules

You and your athletes need to know several main rules when defending the onside kick:

o All players on the hands team must stay behind the 10-yard restraining line until the ball is kicked; otherwise an offside penalty could be called, giving the kicking team a second opportunity to recover the kick. (The kicking team also must stay behind the kickoff line until the ball is kicked.)

o The ball does not become live and legal for the kicking team to recover until it travels 10 yards downfield from the kickoff line or until it touches someone on the receiving team. Hands team members should not touch onside kick attempts that are short and clearly are not going to travel the required 10 yards.

o The kicking team cannot block members of the receiving team (the hands team) until the ball is live, so hands team players are safe from contact until the ball goes 10 yards or until a teammate touches it.

o If one or more players on either team touches the ball but no one gains possession of it and it then goes out of bounds, by rule the ball goes to the receiving team.

Physical Playing Conditions

The physical playing conditions significantly affect the game. Thus, you and your players must pay attention to the following physical conditions when defending the onside kick:

o If the field is wet or slippery, this play becomes even more unpredictable. Players on the hands team must take short, choppy steps as they move into position to recover the kick, being sure not to lose their footing.

o If the ball is wet, the hands team players must be certain to secure the ball against the body immediately after making a play on it so that it does not slip away.

Strengths and Weaknesses of Opponents

You and your players must account for your opponent's strengths and weaknesses to know how to defend the onside kick properly. Consider the following about your opponents:

o How talented is the opposing team's kicker? If the kicker kicks the ball too softly, so that it doesn't go 10 yards, or too hard, so that it quickly goes out of bounds, the job of the hands team is easy. But if the kicker has the ability to kick the ball just past the 10-yard line, putting a high bounce on the ball as it crosses that line, the catch will be difficult and either team could recover the kick.

o What kind of scheme do they use? The hands team is usually not able to scout the opponent's onside kick because they will not use this kick in most games. Therefore, the hands team must be ready for the opponent to line up in any number of sets, using a variety of kicks. An unusual scheme by the kicking team may create confusion.

(continued)

- How fast are the opponent's coverage players? If the opponent has several very fast players and they use them on the onside kick team, the hands team will have little time to react to the kick and make the recovery.

- How disciplined are the opponent's coverage players? If the athletes on the onside kick team all converge on the hands team player who initially tries to catch or recover the ball, they won't be in position to recover deflections. The hands team must take advantage of this mistake and be in position for the recovery if the ball gets loose.

Self-Knowledge

Besides being aware of your opponent's strengths and weaknesses, you and your players need to know about your own team's ability. Teach your players to be aware of the following when defending the onside kick:

- Who has the best hands on your football team? The players on the hands team may play any position but they must have the ability to catch the ball high, low, hard or soft.

- Who is likely to come out of a pile of players with a loose ball? If the ball rolls on the ground, a wild pack of players will converge on it. Some athletes are more tenacious than others in these situations, and their determination helps them make a play at a critical time. Those athletes need to be on the hands team.

- Who can make quick, accurate decisions? Hands team members have just a fraction of a second to decide whether the ball is going to travel 10 yards, whether it is going to go out of bounds, whether they should allow it through to the back line and so on. The athletes on this team need to be quick-thinking, heady players who can react appropriately under pressure.

Decision-Making Guidelines

When deciding how to gain the best advantage when defending the onside kick, you and your players should consider the previous information as well as the following guidelines:

- If the ball is kicked in the air for some reason, the hands team player nearest the ball should fair catch it, using the waving-arm signal before the catch.

- The front line should recover a slow, soft kick, but they must be sure that the ball is going to go 10 yards before they attempt to recover it. If it is definitely going to go 10 yards and is rolling, the nearest hands team member should fall on it at 9 yards, because at that distance, no kicking team member is allowed to touch it (or the hands team player!) yet and he will have an opportunity to recover it before being touched by the kicking team.

- The front line should let all hard, low kicks go through to the second line. These kicks will be easier to field after they have slowed down a bit and have taken at least one big bounce. Also, the kicking team has farther to run to collide with the second-row players, so the hands team should have a chance to make a play before being hit.

- If the front-line players on the hands team let the ball go through to the second line, they each should block a player on the kicking team to stop his progress toward the ball.

- All players on the hands team who are not making a play on the ball should position themselves near the teammate who is about to catch the ball, looking for a deflection that they can recover.

- If the ball is unexpectedly kicked deep, the back-line safety player should secure it properly, then take a knee or go out of bounds to avoid being tackled by the kicking team.

Punt Protection

The primary job of the punt team is to be sure that the punter has time to punt the ball down the field without being rushed or having his punt blocked. This task is called punt protection. After the punter kicks the ball away, the punt team becomes a coverage unit (as discussed in "Punt Coverage" on page 284), sprinting downfield to down the ball or the ball carrier if he fields the ball. Two types of punt protection are commonly used today, the tight punt and the spread punt. In the tight punt, no players align split out from the formation, and all players have protection responsibilities. In the spread punt, two split ends, called bullets, do not have protection responsibilities. Because they have only coverage responsibilities, the bullets will not be discussed in this skill.

The tight punt formation is probably safer than the spread punt for protection purposes, because 10 players block for the punter (instead of 8 in the spread punt). Those 10 players can build a long, wide wall in front of the punter. But because all 10 players have to block before releasing downfield to cover, the tight punt is not as effective for punt coverage as the spread punt, which releases 2 players (the bullets) downfield immediately on every punt. Both the tight punt and the spread punt use zone blocking schemes, in which each man is responsible for the space from his inside foot to the inside foot of the next player outside. In the tight punt, the players immediately plant the inside foot and then take a step to the outside to fill the area that they have to protect. In the spread punt, each player retreats six steps (three backward steps with each foot, beginning with the outside foot), before planting the inside foot and stepping outward to protect his area. With the exception of the initial footwork, the protection concepts are similar.

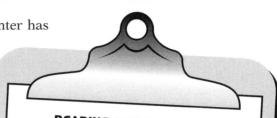

READING THE SITUATION

How can you and your players gain an advantage when protecting the punt? Teach your players to do the following:

- Understand that the protection scheme is a zone scheme and that each blocker is responsible for an area (from his inside foot to the inside foot of the player outside him).
- Ignore twists, slants, angles and other defensive movements. Each player must block his area.
- Before contact, plant the inside foot and step outside with the outside foot.

Note here that every punt team has a personal protector, a designated player who stands a few yards in front of the punter and a few steps behind the line. The player acting as the personal protector has several jobs, such as calling out the signals for the snap, looking for fake opportunities, alerting the blockers to overloads or key opponents and serving as the mop-up blocker against any opponent who penetrates the line. The personal protector does not use the same steps as the other punt team members do, and he must observe one important rule: Never back up after the snap or he may block the punt with his own backside!

⚠ WATCH OUT!

The following circumstances may distract your players:

- Defensive players who jump around and change alignment. Blockers must stay poised and concentrate on the snap of the ball.
- Using the hands before moving the feet. Blockers must not become so excited about blocking a rusher that they attack with the hands and fail to move the feet. They should move the feet first and then attack with the hands.
- Chasing twists, angles or slants by the defenders. Punt protection is a zone scheme; blockers must stay in their areas and not be influenced by defensive movement.
- Getting buried in one rusher. Punt protectors may have to block more than one rusher. They must not be so consumed with one rusher that they leave a gap open for another rusher.
- Being in too big a hurry to get downfield. Each player on the punt team who has protection responsibility must block his gap first before releasing to cover the punt.

(continued)

REMINDER!

When protecting the punt, you and your players must understand the team strategy and game plan. Don't forget to consider the questions on page 172.

ACQUIRING THE APPROPRIATE KNOWLEDGE

When protecting the punt, you and your players should understand the following:

Rules

You and your athletes need to know several main rules when protecting the punt:

- Defensive players are allowed to move before the snap as long as they don't cross the line of scrimmage, but players on the punt team are not allowed to move for at least one full count before the ball is snapped. The punt team must possess great discipline to ignore defensive movement and not jump offside.

- The rules do not allow a defensive player to grab and pull a punt protector out of his area to create an open lane for a teammate to rush the punter. The officials do not see all these infractions and so do not always call them. A punt protector must hold his ground in the zone that he is protecting, even if opponents use illegal tactics to pull him away from his assignment.

- The defense cannot contact the long snapper after the snap until he has time to raise his head and see what is in front of him. This rule, designed to protect the snapper from vicious contact immediately after the snap, is strictly enforced by most officiating crews.

Physical Playing Conditions

The physical playing conditions significantly affect the game. Thus, you and your players must pay attention to the following physical conditions when protecting the punt:

- If the field is wet or slippery, the punt protection team will have to be cautious in their footwork, taking slightly smaller, less dramatic steps to avoid losing their footing and slipping, thus opening a lane for the defenders to rush the punter.

Strengths and Weaknesses of Opponents

You and your players must account for your opponent's strengths and weaknesses to know how to protect the punt properly. Consider the following about your opponents:

- How fast and aggressive are the opponent's rushers? Through scouting and game-day observation, the punt team should be able to identify the location of the opponent's best, fastest rushers. Punt protectors lined up against these rushers must hold their blocks longer before releasing into coverage.

- How and where do the opponents attack when they try to block a punt? Some defenses try to overload an area with two or even three rushers; other defenses try to twist and loop rushers; some defenses try to pull a blocker out of the way (sometimes illegally) and rush a man through the opened gap. Through scouting and game-day observation, the punt team should be able to identify the punt rush schemes that they need to block and be prepared to stop them.

- Are the opponents sound against fakes? Some defenses are so committed to the punt rush and the effort to block the punt that they leave themselves open for a fake punt, such as a quick pass to one of the slots in the spread punt formation or a pass to one of the tight ends in the tight punt formation. The punt protection unit should look for these opportunities and use the fake punt for two purposes: first, to get a first down instead of punting the ball away and second, to deter the defense from mounting an all-out punt rush on future punt attempts.

Self-Knowledge

Besides being aware of your opponent's strengths and weaknesses, you and your players need to know about your own team's ability. Teach your players to be aware of the following when protecting the punt:

At a Glance

The following parts of the text offer additional information on punt protection.

Pass Protection	p. 85
Punt	p. 140
Long Snap	p. 155
Punt Coverage	p. 284

- How fast and accurate is the long snapper? A fast, accurate long snap can help the punt protection immensely by decreasing the operation time for the punt. If the long snapper is erratic or slow, the punt protection unit will have to hold their blocks longer to ensure that the punt gets away (the recommended 14-yard snap time is 0.8 to 1.0 seconds).

- What is the punter's operation time? If the punter's operation time is long, the punt team will have to hold their blocks longer and more punts may be blocked. If the punter has good operation time, the protection unit can release into coverage earlier and fewer punts will be blocked. The punter should execute his punt in two steps after the catch, not three, because the extra step is the most common cause of long operation time (the recommended operation time from catch to kick is 1.4 to 1.5 seconds).

- How disciplined are the punt protectors? The best athletes for the punt team are players who are willing to take the proper steps and consistently fill their gaps without being distracted, influenced or powered out of their areas. These athletes must also be able to release down the field and cover the punt, so they must have the requisite skills for that assignment as well.

Decision-Making Guidelines

When deciding how to gain the best advantage when protecting the punt, you and your players should consider the previous information as well as the following guidelines:

- Players should take their stances in the standard athletic position on the line. They should take splits (the distance from one player to the next) of approximately 2 feet for the tight punt and about 1 foot for the spread punt. Both units have a long snapper, two guards and two tackles. The tight punt also has two tight ends and two upbacks who align in the center guard gap about a yard off the line to protect against a middle rush; the spread punt has no upbacks and no tight ends but has two slots, who align a yard off the line just outside the tackles.

- Blockers protect from inside leg to inside leg (remember that spread punt protectors backpedal first to force the outermost rusher on each side to take a wider, deeper rush). Keeping the inside foot planted, the player firmly punches his inside hand at any rusher who attacks him head up to slightly inside. At the same time, he steps outside with his outside foot and firmly punches with his outside hand against any rusher attacking the gap outside him. He might have to block two rushers at one time, but he does not have to stop them completely; he only has to slow them down and be sure that neither gets past him cleanly. Players need to remember that they are responsible only for rushers who attack them from the inside leg through the gap extending to the next player's inside leg. If they stay low and maintain body position in their gaps, they should be able to execute this assignment.

- Players must block aggressively. Some punt protection players believe that their assignment is a passive play. In reality, after the first positioning steps, the protection player needs to play aggressively, with low pad level, forceful hand contact and tough physical effort.

Punt Coverage

The main responsibility for all punt team players is to protect the punter so that he can get the punt away safely. But after the punt is away, the punt team players become a coverage unit with the important job of minimizing any return of the punt. They must be physical, so that they can escape from defenders; fast, so that they can get quickly down the field; and smart, so that they will be in good coverage lanes with the proper leverage on the ball. Players who have good defensive skills are often the best players to use on the punt team.

Spread punt teams have an advantage in punt coverage over tight punt teams because the spread punt teams have two bullets, split ends, who release immediately on the snap, with no protection responsibilities, and sprint directly to the ball. The bullets try to keep the ball on the inside shoulder, but they are not force players. The slot backs on the spread punt team must fan out and be the more passive, outside-conscious force players. On the tight punt, the tight ends, the outermost players in the alignment, fan out and become the force players for tight punt coverage.

 **WATCH OUT!**

The following circumstances may distract your players:

- Holding a block too long.
  The punter should get the ball away in 2.0 seconds or less.
  Blockers should not hold their blocks longer than that.

- Getting held up by a defender who is no longer rushing the punt. At some point in the play the rusher is no longer trying to block the punt—he's trying to stop the punt team player from releasing! The punt team player must release from his opponent and cover the punt.

- Getting pushed too far back. Punt team players must not think of punt protection as being passive. They should play aggressively and hold their ground so that they can release and get down the field quickly.

- Running straight to the ball after releasing. The ball is like a magnet—players are attracted to it—but after releasing from protection, the coverage players have to fan out into lanes to prevent the return man from outflanking them to the outside.

READING THE SITUATION

How can you and your players gain an advantage when covering punts? Teach your players to do the following:

- Recognize when the rush threat ends. When the defenders across from them are no longer rushing the punter, the punt team players should start their release into coverage.

- Plant the feet and sink the hips. Blockers must not be driven too far back while they are protecting the punter. They must sink their hips and hold their ground.

- Release through the outside gap with an aggressive underarm rip move.

- Fan out into coverage. Players should release on an angle toward the outside as they head downfield to keep the ball carrier from getting outside the coverage.

- Find the ball and adjust to its location. The long snapper runs directly to the ball; all other players keep the ball on the inside shoulder.

- After the return man catches the ball, the long snapper adjusts to stay head up with him. All other players keep the return man on the inside shoulder.

ACQUIRING THE APPROPRIATE KNOWLEDGE

When covering punts, you and your players should understand the following:

REMINDER!

When covering punts, you and your players must understand the team strategy and game plan. Don't forget to consider the questions on page 172.

Rules

You and your athletes need to know several main rules when covering punts:

- All blocks on kicking plays must be initiated in front and above the waist, so punt coverage players should be able to see the players who might be threats to block them and should be ready to take on all blocks with forearms and shoulder pads.

- If the punt hits the ground and is not caught, it still belongs to the receiving team (unless it touched a player on the receiving team after it crossed the line of scrimmage). The punt coverage players must cover the punt as it rolls, in case the return man tries to pick it up and run with it. When it stops rolling, the officials will blow the ball dead, and the receiving team will have the ball.

- If the punt is blocked and stays behind the line of scrimmage, players on the punt team can legally pick up the ball and advance it. If the other team picks up the blocked punt, of course, they also can advance it, so members of the punting team must hustle to catch them and make a tackle.

- If the punt is partially blocked but travels past the line of scrimmage, it is treated the same as a punt that was not blocked. It belongs to the receiving team (unless it touches a player on the receiving team after it crosses the line of scrimmage).

Physical Playing Conditions

The physical playing conditions significantly affect the game. Thus, you and your players must pay attention to the following physical conditions when covering punts:

- In wet and slippery field conditions, the punt coverage unit needs to use careful footwork both on their releases at the line of scrimmage and on their course downfield to cover the punt to be sure that they don't slip and fall.

- If the punter has a strong wind behind him, the punt coverage unit needs to be aware that they will have to run extremely fast and go farther down the field to cover the punt.

- If the punter is facing a strong wind, the punt coverage unit must be aware that the punt may hang up in the wind and not travel very far. The punt coverage unit must adjust to a shorter punt and not overrun the ball.

Strengths and Weaknesses of Opponents

You and your players must account for your opponent's strengths and weaknesses to know how to cover punts properly. Consider the following about your opponents:

- How good is the return man? Fast, shifty and fearless return men are a threat to break open a game with a big return. The punt coverage team must work hard against such a player to release efficiently and hustle down the field to keep him under control. (The punt team also might want to consider punting the ball out of bounds or away from an outstanding return man.)

- What kind of return does the opponent use? Some teams use man blocking schemes for a middle return. Others use a wall return toward one of the sidelines (see "Wall Return"

(continued)

on page 291). Against man returns, every coverage player must defeat his blocker, keeping his outside arm free and keeping the ball inside. Against wall returns, the outermost coverage player (the tight end in tight punt and the slot back in spread punt) must see the wall setting up and get outside the wall. These coverage players are the force players on the coverage unit and they must not allow themselves to be trapped inside the wall (see "Playing Force on Kick Coverage" on page 272).

Self-Knowledge

Besides being aware of your opponent's strengths and weaknesses, you and your players need to know about your own team's ability. Teach your players to be aware of the following when covering punts:

- How much hang time does your punter have? Hang time is measured from the moment the ball is punted until it hits the ground or the return man catches it. The longer the hang time, the better the coverage because the punt coverage players have more time to release and get down the field. If the punt is low and the hang time is short, the punt coverage unit has a much more difficult assignment (the recommended hang time is over 4.0 seconds).

- How fast are the coverage players? In assigning personnel for the punt team, you have a tricky dilemma: you need strong blockers for protection but fast players for coverage. If the punt team does not include fast players, punt coverage will be more difficult because the punt return man will have more room to operate.

- How disciplined are the coverage players? As the punt coverage players release and start to run downfield, the undisciplined ones will take a direct course to the ball and forget to fan out into lanes. This action will leave holes in the coverage that a good return man will find.

Decision-Making Guidelines

When deciding how to gain the best advantage when covering punts, you and your players should consider the previous information as well as the following guidelines:

- Punt team players must recognize when their role changes from punt protection (trying to stop defenders on their rush to block the punt) to punt coverage (trying to release past defenders who are trying to stop them from going downfield to cover the punt). The punt team player must read his opponent's aggressiveness and gauge his forward momentum; when it stops, roles reverse!

- When releasing into coverage, the punt team player should lower his hips, take his inside arm aggressively to the outside and attack any punt rusher in his outside gap. Dipping the shoulders and ripping the arms, the punt team player must escape the defender and release in an outward direction toward his assigned coverage lane.

- The coverage players must fan out to a distance 3 yards apart from each other as they run downfield to form a pocket that will trap the return man. The long snapper is the point man in the pocket, and he runs directly to the punt return man. The other coverage players are on each side of the long snapper, in the same alignment, left to right, as they were for punt protection, but they are farther apart now that they have changed from protection mode to coverage mode.

○ As the return man begins to run laterally to find a seam in the coverage, the coverage players move laterally as well, keeping the ball inside and maintaining their separation from each other. This configuration prevents the return man from getting outside the punt coverage team.

○ When the return man makes a move to run through a seam in the pocket of the punt coverage, the coverage players converge on him and make the open-field tackle. The coverage players must break down when they reach the vicinity of the return man, slowing their forward speed, lowering their center of gravity and balancing their weight on both feet in good athletic position. Breaking down allows them to move laterally and react to the return man's fakes or moves. The first player should go for a high tackle so that he can control the runner and receive help from his teammates.

○ The punter and the personal protector will be the last two players on the punt team to release and run downfield to cover the punt. Consequently, they usually have the role of safeties on the punt coverage unit. In that role, they fan out apart from each other, staying 15 to 20 yards behind the other coverage players. If the return man breaks loose outside, the man on that side tries to force him out of bounds. If the return man breaks loose up the middle, the safeties force him to go between the two of them, squeezing his field. One of them must make the tackle.

At a Glance

The following parts of the text offer additional information on punt coverage.

Punting Inside the 40-Yard Line

The offense has a fourth down inside the opponent's 40-yard line. The line to gain is too far to attempt an offensive play, the distance is too far for the place kicker to try a field goal and the spot is too close for the punter to kick his normal kick. In this situation, the offense may choose to have the punter use a sky punt or corner punt to force the opponent to start their next possession with poor field position. The punter should try to keep the ball in the field of play, but the punt must either be high enough that the other team has to fair catch it (sky punt) or punted away from the return man toward the sideline so that the ball will hit and roll to a stop or go out of bounds before going into the end zone (corner punt).

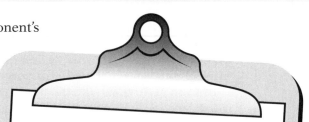

READING THE SITUATION

How can you and your players gain an advantage when punting inside the 40-yard line? Teach your players to do the following:

- The punter should kick the ball high on the sky punt to allow time for coverage.
- The bullets (players on the punt team split away from the formation) should concentrate only on downing the ball, not worrying about covering the punt return.
- Communicate, so that two players from the coverage unit don't bump into each other and allow the ball to roll into the end zone.

⚠ WATCH OUT!

The following circumstances may distract your players:

- An aggressive punt rush team. A tough punt rush might force the punter to rush his punt, a particularly harmful circumstance here because the punter usually executes these types of specialty punts best if he can take his time.
- The short field. Sometimes, punters see the short distance to the goal line and, realizing that they can't use their regular punt, back off too much and punt the ball too short.
- Being too concerned about the outcome of the play. Punters obviously are curious about where the ball will be downed, but they can't be so concerned with the end of the play that they rush the punt, look up too early and cause themselves to make a technical mistake on the punt.
- The return man who makes a fair catch signal. The return man who signals a fair catch may be decoying, trying to slow the coverage team. The coverage players should go past him, because he can't return the ball after he catches it now anyway.

ACQUIRING THE APPROPRIATE KNOWLEDGE

When punting inside the 40-yard line, you and your players should understand the following:

Rules

You and your athletes need to know several main rules when punting inside the 40-yard line:

- Rules for change of possession.
- Players on the punt team must be careful not to jump offside in their eagerness to get downfield to cover the punt.

- If the punted ball touches one of the players on the punt coverage team downfield, a rule called first touching goes into effect. The officials marks the spot where the ball touched the coverage player, but they let play continue. At the end of the play, the receiving team has their choice of the outcome of the play or the spot where the ball was first touched. In effect, this rule gives the receiving team a free return because if they have a poor return or even fumble the ball, they still get the ball back at the spot of the first touch. Both the coverage team and the receiving team must be aware of this rule and keep playing hard until the play ends.

REMINDER!

When punting inside the 40-yard line, you and your players must understand the team strategy and game plan. Don't forget to consider the questions on page 172.

Physical Playing Conditions

The physical playing conditions significantly affect the game. Thus, you and your players must pay attention to the following physical conditions when punting inside the 40-yard line:

- In wet or slippery field conditions, the coverage players have to be sure not to slide into the end zone as they try to down the football. They must realize that stopping on a wet field will take longer.
- If the ball is wet, the coverage players must understand that they won't be able to grab the ball as easily when they try to down it.
- If the punting team has a strong wind at their back, they may consider using a sky punt or corner punt from farther away than the 40-yard line. Conversely, if the punting team is facing a strong wind, the punter may be able to use his regular punt at the 40-yard line. The punter might not use the sky punt or corner punt until his team is closer to the end zone.
- If the punting team is punting into a strong wind, the sky punt may be a better option than the corner punt because the wind may keep the ball from sailing into the end zone.

Strengths and Weaknesses of Opponents

You and your players must account for your opponent's strengths and weaknesses to know how to punt inside the 40-yard line properly. Consider the following about your opponents:

- Is the punt rush team strong? The punt coverage players are eager to get downfield to down the punt, but if the opponent has a strong rush unit or a talented player or two who rush punts, the coverage players will have to hold their blocks longer before releasing into coverage, thus reducing the punt team's chances of downing the ball close to the opponent's goal line.
- Is the return man aggressive? Against an aggressive return man, the punt coverage unit should be prepared, first, for a return. The coverage unit players must stay in their lanes and break down at the return man, not at the end zone, to be sure that he cannot field the ball and make a return. Remember, the bullets do not have coverage responsibilities here, so the rest of the unit must take more responsibility for coverage.
- How willing is the return man to catch the ball in this critical situation? A hesitant or less aggressive punt catcher might back off in this situation, letting the ball bounce instead of taking a chance on a catch that he might fumble. Through scouting and game-day observation, assess the confidence and aggressiveness of the return man. If he appears unwilling to step up and make a catch, use the sky punt whenever possible.
- How good are the players covering the bullets? If the defenders covering the bullets are talented enough to prevent the bullets from getting downfield while the punt is in the air, the sky punt and corner punt are less likely to be effective. The bullets are usually the

(continued)

players who get downfield to down these types of punts before they go into the end zone.

Self-Knowledge

Besides being aware of your opponent's strengths and weaknesses, you and your players need to know about your own team's ability. Teach your players to be aware of the following when punting inside the 40-yard line:

- Is your punter versatile and skilled? Neither the sky punt nor the corner punt will be effective if the punter is inconsistent in executing them. If the punter cannot master at least one of these kicks, the offense may be better off just punting the ball into the end zone and giving the other team the ball on the 20-yard line (this result is better than giving up a long punt return on a poor sky punt or having a shanked corner punt go out of bounds at the 30!).

- Are the bullets fast and heady? If the bullets are quick, talented athletes, they can make great plays for the punt team on sky punts and corner punts by downing the ball inside the 10- or 5-yard line. If the bullets are not fast, or if they don't find and react well to the ball, these specialty punts have far less chance of success.

- How good is your field-goal kicker? If your field-goal kicker is accurate at long range, you will use the sky punt and corner punts less often to allow him a chance to put 3 points on the scoreboard. If your field-goal kicker is erratic or short on leg strength, you will use the sky and corner punts more often.

Decision-Making Guidelines

When deciding how to gain the best advantage when punting inside the 40-yard line, you and your players should consider the previous information as well as the following guidelines:

- Release the bullets from coverage responsibility. When working from a spread punt formation with two players (bullets) split out like wide receivers, give those bullets a call on both the sky punt and corner punt that they do not have coverage responsibility; instead, they are to find the ball and try to down it before it goes into the end zone.

- Bullets should run to the goal line, turn around with their backs to the goal line and find the ball. If the bullets look for the ball while they are running downfield, they will slow down. Likewise, if they try to make a play on the ball while running toward the goal line, their momentum is likely to carry them, and the ball, into the end zone. They should sprint full speed to the goal line and then wheel around, find the football and play goalie, trying to keep the ball from going into the end zone.

- The punter should try to kick the ball very high, hoping for a long hang time (length of time that the ball is in the air on a punt). The better the hang time, the better the coverage and the better the chance to down the ball before it goes into the end zone.

- The punter should try to land the ball at the 10-yard line. Most teams will fair catch a punt at the 10-yard line, which is an excellent outcome for the punting team on this play.

- The coverage team should not be too greedy. The odd shape of the football can cause it to take strange bounces. If the ball hits the ground and rolls, the coverage team should not wait until the ball is inside the 1-yard line to down it, unless it has almost stopped and is rolling slowly. If the punt team waits too long, a bad hop could take the football into the end zone.

A wall return is a punt return in which some of the players on the return unit peel off while the ball is in the air and position themselves a few yards apart near one sideline. Facing inside, they create a wall of blockers between the coverage players and the sideline. If the return man can catch the punt and get to the wall, he should have a clear path to the end zone. The challenge for the players executing a wall return is that they don't have a particular opponent to block; they simply establish their positions and then block any opponent who comes into their area. The wall return also requires a punt that stays in the air long enough for the return team to set up the wall. Finally, the wall return requires a good punt return man—one who catches the ball well and has enough speed to get to the wall. Although the wall return is a difficult tactical skill in the realm of special teams, practicing it may be worth the effort because it can be an exciting, game-changing play.

⚠ WATCH OUT!

The following circumstances may distract your players:

- Being too eager to block. The players setting up the wall have to be patient and poised, hustling to their general area and then evaluating the deployment of the coverage unit's players to see which of them is most likely to run toward their area.

- Setting up the wall too far from the punt return man. The players will not set up the wall in the same place, relative to the sideline, on every punt, so they cannot look for field landmarks to tell them where to set up. Players have to find the ball while it is in the air and adjust the location of the wall accordingly.

READING THE SITUATION

How can you and your players gain an advantage when using a wall return? Teach your players to do the following:

- Slow down the bullets. The wall return will never even get started if the punt return man can't get past the bullets.

- Sprint downfield. The players in the wall have to sprint downfield to set it up before the return man catches the ball and heads their way.

- Follow the leader. The point man, or first man down the field in the wall, determines where to set the wall, and everyone else bases his position on the man in front of him.

- Set up the wall based on the punt catch. The point man should set the wall 15 to 20 yards laterally and about 5 yards short vertically from the return man at the catch.

- Keep proper spacing in the wall. The players setting up the wall must be 4 to 5 yards apart so that they can protect a path of sufficient length for the return man and will be unlikely to block the same coverage man.

- Communicate! If two coverage players are close together, the blockers must let each other know which one they are going to take.

ACQUIRING THE APPROPRIATE KNOWLEDGE

When using the wall return, you and your players should understand the following:

Rules

You and your athletes need to know several main rules when using the wall return:

- All blocks on kicking plays in football have to be above the waist, so players in the wall must stay high when they put on their blocks.

(continued)

REMINDER!

When using the wall return, you and your players must understand the team strategy and game plan. Don't forget to consider the questions on page 172.

○ Players must initiate all blocks with the contact on the front part of the blocked man's body. On the wall return, coverage players are often turning and changing directions to chase the punt return man when they approach the wall. The blockers in the wall must wait until the coverage player turns toward them so that their block legally starts on the front of the coverage player's body.

○ Holding, of course, is not permitted when blocking on any play. On special teams plays such as the wall return, with the players spread out all over the field, the blockers have to concentrate on using good speed and footwork to get in position for a legal block instead of reaching out to push or hold the opponent.

Physical Playing Conditions

The physical playing conditions significantly affect the game. Thus, you and your players must pay attention to the following physical conditions when using the wall return:

○ In wet or slippery field conditions, the wall return blockers must use shorter steps and more cautious footwork to be sure that they don't slip and fall when setting up the wall.

○ If the punter has a strong wind at his back, the wall return might have a better chance to be successful, because a high, deep punt gives the punt return unit more time to set up the wall. The wall might have to be set up deeper down the field, however, because the wind will carry the punt deeper.

○ If the punter is punting into a strong wind, the wall return is probably not a good call. The punt return unit will have little time to set up the wall, and the return man will probably be surrounded by coverage players when he catches the short punt, so he is unlikely to get to the wall.

Strengths and Weaknesses of Opponents

You and your players must account for your opponent's strengths and weaknesses to know how to use the wall return properly. Consider the following about your opponents:

○ How good is the punter? If the opposing punter is strong and consistent, the wall return may be a good strategy to counter his talents. His long, high punts will give the punt return unit more time to set up the wall and give the punt return man a chance to catch the ball, make a move or two to beat the bullets and get to the wall. On the other hand, if the punter is inconsistent or short with his punts, the wall return is probably not a good call because the punt return unit won't have time to set up the wall before the coverage players catch the return man.

○ How fast are the opponent's coverage players? If the bullets are fast, assign another player or two to getting them blocked. If the coverage unit players are also fast, the wall return may be difficult to execute because the coverage players may get to the return man before he can reach the wall. If the opponent's bullets or coverage players are not fast, the wall return has a much better chance to be successful.

○ How well do the opponent's coverage players adjust to blocking schemes on returns? Some coverage units have learned to recognize wall returns, and these units teach players to peel off and get outside the wall, making it tough to execute the return. Other opponents do not look for blocking schemes and do not change the path of their coverage players regardless of the type of return that their opponent is running. These opponents are vulnerable to the wall return because they may not see it coming.

Self-Knowledge

Besides being aware of your opponent's strengths and weaknesses, you and your players need to know about your own team's ability. Teach your players to be aware of the following when using the wall return:

- How talented is your punt return man? A shifty, fast return man who catches punts consistently is a great candidate to run a wall return. If he has the ability to make someone miss, he can sidestep that first bullet or fast coverage player and then have a chance to get to the wall. Conversely, if the return man can catch consistently but does not possess great speed or moves, the wall return is not as good an option.

- How do you match up against the bullets? If the punt return unit can put two players on the field who can cover the bullets and significantly slow them down, the wall return, or any punt return for that matter, can be successful. If the bullets are too good to handle one-on-one, then you have to steal blockers from the return scheme to double up on the bullets, reducing the chances for a big play. (You may get a few yards after the catch by double-teaming the bullets, but you won't be able to block as many of the remaining defenders.)

- How disciplined are the players who are setting up the wall? Overaggressive, impatient players do not execute the wall return as well as heady, patient players do. All players in the wall have to hustle and be physical blockers, but they also need to be in the right spot on the field and be able to pick out the correct defender to block.

At a Glance

The following parts of the text offer additional information on the wall return.

Punt	p. 140
Catching the Punt	p. 148
Bullets	p. 150
Defending Against the Bullets	p. 153
Playing Force on Kick Coverage	p. 272
Punt Protection	p. 281
Punt Coverage	p. 284

Decision-Making Guidelines

When deciding how to gain the best advantage when using the wall return, you and your players should consider the previous information as well as the following guidelines:

- At the beginning of the play, the punt return unit has to line up against the punt team and be sure that they are sound against a possible fake. They can keep the punt team unaware that a wall return is coming if they show a punt block look before the snap.

- When the ball is snapped, at least one player from the return unit has to rush the punter to be sure that he punts the ball on time so that the ball will get to the return man before the coverage players do.

- Players who will be setting up the wall should not start peeling off toward the side of the field to set up the wall until the coverage player nearest them leaves to go down the field and cover the punt. The coverage player is less likely to see the wall player heading to a sideline if the wall player is behind him!

- After taking their positions in the wall, the blockers should shuffle laterally toward the punt return man until he catches the ball. They then shuffle the other way, in the direction of the return, until a coverage man shows up to be blocked.

- In choosing which defender to block, the wall players always choose a man who is farther down the field as opposed to one who is not as far down the field. The idea is to prevent penetration by defenders at the beginning, or top, of the wall. If a coverage player penetrates the wall at the top and makes the tackle, the blocks farther down the wall are wasted.

The most common scheme for a kickoff return is the wedge return. On the wedge return, the five players on the front line of the return team retreat, gather and form a shoulder-to-shoulder wedge whose objective is to clear a path where the return man can carry the ball. A second wedge consisting of four players forms up in similar fashion about 10 yards behind the first wedge, looking to block any defenders who get through the first wedge. The remaining two players on the return team are the deep return men. One of these players catches the kickoff and returns it, while the other watches the catch to be sure that his partner secures the ball. The second deep man then leads the return man toward the wedge. The wedge return is simple to teach and install, and it can produce consistent kickoff returns if the blockers set up properly and block aggressively.

 **WATCH OUT!**

The following circumstances may distract your players:

- Front-line players retreating too early. Although the assignment on the wedge return requires the front-line players on the return team to turn and sprint down the field, those players must remember to watch the ball until it is kicked. If the front-line players leave too early, before they see that the ball is kicked, they could be vulnerable to a surprise onside kick.

READING THE SITUATION

How can you and your players gain an advantage when using a wedge return? Teach your players to do the following:

- Sprint down the field! Front-line players must sprint downfield so that they have time to turn around and locate the approaching defenders.

- Run forward, toward the kickoff team, before contact. After they form the front wedge, all five players run forward toward the onrushing defenders. The players in the wedge won't get far before they run into the defenders, but they must start moving forward before contact occurs to avoid being knocked backward by the onrushing defenders.

- Second-wedge players must see the catch. These players retreat until they are 15 to 20 yards ahead of the return man at the catch, so the deeper the kick, the farther they retreat.

- Turn and attack the coverage team. Like the front-wedge players, the second wedge must turn and establish forward momentum before blocking occurs.

- Stay shoulder to shoulder. Gaps in either wedge spoil the return. Blockers in both wedges must stay together, forcing defenders to go around the wedge or try to run directly over them.

- Watching coverage players instead of sprinting to form the wedge. Blockers forming the wedges must ignore the coverage players initially and concentrate on sprinting to the position on the field where they will meet their teammates.

- Failing to adjust to the depth of the kick. The wedges have to be set up farther down the field on a deep kick than they are on a short kick. Players on the return team cannot be so eager to set up their wedge that they fail to track the course and depth of the kick.

ACQUIRING THE APPROPRIATE KNOWLEDGE

When using the wedge return, you and your players should understand the following:

REMINDER!

When using the wedge return, you and your players must understand the team strategy and game plan. Don't forget to consider the questions on page 172.

Rules

You and your athletes need to know several main rules when using the wedge return:

- All blocks on kicking plays in football have to be above the waist, so players on the wedge return must stay high when they put on their blocks.

- Player must initiate all blocks with contact on the front part of the blocked man's body. The blockers in the wedge must be sure to turn around and face the coverage players so that their blocks legally start on the front of the coverage player's body.

- Holding, of course, is not permitted when blocking. On special teams plays such as the wedge return, blockers have to use good footwork to get in position for a legal block instead of reaching out to push or hold their opponents.

Physical Playing Conditions

The physical playing conditions significantly affect the game. Thus, you and your players must pay attention to the following physical conditions when using the wedge return:

- The wedge return is a good call if the field is wet or slippery. Players in the wedge have to be careful not to retreat so fast that they cannot stop themselves and turn around to form the wedge, but this blocking scheme does not require a lot of planting and cutting, so it should be effective even on a wet field.

- Windy conditions will affect the location of the wedges. If the kicker has a strong wind at his back, the kick should be deep and the return team will have to set up the wedges farther down the field than normal. If the kicker is facing a strong wind, the kick probably won't be as deep, so the return team won't set up the wedges as far down the field as normal.

Strengths and Weaknesses of Opponents

You and your players must account for your opponent's strengths and weaknesses to know how to use the wedge return properly. Consider the following about your opponents:

- How strong is the opponent's kicker? Through scouting and game-day observation, you can establish the depth and hang time of the opponent kicker, so the players on the wedge return will have a better idea of how far they will have to retreat before setting up the wedges.

- How consistent is the opponent's kicker? If the kicker is inconsistent on depth and hang time, the wedge return players will have to be alert and aware of the location and depth of each kickoff so that they will know where to set up the wedges.

- How fast are the kickoff coverage players? The faster the kickoff team, the tougher it will be to run the wedge return. The players on the front line of the kickoff return team have only a 10-yard head start on the kickoff coverage players, and the kickoff return players have to sprint downfield, turn around and start going the other direction before the kickoff coverage players arrive. If the opponent's kickoff team has fast players, then the wedge return team must use fast players in the front line for the return to work.

(continued)

Self-Knowledge

Besides being aware of your opponent's strengths and weaknesses, you and your players need to know about your own team's ability. Teach your players to be aware of the following when using the wedge return:

- How fast are the players on the wedge return unit? Speed is an important factor in assigning players to this unit, especially on the front line. Defensive backs and wide receivers are usually good candidates for these positions.

- How aggressive and tough are the players on the wedge return team? The wedge return scheme requires players to run directly at onrushing coverage players, and the collisions can be ferocious. Players selected for duty on this unit have to love contact and be willing to play with aggressiveness and courage.

- What are the characteristics of the return man? Of course, the most important job for the return man is to catch the ball and hang on to it throughout the return. But beyond that, the wedge return requires a powerful return man who is somewhat of a daredevil. He must be willing to sprint toward the two wedges, knowing that there might not be much of an opening. Sometimes, he will run into an impassable mass of bodies. But other times, the wedges will clear a path through the kickoff coverage players, and an opening will appear that the return man has to hit at full speed. For this scheme to work, the return man must believe in it and attack the location where the opening may appear.

Decision-Making Guidelines

When deciding how to gain the best advantage when using the wedge return, you and your players should consider the previous information as well as the following guidelines:

- For the wedge return to be successful, the wedges have to be set up properly, based on the depth and location of the kick. The most common mistake is setting up one or both wedges too early on a deep kick. By the time the return man gets there, coverage players have run around the wedge or the wedge is starting to break up. Conduct drills with the players in both wedges to get them used to going far enough down the field on deep kicks, but not so far on shallow kicks.

- Blockers in the two wedges cannot "catch" defenders and expect to be successful. If the blockers are not moving forward at impact, the kickoff coverage defenders will knock them backward.

- Blockers in the wedges must stay shoulder to shoulder. Again, use drills "on air" in practice to teach the players to sprint to a spot (usually chosen by the group leader in the wedge), get close together and then turn and charge back upfield as a unit, not getting separated as they go.

- The job of the return man who does not catch the ball is important. He must be sure to block any onrushing coverage defender who tries to get around the wedges and attack the ball carrier from the outside. His job is to ensure that the return man who has the ball gets to the wedge and has a chance to find an opening behind those blockers.

PAT and FG Protection

Blockers on the PAT–FG (point after touchdown field goal) unit must be big, strong players who can hold their ground when the defensive players rush the kick. Lining up in a two tight end, double wing formation, these blockers create a solid wall between the kicker and the defensive rushers so that the only possible place for a defender to get past them is outside the wing blockers. (Each blocker on the line is responsible for protecting the area from his outside foot to the outside foot of the next player inside.) If the snap, hold and kick can be completed in less than two seconds, the outside rushers simply do not have enough time to get around the wing blockers and block the kick.

⚠ WATCH OUT!

The following circumstances may distract your players:

- Movement by defensive players. Defensive shifting and jumping around may cause a member of the PAT–FG protection unit to flinch, resulting in a penalty and loss of yards.

- Being preoccupied with one rusher. If two rushers attack one blocker, the blocker must slow down both of them, although only one of the rushers may be immediately in front of him.

ACQUIRING THE APPROPRIATE KNOWLEDGE

When protecting the PAT or FG attempt, you and your players should understand the following:

Rules

You and your athletes need to know several main rules when you are protecting the PAT or FG attempt:

- Defensive players can move around before the snap, as long as they don't cross the line of scrimmage. But because the PAT FG protection unit is in possession of the ball, all players on that unit must be set for one full count before the snap. Blockers on the PAT–FG unit cannot let defensive movement cause them to move, which would result in a penalty and a longer kick.

- Blockers on the PAT–FG unit cannot grab or hold the rushers. The wing blockers especially have to resist the temptation to grab the outermost rusher as he goes by.

- Defenders rushing the kick are not allowed to pull a blocker out of his area to create a gap for another defender to rush the kick. But the officials do not always see or call this infraction. Blockers on the PAT–FG unit must hold their ground firmly, even if they are being illegally pulled by a defender, to prevent a seam from being opened up in the wall.

READING THE SITUATION

How can you and your players gain an advantage when protecting the PAT or FG attempt? Teach your players to do the following:

- Focus on keeping pads low and body weight forward.

- At the snap, step inside with the inside foot to completely seal the front wall of the unit.

- Prepare for a physical rush and be ready to strike forward aggressively.

- Check the opposing team's alignment and anticipate when your gap will be threatened.

REMINDER!

When blocking on PAT and FG attempts, you and your players must understand the team strategy and game plan. Don't forget to consider the questions on page 172.

(continued)

- Defenders are not allowed to step on top of other players and then jump to try to block the kick. Nor are they allowed to land on top of other players after they jump in the air, so if they do jump to make a block, they have to take off from the ground and land on the ground.

- Defenders trying to block the kick cannot run into the kicker unless they also touch the ball. Therefore, the holder should place the tee no farther than 7 yards behind the line of scrimmage so that a defender rushing around the wing blocker has to negotiate a very tight corner to avoid running into the kicker.

Physical Playing Conditions

The physical playing conditions significantly affect the game. Thus, you and your players must pay attention to the following physical conditions when protecting the PAT or FG attempt:

- In wet or slippery field conditions, the PAT–FG blockers have to be sure to keep their weight over their feet, possibly shortening their splits a bit, so that they don't overextend themselves and lose their footing.

- If the ball is wet, the PAT–FG blockers might have to hold the blocks slightly longer because the snap and hold might be slower than usual.

Strengths and Weaknesses of Opponents

You and your players must account for your opponent's strengths and weaknesses to know how to protect the PAT or FG attempt properly. Consider the following about your opponents:

- How fast is the outermost rusher? The greatest threat to a PAT or FG try is an extremely quick outermost rusher who can get around the wing and dive for the block. If the opponent has a great outside rusher, the PAT–FG unit could consider taking wider splits to make his course longer, as long as the protection remains solid inside. The wing blocker also has to be sure to get a good punch on the outermost rusher as he goes by.

- How powerful are the inside rushers? Through scouting and game-day observation, the PAT–FG unit should be able to evaluate the strength and power of the inside rushers and identify any mismatches. If they find mismatches, the PAT FG unit could move players around to put their best blockers in front of the best rushers.

- Does the opponent have a great leaper who is a threat to jump and block a kick? A tall athlete who jumps well can be a particular threat to a longer field-goal try that will have a lower trajectory. The kicker has to be aware of this threat and be sure that he gets good elevation on his kick.

Self-Knowledge

Besides being aware of your opponent's strengths and weaknesses, you and your players need to know about your own team's ability. Teach your players to be aware of the following when blocking on PAT or FG protection:

- How fast is your operation time on PAT or FG tries? If the operation time is longer than two seconds, the PAT–FG unit will have tough assignment protecting for the kicks. The snapper, holder and kicker must work to improve operation time.

- How good is your kicker's elevation? The kicker must put elevation on the ball immediately to avoid being blocked by an inside rusher or jumper. The kicker should work on elevation drills in which he practices getting the ball 10 feet in the air by the time it travels 10 yards down the field. (In practice, he can place the ball on the goal line and kick it over the crossbar.)

- How disciplined are your blockers? The PAT–FG unit requires athletes who will consistently align with the proper split, take the proper inside step and punch with the correct technique. Watching tape of this unit will reveal whether the blockers are using consistent form.

Decision-Making Guidelines

When deciding how to gain the best advantage when protecting the PAT or FG, you and your players should consider the previous information as well as the following guidelines:

- Blockers should line up with at least 6-inch splits so that the formation is as wide as possible from one wing to the other without creating seams between players.

- Each blocker should take a stance slightly wider than normal, partly to keep the formation as wide as possible but also to establish a strong base for the anticipated rush.

- The blockers' forearms should rest comfortably on the knees. The blockers should lower their body weight by sinking the hips and bending the knees, but their heads should be up so that they can see the rushers.

- On the snap, the blockers must take a quick 6-inch step to the inside to fill the gaps between them. Each blocker must concentrate on getting his inside foot down on the ground quickly, so that he establishes a solid base before any of the rushers make contact. This step also gives the blocker a bit of forward lean and forward momentum that will help him withstand the pressure from the rushers. When he makes this step, he must also keep his outside foot planted firmly on the ground.

- As the blockers step inside, they punch to the inside with both hands against any oncoming rushers. This punch must be physical and aggressive to slow the charge of the rushers.

- While punching, the blockers must be sure not to lean inside and create a gap to the outside. In other words, the blocker must keep his outside shoulder square to the line of scrimmage while stopping any inside rush threat.

- The wing blockers take the same inside step as everyone else on the unit does, but they use a different hand punch. They punch inside hard with the inside hand as they step that way, and then they take a small step outside with the outside foot and punch outside with the outside hand. The idea is to make contact with any inside rusher first to prevent penetration in the tight end wing gap and then to contact the outermost rusher to force him to alter his course slightly to the outside, making his path to the block point longer and more improbable.

- If a rusher runs over a blocker, the blocker probably took too narrow a base on his stance or stood up too high on the snap. Either error will make it difficult for him to stay upright against a full-speed rush.

At a Glance

The following parts of the text offer additional information on PAT and FG protection.

Short Snap	p. 158
Holding for the Place Kick	p. 160
Place Kick	p. 162
Blocking the Kick	p. 166

Planning for Teaching

Part IV helps you apply what you learned in the previous chapters to developing a plan for the upcoming season. By having a good season plan that outlines your practices for the year and then creating specific practice plans that make up your season plan, you will be ready to coach and get the most out of your season.

In chapter 9 you learn how to create your season plan, which is a framework for the practices that make up your season. Besides teaching you about the six essential steps to developing the season plan, this chapter provides a sample games approach season plan.

After you have your season plan, you must create what is called a practice plan, which outlines how you will approach each practice. Chapter 10 helps you do this by explaining the important components of a good practice plan and then providing you with samples of the first eight practices of your season based on the season plans.

Season Plans

chapter 9

The preceding chapters of this book have described the complexity of football and the myriad skills that you must teach in building your team. The process of teaching these numerous and varied skills to the variety of players and positions that make up the game of football requires a comprehensive, systematic approach. Putting a team together is like assembling a jigsaw puzzle. When you open the puzzle box and dump the pieces on the table, the prospect of making order out of the chaos seems overwhelming. Facing the job of teaching dozens of skills, you may feel a similar sense of despair.

The solution for this situation is to develop a plan. Before touching any of the pieces, you must have a vision of the completed project—what the puzzle will look like—which is provided by the picture on the cover of the box. For you as a football coach, this picture is your coaching philosophy, what you want your team to look like, garnered from your own experience and exposure to other coaches' ideas through clinics, camps and conversations. You must decide if you will emphasize offense, defense or balance; use a wide-open passing attack or a powerful run and play-action attack; run a blitzing, big-play defense or a sound, bend-but-don't-break defense. You must decide how you want your team to dress, on and off the field; how much to try to control their emotions and reactions, on and off the field; how regimented to be with policies, practice sessions and side-line behavior; and how involved you want to be in their lives away from football. You must consciously and systematically review your philosophy every year so that you have an up-to-date blueprint for your program. Just as the picture on the puzzle box constantly guides you as the puzzle takes shape, you frequently refer to this philosophy to be sure that your teaching strategies are producing the look that you desire.

After the picture, or the philosophy, is clear, you must organize and prioritize the pieces of the puzzle so that the project has some starting points. You first find all the pieces with at least one straight edge to give the puzzle its shape and its borders. Next, you sort the pieces into groups by colors and design. Finally, you analyze the particular lines and curves of each piece and work diligently to match that piece with its adjacent pieces. This chapter provides you with the straight edges and color groupings of your project, giving you a place to start planning and a method for prioritizing your teaching. Then, with the plan in place, you can take each piece of the puzzle—each isolated skill required to play the game—and fit that piece into the larger picture. And just as the completed puzzle transforms a chaotic pile of cardboard pieces into a beautiful picture, the well-coached football team, built by following an organized plan, miraculously blends a diversity of skills into a fascinating, systematic team effort.

Six Steps to Instructional Planning*

As with building a puzzle, using a systematic approach can help you put together your season plan. After you have articulated your philosophy, you can begin planning for the season ahead by following a simple six-step procedure called "Six Steps to Instructional Planning":

Step 1: Identify the skills that your athletes need

Step 2: Know your athletes

Step 3: Analyze your situation

Step 4: Establish priorities

Step 5: Select the methods for teaching

Step 6: Plan practices

Step 1: Identify the Skills That Your Athletes Need

The first step in organizing the season plan is to identify the specific skills that the athletes must be able to execute for the team to be successful, as shown in column one of figure 9.1. This list of skills is based on the technical and tactical skills in this book as well as the information on communication and physical, character and mental skills from *Successful Coaching, Third Edition.* In the following steps, you will be examining the list of skills and adding others if necessary. Step 4 of the planning process will then explain further how you can put this list to work for yourself.

Step 2: Know Your Athletes

The next step in the planning process is to work with your coaching staff to refine the list of skills that you are planning to teach, based on an evaluation of the strengths, weaknesses and ability of the athletes in your program. For example, assume that you want to run an option offense because you think that it creates strategic advantages on the field. Before installing this offense, you and your staff must evaluate the ability of the quarterbacks (both the starter and alternates) in your program to determine if they have the speed, quickness and decision-making ability to run an option offense effectively.

---

*Reprinted, by permission, from R. Martens, 2004, *Successful Coaching*, 3rd Ed. (Champaign, IL: Human Kinetics), 237.

Figure 9.1 Identifying and Evaluating Skills

STEP 1	STEP 4							
	Teaching priorities			Readiness to learn		Priority rating		
Skills identified	**Must**	**Should**	**Could**	**Yes**	**No**	**A**	**B**	**C**
Offensive technical skills								
Stance and Start for Offense (1)	M	S	C	Yes	No	A	B	C
Center–Quarterback Exchange (2)	M	S	C	Yes	No	A	B	C
Ball Security (3)	M	S	C	Yes	No	A	B	C
Option Pitch Mechanics (4)	M	S	C	Yes	No	A	B	C
Quarterback Drops (5)	M	S	C	Yes	No	A	B	C
Throwing (6)	M	S	C	Yes	No	A	B	C
Faking (7)	M	S	C	Yes	No	A	B	C
Catching (8)	M	S	C	Yes	No	A	B	C
Running Shallow and Intermediate Routes (9)	M	S	C	Yes	No	A	B	C
Running Deep Routes (10)	M	S	C	Yes	No	A	B	C
Releases (11)	M	S	C	Yes	No	A	B	C
Drive Block (12)	M	S	C	Yes	No	A	B	C
Reach Block (13)	M	S	C	Yes	No	A	B	C
Cutoff Block (14)	M	S	C	Yes	No	A	B	C
Down Block (15)	M	S	C	Yes	No	A	B	C
Double-Team Block (16)	M	S	C	Yes	No	A	B	C
Mirror Block (17)	M	S	C	Yes	No	A	B	C
Lead Block (18)	M	S	C	Yes	No	A	B	C
Pulling (19)	M	S	C	Yes	No	A	B	C
Pass Protection (20)	M	S	C	Yes	No	A	B	C
Defensive technical skills								
Stance and Start for Defense (21)	M	S	C	Yes	No	A	B	C
Tackling (22)	M	S	C	Yes	No	A	B	C
Defending Basic Run Blocks (23)	M	S	C	Yes	No	A	B	C
Defending the Double-Team Block (24)	M	S	C	Yes	No	A	B	C
Spilling Blocks (25)	M	S	C	Yes	No	A	B	C
Squeezing Blocks (26)	M	S	C	Yes	No	A	B	C
Pass Rush (27)	M	S	C	Yes	No	A	B	C
Feathering (28)	M	S	C	Yes	No	A	B	C
Zone Pass Drops (29)	M	S	C	Yes	No	A	B	C
Man Pass Coverage (30)	M	S	C	Yes	No	A	B	C
Speed Turn (31)	M	S	C	Yes	No	A	B	C
Press Man Coverage (32)	M	S	C	Yes	No	A	B	C
Blitzing (33)	M	S	C	Yes	No	A	B	C
Special teams technical skills								
Kickoff (34)	M	S	C	Yes	No	A	B	C
Onside Kick (35)	M	S	C	Yes	No	A	B	C

(continued)

Figure 9.1 *(continued)*

STEP 1	STEP 4							
	Teaching priorities			**Readiness to learn**		**Priority rating**		
Skills identified	**Must**	**Should**	**Could**	**Yes**	**No**	**A**	**B**	**C**
Special teams technical skills *(continued)*								
Catching the Kickoff (36)	M	S	C	Yes	No	A	B	C
Punt (37)	M	S	C	Yes	No	A	B	C
Sky Punt (38)	M	S	C	Yes	No	A	B	C
Corner Punt (39)	M	S	C	Yes	No	A	B	C
Catching the Punt (40)	M	S	C	Yes	No	A	B	C
Bullets (41)	M	S	C	Yes	No	A	B	C
Defending Against the Bullets (42)	M	S	C	Yes	No	A	B	C
Long Snap (43)	M	S	C	Yes	No	A	B	C
Short Snap (44)	M	S	C	Yes	No	A	B	C
Holding for the Place Kick (45)	M	S	C	Yes	No	A	B	C
Place Kick (46)	M	S	C	Yes	No	A	B	C
Blocking the Kick (47)	M	S	C	Yes	No	A	B	C
Open-Field Tackling (48)	M	S	C	Yes	No	A	B	C
Offensive tactical skills								
Progression of Receivers (49)	M	S	C	Yes	No	A	B	C
Option Pitch Read (50)	M	S	C	Yes	No	A	B	C
Pass–Run Option (51)	M	S	C	Yes	No	A	B	C
Scramble (52)	M	S	C	Yes	No	A	B	C
Running to the Gap (53)	M	S	C	Yes	No	A	B	C
Running to Daylight (54)	M	S	C	Yes	No	A	B	C
Evading Tacklers (55)	M	S	C	Yes	No	A	B	C
Picking Up the Blitz (56)	M	S	C	Yes	No	A	B	C
Crossing Route Adjustments (57)	M	S	C	Yes	No	A	B	C
Curl Route Adjustments (58)	M	S	C	Yes	No	A	B	C
Hard Corner Route Adjustments (59)	M	S	C	Yes	No	A	B	C
Press Man Route Adjustments (60)	M	S	C	Yes	No	A	B	C
Reach Blocking Against Defensive Movement (61)	M	S	C	Yes	No	A	B	C
Combination Block (62)	M	S	C	Yes	No	A	B	C
Pass Protection Against a Twist (63)	M	S	C	Yes	No	A	B	C
Pass Protection on the Edge (64)	M	S	C	Yes	No	A	B	C
Defensive tactical skills								
Controlling the Gap (65)	M	S	C	Yes	No	A	B	C
Taking the Inside Rush (66)	M	S	C	Yes	No	A	B	C
Reacting When Unblocked (67)	M	S	C	Yes	No	A	B	C
Defending the Option (68)	M	S	C	Yes	No	A	B	C
Linebacker Reads (69)	M	S	C	Yes	No	A	B	C
Choosing to Spill or Squeeze (70)	M	S	C	Yes	No	A	B	C

STEP 1	STEP 4							
	Teaching priorities			Readiness to learn		Priority rating		
Skills identified	Must	Should	Could	Yes	No	A	B	C
Defensive tactical skills (continued)								
Finishing Plays in Man Pass Coverage (71)	M	S	C	Yes	No	A	B	C
Reads and Reactions in Zone Pass Coverage (72)	M	S	C	Yes	No	A	B	C
Force (73)	M	S	C	Yes	No	A	B	C
Defending the Play-Action Pass (74)	M	S	C	Yes	No	A	B	C
Defending the Draw Play (75)	M	S	C	Yes	No	A	B	C
Playing the Long-Yardage Situation (76)	M	S	C	Yes	No	A	B	C
Pursuit Angles (77)	M	S	C	Yes	No	A	B	C
Special teams tactical skills								
Kickoff Coverage (78)	M	S	C	Yes	No	A	B	C
Playing Force on Kick Coverage (79)	M	S	C	Yes	No	A	B	C
Recovering the Onside Kick (80)	M	S	C	Yes	No	A	B	C
Defending the Onside Kick (81)	M	S	C	Yes	No	A	B	C
Punt Protection (82)	M	S	C	Yes	No	A	B	C
Punt Coverage (83)	M	S	C	Yes	No	A	B	C
Punting Inside the 40-Yard Line (84)	M	S	C	Yes	No	A	B	C
Wall Return (85)	M	S	C	Yes	No	A	B	C
Wedge Return (86)	M	S	C	Yes	No	A	B	C
PAT and FG Protection (87)	M	S	C	Yes	No	A	B	C
Physical training skills								
Strength	M	S	C	Yes	No	A	B	C
Speed	M	S	C	Yes	No	A	B	C
Agility	M	S	C	Yes	No	A	B	C
Power	M	S	C	Yes	No	A	B	C
Flexibility	M	S	C	Yes	No	A	B	C
Other	M	S	C	Yes	No	A	B	C
Mental skills								
Emotional control—anxiety	M	S	C	Yes	No	A	B	C
Emotional control—anger	M	S	C	Yes	No	A	B	C
Maturity	M	S	C	Yes	No	A	B	C
Self-confidence	M	S	C	Yes	No	A	B	C
Motivation to achieve	M	S	C	Yes	No	A	B	C
Ability to concentrate	M	S	C	Yes	No	A	B	C
Experience	M	S	C	Yes	No	A	B	C
Other	M	S	C	Yes	No	A	B	C
Communication skills								
Sends positive messages	M	S	C	Yes	No	A	B	C
Sends accurate messages	M	S	C	Yes	No	A	B	C
Listens to messages	M	S	C	Yes	No	A	B	C

(continued)

Figure 9.1 *(continued)*

STEP 1	STEP 4							
	Teaching priorities			Readiness to learn		Priority rating		
Skills identified	Must	Should	Could	Yes	No	A	B	C
Communication skills *(continued)*								
Understands messages	M	S	C	Yes	No	A	B	C
Receives constructive criticism	M	S	C	Yes	No	A	B	C
Receives praise and recognition	M	S	C	Yes	No	A	B	C
Credibility with teammates	M	S	C	Yes	No	A	B	C
Credibility with coaches	M	S	C	Yes	No	A	B	C
Character skills								
Trustworthiness	M	S	C	Yes	No	A	B	C
Respect	M	S	C	Yes	No	A	B	C
Responsibility	M	S	C	Yes	No	A	B	C
Fairness	M	S	C	Yes	No	A	B	C
Caring	M	S	C	Yes	No	A	B	C
Citizenship	M	S	C	Yes	No	A	B	C

From *Coaching Football Technical and Tactical Skills* by ASEP, 2006, Champaign, IL: Human Kinetics. Adapted, by permission, from R. Martens, 2004, *Successful Coaching*, 3rd ed. (Champaign, IL: Human Kinetics), 250-251.

As you learned previously, this evaluation takes place in many forms. You should study videotapes of the previous season's games, focusing on the strengths and weaknesses of the individual athletes instead of analyzing schemes. The results of off-season testing for speed, strength and agility also provide useful information during this evaluation. Summer workouts, including weightlifting sessions as well as camps and passing leagues, also reveal the ability of the athletes who will be competing during the season.

Using all this information, you and your coaching staff need to add or delete skills on the list that you began developing in step 1, based on the ability of the athletes in your program.

Step 3: Analyze Your Situation

As you prepare for the season, you must also weigh the external factors that will both guide and limit you. Budgetary issues and related fund-raising options will affect scheduling, training facilities, practice equipment and professional development opportunities. Administrative and community support will influence goal setting and expectations. Teaching loads and staffing structure regarding assistant coaches will set parameters for both off-season and in-season programming. Clearly, then, many factors influence your planning. In evaluating these factors, you will find it helpful to spend some time working through the questions in figure 9.2.

Step 4: Establish Priorities

Steps 1, 2 and 3 of the six steps to planning describe general factors that provide an important base of information regarding your players and your program. Now in step 4, you must make a decision about where to start and how to progress in the teaching of skills. Refer back to figure 9.1 and notice the three columns under "Step 4." You are asked to evaluate each essential skill based on two factors—teaching priority and the athletes' readiness to learn. To assess the teaching priority,

Figure 9.2 Evaluating Your Team Situation

How many practices will you have over the entire season? How long can practices be?

How many contests will you have over the entire season?

What special events (team meetings, parent orientation sessions, banquets, tournaments) will you have and when?

How many athletes will you be coaching? How many assistants will you have? What is the ratio of athletes to coaches?

What facilities will be available for practice?

What equipment will be available for practice?

How much money do you have for travel and other expenses?

What instructional resources (videos, books, charts, CDs) will you need?

What other support personnel will be available?

What other factors may affect your instructional plan?

From *Coaching Football Technical and Tactical Skills* by ASEP, 2006, Champaign, IL: Human Kinetics. Reprinted, by permission, from R. Martens, 2004, *Successful Coaching*, 3rd ed. (Champaign, IL: Human Kinetics), 247-248.

you must think of your overall scheme and plan for the season and, for each skill, ask yourself, "Is this a skill that I must, should or could teach?" Then, you must think about each skill and your athletes and ask yourself, "Are my athletes ready to learn this skill?"

Take some time now to rate the skills on your form. These ratings will divide the skills into three groups. Skills that are A-rated are obviously priority skills that you must teach immediately and emphasize. Include B-rated skills in the planning process and teach them periodically. Finally, depending on the progress of the season and of the athletes, you can incorporate instruction for the C-rated skills.

After you have finished your A, B and C ratings, you will want to create an installation schedule, as discussed in "Developing Installation Schedules," to ensure that during the season you will teach all your A-rated skills, most of your B-rated skills and some of your C-rated skills.

DEVELOPING INSTALLATION SCHEDULES

Installation schedules provide you with a timetable for planning your practices. They are based on your playbook and your list of skills that you began developing in step 1. They help you focus your season planning to ensure that you cover all your A-rated skills, most of your B-rated skills and some of your C-rated skills before you begin your season.

You should create an installation schedule for both offense and defense. Set up an offensive installation schedule, as shown in figure 9.3a, for each of the following aspects: running plays, passing plays, formations, motions, pass protections and special plays. Set up a defensive installation schedule, as shown in figure 9.3b, for fronts, coverages, line games, blitzes and defending certain concepts such as screens, draws and the option.

When developing your installation schedules, you want to keep them basic and just list the key plays that you want to cover during your practices and the skill numbers (based on the chart that you began developing in step 1) associated with those plays. You also should schedule a time to work on special situations, such as the red zone, goal line and the two-minute drill (no huddle) for both offense and defense. Of course, you want the offense and defense to work together to merge their schedules so that, for example, the offense is introducing blitz pickup drills on the same day that the defense is introducing blitzes. You may use the sample installation schedules for the first eight practices, as shown in figure 9.3, a and b, to guide you as you and your staff develop your own schedules.

Step 5: Select the Methods for Teaching

Now that you have a complete installation schedule, you should go through the schedule and determine the methods that you will use in daily practices to teach the skills that you have decided are necessary to your team's success. As you learned previously, the traditional approach to practice emphasizes technical skill development and usually involves using daily drills to teach skills, interspersed with group and team drills, whereas in the games approach, players learn to blend decision making with skill execution as you add the elements of pressure, competition and game-day nuance to the performance of essential skills.

The traditional method might cover all the techniques of football adequately and may even cover most of the skills that players would typically use during games, but it does have at least two glaring shortcomings: First, traditional practice sessions by their very nature emphasize techniques at the expense of tactics, and, second, they involve too much direct instruction. Typically, a coach explains a skill, shows the players how they are to perform the skill and then sets up situations in

Figure 9.3a Offensive Installation Schedule Template

Practice	Run plays	Pass plays	Formations	Motion	Pass protection	Special situations*
1						
2						
3						
4						
5						
6						
7						
8						

From *Coaching Football Technical and Tactical Skills* by ASEP, 2006, Champaign, IL: Human Kinetics.

*such as: screens, draws, option, play action, long yardage, red zone, goal line

Figure 9.3b Defensive Installation Schedule Template

Practice	Fronts	Coverages	Line games	Blitzes	Special situations*
1					
2					
3					
4					
5					
6					
7					
8					

From *Coaching Football Technical and Tactical Skills* by ASEP, 2006, Champaign, IL: Human Kinetics.

*such as: screens, draws, option, play action, long yardage, red zone, goal line

which the players can learn the skill, without placing that skill in the context of game-day, tactical decision making.

Recent educational research has shown that students who learn a skill in one setting, say the library, have difficulty performing it in another setting, like the classroom. Compare this finding to the common belief among coaches that today's young players don't have football sense, the basic knowledge of the game that players used to have. For years, coaches have been bemoaning the fact that players don't react as well to game situations as they used to, blaming everything from video games to the increasing popularity of other sports. But external forces may not be entirely to blame for the decline in football logic. Bookstores offer dozens of drill books to help coaches teach the technical skills of football, and teams around the country practice those drills ad infinitum. If drills are so specific, numerous and clever, why aren't players developing that elusive football sense? Perhaps just learning techniques and performing drill after drill creates not expertise but the ability to do drills.

An alternative way to teach football skills is the games approach. As outlined in chapter 1, the games approach allows players to take responsibility for learning skills. A good analogy is to compare the games approach in sports to the holistic method of teaching writing. Traditional approaches to teaching students to write included doing sentence-writing exercises, identifying parts of speech and working with different types of paragraphs. After drilling students in these techniques, teachers assigned topics to write about. Teachers used this method of teaching for years. When graduating students could not write a competent essay or work application, educators began questioning the method and began to use a new approach, the holistic method. In the holistic method of teaching writing, students wrote compositions without learning parts of speech or sentence types or even ways to organize paragraphs. Teachers looked at the whole piece of writing and made suggestions for improvement from there, not worrying about spelling, grammar or punctuation unless it was germane. This method emphasized seeing the forest instead of the trees.

This forest-versus-trees approach is applicable to teaching football skills as well. Instead of breaking down skills into their component parts and then waiting until game day for the athletes to put the pieces together, you can impart the whole skill to the team and then let the athletes discover how the parts relate. This method resembles what actually occurs in a game more than the traditional drill method does, and learning occurs at game speed. These latter two concepts are crucial to understanding the games approach.

This method does not take you out of the equation; in fact, you must take a more active approach. You must shape the play of the athletes to get the desired results, focus their attention on the important techniques and components of the game and enhance the skill involved by attaching various challenges to the games played.

You can use the games approach to teach almost any area of the game. For example, instead of having quarterbacks and receivers work endlessly on route timing drills and one-on-one drills against a defender, you can create games around pass routes and reads, and encourage competition.

Step 6: Plan Practices

At this stage you should sketch out a brief overview of what you want to accomplish during each practice for your season. You will pull all the information that you have gathered from the previous steps. Your installation schedules should also help you greatly at this stage in the process.

Figure 9.4 shows a season plan for the games approach, using a 12-week season plan that includes a two-week period for postseason playoffs (for a sample traditional approach season plan, please refer to the *Coaching Football Technical and Tactical Skills* online course). Although this season plan was created in isolation, you can use it in your season planning. You may find that you are more comfortable teaching blocking using the traditional approach but that the games approach works best for teaching pass reads. Use these season plans as templates to help you to create the plan that works best for you and your team.

In the sample season plan, you will notice that the first two weeks are completed. After the games begin in the season, the practice plans are more open ended so that you can focus on problems that may have occurred in past games and can develop practices according to your game plan (we will discuss this further in chapter 11). You will also notice that we have identified some technical and tactical skills that are important to teach during those later practices. Keep those skills in mind as you are further fine-tuning your practices during the season. The main objective of your practices at this point is to focus on your game plan, but as time permits you should fit in these key skills to help your players continue to learn throughout the season.

Keep in mind that this season plan was based on the skills in the book rather than on an individual installation schedule. Although this season plan provides a good example, you should use your installation schedule and the information that you gained in the other five steps of the process to create a detailed plan tailored to your program.

After you have developed your season plan, you can further refine individual practices. We will help you do that in the next chapter by showing you the components of a practice and providing a sample practice plan for the games approach.

Figure 9.4 Games Approach Season Plan

	Practice dress	Purpose	New skills to introduce
Week 1 (preseason)			
Practice 1 (offense)	Helmets only	Introduce basic offensive skills for all position groups that support gap running plays, as well as working on basic passing; introduce basic skills for special teams that focus on punt protection.	Stance and Start for Offense Center–Quarterback Exchange Ball Security Quarterback Drops Throwing Catching Running Shallow and Intermediate Routes Drive Block Double-Team Block Mirror Block Lead Block Punt Long Snap Punt Protection Running to the Gap
Practice 2 (defense)	Helmets only	Introduce basic defensive skills for all position groups; review basic special teams skills from practice 1, adding punt coverage.	Stance and Start for Defense Defending Basic Run Blocks Defending the Double-Team Block Pass Rush Zone Pass Drops Bullets Long Snap Linebacker Reads Reads and Reactions in Zone Pass Coverage Force Pursuit Angles Punt Coverage
Practice 3 (offense)	Helmets only	Introduce basic offensive skills that support passing (the short game). Build on skills for gap plays or add to gap running plays; introduce basic skills for special teams that focus on the punt return.	Pulling Pass Protection Catching the Punt Defending Against the Bullets Wall Return
Practice 4 (defense)	Helmets only	Build on skills from practice 2 for defending gap running plays; introduce man pass coverage; review basic special teams skills from practice 3, focusing on the punt return.	Spilling Blocks Squeezing Blocks Man Pass Coverage Finishing Plays in Man Pass Coverage
Practice 5 (offense)	Helmets only	Build on the offensive skills from practice 1 by focusing on skills that support zone running plays for all position groups; continue to refine special teams by working on the kickoff.	Reach Block Cutoff Block Kickoff Open-Field Tackling Running to Daylight Combination Block Kickoff Coverage Playing Force on Kick Coverage

	Practice dress	Purpose	New skills to introduce
Week 1 (preseason) *(continued)*			
Practice 6 (defense)	Helmets and shoulder pads	Introduce skills to defend zone running plays; introduce intermediate skills for pass defense; review basic special teams skills from practice 5, focusing on the kickoff.	Speed Turn Controlling the Gap
Practice 7 (offense)	Helmets and shoulder pads	Build on the skills from practice 3 by adding skills that support offensive passing (the deep game); continue to refine the zone running game; continue to refine special teams skills by focusing on the kickoff return.	Running Deep Routes Catching the Kickoff Crossing Route Adjustments Curl Route Adjustments Reach Blocking Against Defensive Movement Pass Protection Against a Twist Pass Protection on the Edge Wall Return Wedge Return
Practice 8 (defense)	Full pads	The primary focus of this practice is to refine tackling mechanics; this is the first opportunity for live tackles. Introduce skills for defending the option, and refine special teams skills from practice 7, kickoff return.	Tackling Feathering Evading Tacklers Defending the Option
Practice 9 (offense)	Full pads	Introduce the skills for running the option; focus special teams on PAT.	Option Pitch Mechanics Short Snap Holding for the Place Kick Place Kick Option Pitch Read PAT and FG Protection
Practice 10 (offense and defense)	Full pads	This practice focuses on both the offense and the defense. Emphasize full-contact drills in gradually larger groups (two-on-two, inside run); reserve time for a controlled team scrimmage.	Reacting When Unblocked Choosing to Spill or Squeeze
Week 2 (preseason)			
Practice 11 (offense)	Full pads	Focus on skills that support play-action routes; review gap run plays; introduce punt variations.	Faking Sky Punt Corner Punt Pass–Run Option Punting Inside the 40-Yard Line
Practice 12 (defense)	Full pads	Instruct defense on down and distance; practice punt protection and coverage full speed in pads.	Defending the Play-Action Pass Defending the Draw Play Playing the Long-Yardage Situation
Practice 13 (offense)	Full pads	Refine the passing game by introducing how to handle blitzes, press coverage and line games; review zone run plays; practice kickoff coverage full speed in pads.	Picking Up the Blitz Press Man Route Adjustments Playing Force on Kickoff Coverage

(continued)

Figure 9.4 *(continued)*

	Practice dress	Purpose	New skills to introduce
Week 2 (preseason) *(continued)*			
Practice 14 (defense)	Full pads	Refine the defensive game by adding blitzing; review down and distance situations. Review punt return, live and full speed in pads.	Press Man Coverage Blitzing Taking the Inside Rush Playing the Long Yardage Situation Zone Pass Drops
Practice 15 (offense)	Full pads	Refine passing game; discuss red zone and goal line; introduce special plays such as the scramble situation; build on skills from previous running practices; review PAT and FG and introduce the onside kick.	Onside Kick Place Kick Blocking the Kick Pass-Run Option Scramble Hard Corner Route Adjustments Holding for the Place Kick PAT and FG Protection Recovering the Onside Kick Defending the Onside Kick
Practice 16	Full pads	Conduct a game-style scrimmage (include officials and simulate an overtime). Include live PAT/FG work.	
In-season			**In-season skills are TBD**
Mondays	Helmets and shoulder pads	Review scouting report on next opponent; run opponent's offensive plays on your defense (walk-through of carded plays). Review special teams, hurry-up offense, conditioning.	*TBD
Tuesdays	Full pads	Review individual offensive skills; review crossover in groups, seven-on-seven, inside run; review special teams; conduct team vs. scouts scrimmage with emphasis on offensive blocking adjustments and defensive alignments and reactions.	*TBD
Wednesdays	Full pads	Review individual defensive skills; review crossover in groups, seven-on-seven, pass rush; review special teams; conduct team vs. scouts scrimmage with emphasis on down and distance, red zone, goal line.	*TBD
Thursdays	Helmets and shoulder pads	Review game plan; review special teams.	*TBD

From *Coaching Football Technical and Tactical Skills* by ASEP, 2006, Champaign, IL: Human Kinetics.

chapter 10

Practice Plans

To get the most out of your practice sessions, you must plan every practice. Completing the season plan, as described in the last chapter, helps you do this. But you have to take that season plan a step further and specify in detail what you will be doing at every practice.

As described in *Successful Coaching, Third Edition,* every practice plan should include the following:

- Date, time of practice and length of practice session
- Objective of the practice
- Equipment needed
- Warm-up
- Practice of previously taught skills
- Teaching and practicing new skills
- Cool-down
- Coaches' comments
- Evaluation of practice

Using those elements, eight practice plans were developed based on the games approach season plan in chapter 9 (figure 9.4, page 314). The early practices focus on football as a whole, including the essential tactical skills. Then, as players need to refine technical skills, those skills are brought into the practices. When athletes play focused games early in the season, they quickly discover their weaknesses and become more motivated to improve their skills so that they can perform better in game situations.

Please note that the equipment listed in the practice plans does not include large equipment such as gauntlets, linemen and tackling sleds, but rather focuses on the equipment that needs to be brought to practice each day.

Also note that these practice plans have been developed based on a program of 40 to 50 players and approximately four coaches. You may need to tailor your practices to fit your situation better.

PRACTICE 1

Date:

Monday, August 15

Practice Start Time:

6:45 a.m.

Length of Practice:

2 hours, 15 minutes

Practice Objectives:

- Introduce basic offensive skills for all position groups that support inside running plays.
- Introduce basic skills for special teams that focus on the punt.

Equipment:

Balls, agility bags, spacing hoses, hand shields, cones, helmet caps, stand-up bags

Practice Dress:

Helmets only

Time	Position	Name of activity	Description	Key teaching points
6:45–7:00	All players	Prepractice meeting and team building	Review of coaches' expectations of players.	• Hustle • Teamwork
7:00–7:15	All players	Warm-up game	A 10-minute relay run in which the back runner jogs at a moderate pace to overtake the front runner, followed by 5 minutes of dynamic stretching. Break team into position groups for the game.	• Good running form • Full range of movement
7:15–7:25	QB, centers	Center–Quarterback Exchange	Center–quarterback exchange drills.	• Hand positioning • Heels of the hands touching • Passing hand on top • Feet parallel • Weight on the balls of the feet • Receiving the snap
	RB, TE, WR, OL	Stance and Start for Offense	Drills to work on footwork for gap run plays.	• Achieving balance • Comfortable stance • Head and eyes up
7:25–7:30	All players	Water break		
7:30–7:45	WR, OL, TE, half of RBs	Blocking	Mirror blocking drill for the WR.	• Reacting • Breaking down • Engaging the defender
			Drive, down and double-team blocking drills for the OL or TE.	• Identifying the defender • Proper footwork • Creating movement • Preventing the split • Follow-through
			Lead blocking drill for RBs.	• Taking the proper course • Focusing on the target • Contacting the defender • Follow-through

Time	Position	Name of activity	Description	Key teaching points
	QB, half of RBs	Gap Run Plays	Installation of 2 or 3 run plays against air.	• Exchanges • Aiming points • Ball security
7:45–8:00	OL, RB, half of TEs	Simon Says Game	Use the run plays that were installed with the RBs in earlier time slot and call out the plays going either right or left (giving you 4 to 6 possible plays). OLs and TEs work on using appropriate blocks based on the plays called (they will need much help with this in the beginning). Award 1 point for correct execution.	• Drive blocks • Down blocks • Double-team blocks
	WR, QB, half of TEs	Throw and Catch Game	Stationary partners throwing 10, 15, 20 yards at various angles. Partners are aiming for completions with quarterbacks working on taking the proper step toward their target and receivers working on using the proper hand placement.	• Foot positioning • Hand positioning
8:00–8:05	All players	Water break		
8:05–8:25	All players	Perfect Play Game	Run gap plays on air. Reward for perfect plays, quick penalty for mistakes.	• Blocking assignments • Exchanges • Aiming points • Fakes
8:25–8:45	All players except punters, QBs, WRs	Punt Protection Game	Punt team versus coaches or scout players. Snappers snap the ball to a coach who simulates the punter. Defenders have 4 seconds to try to reach the coach.	• Understanding the protection scheme • Ignoring twists, slants, angles and other defensive movement • Planting the inside foot and stepping with the outside foot before contact
	Punters	Kick the Cone Game	Three chances for punter to try to kick over various cones.	• Leg alignment • Balanced stance • Making the catch • Hand positioning • Punt approach • Making the kick • Follow-through
	QB, WR	Introduce Routes	Build on stationary drilling game by having quarterback drop and throw to receivers who are running routes. Install 2 or 3 shallow routes.	• Quarterback drops • Running shallow and intermediate routes • Throwing • Catching
8:45–8:55	All players	Cool-down	Light jog followed by static stretching.	• Relaxing muscles • Controlled movement
8:55–9:00	All players	Practice wrap-up	Review of practice.	• Enthusiasm • Patience with players in this learning phase

PRACTICE 2

Date:

Tuesday, August 16

Practice Start Time:

3:45 p.m.

Length of Practice:

2 hours, 15 minutes

Practice Objectives:

- Introduce basic defensive skills for all position groups.
- Review basic special teams skills from practice 1 with focus on the punt.

Equipment:

Balls, agility bags, spacing hoses, cones, helmet caps, stand-up bags

Practice Dress:

Helmets only

Time	Position	Name of activity	Description	Key teaching points
3:45–4:00	All players	Prepractice meeting and team building	Review of coaches' expectations of players.	• Hustle • Teamwork
4:00–4:15	All players	Warm-Up Game	A 10-minute relay run in which the back runner jogs at a moderate pace to overtake the front runner, followed by 5 minutes of dynamic stretching. Break team into groups based on birthdays for the game.	• Good running form • Full range of movement
4:15–4:25	LB	Stance and Start for Defense	Drills to work on balance and release.	• Two-point squared stance • Eliminating false steps • Moving out of the stance
	DB	Stance and Start for Defense	Drills that focus on backpedaling and breaking to the ball.	• Two-point staggered stance • Eliminating false steps • Moving out of the stance
	DL	Stance and Start for Defense	Drills to encourage quick reactions to the snap.	• Three- or four-point stance • Eliminating false steps • Moving out of the stance
4:25–4:30	All players	Water break		
4:30–4:45	All players	Defensive keys	Walk-through of base defensive alignment against offensive formations.	• Alignments • Assignments • Coverages

Time	Position	Name of activity	Description	Key teaching points
4:45–5:00	LB, DB	Reads and Reactions Game	Full-field 7-on-7 or half-field 4-on-3 game in which the defensive players focus on incompletions, knockdowns, and interceptions as well as reading run or pass correctly.	• Zone pass drops • Reads and reactions in zone pass coverage • Defending basic run blocks • Linebacker reads
	DL, OL	Pass or Run Game	A 4-on-5 game (4 DLs vs. 5 OLs) in which the defense focuses on reading pass or run.	• Pass rush • Defending basic run blocks • Defending the double-team block
5:00–5:05	All players	Water break		
5:05–5:25	All players	Team Pursuit Angle Game	A 1-on-11 game in which the 11 defenders read right or left and stay in their pursuit angles until they reach their target.	• Proper lanes • Executing until the play is dead • Pursuit angles • Force
5:25–5:45	All players except punters, OL	Punt Coverage Game	Full team versus air working on long snap, bullets and punt coverage.	• Releasing from protection • Fanning into the lanes • Maintaining outside leverage • Breaking down and getting under control to make the tackle
	Punters	Operation Time Contest	A game to see who can achieve the best hang time; focus on good technique.	• Leg alignment • Balanced stance • Making the catch • Hand positioning • Punt approach • Making the kick • Follow-through
	OL	Blocking Drills	Install the third gap play.	• Reacting • Breaking down • Engaging the defender
	QB, WR	Throw and Catch Game	Install 2 or 3 additional shallow to intermediate routes.	• QB drops • Shallow routes
5:45–5:55	All players	Cool-down	Light jog followed by static stretching.	
5:55–6:00	All players	Practice wrap-up	Emphasis on players' executing their assignments.	• Alignments • Assignments • Coverages

PRACTICE 3

Date:

Wednesday, August 17

Practice Start Time:

6:45 a.m.

Length of Practice:

2 hours, 15 minutes

Practice Objectives:

- Introduce basic offensive skills that support passing based on the offensive installation schedule.
- Introduce basic skills for special teams that focus on the punt return.

Equipment:

Balls, agility bags, spacing hoses, hand shields, cones, helmet caps, stand-up bags

Practice Dress:

Helmets only

Time	Position	Name of activity	Description	Key teaching points
6:45–7:00	All players	Prepractice meeting and team building	Review of coaches' expectations of players.	• Teamwork • Effort
7:00–7:15	All players	Warm-Up Game	A 10-minute relay run in which the back runner jogs at a moderate pace to overtake the front runner, followed by 5 minutes of dynamic stretching. Break team into groups based on height for the game.)	• Good running form • Full range of movement
7:15–7:25	QB	Center–Quarterback Exchange	Center–Quarterback Exchange Drill.	• Hand positioning • Heels of the hands touching • Passing hand on top • Feet parallel • Weight on the balls of the feet • Receiving the snap
	QB, RB, TE, WR	Stance and Start for Offense	Stance and Start for Offense Drill.	• Achieving balance • Comfortable stance • Head and eyes up
	OL	Center–Quarterback Exchange	Center–Quarterback Exchange Drill.	• Laces up • Forceful execution • Forward hip movement
7:25–7:30	All players	Water break		

Time	Position	Name of activity	Description	Key teaching points
7:30–7:45	QB, RB, WR, TE	Throwing Game	A 2-on-1 game in which the offense focuses on three-step drops, throwing, routes, catching (WR, RB, and TE alternating plays).	• Foot positioning • Hit and throw versus hitch and throw • Route running
	OL	Two-Step Pass Protection Game	A 5-on-4 game in which the five offensive players check their pass protection assignments by placing two hands on the defensive rushers.	• Balanced stance • Body positioning and footwork • Pop and set • Punch
7:45–8:00	QB, RB	Frame Run Game	QBs and RBs work together to execute various gap run plays, focusing on ball exchanges and aiming points.	• Ball exchanges • Aiming points
	TE, OL	Gap Run Drills	Review blocking techniques for all gap running plays while also focusing on pulling.	• Down block • Drive block • Double-team block • Pulling
	WR	Mirror Blocking Game	Set up two cones 4 to 5 yards apart on the field to act as a goal for the game. One WR plays defense, trying to fake out the other WR, who is acting as an offensive blocker protecting the goal. The defensive player tries to get past the offensive blocker through the cones to score a point.	• Reacting • Breaking down • Engaging the defender
8:00–8:05	All players	Water break		
8:05–8:25	All players	Perfect Pass Play Game	Pass plays on air; reward for perfect plays, quick penalty for mistakes.	• Protection • Route timing • Throwing and catching
8:25–8:45	Punters	Snap and Punt Hang-Time Game	One point for punters for every half second that the ball is in the air from the punter's foot to the time the receiver catches the ball.	• Punt • Catching the punt
	All other players	Get to the Wall Game	A 10-on-11 game in which the 11 punt return players work on defending against the bullets and executing the wall return. The coach throws the ball to the punt return man (at various difficulties) and the punt return man focuses on getting to the wall before being tagged by the punt coverage players.	• Defending against the bullets • Wall return
8:45–8:55	All players	Cool-down	Light jog followed by static stretching.	
8:55–9:00	All players	Practice wrap-up	Emphasis on pass protection, proper route execution and timing.	• Highlighting of strengths • Statement about areas to improve but ending with a positive note

PRACTICE 4

Date:

Thursday, August 18

Practice Start Time:

3:45 p.m.

Length of Practice:

2 hours, 15 minutes

Practice Objectives:

- Build on skills from practice 2 by adding new skills based on the defensive installation schedule.
- Review basic special teams skills from practice 3 with focus on the punt return.

Equipment:

Balls, agility bags, spacing hoses, cones, helmet caps, stand-up bags

Practice Dress:

Helmets only

Time	Position	Name of activity	Description	Key teaching points
3:45–4:00	All players	Prepractice meeting and team building	Review of coaches' expectations of players.	• Hustle • Teamwork
4:00–4:15	All players	Warm-Up Game	A 10-minute relay run in which the back runner jogs at a moderate pace to overtake the front runner, followed by 5 minutes of dynamic stretching. Break team up into groups based on speed for the game.	• Good running form • Full range of movement
4:15–4:25	LB	Stance and Start for Defense	Drills to work on balance and release.	• Two-point square stance • Eliminating false steps • Moving out of the stance
	DB	Stance and Start for Defense	Drills that focus on backpedaling and breaking to the ball.	• Two-point staggered stance • Eliminating false steps • Moving out of the stance
	DL	Stance and Start for Defense	Drills to encourage quick reactions to the snap.	• Three- or four-point stance • Eliminating false steps • Moving out of the stance
4:25–4:30	All players	Water break		
4:30–4:45	DL	Defending basic run blocks	Defensive linemen spend half the time working on pass rush and half the time working on defending blocks.	• Pass rush • Squeezing blocks • Spilling blocks
	LB	Defending basic run blocks	Linebackers spend half the time working on man coverage and the other half working on defending blocks	• Man coverage • Squeezing blocks • Spilling blocks

Time	Position	Name of activity	Description	Key teaching points
	DB	Man Pass Coverage	.	• Keying the quarterback • Understanding the assignment • Maintaining proper cushion and leverage • Adjusting to the route • Closing the gap • Finishing plays in man pass coverage
4:45–5:00	DL	Pass Rush	Pass rush drills.	• Recognizing pass protection • Staying in the lane • Using the rip and the swim • Using other moves
	LB	Pass Coverage Game	A 1-on-1 or 2-on-2 game where the linebackers play against running backs and tight ends working on pass routes and coverages.	• Keying the quarterback • Understanding the assignment • Maintaining proper cushion and leverage • Adjusting to the route • Closing the gap • Finishing plays in man pass coverage
	DB	Pass Coverage Game	A 1-on-1 or 2-on-2 game where the defensive backs play against wide receivers working on pass routes and coverages.	• Keying the quarterback • Understanding the assignment • Maintaining proper cushion and leverage • Adjusting to the route • Closing the gap • Finishing plays in man pass coverage
5:00–5:05	All players	Water break		
5:05–5:25	All players	Defensive keys	Review defensive base alignment and assignments; finish with 5 to 10 minutes of the pursuit angle game.	• Alignments • Assignments • Coverages
5:25–5:45	Punters and snappers	Snap and Punt Operation Time Game	One point for punters for every half second that the ball is in the air from the snap to the kick. Low score wins.	• Punt • Catching the punt • Long snap
	All other players	Get to the Wall Game	A 10-on-11 game in which the 11 punt return players work on defending against the bullets and executing the wall return. The coach throws the ball to the punt return man (at various difficulties) and the punt return man focuses on getting to the wall before being tagged by the punt coverage players.	• Punt coverage • Defending against the bullet • Wall return
5:45–5:55	All players	Cool-down	Light jog followed by static stretching.	
5:55–6:00	All players	Practice wrap-up	Emphasis on gap responsibility, assignments and importance of special teams.	• Highlighting of strengths • Statement about areas to improve but ending with a positive note

PRACTICE 5

Date:

Friday, August 19

Practice Start Time:

6:45 a.m.

Length of Practice:

2 hours, 15 minutes

Practice Objectives:

- Build on the offensive skills from practice 1 with focus on skills that support perimeter running plays for all position groups.
- Refine special teams by working on the kickoff.

Equipment:

Balls, agility bags, spacing hoses, hand shields, cones, helmet caps, stand-up bags

Practice Dress:

Helmets only

Time	Position	Name of activity	Description	Key teaching points
6:45–7:00	All players	Prepractice meeting and team building	Review of coaches' expectations of players.	• Horizontal game • Team effort
7:00–7:15	All players	Warm-Up Game	A 10-minute relay run in which the back runner jogs at a moderate pace to overtake the front runner, followed by 5 minutes of dynamic stretching. Break team up into position groups for the game.	• Good running form • Full range of movement
7:15–7:25	QB	Center–Quarterback Exchange	Center–Quarterback Exchange Drill.	• Hand positioning • Heels of the hands touching • Passing hand on top • Feet parallel • Weight on the balls of the feet • Receiving the snap
	QB, RB, TE, WR	Stance and Start for Offense	Stance and Start for Offense Drill.	• Achieving balance • Comfortable stance • Head and eyes up
	OL	Center–Quarterback Exchange	Center–Quarterback Exchange Drill.	• Laces up • Forceful execution • Forward hip movement
7:25–7:30	All players	Water break		

Time	Position	Name of activity	Description	Key teaching points
7:30–7:45	QB, RB	Zone Read Game	A 4-on-3 game (The "4" on offense are quarterback, running back, and two other running backs acting as blockers. The "3" on defense are two running backs acting as defensive linemen and one running back acting as a linebacker) in which the ball carrier takes a handoff from a quarterback and then reads the blocks of two teammates who are simulating offensive line blockng on zone plays. The ball carrier runs to daylight based on the success of the reach or combination block by his two teammates against two "defenders" and then reacts to the unblocked linebacker. There are two possible points for the ball carrier, one for using proper initial footwork and one for making the proper cut on the heels of the blockers.	• Ball security • Running to daylight
	WR	Mirror Block	Drill using hand shields.	• Reaction • Breaking down • Engaging the defender
	OL, TE	Reach Blocking Game	A 1-on-1 game played on a 10-yard straight-line course between two cones. Players start at one cone trying to reach each other. A point will be provided to the player who has his head on the outside of his opponent by the time he reaches the last cone.	• Creating a base of power • Proper footwork • Contacting the defender • Follow-through
7:45–8:00	QB, RB, TE	Zone run plays	Installation of two or three run plays against air.	• Exchanges • Aiming points • Fakes
	OL	Blocking	Reach blocking drill for the OL. Cutoff blocking drill for the OL. Combination blocking drill for the OL. Mirror blocking drill for the WR.	• Creating a base of power • Proper footwork • Contacting the defender • Follow-through
	WR	Catching and Mirror Blocking Drills	Catching and mirror blocking drill for the WR (half practice catching; half practice mirror blocking).	• Proper hand position • Catching the ball away from the body
8:00–8:05	All players	Water break		
8:05–8:25	All players	Perfect Play Game	Run zone plays on air; reward for perfect plays, quick penalty for mistakes.	• Exchanges • Aiming points • Fakes
8:25–8:45	Kickers	Distance and Direction Game	Game in which kickers have three chances to kick toward cones spread out over the field and receive points for accuracy and distance.	• Consistent alignment • Approaching the ball • Planting the foot • Contacting the ball • Follow-through
	All other players	Kickoff Coverage Game	A 9-on-9 game emphasizing kickoff coverage.	• Kickoff • Kickoff coverage • Playing force on kick coverage • Open-field tackling
8:45–8:55	All players	Cool-down	Light jog followed by static stretching.	
8:55–9:00	All players	Practice wrap-up	Emphasis on stretching the field horizontally with the perimeter run game.	• Highlighting of strengths • Statement about areas to improve but ending with a positive note

PRACTICE 6

Date:

Monday, August 22

Practice Start Time:

3:45 p.m.

Length of Practice:

2 hours, 15 minutes

Practice Objectives:

- Introduce skills to defend the option.
- Review basic special teams skills from practice 5 with focus on the kickoff.

Equipment:

Balls, agility bags, spacing hoses, cones, helmet caps, stand-up bags

Practice Dress:

Helmets and shoulder pads

Time	Position	Name of activity	Description	Key teaching points
3:45–4:00	All players	Prepractice meeting and team building	Review of coaches' expectations of players.	• Hustle • Teamwork
4:00–4:15	All players	Warm-Up Game	A 10-minute relay run in which the back runner jogs at a moderate pace to overtake the front runner, followed by 5 minutes of dynamic stretching. Break team up randomly for the game, counting off based on how they are standing on the field.	• Good running form • Full range of movement
4:15–4:25	LB	Stance and Start for Defense	Drills to work on balance and release.	• Two-point squared stance • Eliminating false steps • Moving out of the stance
	DB	Stance and Start for Defense	Drills that focus on backpedaling and breaking to the ball.	• Two-point staggered stance • Eliminating false steps • Moving out of the stance
	DL	Stance and Start for Defense	Drills to encourage quick reactions to the snap.	• Three- or four-point stance • Eliminating false steps • Moving out of the stance
4:25–4:30	All players	Water break		

Time	Position	Name of activity	Description	Key teaching points
4:30–4:45	LB, DB	Zone Pass Defense Game	A 7-on-7 game in which the defense earns points for defending various carded plays.	• Zone pass drops • Reads and reactions in zone pass coverage
	DL	Gap Control Game	A 1-on-1 or 2-on-2 game where the coach indicates to the offense the direction of the block. Defensive players are rewarded for maintaining proper gap control while defending themselves against the block.	• Controlling the gap • Defending basic run blocks
4:45–5:00	All players	Prevent Game	An 11-on-11, third-and-long game in which the defense receives 1 point every time they stop the offensive pass play short of a first down.	• Linebacker reads • Zone pass drops • Speed turn • Pass rush • Reads and reactions in zone pass coverage • Playing the long-yardage situation
5:00–5:05	All players	Water break		
5:05–5:25	All players	Defensive keys	Team Alignment and Pursuit Game (with conditioning reward).	• Alignments • Assignments • Coverages
5:25–5:45	Kickers	Hang Time Game	Game in which kickers receive a point for having the ball in the air for half a second or more.	• Consistent alignment • Approaching the ball • Planting the foot • Contacting the ball • Follow-through
	All other players	Kickoff Coverage Game	A 10-on-10 game emphasizing kickoff coverage.	• Kickoff • Kickoff coverage • Playing force on kick coverage • Open-field tackling
5:45–5:55	All players	Cool-down	Light jog followed by static stretching.	
5:55–6:00	All players	Practice wrap-up	Emphasize importance of defending long yardage situations and gap control. Remind players about checking equipment.	• Highlighting of strengths • Statement about areas to improve but ending with a positive note

PRACTICE 7

Date:

Tuesday, August 23

Practice Start Time:

6:45 a.m.

Length of Practice:

2 hours, 15 minutes

Practice Objectives:

- Build on the skills from practice 3 by adding skills that support offensive passing based on the offensive installation schedule.
- Refine special teams skills with focus on the kickoff return.

Equipment:

Balls, agility bags, spacing hoses, cones, helmet caps, stand-up bags

Practice Dress:

Helmets and shoulder pads

Time	Position	Name of activity	Description	Key teaching points
6:45–7:00	All players	Prepractice meeting and team building	Review of coaches' expectations of players.	• Horizontal game • Team effort
7:00–7:15	All players	Warm-Up Game	A 5-minute relay run in which the back runner jogs at a moderate pace to overtake the front runner, followed by 10 minutes of dynamic stretching. Break team up into groups based on speed for the game.	• Good running form • Full range of movement
7:15–7:25	QB	Quarterback Drops—three and five step	Quarterback Drops Drill.	• Escaping • Foot positioning • Hit and throw versus hitch and throw
	RB, TE, WR, OL	Stance and Start for Offense	Stance and Start for Offense Drill.	• Achieving balance • Comfortable stance • Head and eyes up
7:25–7:30	All players	Water break		
7:30–7:45	QB, RB, WR, TE	Curl Read Game	A 4-on-3 game in which the 4 offensive players try to get a first down based on the coach's down-and-distance call.	• Running shallow and intermediate routes • Running deep routes • Quarterback drops • Throwing • Progression of receivers • Catching
	OL	Pass Protection Game	A 5-on-4 game in which the offense tries to protect the quarterback for four seconds.	• Pass protection • Pass protection against a twist • Pass protection on the edge

Time	Position	Name of activity	Description	Key teaching points
7:45–8:00	QB, RB, WR, TE	Seven-on-Seven Game	A 7-on-7 game in which the offensive players try to get a first down based on the coach's down-and-distance call; defense mixes man and zone.	• Running shallow and intermediate routes • Running deep routes • Adjustments to curl route • Adjustments to crossing route • Quarterback drops • Progression of receivers • Catching • Releases
	OL	Reach Block Game	A 1-on-1 or 2-on-2 game focusing on reach and cutoff blocking against defensive movement, such as slants or angles. Offense receives 1 point for getting the right assignment and 1 point for executing the proper technique.	• Reach block • Cutoff block • Reach blocking against defensive movement
8:00–8:05	All players	Water break		
8:05–8:25	All players	Third Down Game	An 11-on-11 game in which offense focuses on both the running and passing game. Coach varies the third-down yardage to create different situations. (*Note:* Since the first tackling drills are not introduced until afternoon practice, focus for this practice is on framing up rather than actual tackles.) Offense is awarded 1 point each time it makes a first down.	• Protection • Route execution • Progression of receivers
8:25–8:45	All players	Special teams: kickoff returns	An 11-on-11 game in which the offensive players focus on catching the kickoff and the defensive players focus on kickoff coverage.	• Kickoff • Catching the kick • Wall return • Wedge return • Kickoff coverage • Playing force on kick coverage
8:45–8:55	All players	Cool-down	Light jog followed by static stretching.	
8:55–9:00	All players	Practice wrap-up	Emphasis on stretching the field vertically.	• Highlighting of strengths • Statement about areas to improve but ending with a positive note

PRACTICE 8

Date:

Wednesday, August 24

Practice Start Time:

3:45 p.m.

Length of Practice:

2 hours, 15 minutes

Practice Objectives:

- Refine tackling mechanics, with this being the first opportunity for live tackling.
- Review gap plays, deep balls.
- Refine special team skills from practice 7 with focus on the kickoff return.

Equipment:

Balls, agility bags, spacing hoses, cones, helmet caps, stand-up bags

Practice Dress:

Full pads

Time	Position	Name of activity	Description	Key teaching points
3:45–4:00	All players	Prepractice meeting and team building	Review of coaches' expectations of players.	• Hustle • Teamwork • Tackling safely using proper technique
4:00–4:15	All players	Warm-Up Game	A 5-minute relay run in which the back runner jogs at a moderate pace to overtake the front runner, followed by 10 minutes of dynamic stretching. Break team up into position groups for the game.	• Good running form • Full range of movement
4:15–4:25	LB	Stance and Start for Defense	Drills to work on balance and release.	• Two-point squared stance • Eliminating false steps • Moving out of the stance
	DB	Stance and Start for Defense	Drills focusing on backpedaling and breaking to the ball.	• Two-point staggered stance • Eliminating false steps • Moving out of the stance
	DL	Stance and Start for Defense	Drills to encourage quick reactions to the snap.	• Three- or four-point stance • Eliminating false steps • Moving out of the stance
4:25–4:30	All players	Water break		

Time	Position	Name of activity	Description	Key teaching points
4:30–4:45	LB, DB, DL	Tackling	A 1-on-1 drill emphasizing proper technique, slowly progressing to full tackling.	• Approaching the ball carrier • Squaring up • Contacting the defender • Wrapping the arms
4:45–5:00	DL, LB, DB	Half-Line Option Drill	Separate players by left side and right side of the defense. The offense alternates going to the left and right, using carded option plays. No football is used in this game. Rather the focus for the players is on covering each phase of the option play that they are assigned to defend.	• Feathering • Defending the option • Linebacker reads • Pursuit angles • Force • Pursuit angles
5:00–5:05	All players	Water break		
5:05–5:25	All players	Full-Team Oklahoma Game	An 11-on-11 game, third down and three, in which the defense receives 1 point for stopping the first down and 3 points for using proper tackling techniques.	• Spilling blocks • Squeezing blocks • Force • Tackling • Defending basic run blocks
5:25–5:45	All players except for snapper, holder and kicker	PAT/FG Protection	Drills that focus on alignment and technique.	• Keep pads low and body weight forward. • Be ready to strike forward aggressively. • Anticipate when the gap will be threatened.
	Snapper, holder and kicker	Snap, Hold, Kick	Drills that focus on proper execution of PAT or FG.	• Short snap • Holding for the place kick • Place kick
5:45–5:55	All players	Cool-down	Light jog followed by static stretching.	
5:55–6:00	All players	Practice wrap-up	Emphasis on proper tackling techniques and the need to go all out.	• Highlighting of strengths • Statement about areas to improve but ending with a positive note

Game Coaching

You can plan and you can practice all day long. But if your team does not perform to the best of its ability during your games, what has all that planning done for you? Part V will help you prepare for game situations.

Chapter 11 teaches you how to prepare long before the first game, including issues such as communication, scouting your opponent and creating your game plan. Chapter 12 teaches you how to be ready to make decisions during and after the game about items like the coin toss, making substitutions, managing the sideline area, meeting with the media and speaking with your players after the game.

After all the preparation that you have made, game day is when it really becomes exciting, especially if you and your team are ready for the challenge.

Preparing for Games

The performance of a football team on game day reflects its preparation. A well-prepared team will be fundamentally sound, organized and efficient, opening the game with a strong attack and handling crucial situations effectively because the players have rehearsed those skills and situations. Following are the areas that you should consider when preparing yourself and your team for a game.

Communication

As a coach, you must communicate well at many levels—with players, team captains, coaching staff, parents, school and community officials, officials and the media. You must be aware of your nonverbal communication, which can be just as loud as what you say with your mouth.

Players

When you communicate well, you engage your players in the learning process. When players become partners and have a stake in their own development, you become a facilitator, not merely a trainer. The players' participation in the learning process is the key to the games approach and what makes it such a valuable approach to coaching. Although shaping, focusing and enhancing play is difficult, it is ultimately more rewarding because it allows players to take ownership of their development.

As part of the communication process, you should assemble a team manual that covers basic offensive and defensive alignments, notes on the season plan, team terminology, basic techniques and summarized versions of tactics. Distribute this resource to players several weeks before the first day of practice. The manual should not be too long because the longer it is, the less apt the athletes are to read it. Meet with players often and encourage them to study the manual thoroughly.

Before the beginning of a season, you should prepare a list of expectations, which outlines the policies that you expect players to follow. The term *expectations* is preferable to the term *rules*, which conveys a sense of rigidity. The term *expectations* also communicates to players that they are responsible for living up to them. The coaching staff must reinforce expectations daily so that they become second nature to the team. Any breaches of discipline that arise should be handled immediately and evenhandedly. You must treat all players alike, starters no differently than subs. Finally, you should make sure that your list of expectations covers any exigency that may occur in your local situation.

You may decide to have the team elect captains, who can then assist you in communicating to the team. Emphasize to captains that their main role is to help make their teammates better players, not order them around. Show captains the many ways to accomplish that—by encouraging teammates, helping them work on their skills, supporting them and modeling good practice habits.

Parents

Before the season begins, you should schedule a preseason meeting with parents of all football candidates, separate from the meeting that most schools already sponsor during each sport season. A few weeks before the season begins, mail a letter to the homes of players with an RSVP enclosed. This personal touch will pique the interest of parents and make them feel valuable to the program. A special invitation letter should go to the superintendent, the principal and the athletic director, who should be present to explain school policies, athletic codes and general school issues.

Prepare a simple agenda for this meeting and follow it to keep the meeting on track and to convey to parents a sense of your organizational ability. Besides setting an agenda, you should prepare and distribute a simple list, outlining the roles of parents, players and coaches. Parents want to be involved in their child's progress, so stating the method of communication between parent and coach is important.

Coaching Staff

Coaches need to communicate well with their assistants. Each season, you should hold a formal preseason meeting with your coaching staff to outline expectations. Discuss season philosophy and specific techniques that you will emphasize, especially if changes have occurred from the previous year or if new members have joined the staff. You should spell out, or even write out, the roles of assistants or volunteer coaches, including how to deal with parents, who should be referred to you. Assistants should be firm and fast in noting breaches of discipline and bringing them to your attention.

Officials

Coaches must also communicate well with officials. You should treat officials as the professionals that they are, even when they are wrong. When questioning a ruling, approach the official slowly and respectfully. Players will model your behavior with officials. Because most states and leagues provide outlets for official evaluations, you can address shortcomings and commendations of officials through that process.

Community and Media

Involvement with the community and the media demands that you be a good communicator. You speak each day with your demeanor. If you become rattled or easily frustrated, players will assume that demeanor. If you are cool-headed, the players will be calm too. By maintaining composure, you convey an attitude of control under pressure even in intense, challenging situations.

You should be accommodating to the press and instruct players in tactics for talking to media. Players need to understand that the role of the media may come in conflict with the goals and expectations of the team. Players should respectfully answer questions that deal with games but defer questions about philosophy or game management to the coaching staff. Players must be careful not to say anything derogatory about an opponent that might find its way onto an opponent's locker room bulletin board.

Scouting an Opponent

An essential step in preparing for games is scouting. Scouting helps eliminate the element of surprise from the game equation. Most of the scouting for football teams today is done using videotapes. By reviewing tapes, you can develop more accurate scouting reports than you can by watching games in person, allowing you to prepare your team better for competition.

The most important element of scouting is the breakdown, or evaluation, of the tape. The final scouting report may come in different forms, from fancy computer spreadsheets to hand-written notes, but it will be only as accurate and meaningful as the information recorded on the original breakdown.

The coaching staff on each side of the ball must first decide what elements they are going to chart as they break down the tape. Most breakdowns include the following:

- Down and distance
- Yard line and hash mark
- Offensive formation, motion and play
- Defensive front, coverage and stunts, if any
- Result of the play

Coaches should use the same terminology throughout the season to describe the opponents' schemes. Every formation, motion, running play, pass route, front, coverage and blitz should have a name that all coaches on the staff understand and know. Obviously, the defensive coaches will be more detailed in their breakdown of the opponent's offense, and offensive coaches will be more detailed in their breakdown of the opponent's defense, but at least on their side of the ball they should use terms consistently when describing what they see on scouting tapes.

After capturing the information for each play of the game, you should use computer programs or other means to produce reports on the opponent. Often these reports will be simple spreadsheets that list, for example, the plays or defenses that the opponent runs on third-and-long situations (see "Sample Scouting Report List" for additional reports). Sometimes, however, you may want to produce hand-drawn diagrams of blocking schemes or complicated blitzes so that the players get a visual impression of the concept that the opponent uses.

SAMPLE SCOUTING REPORT LIST

A general list of defensive and offensive scouting reports might include the following:

Defensive Scouting Reports

- Two-deep lineup
- Plays by down and distance
- Most frequent formations
- Favorite runs (by formation)
- Favorite passes (by formation)
- Screens
- Red-zone runs
- Red-zone passes
- Goal-line plays
- Two-point plays
- Favorite pass protections
- Motion

Offensive Scouting Reports

- Two-deep lineup
- Defenses by down and distance
- Favorite fronts (by formation)
- Favorite coverages (by formation)
- Favorite blitzes (by formation)
- Line games and movement
- Red-zone defenses
- Goal-line defenses
- Two-point play defenses
- Adjustments to motion

The scouting report also must include an evaluation of the opponent's kicking game because many games are won or lost on kicking-game plays. Each assistant coach should analyze one facet of the kicking game by evaluating that area on the opponent's tapes and reporting to the rest of the staff. Besides charting kick distances and hang times, coaches should note operation times for both the punters and place kickers and be aware of how those times compare to their own. Other areas of the opponent's kicking game to evaluate include the following:

- Punt rush schemes
- Punt return concept
- Punt protection scheme
- Punt coverage concept
- PAT and FG block schemes
- PAT and FG protection scheme
- Kickoff coverage concept
- Kickoff return scheme

○ Fakes

○ Special situations (onside kick, hands team, sky punt and so on)

After compiling these scouting reports, the coaching staff must return to the videotapes and evaluate the opponent's personnel. Although this aspect of scouting cannot easily be captured on charts or computers, it is crucial to a successful game plan and game-day performance. You must also evaluate matchups, trying to determine how your players will compare in size, strength and speed (or quickness) to the players whom they will be facing on the opposing team. In matchups that do not favor your player, you might consider double-teaming a lineman or double-covering a receiver. Conversely, with favorable matchups, you should make sure that your game plan features those advantages.

Finally, no scouting report is complete until you have completed a self-scout of your team's tendencies, which your opponent will be evaluating. Although the self-scout doesn't have to be as elaborate or detailed as the scouting report on the opponent, you should prepare it carefully, consider it in the game plan and make an effort to break the tendencies that your team has established in previous games. Otherwise, the opponent will have the advantage on game day of knowing what you are going to do before you do it!

Developing the Game Plan

After completing and analyzing the scouting report, the coaching staff begins the process of developing a game plan for the opponent. You formulate the game plan by carefully considering the scouting report, your overall strategy and your team's offensive and defensive capabilities. The game plan, simply put, is the particular concepts that you have chosen to give your team the best chance for success against the schemes that the opponent uses.

Game planning, however, can be haphazard and inefficient unless you use an organized, systematic timetable. Figure 11.1 is a sample timetable that provides a method for developing a game plan. Essentially, the concept is to break down the development of the game plan into several smaller parts and work on a few of those parts each day. Of course, transferring the game plan from your notepad to the players' performance on the field is one of the great challenges of coaching football. For the game plan to be successful, the players must understand it and execute it under pressure. The only way this can happen is by giving them the opportunity to learn the plan in practice sessions during the week and try it out against simulated opponent looks. Keep in mind that they cannot learn the game plan all at once. Rather, if you present the plan in stages so that they can learn one facet at a time, they have an excellent chance to absorb the concepts and perform them on game day.

Simultaneously, the coaching staff should prepare the game-day call sheet with the elements of the game plan that you are drilling the players on, so that the call sheet ends up including the best, most well-prepared elements of the game plan. The call sheet is a way to prepare and organize your calls before game day. You can use this sheet during the game to assist you in making quick, yet well-thought-out calls. Figures 11.2 and 11.3 provide sample offensive and defensive call sheet templates that you can use to organize your thoughts. You will be filling out the call sheets throughout your preparation for the game and incorporating the plays in your practices.

Figure 11.1 Sample Game-Plan Timetable

	Staff assignments	Offensive game plan	Defensive game plan	Practice structure
Sunday	• Grading of tape from previous game • Breakdown of opponent tape • Special teams meeting	Review of preliminary game-plan ideas	Review of preliminary game-plan ideas	(No practice)
Monday	• Review of scouting reports • Review of self-scout • Review of motivation plan • Review of blocking adjustments	1. Runs by formation 2. Run checks 3. Pass protection 4. Blitz pickup 5. Goal-line package	1. Formation adjustments 2. Motion adjustments 3. Goal line 4. Red zone 5. Blitz package	*Dress*: half pads *Activity level*: moderate *Objective*: introduction of game-plan concepts and review of all special teams units
Tuesday	• Scripting of practice • Preparation of call sheet for goal line and run checks	1. Final run checks 2. Passes by formation 3. Play-action passes 4. Checks and choices	1. Final blitz package 2. Run game by personnel 3. Line games 4. Two-point plays	*Dress*: full pads *Activity level*: heavy *Objective*: installation of game plan for Monday and Tuesday and review of two special teams units
Wednesday	• Scripting of practice • Preparation of call sheet for down and distance calls	1. Third-down calls 2. Fourth-down calls 3. First 10 plays	1. Review of personnel 2. Third-down calls 3. Fourth-down calls	*Dress*: full pads *Activity level*: heavy *Objective*: installation of third- and fourth-down calls and review of two special teams units
Thursday	• Scripting of practice • Preparation of final call sheet • Breakdown of opponent tape	1. Hunch plays 2. Two-point plays	1. Calls by personnel 2. Special situations	*Dress*: helmet only *Activity level*: light *Objective*: review of opening script, game plan and all special teams units
Friday	• Final review of game plan and chair drill • Team stretch • Pregame warm-up	(Game)	(Game)	(Game)

From *Coaching Football Technical and Tactical Skills* by ASEP, 2006, Champaign, IL: Human Kinetics.

Structuring Practices

With only four days available for practice between one game and the next, organization and scheduling of practice sessions is crucial. You must teach your players the game plan, of course, but you also must allow them ample recovery time from the previous game, maintain their fitness and keep them fresh for the upcoming game.

Figure 11.2 Offensive Call Sheet

First 10 plays	First 10 companions	Third and 7 or more
1.	1.	
2.	2.	
3.	3.	
4.	4.	
5.	5.	**Third and 4 to 6**
6.	6.	
7.	7.	
8.	8.	
9.	9.	
10.	10.	
Hunch plays	**Fourth-down calls**	**Third and 1 to 3**
Red-zone runs	**Red-zone passes**	**Goal-line plays**

Figure 11.3 Defensive Call Sheet

First and 10	Second and 8+	Second and 4-7	Second and 1-3
Base	Base	Base	Base
Pressure	Pressure	Pressure	Pressure

Third and 8+	Third and 4-7	Third and 1-3	Fourth and 1-3
Base	Base	Base	Base
Pressure	Pressure	Pressure	Pressure

Red zone (20 to 11)	Red zone (10 to 3)	Goal line (1 to 3)	2-point play
Base	Base	Base	Base
Pressure	Pressure	Pressure	Pressure

From *Coaching Football Technical and Tactical Skills* by ASEP, 2006, Champaign, IL: Human Kinetics.

Monday

On Mondays the game plan begins to take shape. The coaching staff should use this practice to introduce the players to some of the important concepts. This session gives the players a solid background on the upcoming opponent and prepares them for the more detailed elements of the game plan that are coming up.

Defensive coaches can show their players the opponent's top three runs and top three passes and show them how to defend those plays. Offensive coaches can show their players the opponent's favorite blitzes and how to pick them up, or they can show the players the blocking adjustments that they will need to use in the game.

Physically, Monday is a transition day for the players. They loosen up their bodies from the previous game and prepare for the upcoming week of practice. Practice is not at full speed, and the athletes are not in full pads, but the units can jog through assignments on offense and defense, and perhaps run a quick two-minute (no-huddle) drill to keep the activity level where you want it. A long flexibility session should be followed by a series of 40- to 80-yard striders in which the players start slow, build up to top speed and then coast to the finish. Striders give the players some conditioning benefit and, because no quick starts, stops or turns are involved, their legs feel loose and fresh after the workout.

Monday is also a good day to review each special teams unit—assessing the performance of those units in the previous game, correcting mistakes, working on techniques involved with the technical skills of the kicking game and previewing the opponent's schemes on each special teams unit. These periods in practice should be active, with players covering kicks, working on protection techniques, kicking and catching the ball, and so on. Contact should be minimal, but the players need to perform their assignments, not just listen to a description of what they will be assigned to do.

Tuesday

On Tuesdays the coaching staff begins to move the game plan from general concepts to specific calls that will be made in the game. On these days, the offensive and defensive staffs each begin to develop a call sheet that lists the play calls that they want to make in the game and the situations in which they will make those calls. They then script the calls into the practice plan so that the players have a chance to learn them.

The call sheet for the game is a work in progress. By Tuesday's practice, only part of the call sheet will be complete, and those are the calls that you will rehearse in practice. As a coach, you have freedom to choose which aspects of your call sheet you want to emphasize on Tuesday. The outline provided in figure 11.1 on page 342 suggests that the offensive emphasis should be on runs by formation and run checks, pass protection and blitz pickup, and goal-line plays. Defensively, the outline recommends focusing on formation and motion adjustments, goal-line defense, red-zone defenses and the blitz package.

Regardless of which aspects you choose for Tuesday, those aspects guide the structure of practice. Set up individual and group drills to practice the technical and tactical skills that the players need to know so that they can execute the plays on the script for the day. Organize team segments into game-plan components so that the players understand the emphasis of the segment.

Tuesday's practice should be the most demanding of the week. Dress should be full pads, and the tempo should be full speed throughout the practice, without tackling the ball carrier to the ground. Schedule the players for enough reps that they gain significant conditioning benefit from the practice. If the players need additional conditioning after the team period ends, consider a drill that would provide conditioning benefit while also rehearsing some part of the game plan. For example, the offense could practice throwing deep passes for the week, throwing the ball downfield and then having the quarterback and the linemen sprint down the field to meet the receiver. They would run the next play back the other direction. Defensively, the unit could practice a pursuit drill that begins with the formation and motion adjustments of the day and continues with a simulated play that all defenders would have to chase.

Because Tuesday's practice includes so much teaching and so many team reps, usually only two special teams units can perform practice reps—the punt team and the punt block–return unit. The specialists (punters, kickers, snappers, holders, kick catchers) must work on their specialties before or after practice if they play an offensive or defensive position, or during practice if they are truly specialists.

Wednesday

Wednesday's practice is similar to Tuesday's, but the team will rehearse different aspects of the game plan. The coaching staff moves on to another section of the call sheet, filling in the calls for the game, and those calls become the outline for practice.

Wednesday is an excellent day to practice calls by down and distance, particularly third-down calls. Of course, third down is crucial in the game, and these calls, and their execution by the players, are critical for a successful performance. On Tuesday night the coaching staff reviews the scouting report of the opponent's tendencies on third down as well as the self-scout regarding their own third-down calls. Then, working with the list of plays and concepts chosen for the game plan, the coaches choose the calls that they want to make on third and short, third and medium, and third and long. The staff lists these calls on the call sheet for the week and scripts them into Wednesday's practice so that the team rehearses the actual plays that they will be running in the game. To improve the players' chances to be successful, coaches should emphasize the technical and tactical skills necessary for executing those crucial plays during the introductory individual and group periods. At practice, and again at night when watching the tape of practice, if available, the coaches evaluate the calls and the players' ability to execute them. They then settle on the final list of third-down calls for the game.

As on Tuesday's practice, dress for Wednesday's practice should be full pads, and the tempo should be full speed, again without tackling the ball carrier to the ground. If the practice is scheduled and implemented properly, with the reps scripted ahead of time and a minimal amount of dead time when players are inactive, no extra conditioning should be necessary.

The special teams emphasis for Wednesday should be the kickoff and kickoff return teams. Again, the specialists should work on their individual skills. You should strongly consider videotaping the special teams during each practice, because evaluating the 11 players on the kickoff coverage and return teams as the drills happen on the field is difficult. But by watching a few minutes of tape of those drills, you can evaluate individual players very effectively. If videotape is not available, then individual coaches can each watch two or three specific players on each rep of the special team and then provide immediate feedback to those players regarding their assignments and techniques.

Thursday

Thursday's practice, if the game is on Friday night, should be light in both contact and activity, but the game plan can and should be reviewed in detail. The coaching staff should finish the final call sheet for Friday's game before Thursday's practice so that the players can rehearse all the most important plays—the opening script, third-down calls, red-zone calls, goal-line calls and so on. The tempo is quick but light, and the review, although more mental than physical, is extremely valuable.

On Thursday you should review every special teams unit. You must check the final depth chart for each unit, so that all players know who is supposed to be on the field for each unit and who the backups are for that unit. You should also run every unit through their schemes for that week against the opponent's concepts.

Thursday is also a good day for review of videotape of the opponent. Now that you have implemented and prepared the game plan, the players can watch the opponent on tape and mentally rehearse the plays and concepts that they will be using in the game. Because the players need to have fresh legs for the game, this meeting accomplishes the dual purpose of reviewing game concepts while keeping the players off their feet and rested for the game.

Controlling Your Team's Performance

By establishing a consistent routine on game day, you help your athletes prepare themselves physically, mentally and emotionally for their best possible performance. You have great flexibility in designing your pregame ritual. Whatever schedule you choose, staying with that schedule for the entire season is more important than its actual elements. When the team is on the road, the outline should remain as similar as possible to the routine at home. This regularity produces consistency in performance that might not exist if the timetable were erratic. See "Sample Pregame Routine" for a routine that you may want to use with your team.

You should understand that game day is not the time to offer criticism. You may desire outstanding performance during the game, but if you berate players' mistakes on game day, their performance will likely diminish rather than improve for the rest of that day. Instead, allow time during the practices in the first few days after a game to critique the players, point out errors and provide suggestions for improvement and elimination of mistakes.

Team Building and Motivation

All the best game planning and physical training will not produce successful performance on game day unless the athletes work together and are motivated to play hard. We talked earlier in this chapter about preparing players for their assignments in the game plan, but we need to extend our planning for the game into the mental area as well. Although an inspiring message right before the game might produce an early burst of energized play, the physical demands of the game require a more substantial basis for the players to keep playing hard.

The underlying point is that you must motivate your players to practice so that they will be motivated to play well in the game. As they rehearse the game plan each week, they have to know why it is important for them to grasp the concepts and learn how to execute them. They must make the connection between preparation and performance, and realize that they can reach their goals only if they practice diligently. Then, when game time comes, they are confident in their abilities, committed to the goal and ready to play an entire game.

Despite your best efforts to plan and prepare your team, one factor trumps everything else in the game of football. One of the main reasons that young men play football is that they enjoy the friendship, camaraderie, competition and life

SAMPLE PREGAME ROUTINE

Routine should become part of the events leading up to the game itself to breed a comfortable atmosphere and help players feel relaxed and ready to give their best. Following is a suggested routine for the hours leading up to a game.

Four Hours Before the Game

Players should eat a training meal that provides them with the proper diet and nutrition for football performance. This meal should include moderate portions of carbohydrates, low fat, no sugars and so on. If players get in a habit of eating the same meal at the same time before every game, they will learn exactly how much to eat and what choices to make so that they feel their best throughout the contest. For more information on your athletes' diet, refer to chapter 16, "Fueling Your Athletes," beginning on page 357 of *Successful Coaching, Third Edition.*

Three Hours Before the Game

Players should gather at the school in two separate rooms (one for offense and one for defense, or a single classroom if players play both ways) for the final review of the game plan. Some coaches choose to present this final review in the form of interactive tools or drills. Clear the room except for four or five chairs lined up as the opponent's offensive or defensive line. Behind the line of chairs, place a white board with the opponent's favorite alignments diagrammed on it. Give the starting players a play call, either offensive or defensive, and line up the chairs to simulate the proper formation. In the offensive drill, point to a defense drawn on the board. The quarterback then makes his checks, if any, and the linemen make their calls. The quarterback voices the snap count, the center snaps an imaginary ball and every player walks two or three steps to his proper assignment. In the defensive drill, point to an offensive formation on the board. The defensive players make their calls and their checks against any shifts or motion. You then snap an imaginary ball, and every player steps to his gap or coverage assignment. By allowing the players to review 25 to 30 plays in about 15 minutes, this drill provides excellent mental rehearsal and focuses the players on the game and the opponent.

Two Hours Before the Game

Players should gather in a wrestling room, gymnasium or large locker room for a team stretch. They should be dressed in sweats or shorts and should not be wearing any football equipment. Although they will stretch again closer to game time, a short 10- or 15-minute stretch relaxes them, focuses them on the game and the opponent, and begins a long, slow process of warming up that will give their bodies the best chance to perform safely and productively. After the stretch, they should begin the process of getting taped and dressed in their pads for the game.

One Hour Before the Game

Players should start to take the field an hour before the game. The first players out should be the specialists—kickers, punters, snappers, holders, kick catchers, quarterbacks and receivers. A second group of non-specialists can take the field later. When the entire team is on the field, a moving (ballistic) team stretch should be conducted, followed by individual warm-up drills, some small group drills, a few team snaps and a couple of kicking plays. The warm-up should end about 15 minutes before the game so that the team has time to return to the locker room for final details and instructions.

Finally, after a long and complete week of scouting, game planning, practicing, motivating and focusing, game time arrives. By following a predetermined pregame routine, your players should be physically and mentally prepared to give their best effort.

lessons that they share with their teammates. Because they go through tough and exciting experiences together, both positive and negative, they develop deep and committed bonds of friendship. The commitment of team members to each other is the most powerful form of motivation in sport. You must strive to find ways to encourage and enhance opportunities for players to spend time together, work to break down barriers between isolated groups on the team and help players develop the kind of friendships that move mountains.

chapter 12

During and After the Game

One of the great challenges of coaching football is that the season comprises fewer games than the season of any other sport. Rarely does a team play an opponent more than once per year. Second chances are few, and every regular season game figures prominently in the race to the conference or district title or the playoffs. Every game is intense and emotional, packed with pressure-filled, crucial decisions. The coach must manage this game-day cauldron wisely—trusting that planning and practicing has prepared the team for the competition, and relying on a structured administrative protocol to keep the team organized during the game.

The three-step tactical triangle approach to analyzing a game situation detailed earlier in this book creates a blueprint for you and your players to follow in making important decisions during a game. While the game is in progress, you must accurately read the cues presented, apply technical and tactical knowledge on the spot, adjust the game plan accordingly and make immediate decisions. The logical format of the triangle helps you slow the speed of the game and apply organized, logical thinking to the situation. The following sections show how to apply the tactical triangle to several key situations that commonly occur in games.

Leadership does not just happen; it is a gradual process of education and experience. You should prepare your team to be led in the way that you expect them to behave. You should describe to the team how you expect them to look on game day—how they should act on the sideline, how they should talk (or not talk) to the officials or the opponents, how they should react to adverse situations and how they should respond to success. You must subsequently follow up by insisting on those behaviors through reinforcement during and after the game. Everything that your team does on game day is something that you have taught or something that you have allowed to happen. Teach game day the right way, and your team will perform admirably.

Field Management

Field management is a critical aspect of a successful game. Your staff and your players need know what you expect of them on game day. Ensure that they understand how you want things to be on the sideline. Make sure that they know the location and purposes of the meeting areas and ready areas.

Sideline

The sideline during a game is congested, with players and coaches crowding toward the field and officials working the lines and down markers. This crowding and congestion can negatively affect the coaches' ability to make calls and substitutions as well as the officials' ability to work a good game. To help eliminate these problems, you should assign one coach—a disciplined, respected and vocal member of the staff—to patrol the sideline throughout the game and move players (and coaches) back to the line where they are supposed to stand.

On the subject of sideline management, you should work to enforce a rule that no players or assistant coaches are permitted to direct any comment to the officials or opposing players. The result will be that officiating crews and opponents will respect your team, and your players will not be deterred or distracted by mindless bickering and taunting.

Meeting Area

Farther back from the sideline you should set up two meeting areas, one for offense and one for defense, one on each side of the 50-yard line, where the trainers' table and watering station are usually located. These meeting areas should consist of two benches and a white board with towels and markers. After every series in the game, the players should get a drink of water and then go immediately to the adjustment meeting. Here, coaches can exchange information with players about the opponent's alignments and schemes, and correct problems that have arisen. Depending on the size of the coaching staff, you can break down these meetings into smaller groups.

As a coach, you must develop the personal discipline to go to the adjustment meeting faithfully after every series, no matter how exciting and tense the game might be, and you must insist that the players report to the meeting as well. This protocol is critical to the process of adapting the game plan to the game, and it provides you with an opportunity to bolster egos, offer encouragement, inspire persistence and otherwise coach some things that are not Xs and Os. The meeting may be short, or it may last until the next possession, but it must take place each time a unit comes off the field.

Ready Area

The ready area is a staging area on the sideline, marked off by four cones set up in a square, where each special teams unit gathers before going on the field. Assign one coach to manage the ready area and perform no other job during the game.

The ready-area coach should have a complete list of starters and backups for each special teams unit and should call the roll for the unit every time they are about to go on the field. If a player on the unit is already on the field, the ready-area coach assigns one player on the sideline to pick up the player on the field and remind him to stay out there for the special teams play. The ready area, when organized and run properly, saves time-outs and prevents penalties because the players will be assembled and ready to go on the field for each special teams play.

By keeping track of injuries during the game, the ready-area coach will know whether a player on one of the special teams units needs to be replaced. The coach should establish a line of communication with the athletic trainer on duty for each game so that the trainer knows to tell the coach when a player is unable to play.

Coin Toss

The officials and the team captains always administer the coin toss, without coaches present, so the coaching staff must educate the captains about the proper choices for each game. Obviously, the four possible choices at the beginning of the game are to kick, to receive, to choose a goal to defend or to defer the option to the second half. Although the team that wins the toss usually chooses the defer option, some teams prefer to start the game with the ball. Other teams place a priority on having the wind or the sun at their backs if those conditions are significant.

Regardless of your preference, one option that your captains should never choose is to kick. Your team may end up kicking because of your choice to defend a certain goal, but if you just choose to kick, you have gained absolutely nothing. Instruct your captains at the beginning of the season never to choose the option to kick at the coin toss.

The list of instructions to the captains can be cumbersome, especially if you decide, for example, that you would like to defend a certain goal because of the wind. Some coaches have a lengthy meeting with their captains to rehearse all possible options. One simple and easy method of instructing the captains for the coin toss is to give them a list of the top three priorities. So, if you tell your captains, "Defer, ball, scoreboard," they will know that the first choice is to defer. If that's not available they will take the ball, and if the other team takes the ball they will defend the scoreboard. The list can change each week, and it might include just two words if you want the ball or the wind whether you win the toss or not. In any event, this simple priority system takes the uncertainty out of the coin toss.

MESSENGERS AND SIGNALS

As we learned in chapter 11, proper communication is vital. The two most common forms of communicating play calls are messengers and hand signals. Using a messenger is somewhat more reliable, but hand signals are far quicker and allow you more time to make up your mind about a call. Regardless of the style of communication that you choose to use, you must rehearse the message system in practice consistently or errors will occur during games.

If you use messengers, you may want to consider having the quarterback or linebacker wear a simple wristband on which longer and more complicated calls might be written and numbered. Then the messenger could simply run on the field and say, "Play number seven" instead of attempting to communicate the more complex call. The play caller in the huddle can then correctly read the call.

If you use hand signals, you should teach the signals to every player on the unit so that if they do not have time to huddle, they can all get the call from the sideline by watching you and reading the hand signals. If you use hand signals, rehearse them frequently in practice to ensure that your athletes will be ready to use them during the game.

Substitutions

Given the large number of players and positions in football, substituting players can be a massive task. Many solve the problem by not substituting often, but fatigue and specialization are two considerations that warrant it.

Football is a demanding game, so players must expend great energy on every play to be effective. Players can be conditioned to last through a game playing both ways or to participate in every play on one unit and play on several special teams. But you should analyze the game tape to evaluate whether the athletes who are playing all the time are performing at their highest level on every play. Frequently, the backup player who plays at 100 percent may be more effective than the starter who is tired. In addition, football is a specialized game, so you should consider putting players on the field whose talents closely match the situation. On third and long, defensive coaches should consider inserting an extra defensive back or two and perhaps a smaller, quicker defensive lineman who can really rush the quarterback. The game allows free substitution after every play so you should use that rule to the team's advantage.

The coaching staff should handle substitutions on the sideline using a decentralized system. As a head coach, you have too many obligations during the game to handle every substitution, so you should delegate that job to the offensive and defensive coordinators or their assistants on the sideline and to the ready-area coach for special teams. On larger staffs, position coaches can and should handle substitutions for their players. These coaches are more familiar with the particular strengths and weaknesses of their players than you are, and they should be responsible for getting the right players on the field.

Halftime Adjustments

You have a lot to accomplish during the short halftime break. The coaching staff should orchestrate every minute of the break and follow that schedule exactly. In general, the coaches on each side of the ball should meet and discuss adaptations to the game plan while the players use the facilities, get water, see the trainer if needed and then go to assigned areas of the locker room. After seven or eight minutes of discussion, you and your staff must settle on the changes that you will make at halftime. Your assistants then go to their position groups (or units, on smaller staffs) to discuss those changes. After an additional seven or eight minutes of discussion, the team should gather for brief comments from you before heading back out onto the field.

You must remember to give players sufficient time to warm up and stretch again for the second half. Frequently, coaches become so engrossed in halftime adjustments that they keep the team too long in the locker room and leave them too little time to get ready physically for the second half. Mental adjustments are key, but the physical preparedness to perform is important as well.

Crucial Calls and End-of-Game Decisions

As the game reaches its climax, you will have to make crucial decisions that can directly affect the outcome. Frequently, you don't have much time to make those decisions. In these key situations, the coaching staff must follow the rule of chain of command. As the head coach, you must be present, in person or on the headsets, as the offensive or defensive coordinator decides on the fourth-down call. You must voice your assent or disagreement with the call or place the call clearly in the hands of the next coach in the chain. After the game, the coaching staff must know that they made the crucial calls together and must stand by each other regarding those calls. In particular, you cannot dissociate yourself from the call-making process; you must actively participate or clearly pass the authority down.

Time-outs are extremely important in end-of-game scenarios, so you must have rules in place about using them. You should not allow players to call time-outs without permission, except in predetermined situations such as when a linebacker realizes that only 10 defenders are on the field on third down and 10. You must communicate to the team about situations in which time-outs should never be called, such as a PAT when only 10 men are on the field, so that they know that the 5-yard penalty is less harmful than using a time-out. You should also spend ample time on your play calling and messaging system so that you don't have to use time-outs wastefully early in each half of the game.

Clock management is also critical at the end of the game. The team with the lead must run the clock down by staying in bounds, not throwing incomplete passes and getting up from the pile slowly, whereas the team that trails must play hurry-up by getting out of bounds, killing the clock with the spiked pass and hustling back to the line of scrimmage. Players must have rehearsed these situations and must understand the value of each second that they use, or save, on the clock. Ultimately, however, you must communicate to the players that few games are truly decided by the clock running down to zero seconds. A touchdown, field goal, defensive stop or turnover decides most games. In other words, teams cannot play only against the clock; they must still get first downs, make defensive stops, execute in the kicking game and make plays just as they do at any other time in the game.

After the Game

When the game is over, the coaches and players should meet in the middle of the field and shake hands. When the teams meet at the center of the field, the players' actions will reflect the training, or lack thereof, that you have given them about this ceremony. Long before this moment, preferably at the beginning of the season before the first game, you should address this situation to the players. A simple formula for the handshake is to be brief and, in defeat, to extend congratulations and quickly move on. Any further comments could be perceived as either provocative or patronizing.

After the handshake ceremony, you must always meet with your team, either on the field if you can cordon off an area, or in the locker room. At this time, you must address the team, regardless of the outcome. Remember to take a deep breath, think before you speak and be careful and understated whatever your emotional condition. In defeat, console the team and praise their effort without indicating that you are satisfied with the outcome. Find positives to build on and move forward to the next opponent. In victory, let the team know that you are happy but follow up by pointing out any areas where they need to improve. Refer to the game plan and reinforce how a productive week of practice prepared them for their performance.

You can allow players to speak to the team at the postgame meeting, and they often provide the most poignant messages. At the beginning of the year, you must set up a team policy that players' comments must be positive and sincere. Players should keep their comments brief, compliment teammates who played hard and well, and try to motivate the team for the next game.

When the player meeting ends, you and certain players may have to meet with the media. Again, you must train the players before the season starts about how to handle interviews. They must be complimentary of their teammates and their opponents, and avoid making excuses or commenting about the officials. They should be polite, brief and positive about future games but not overconfident. They should answer only the specific questions that are asked, and they should not provide extraneous information. They should also decline to comment about injuries, player dissension, coaching decisions and playing time.

As the head coach, you should again take a deep breath and slow the racing tempo of your thoughts before beginning to answer questions. Many of the instructions for the players apply to you as well, but the media will ask you about your team. In victory, give your players the credit. Talk about how hard they practiced, how well they executed, how they battled back and so on. In defeat, deflect the blame from your players by talking about how well the opponent played and possibly referring to what the coaching staff might have done to change the outcome.

At all costs, avoid two common pitfalls of the postgame interview—first, the comment that "our team didn't show up today" or "we didn't come to play," and, second, the comment that "the players just didn't execute today." Both comments blame the players for the loss; either they lacked motivation or they played poorly. But it is your job to motivate the players and teach them the skills of the game. If the players aren't motivated, you have to do a better job of motivating; if the players aren't executing, you have to do a better job of teaching. We can't separate ourselves from our teams, even when we are tempted to do so after a heartbreaking loss. We are in this game together, all the time, especially in the postgame crucible.

Finally, the postgame media session ends, but you have one final, important task. You make your trip to the locker room and spend time with the players who just gave everything they had to try to win the game. If the game went in your favor, tell them how proud you are and how happy you are for them. If the game ended in a loss, tell them how proud you are and how much you appreciated their effort. Your players will vividly remember these postgame moments. They will never forget that you coached them in life as much as you did in football.

appendix a

Passing Routes

Passing Route Tree
for Shallow, Intermediate and Deep Routes

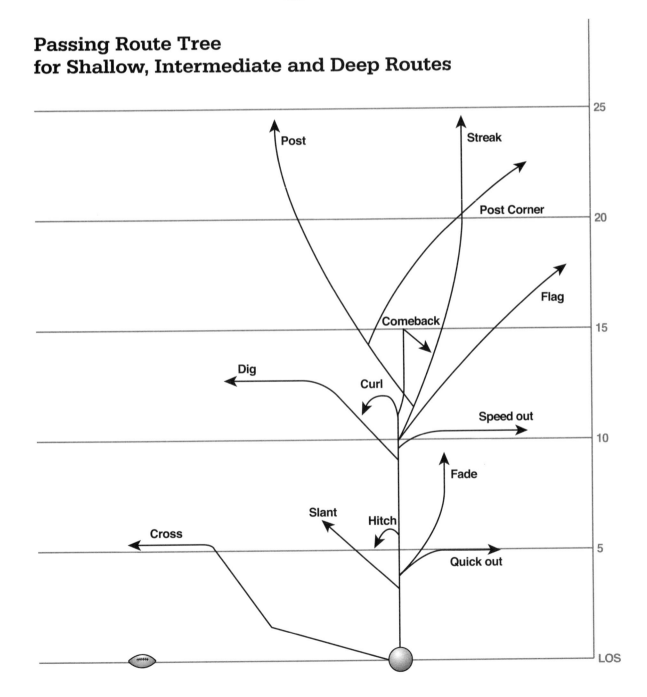

Curl and Comeback Route Adjustments

Soft Corner

Hard Corner

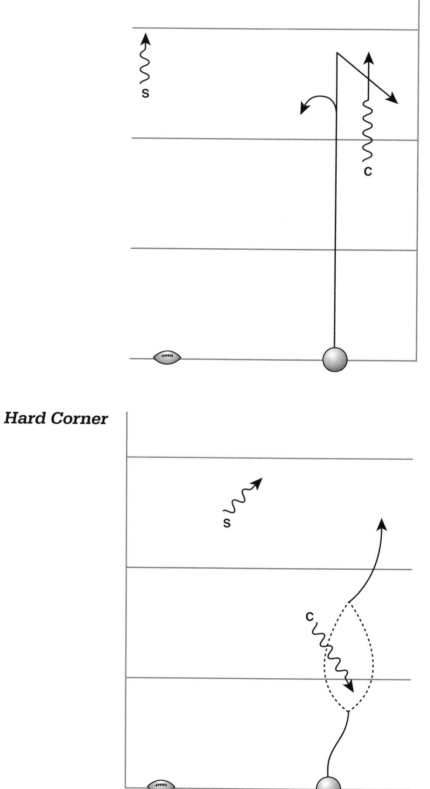

Gap Plays

Gap Plays Versus 4-Man Line (4-3 Defense)

Trap

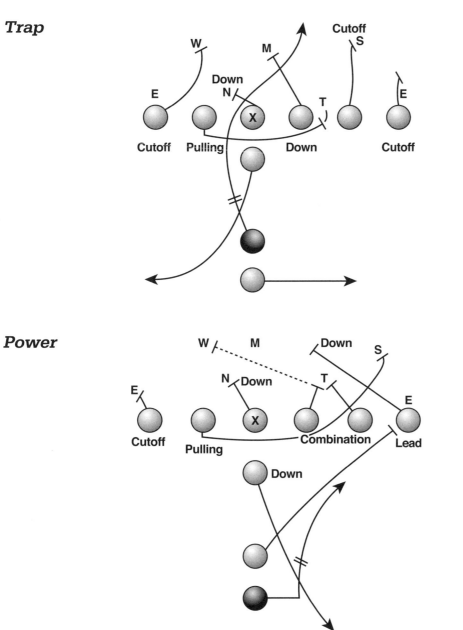

Power

Isolation

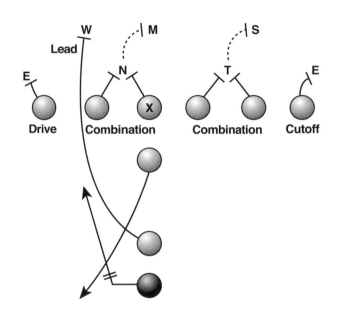

Counter

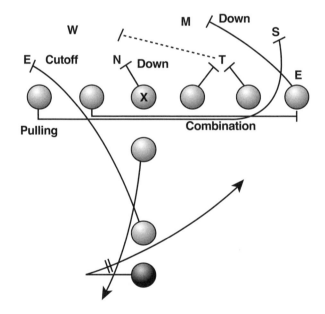

Gap Plays Versus 5-Man Line (Eagle Defense)

Trap

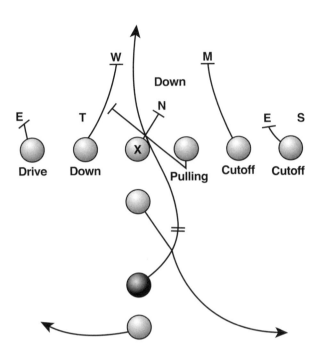

Power

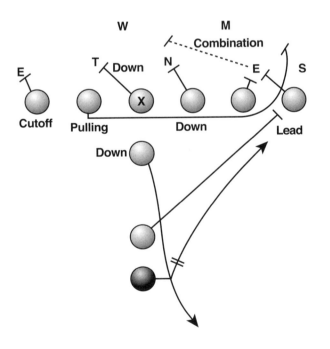

Gap Plays Versus 5-Man Line (Eagle Defense) *(continued)*

Isolation

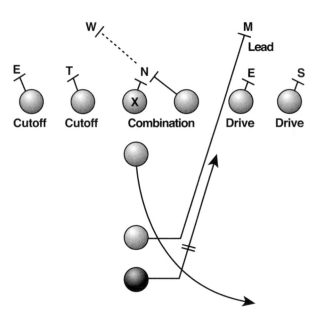

Counter

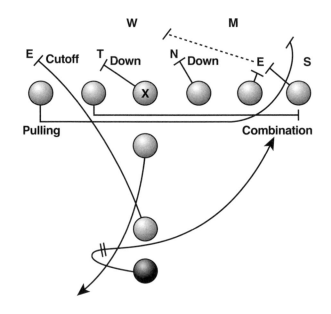

Running to Daylight Plays (Zone)

Inside Zone

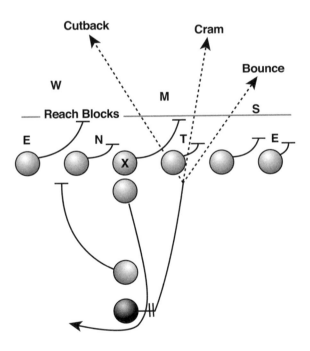

Off-Tackle Zone

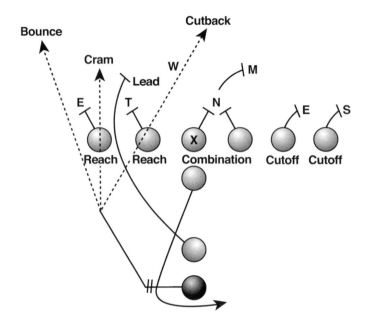

Outside Zone

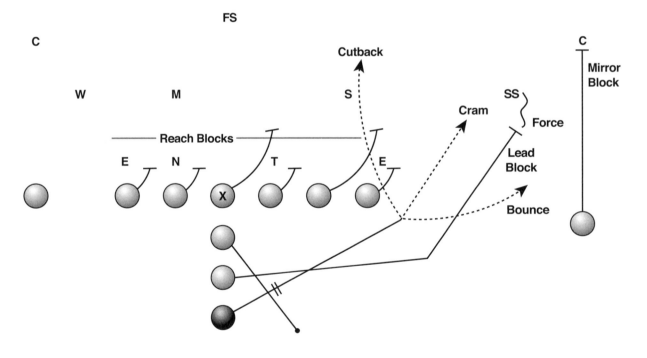

about asep

Coaching Football Technical and Tactical Skills was written by the American Sport Education Program (ASEP) with the assistance of Rob Ash, head football coach at Drake University.

ASEP has been developing and delivering coaching education courses since 1981. As the nation's leading coaching education program, ASEP works with national, state, and local youth sport organizations to develop educational programs for coaches, officials, administrators, and parents. These programs incorporate ASEP's philosophy of "athletes first, winning second."

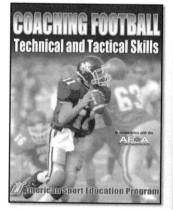

IT STARTS WITH THE COACH

Much is expected of today's high school coach. On any given day, you may play the role of mentor, motivator, mediator, medic, psychologist, strategist, or trainer. Each requiring a separate set of skills and tactics that together make you a "coach."

The **Bronze Level** credential—offered through the ASEP Professional Coaches Education Program—is designed with all of these roles in mind. It includes courses on coaching principles, sport first aid, and sport-specific techniques and tactics, and requires CPR certification. The Bronze Level prepares you for all aspects of coaching and is a recognized and respected credential for anyone who earns it.

To enroll in any of these courses, visit the Course Catalog on the ASEP Web site at **www.ASEP.com** or contact your state association.

To learn more about how you can adopt the program for your state association or organization, contact ASEP at **800-747-5698** or e-mail **ASEP@hkusa.com**.

Developed, delivered, and supported by the American Sport Education Program, a 25-year leader in the sport education field, the ASEP Professional Coaches Education Program fulfills the coaching education requirements of nearly 40 state high school associations.

American Sport Education Program

A DIVISION OF HUMAN KINETICS